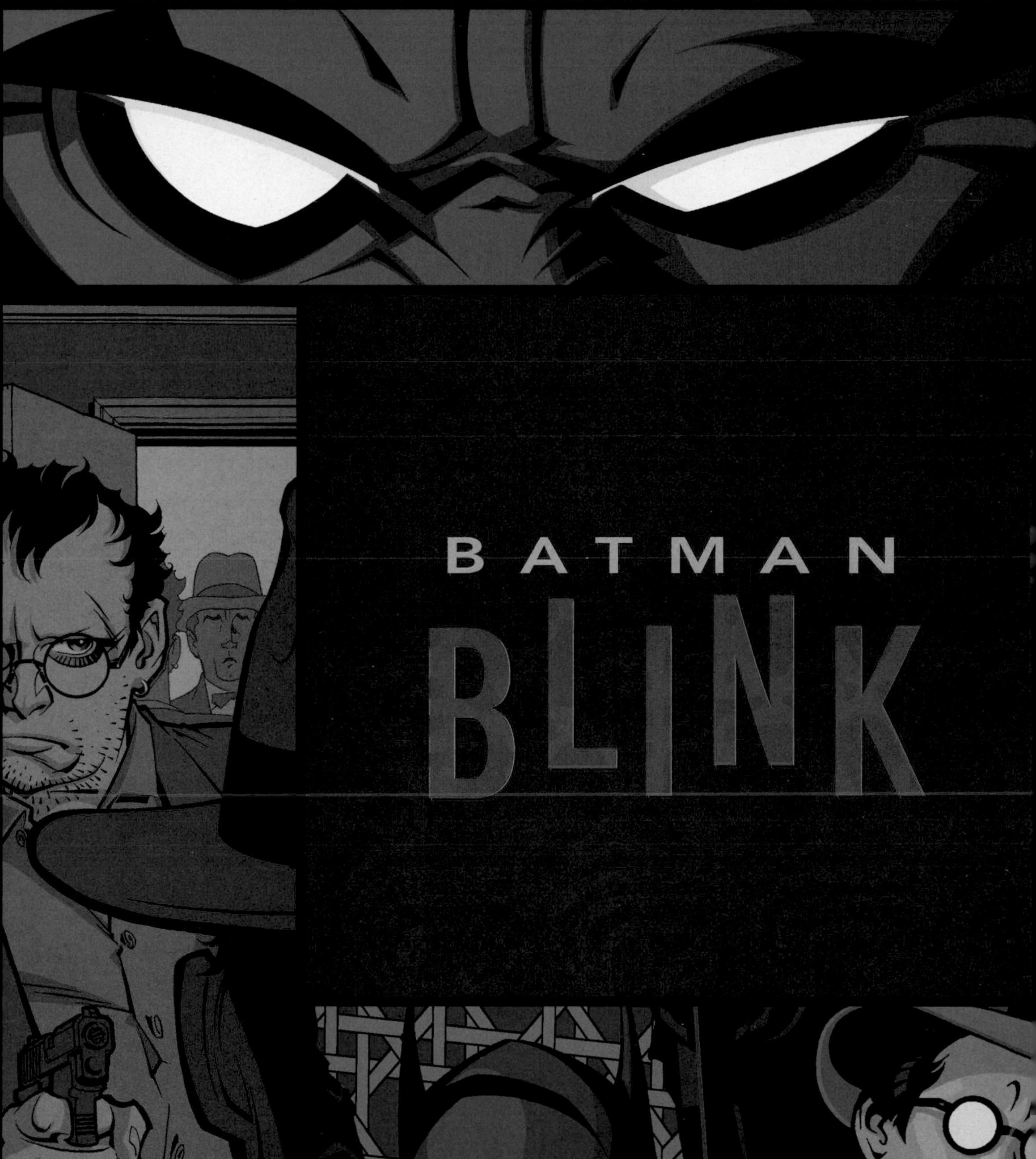
BATMAN
BLINK

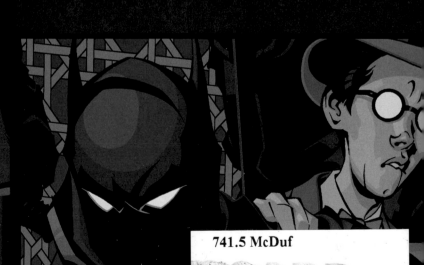

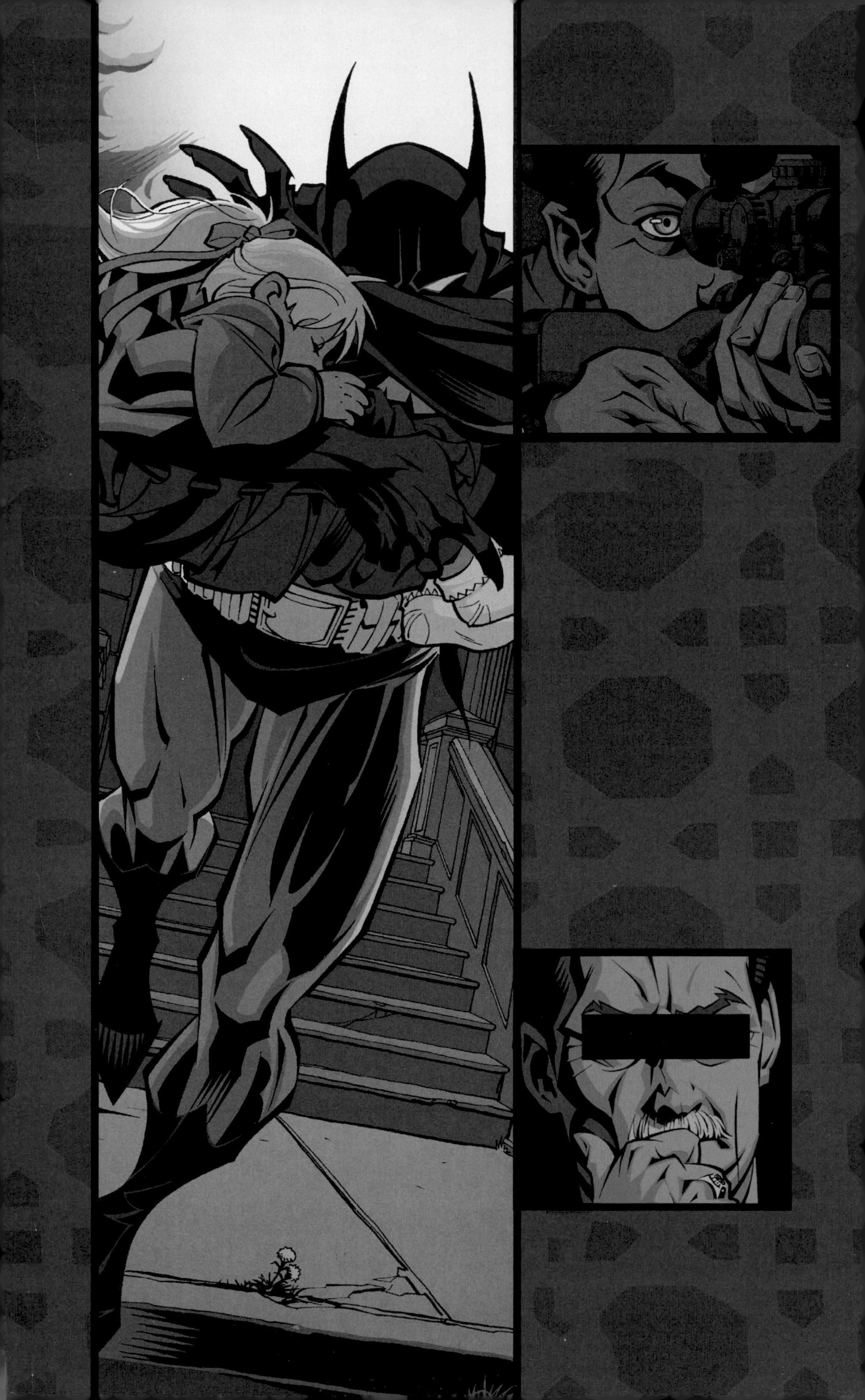

BATMAN
BLINK

Written by
Dwayne McDuffie

Art by
Val Semeiks and **Dan Green**

Coloring by
James Sinclair

Lettering by
Kurt Hathaway

Cover Art and Original Series Covers by
Brian Stelfreeze

Batman created by **Bob Kane**

ANDREW HELFER Editor – Original Series
HARVEY RICHARDS Assistant Editor – Original Series
SCOTT NYBAKKEN Editor
ROBBIN BROSTERMAN Design Director – Books
SARABETH KETT Publication Design

BOB HARRAS Senior VP – Editor-in-Chief, DC Comics

DIANE NELSON President
DAN DIDIO and JIM LEE Co-Publishers
GEOFF JOHNS Chief Creative Officer
AMIT DESAI Senior VP – Marketing and Franchise Management
AMY GENKINS Senior VP – Business and Legal Affairs
NAIRI GARDINER Senior VP – Finance
JEFF BOISON VP – Publishing Planning
MARK CHIARELLO VP – Art Direction and Design
JOHN CUNNINGHAM VP – Marketing
TERRI CUNNINGHAM VP – Editorial Administration
LARRY GANEM VP – Talent Relations and Services
ALISON GILL Senior VP – Manufacturing and Operations
HANK KANALZ Senior VP – Vertigo and Integrated Publishing
JAY KOGAN VP – Business and Legal Affairs, Publishing
JACK MAHAN VP – Business Affairs, Talent
NICK NAPOLITANO VP – Manufacturing Administration
SUE POHJA VP – Book Sales
FRED RUIZ VP – Manufacturing Operations
COURTNEY SIMMONS Senior VP – Publicity
BOB WAYNE Senior VP – Sales

BATMAN: BLINK

Originally published in single magazine form in BATMAN: LEGENDS OF THE DARK
KNIGHT 156-158 and 164-167. Copyright © 2002, 2003 DC Comics.
All Rights Reserved. All characters, their distinctive likenesses and related
elements featured in this publication are trademarks of DC Comics. The stories,
characters and incidents featured in this publication are entirely fictional.
DC Comics does not read or accept unsolicited submissions of ideas,
stories or artwork.

DC Comics, 1700 Broadway, New York, NY 10019
A Warner Bros. Entertainment Company
Printed by RR Donnelley, Owensville, MO, USA. 1/16/15. First Printing.
ISBN: 978-1-4012-5126-0

Library of Congress Cataloging-in-Publication Data

McDuffie, Dwayne.
   Batman : blink / Dwayne McDuffie, writer ; Val Semeiks, artist.
     pages cm
   ISBN 978-1-4012-5126-0 (paperback)
   1. Graphic novels. I. Semeiks, Val, illustrator. II. Title.
   PN6728.B36M35 2015
   741.5'973—dc23
                                          2014042085

TABLE OF CONTENTS

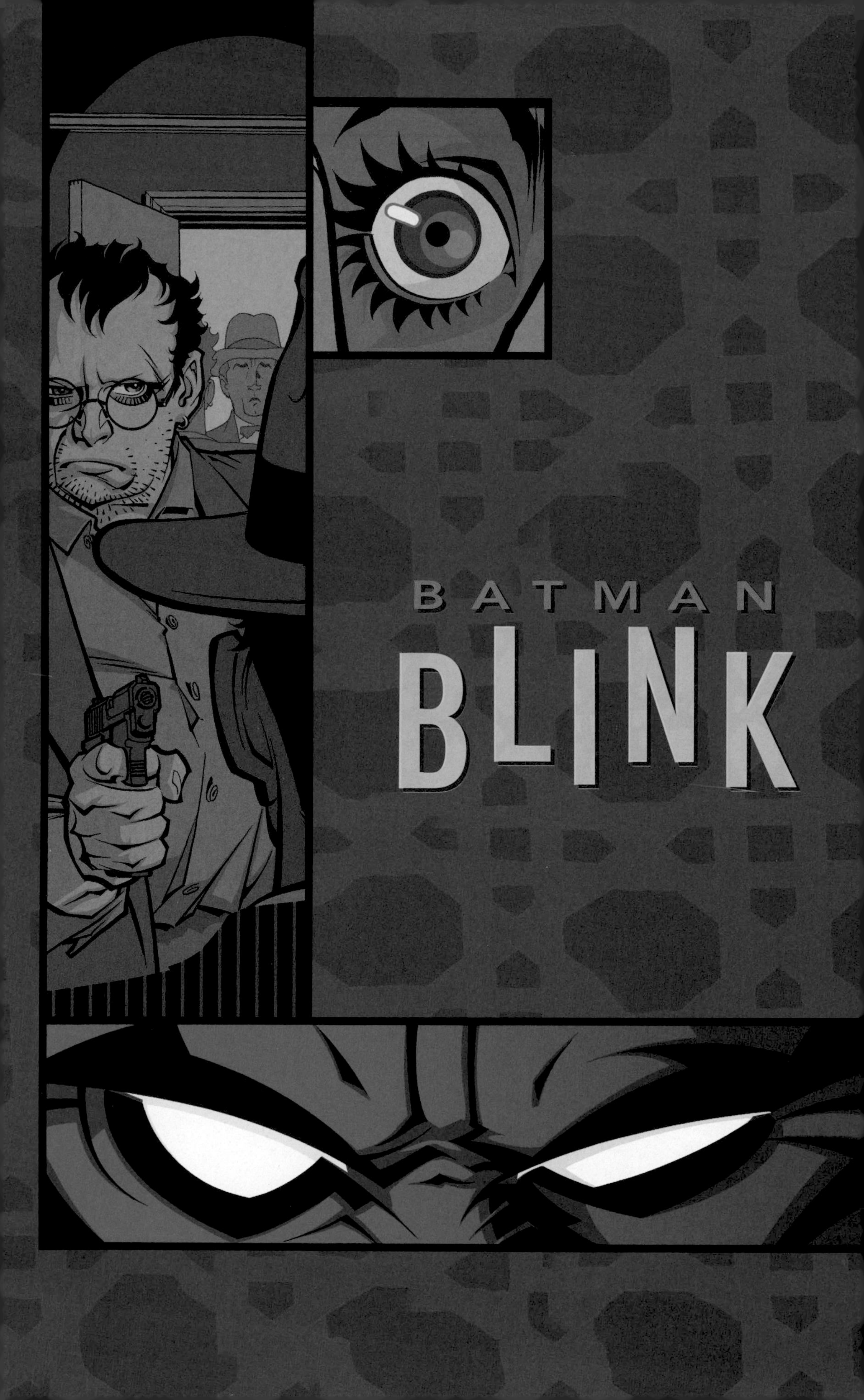
BATMAN
BLINK

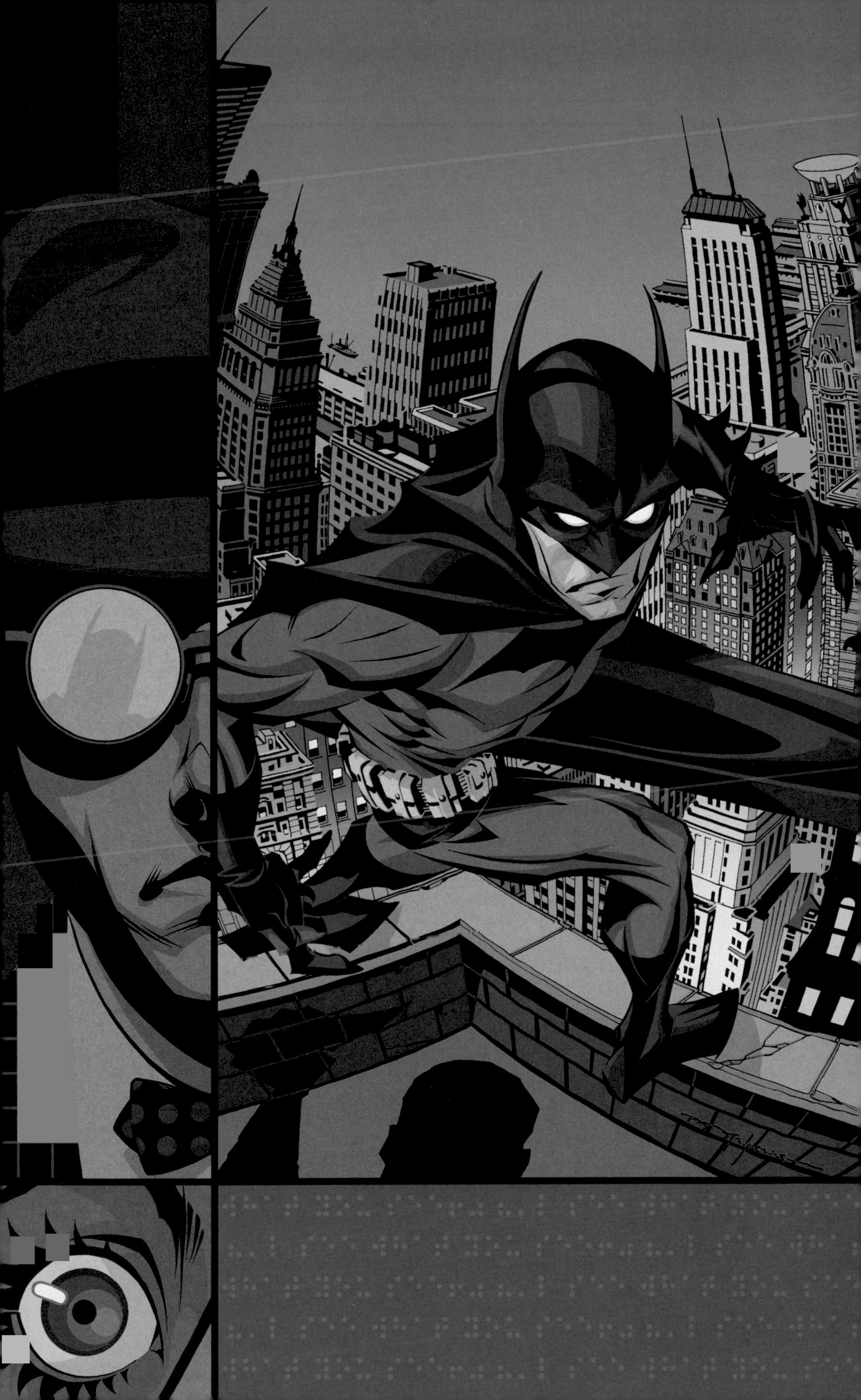

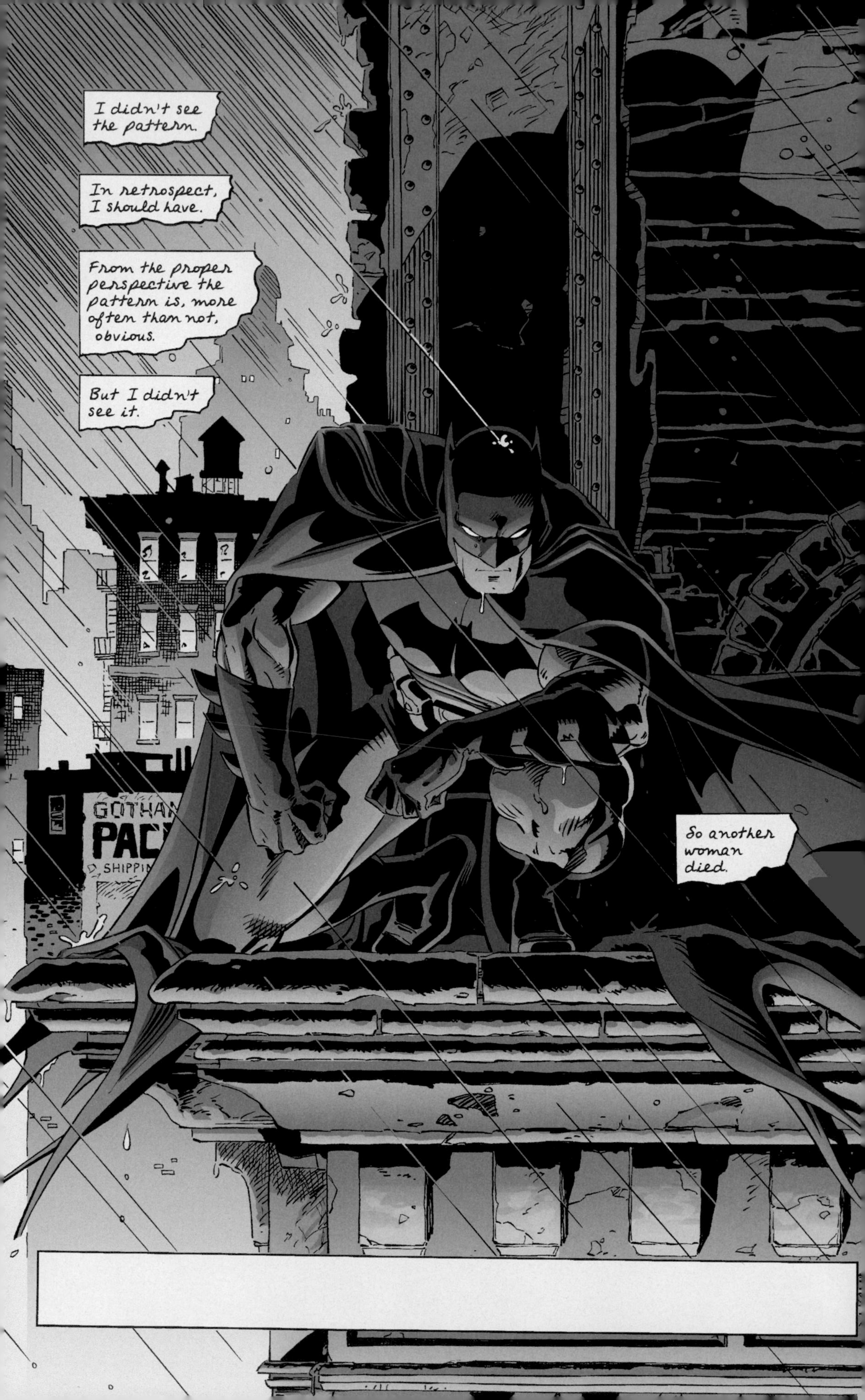
I didn't see the pattern.
In retrospect, I should have.
From the proper perspective the pattern is, more often than not, obvious.
But I didn't see it.
So another woman died.

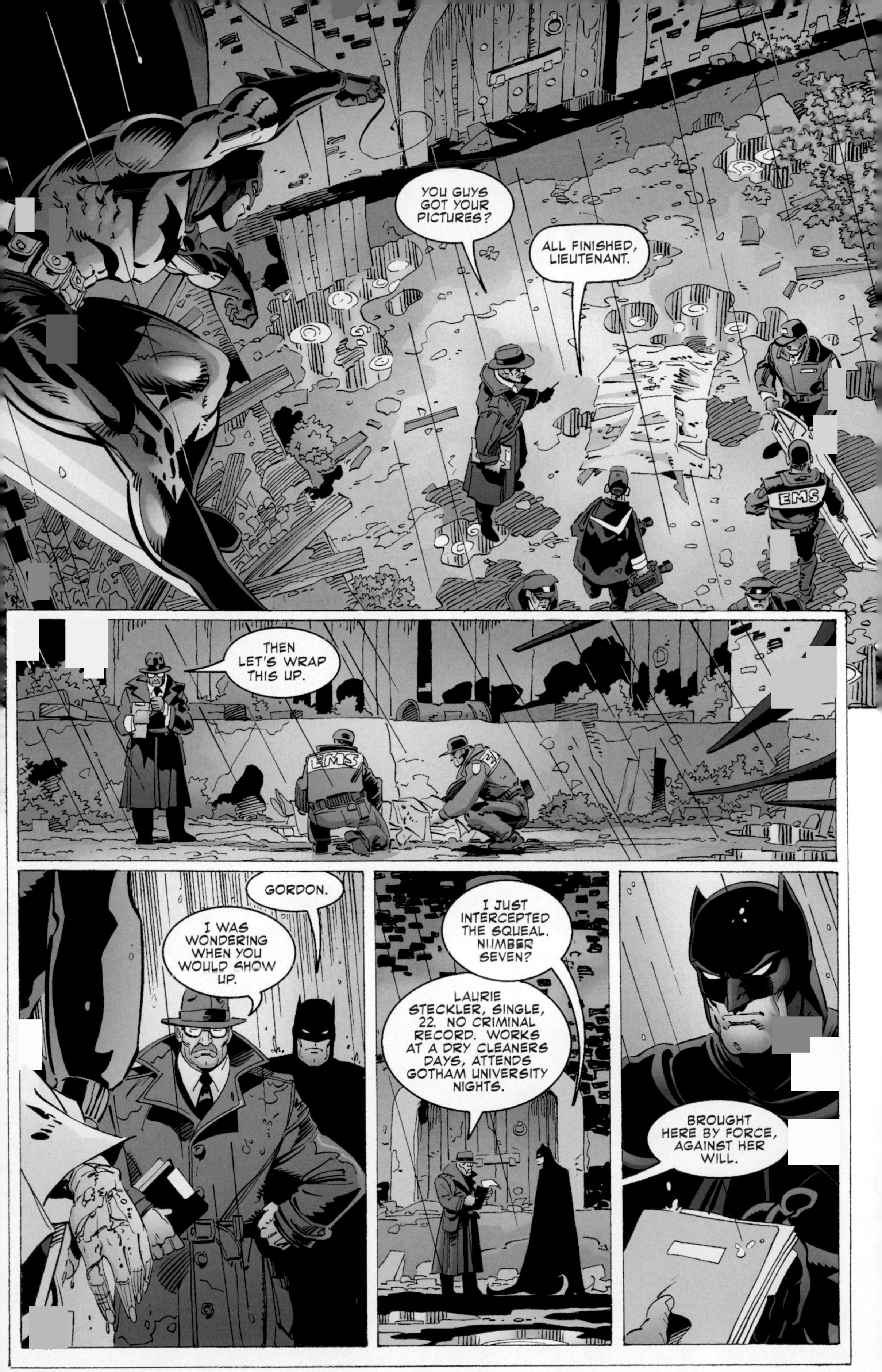
YOU GUYS GOT YOUR PICTURES?
ALL FINISHED, LIEUTENANT.
THEN LET'S WRAP THIS UP.
GORDON.
I WAS WONDERING WHEN YOU WOULD SHOW UP.
I JUST INTERCEPTED THE SQUEAL. NUMBER SEVEN?
LAURIE STECKLER, SINGLE, 22. NO CRIMINAL RECORD. WORKS AT A DRY CLEANERS DAYS, ATTENDS GOTHAM UNIVERSITY NIGHTS.
BROUGHT HERE BY FORCE, AGAINST HER WILL.

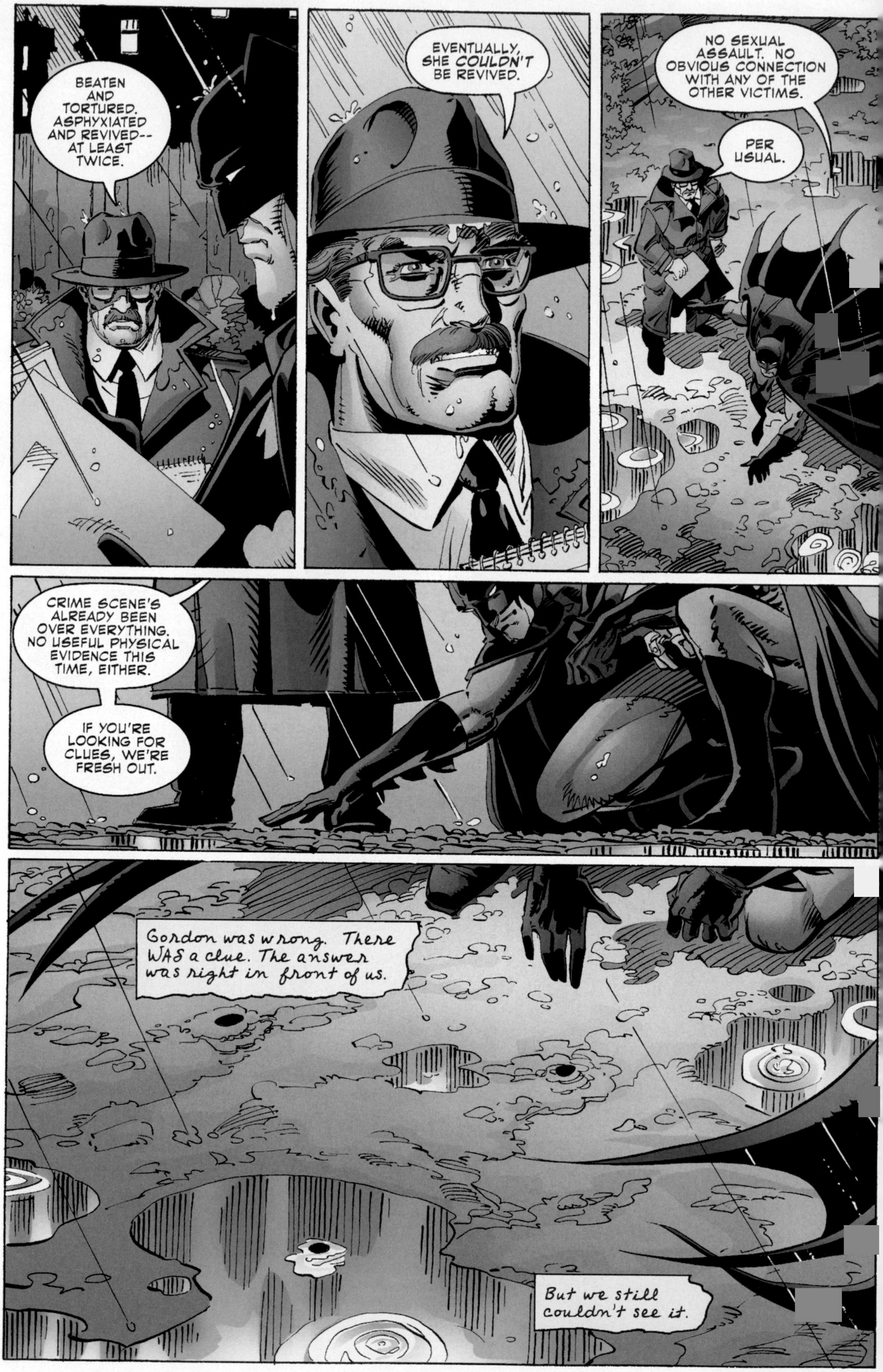
BEATEN AND TORTURED. ASPHYXIATED AND REVIVED-- AT LEAST TWICE.
EVENTUALLY, SHE COULDN'T BE REVIVED.
NO SEXUAL ASSAULT. NO OBVIOUS CONNECTION WITH ANY OF THE OTHER VICTIMS.
PER USUAL.
CRIME SCENE'S ALREADY BEEN OVER EVERYTHING. NO USEFUL PHYSICAL EVIDENCE THIS TIME, EITHER.
IF YOU'RE LOOKING FOR CLUES, WE'RE FRESH OUT.
Gordon was wrong. There WAS a clue. The answer was right in front of us.
But we still couldn't see it.

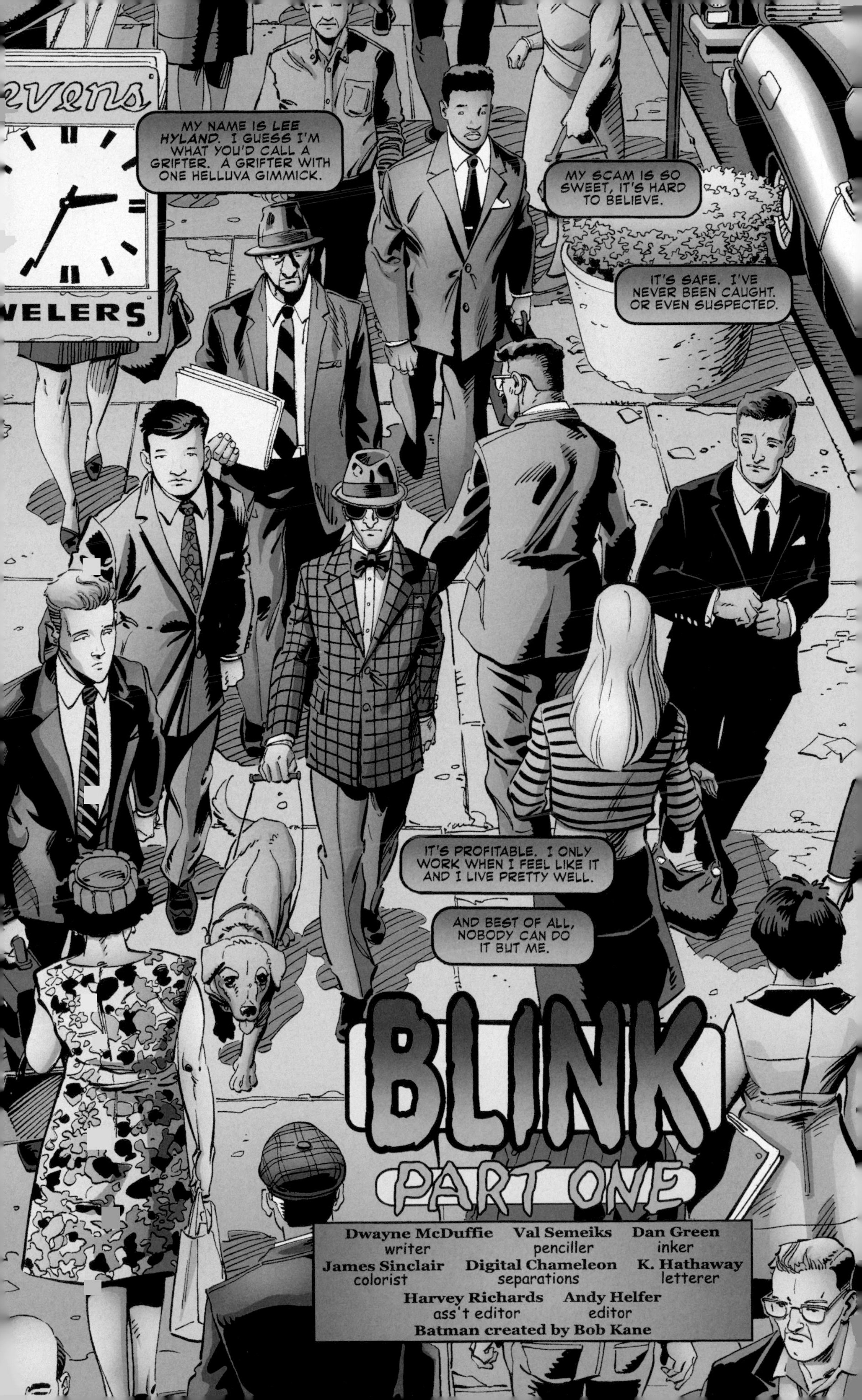

MY NAME IS LEE HYLAND. I GUESS I'M WHAT YOU'D CALL A GRIFTER. A GRIFTER WITH ONE HELLUVA GIMMICK.
MY SCAM IS SO SWEET, IT'S HARD TO BELIEVE.
IT'S SAFE. I'VE NEVER BEEN CAUGHT. OR EVEN SUSPECTED.
IT'S PROFITABLE. I ONLY WORK WHEN I FEEL LIKE IT AND I LIVE PRETTY WELL.
AND BEST OF ALL, NOBODY CAN DO IT BUT ME.
BLINK
PART ONE
Dwayne McDuffie writer
Val Semeiks penciller
Dan Green inker
James Sinclair colorist
Digital Chameleon separations
K. Hathaway letterer
Harvey Richards ass't editor
Andy Helfer editor
Batman created by Bob Kane

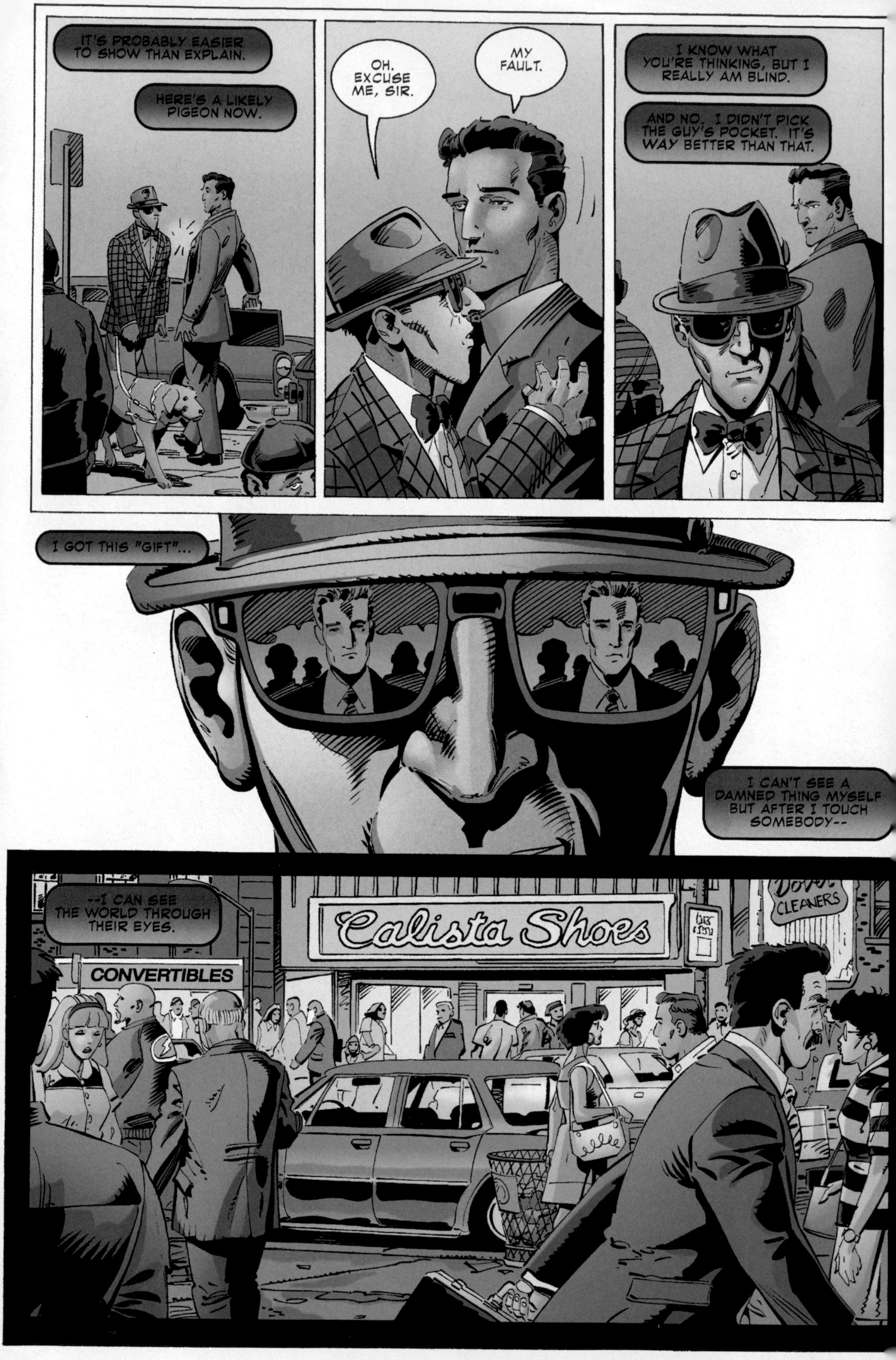
IT'S PROBABLY EASIER TO SHOW THAN EXPLAIN.
HERE'S A LIKELY PIGEON NOW.
OH. EXCUSE ME, SIR.
MY FAULT.
I KNOW WHAT YOU'RE THINKING, BUT I REALLY AM BLIND.
AND NO. I DIDN'T PICK THE GUY'S POCKET. IT'S WAY BETTER THAN THAT.
I GOT THIS "GIFT"...
I CAN'T SEE A DAMNED THING MYSELF BUT AFTER I TOUCH SOMEBODY--
--I CAN SEE THE WORLD THROUGH THEIR EYES.
CONVERTIBLES
Calista Shoes
CLEANERS

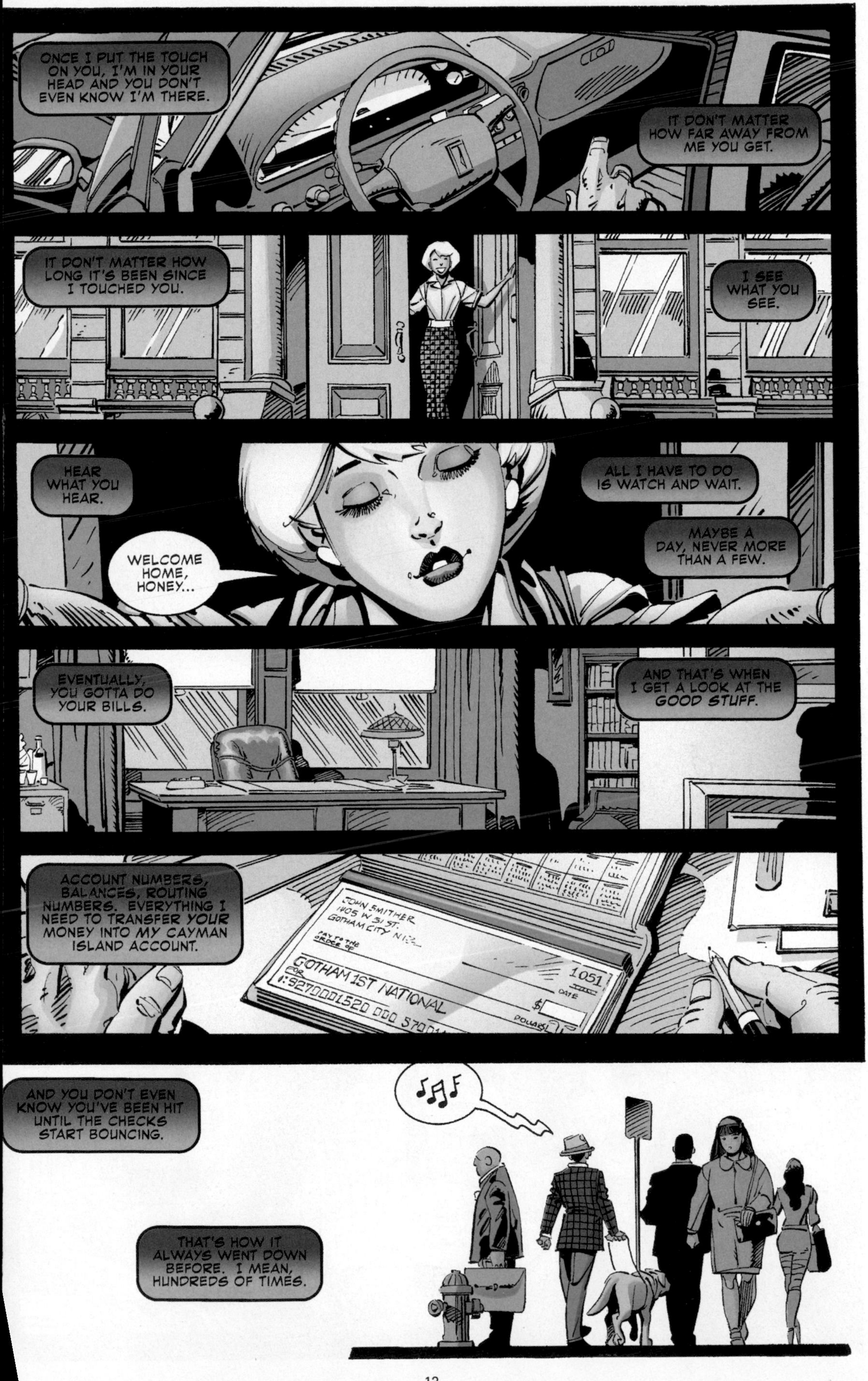
ONCE I PUT THE TOUCH ON YOU, I'M IN YOUR HEAD AND YOU DON'T EVEN KNOW I'M THERE.
IT DON'T MATTER HOW FAR AWAY FROM ME YOU GET.
IT DON'T MATTER HOW LONG IT'S BEEN SINCE I TOUCHED YOU.
I SEE WHAT YOU SEE.
HEAR WHAT YOU HEAR.
WELCOME HOME, HONEY...
ALL I HAVE TO DO IS WATCH AND WAIT.
MAYBE A DAY, NEVER MORE THAN A FEW.
EVENTUALLY, YOU GOTTA DO YOUR BILLS.
AND THAT'S WHEN I GET A LOOK AT THE GOOD STUFF.
ACCOUNT NUMBERS, BALANCES, ROUTING NUMBERS. EVERYTHING I NEED TO TRANSFER YOUR MONEY INTO MY CAYMAN ISLAND ACCOUNT.
JOHN SMITHER
1405 W. 31 ST.
GOTHAM CITY, N.J.
PAY TO THE ORDER OF
1051
DATE
GOTHAM 1ST NATIONAL
FOR
DOLLARS
AND YOU DON'T EVEN KNOW YOU'VE BEEN HIT UNTIL THE CHECKS START BOUNCING.
THAT'S HOW IT ALWAYS WENT DOWN BEFORE. I MEAN, HUNDREDS OF TIMES.

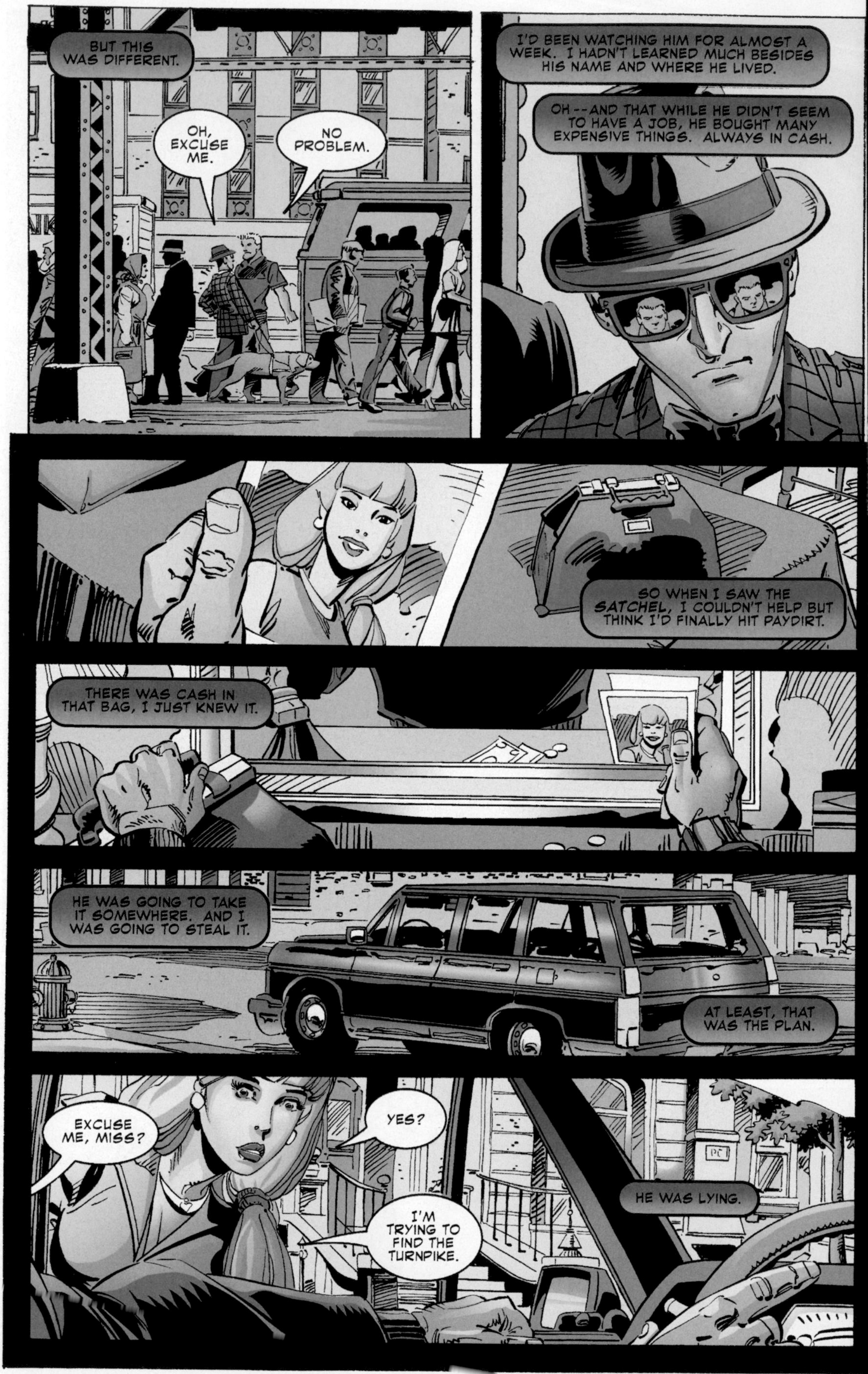
BUT THIS WAS DIFFERENT.
OH, EXCUSE ME.
NO PROBLEM.
I'D BEEN WATCHING HIM FOR ALMOST A WEEK. I HADN'T LEARNED MUCH BESIDES HIS NAME AND WHERE HE LIVED.
OH--AND THAT WHILE HE DIDN'T SEEM TO HAVE A JOB, HE BOUGHT MANY EXPENSIVE THINGS. ALWAYS IN CASH.
SO WHEN I SAW THE SATCHEL, I COULDN'T HELP BUT THINK I'D FINALLY HIT PAYDIRT.
THERE WAS CASH IN THAT BAG, I JUST KNEW IT.
HE WAS GOING TO TAKE IT SOMEWHERE. AND I WAS GOING TO STEAL IT.
AT LEAST, THAT WAS THE PLAN.
EXCUSE ME, MISS?
YES?
I'M TRYING TO FIND THE TURNPIKE.
HE WAS LYING.

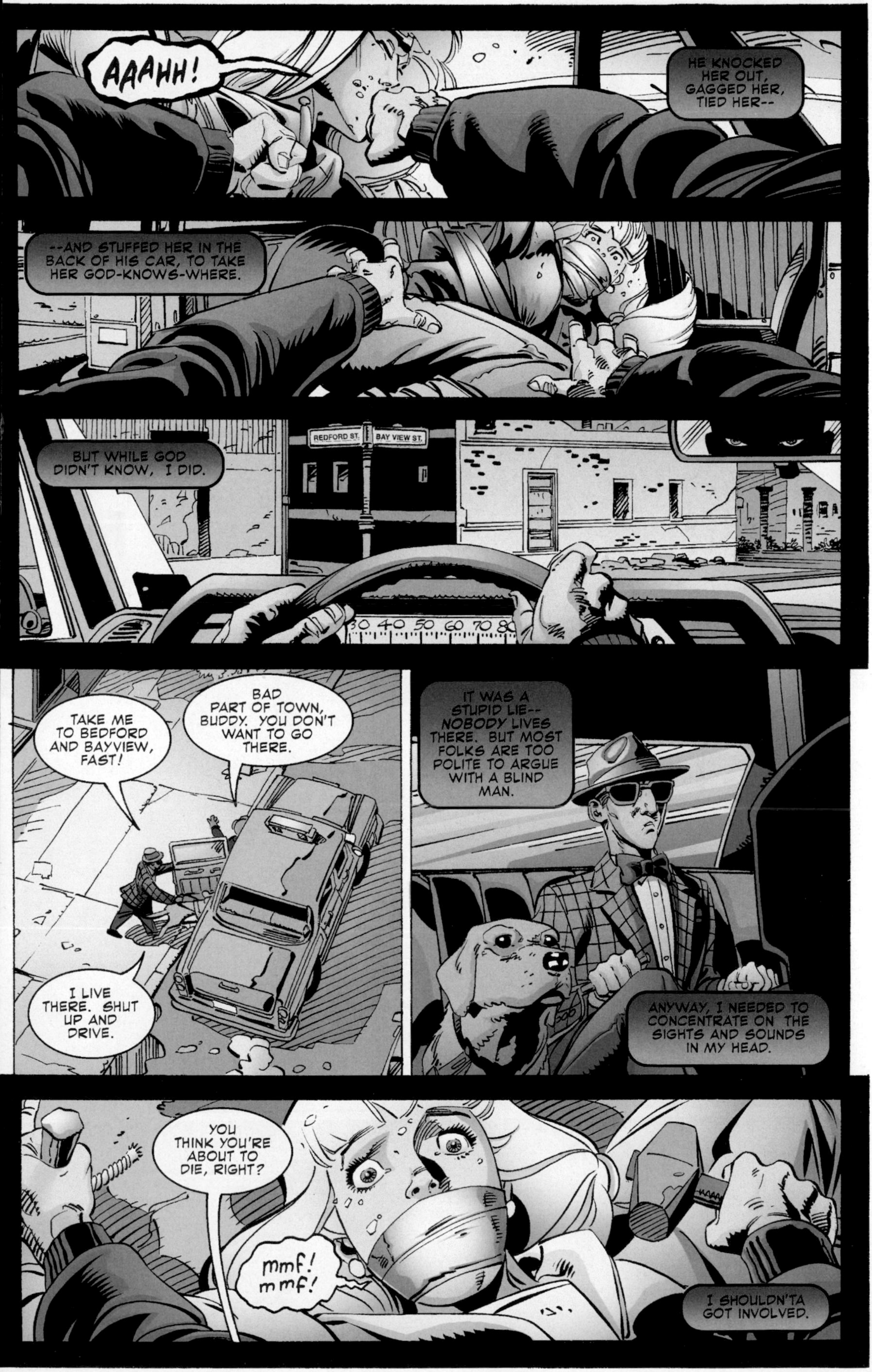
AAAHH!
HE KNOCKED HER OUT, GAGGED HER, TIED HER--
--AND STUFFED HER IN THE BACK OF HIS CAR, TO TAKE HER GOD-KNOWS-WHERE.
BUT WHILE GOD DIDN'T KNOW, I DID.
REDFORD ST.
BAY VIEW ST.
TAKE ME TO BEDFORD AND BAYVIEW, FAST!
BAD PART OF TOWN, BUDDY. YOU DON'T WANT TO GO THERE.
I LIVE THERE. SHUT UP AND DRIVE.
IT WAS A STUPID LIE-- NOBODY LIVES THERE. BUT MOST FOLKS ARE TOO POLITE TO ARGUE WITH A BLIND MAN.
ANYWAY, I NEEDED TO CONCENTRATE ON THE SIGHTS AND SOUNDS IN MY HEAD.
YOU THINK YOU'RE ABOUT TO DIE, RIGHT?
mmf! mmf!
I SHOULDN'TA GOT INVOLVED.

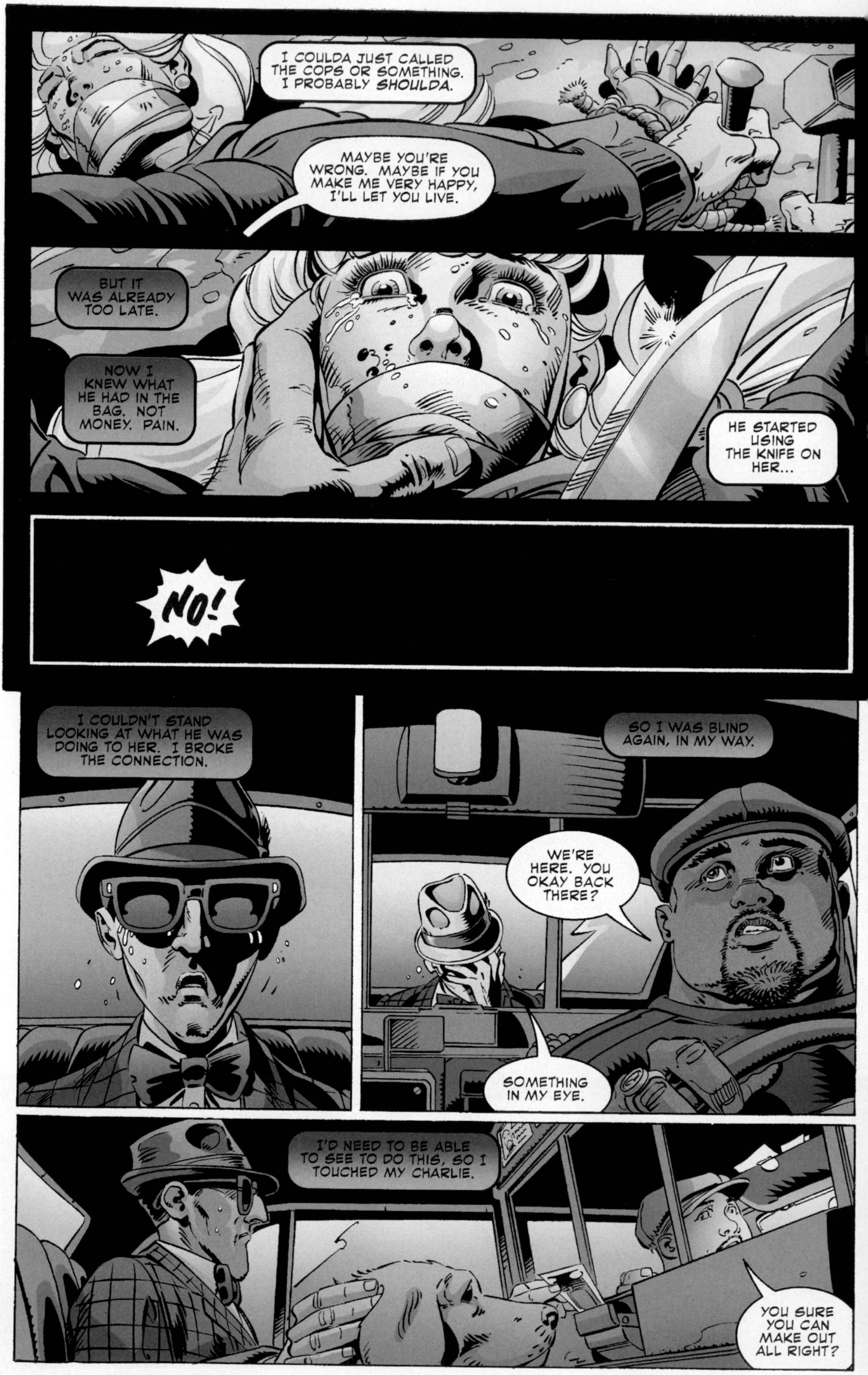
I COULDA JUST CALLED THE COPS OR SOMETHING. I PROBABLY SHOULDA.
MAYBE YOU'RE WRONG. MAYBE IF YOU MAKE ME VERY HAPPY, I'LL LET YOU LIVE.
BUT IT WAS ALREADY TOO LATE.
NOW I KNEW WHAT HE HAD IN THE BAG. NOT MONEY. PAIN.
HE STARTED USING THE KNIFE ON HER...
NO!
I COULDN'T STAND LOOKING AT WHAT HE WAS DOING TO HER. I BROKE THE CONNECTION.
SO I WAS BLIND AGAIN, IN MY WAY.
WE'RE HERE. YOU OKAY BACK THERE?
SOMETHING IN MY EYE.
I'D NEED TO BE ABLE TO SEE TO DO THIS, SO I TOUCHED MY CHARLIE.
YOU SURE YOU CAN MAKE OUT ALL RIGHT?

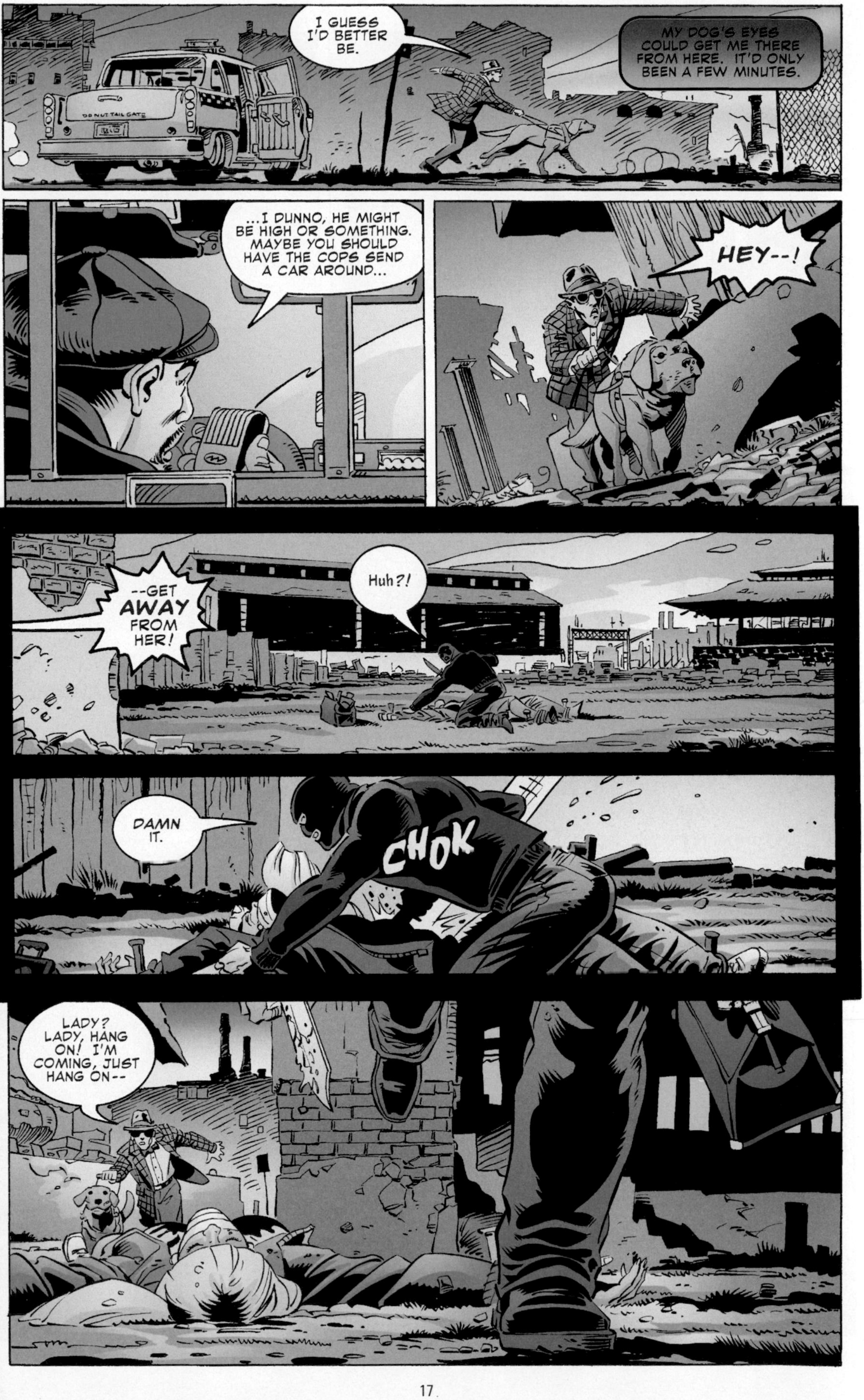

I GUESS I'D BETTER BE.
MY DOG'S EYES COULD GET ME THERE FROM HERE. IT'D ONLY BEEN A FEW MINUTES.
DO NUT TAIL GATE
...I DUNNO, HE MIGHT BE HIGH OR SOMETHING. MAYBE YOU SHOULD HAVE THE COPS SEND A CAR AROUND...
HEY--!
--GET AWAY FROM HER!
Huh?!
DAMN IT.
CHOK
LADY? LADY, HANG ON! I'M COMING, JUST HANG ON--

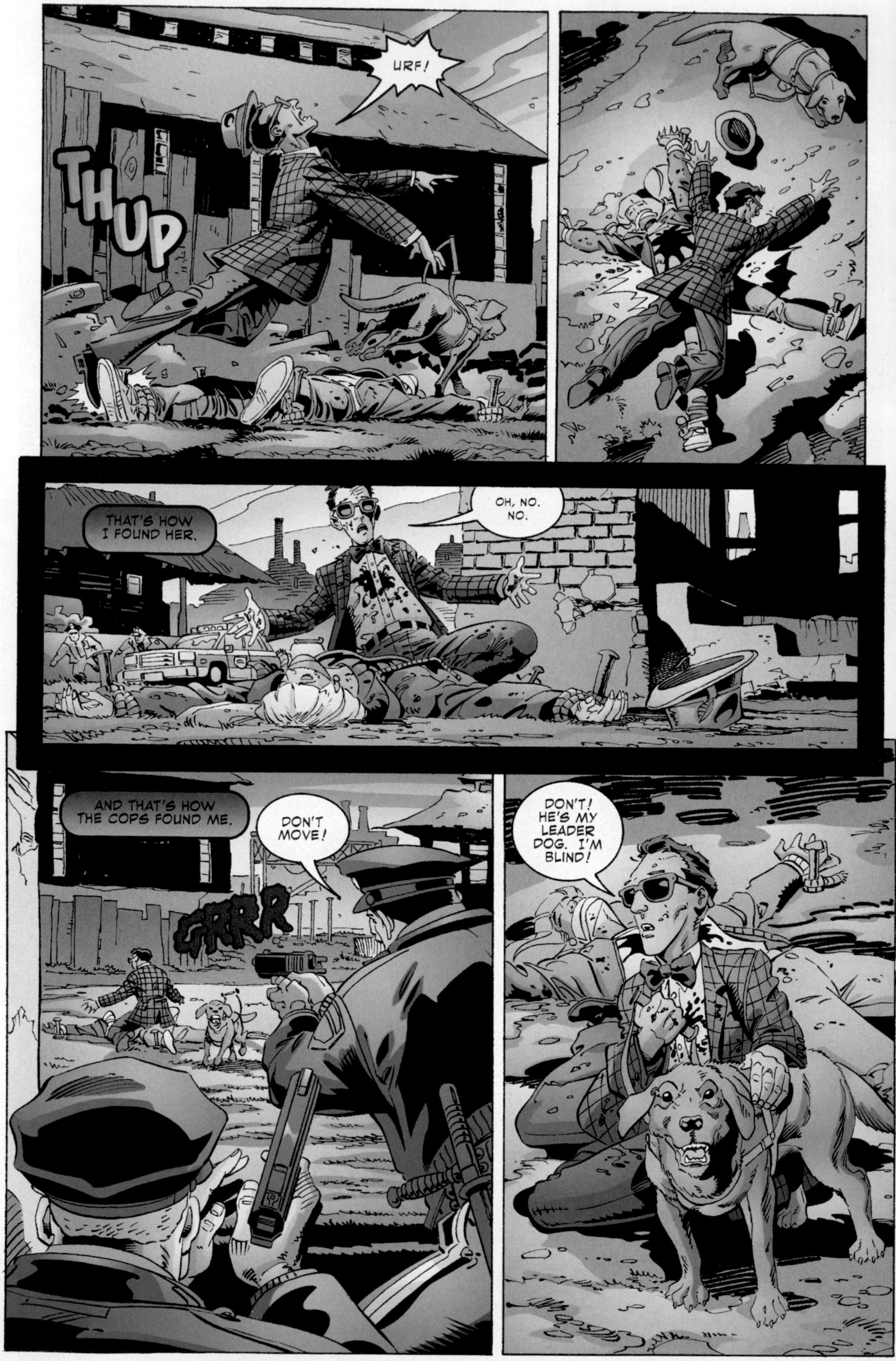
URF!
THUP
THAT'S HOW I FOUND HER.
OH, NO. NO.
AND THAT'S HOW THE COPS FOUND ME.
DON'T MOVE!
GRRR
DON'T! HE'S MY LEADER DOG. I'M BLIND!

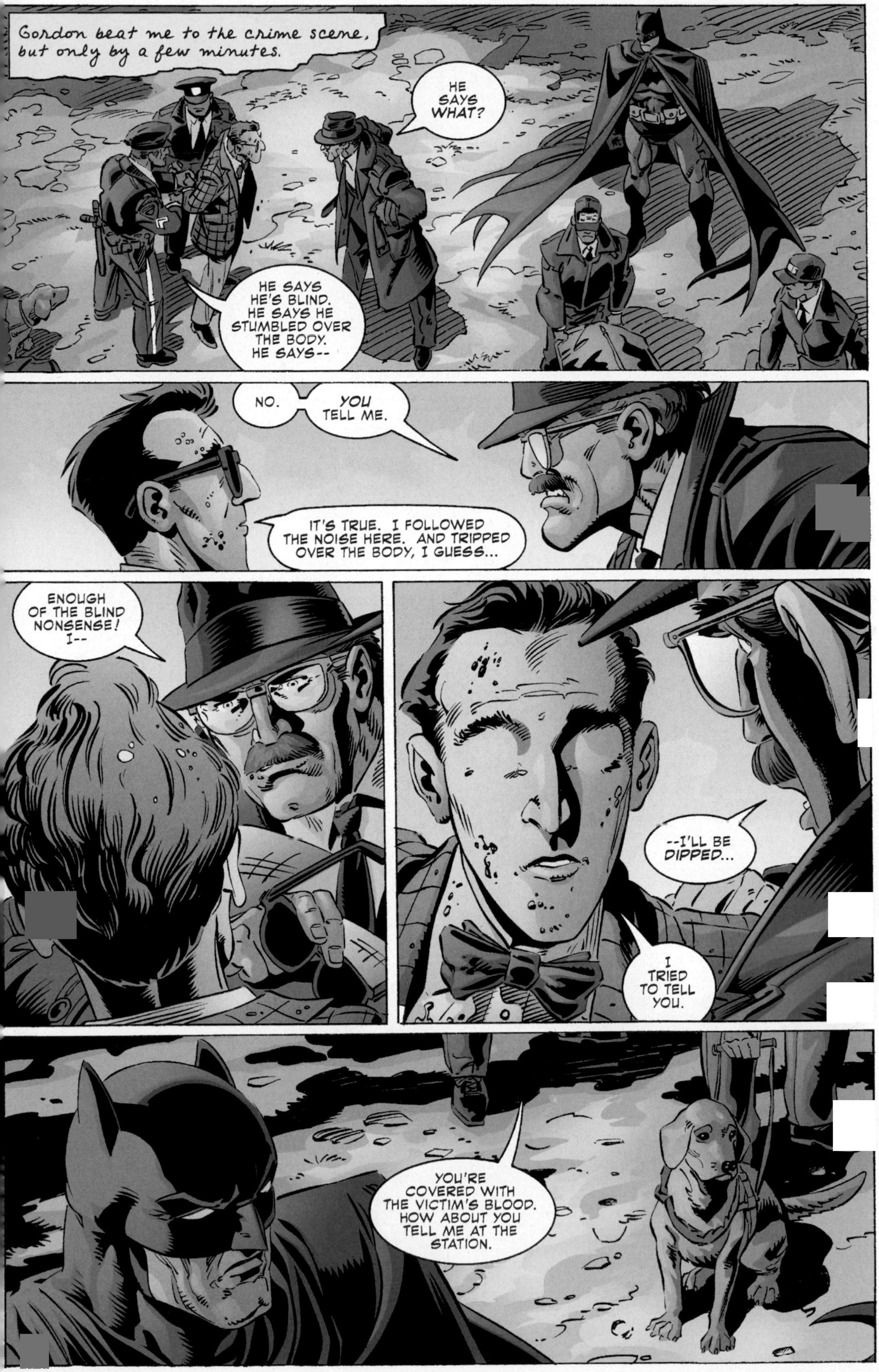

Gordon beat me to the crime scene, but only by a few minutes.
HE SAYS WHAT?
HE SAYS HE'S BLIND. HE SAYS HE STUMBLED OVER THE BODY. HE SAYS--
NO.
YOU TELL ME.
IT'S TRUE. I FOLLOWED THE NOISE HERE. AND TRIPPED OVER THE BODY, I GUESS...
ENOUGH OF THE BLIND NONSENSE! I--
--I'LL BE DIPPED...
I TRIED TO TELL YOU.
YOU'RE COVERED WITH THE VICTIM'S BLOOD. HOW ABOUT YOU TELL ME AT THE STATION.

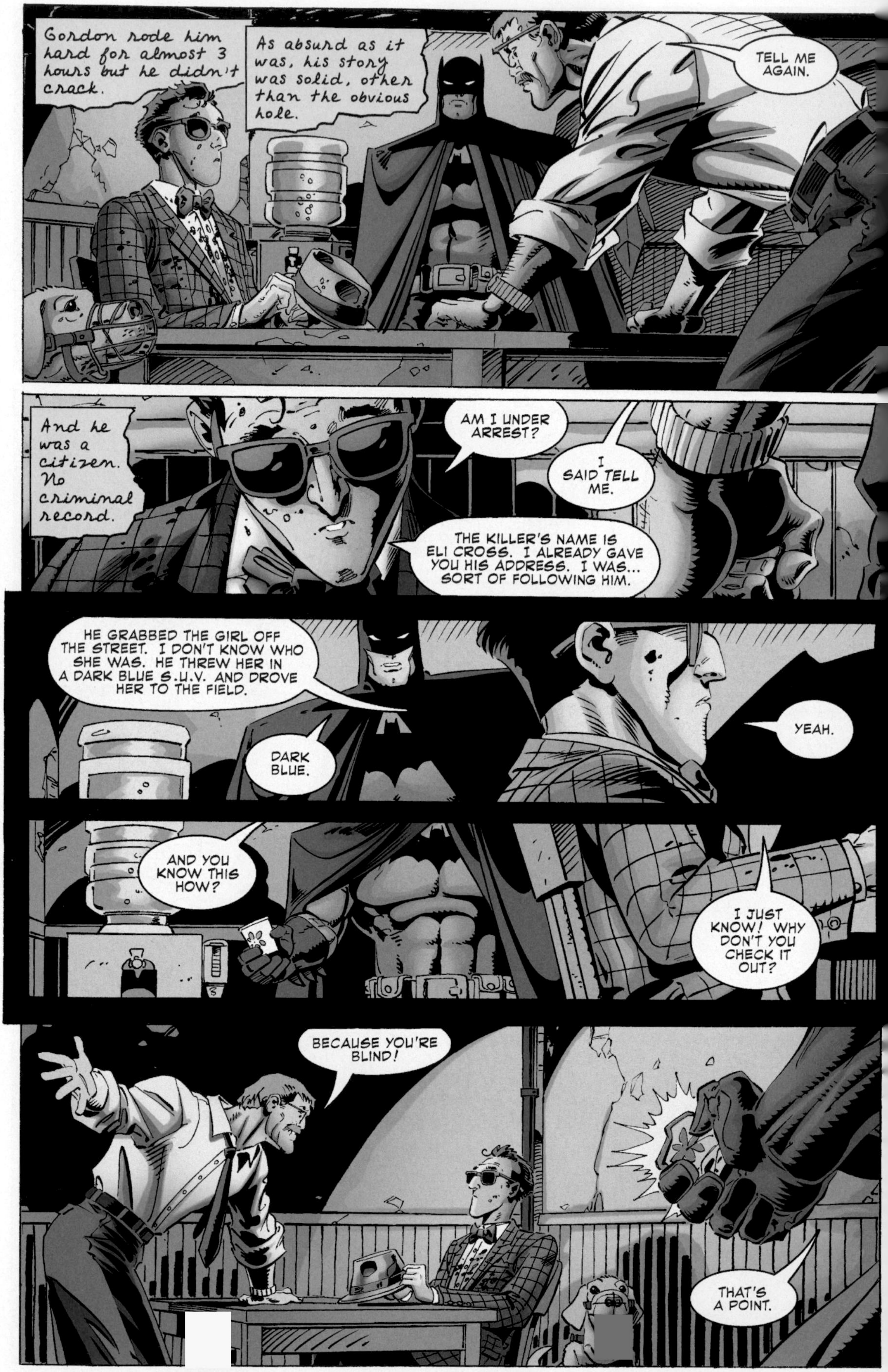
Gordon rode him hard for almost 3 hours but he didn't crack.
As absurd as it was, his story was solid, other than the obvious hole.
TELL ME AGAIN.
And he was a citizen. No criminal record.
AM I UNDER ARREST?
I SAID TELL ME.
THE KILLER'S NAME IS ELI CROSS. I ALREADY GAVE YOU HIS ADDRESS. I WAS... SORT OF FOLLOWING HIM.
HE GRABBED THE GIRL OFF THE STREET. I DON'T KNOW WHO SHE WAS. HE THREW HER IN A DARK BLUE S.U.V. AND DROVE HER TO THE FIELD.
DARK BLUE.
YEAH.
AND YOU KNOW THIS HOW?
I JUST KNOW! WHY DON'T YOU CHECK IT OUT?
BECAUSE YOU'RE BLIND!
THAT'S A POINT.

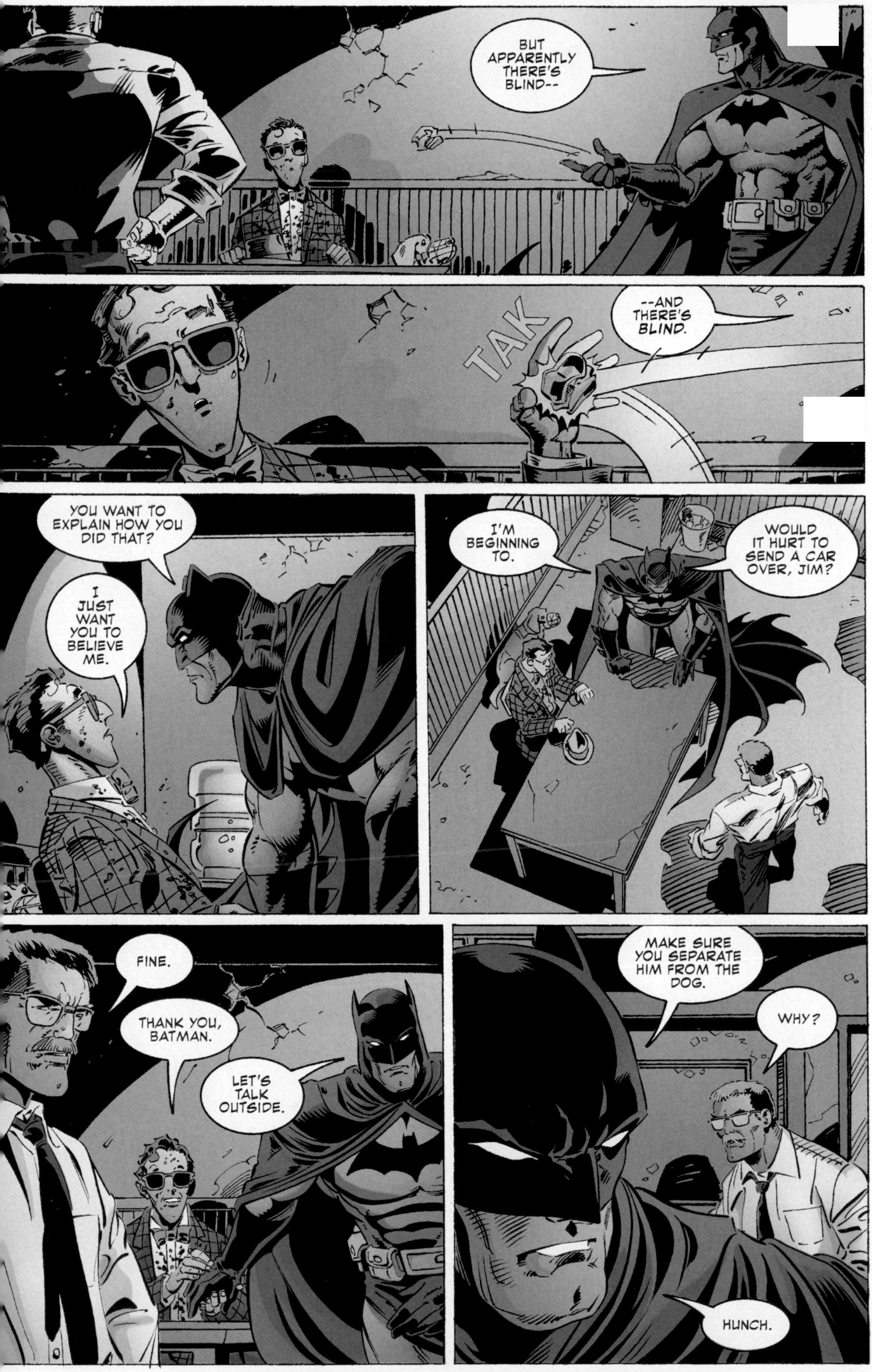

BUT APPARENTLY THERE'S BLIND--
--AND THERE'S BLIND.
TAK
YOU WANT TO EXPLAIN HOW YOU DID THAT?
I JUST WANT YOU TO BELIEVE ME.
I'M BEGINNING TO.
WOULD IT HURT TO SEND A CAR OVER, JIM?
FINE.
THANK YOU, BATMAN.
LET'S TALK OUTSIDE.
MAKE SURE YOU SEPARATE HIM FROM THE DOG.
WHY?
HUNCH.

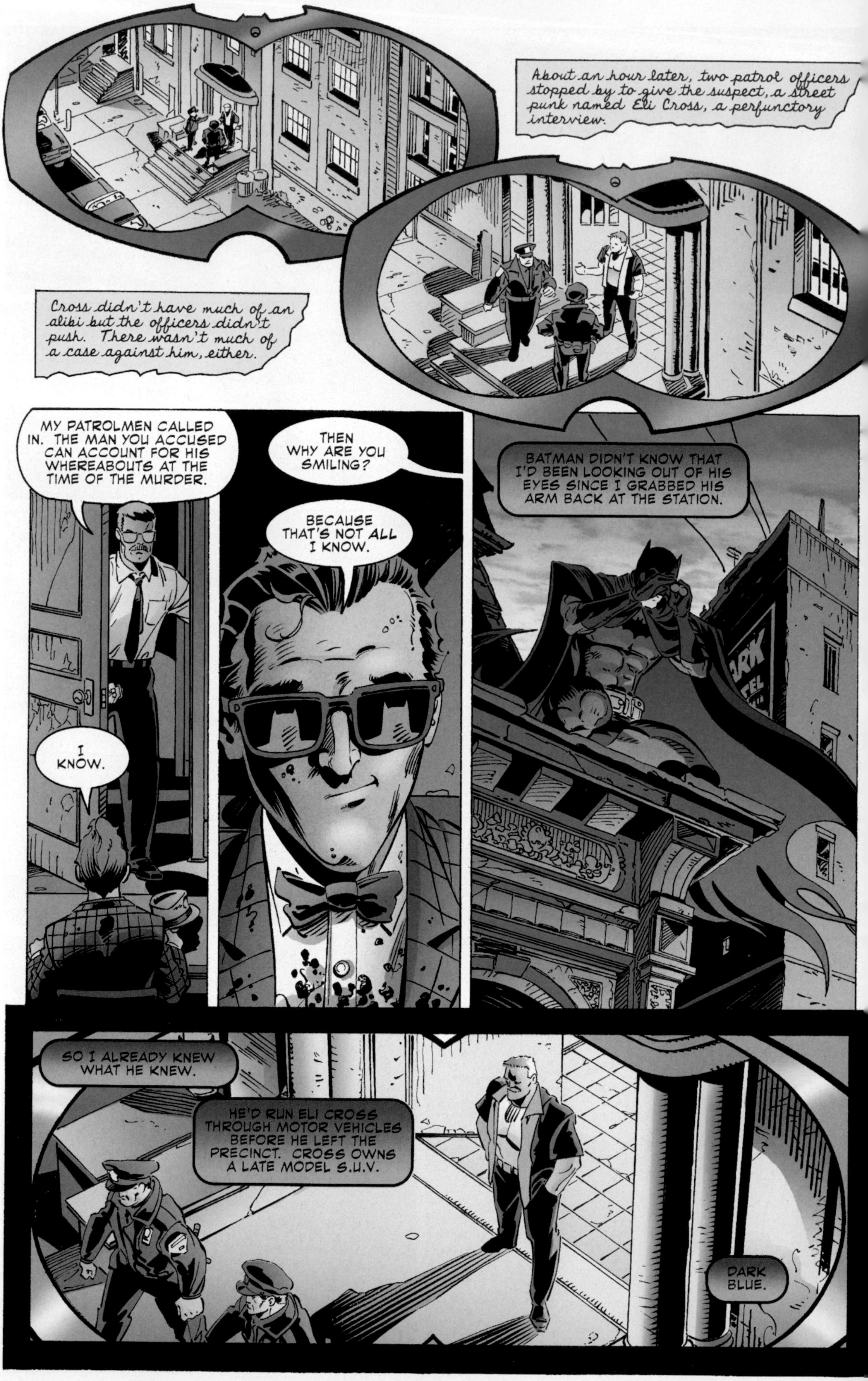
About an hour later, two patrol officers stopped by to give the suspect, a street punk named Eli Cross, a perfunctory interview.
Cross didn't have much of an alibi but the officers didn't push. There wasn't much of a case against him, either.
MY PATROLMEN CALLED IN. THE MAN YOU ACCUSED CAN ACCOUNT FOR HIS WHEREABOUTS AT THE TIME OF THE MURDER.
I KNOW.
THEN WHY ARE YOU SMILING?
BECAUSE THAT'S NOT ALL I KNOW.
BATMAN DIDN'T KNOW THAT I'D BEEN LOOKING OUT OF HIS EYES SINCE I GRABBED HIS ARM BACK AT THE STATION.
SO I ALREADY KNEW WHAT HE KNEW.
HE'D RUN ELI CROSS THROUGH MOTOR VEHICLES BEFORE HE LEFT THE PRECINCT. CROSS OWNS A LATE MODEL S.U.V.
DARK BLUE.

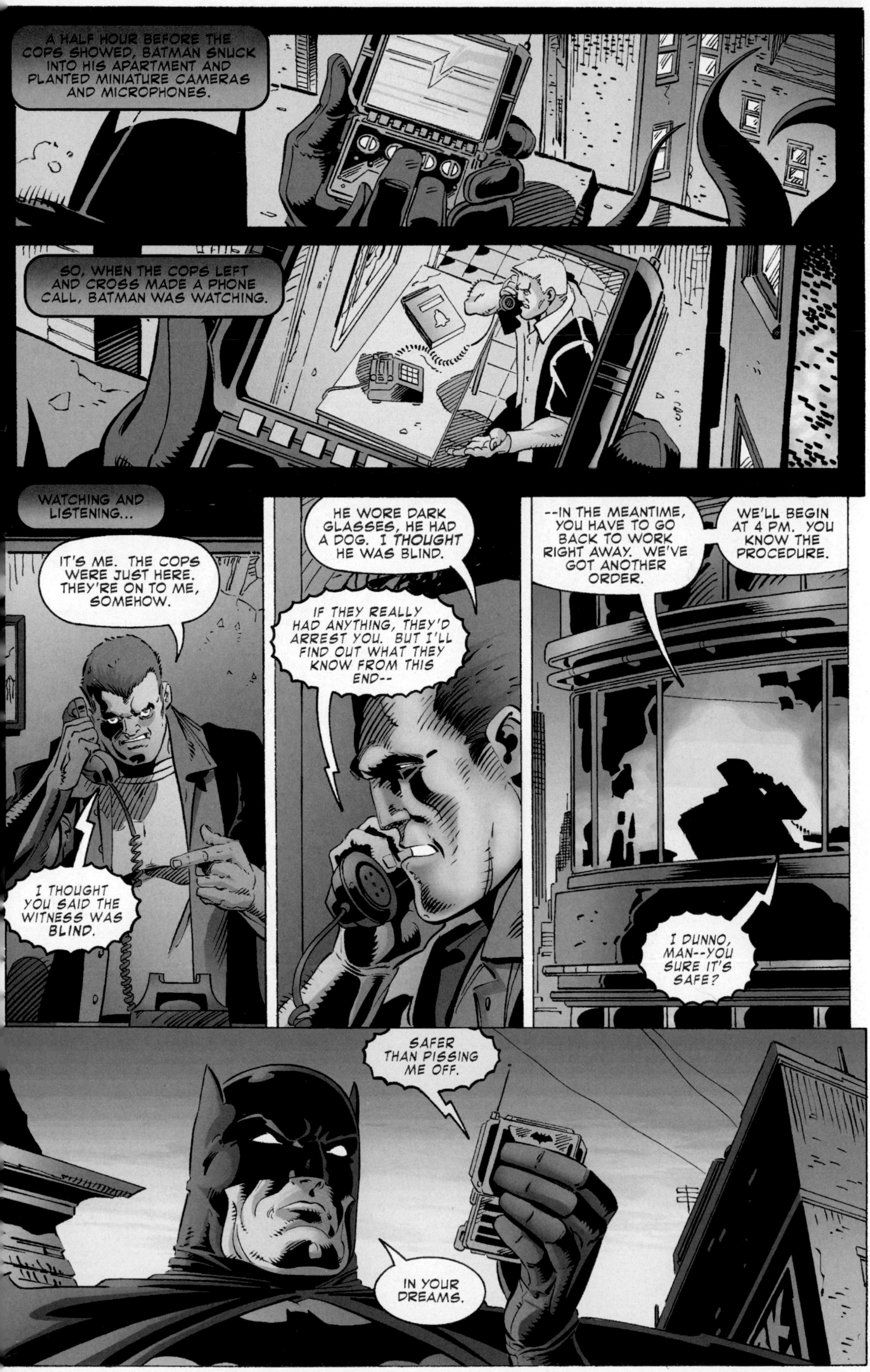
A HALF HOUR BEFORE THE COPS SHOWED, BATMAN SNUCK INTO HIS APARTMENT AND PLANTED MINIATURE CAMERAS AND MICROPHONES.
SO, WHEN THE COPS LEFT AND CROSS MADE A PHONE CALL, BATMAN WAS WATCHING.
WATCHING AND LISTENING...
IT'S ME. THE COPS WERE JUST HERE. THEY'RE ON TO ME, SOMEHOW.
I THOUGHT YOU SAID THE WITNESS WAS BLIND.
HE WORE DARK GLASSES, HE HAD A DOG. I THOUGHT HE WAS BLIND.
IF THEY REALLY HAD ANYTHING, THEY'D ARREST YOU. BUT I'LL FIND OUT WHAT THEY KNOW FROM THIS END--
--IN THE MEANTIME, YOU HAVE TO GO BACK TO WORK RIGHT AWAY. WE'VE GOT ANOTHER ORDER.
WE'LL BEGIN AT 4 PM. YOU KNOW THE PROCEDURE.
I DUNNO, MAN--YOU SURE IT'S SAFE?
SAFER THAN PISSING ME OFF.
IN YOUR DREAMS.

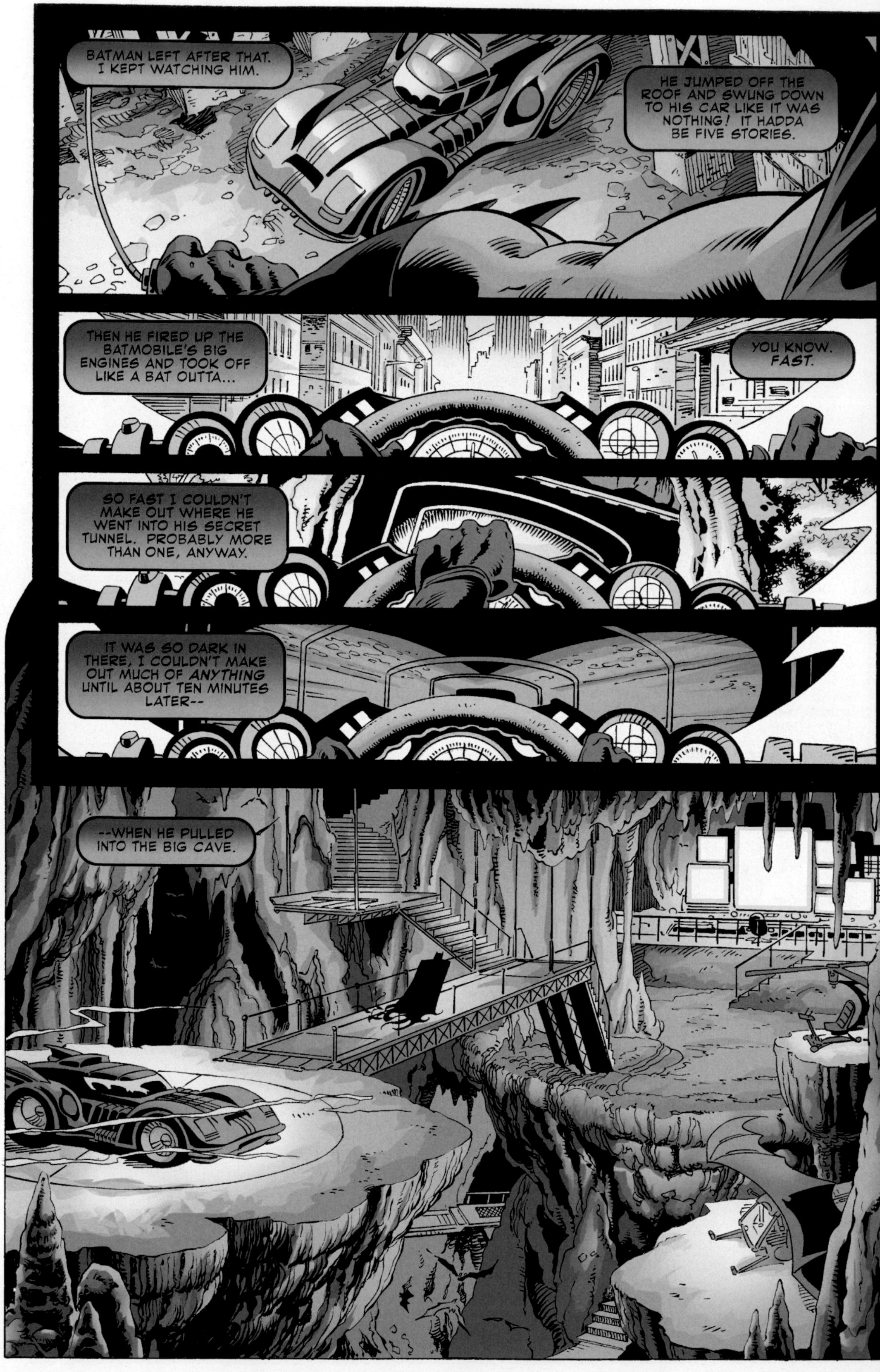
BATMAN LEFT AFTER THAT. I KEPT WATCHING HIM.
HE JUMPED OFF THE ROOF AND SWUNG DOWN TO HIS CAR LIKE IT WAS NOTHING! IT HADDA BE FIVE STORIES.
THEN HE FIRED UP THE BATMOBILE'S BIG ENGINES AND TOOK OFF LIKE A BAT OUTTA...
YOU KNOW. *FAST.*
SO FAST I COULDN'T MAKE OUT WHERE HE WENT INTO HIS SECRET TUNNEL. PROBABLY MORE THAN ONE, ANYWAY.
IT WAS SO DARK IN THERE, I COULDN'T MAKE OUT MUCH OF *ANYTHING* UNTIL ABOUT TEN MINUTES LATER--
--WHEN HE PULLED INTO THE BIG CAVE.

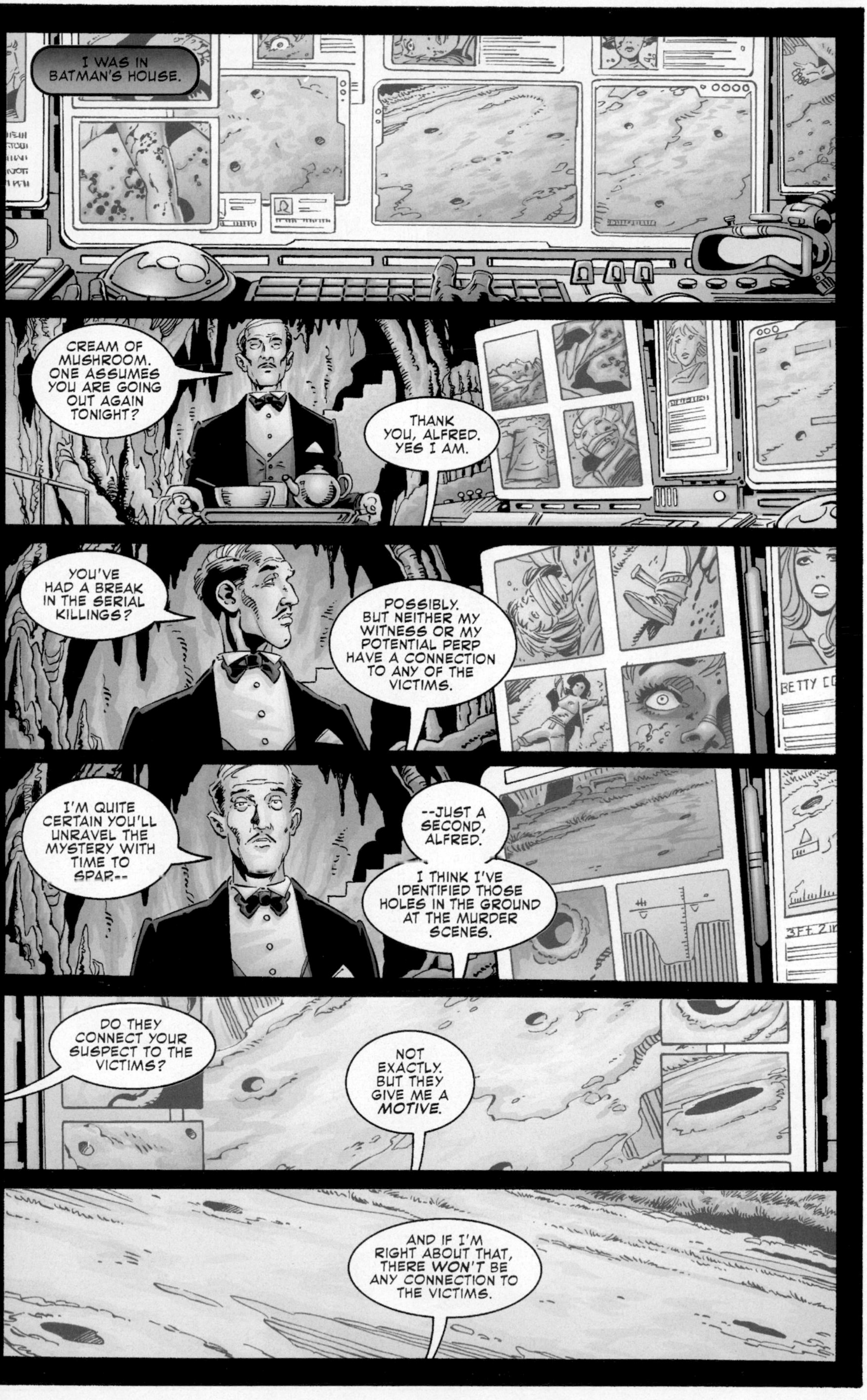
I WAS IN BATMAN'S HOUSE.
CREAM OF MUSHROOM. ONE ASSUMES YOU ARE GOING OUT AGAIN TONIGHT?
THANK YOU, ALFRED. YES I AM.
YOU'VE HAD A BREAK IN THE SERIAL KILLINGS?
POSSIBLY. BUT NEITHER MY WITNESS OR MY POTENTIAL PERP HAVE A CONNECTION TO ANY OF THE VICTIMS.
BETTY C
I'M QUITE CERTAIN YOU'LL UNRAVEL THE MYSTERY WITH TIME TO SPAR--
--JUST A SECOND, ALFRED.
I THINK I'VE IDENTIFIED THOSE HOLES IN THE GROUND AT THE MURDER SCENES.
DO THEY CONNECT YOUR SUSPECT TO THE VICTIMS?
NOT EXACTLY. BUT THEY GIVE ME A *MOTIVE*.
AND IF I'M RIGHT ABOUT THAT, THERE *WON'T* BE ANY CONNECTION TO THE VICTIMS.

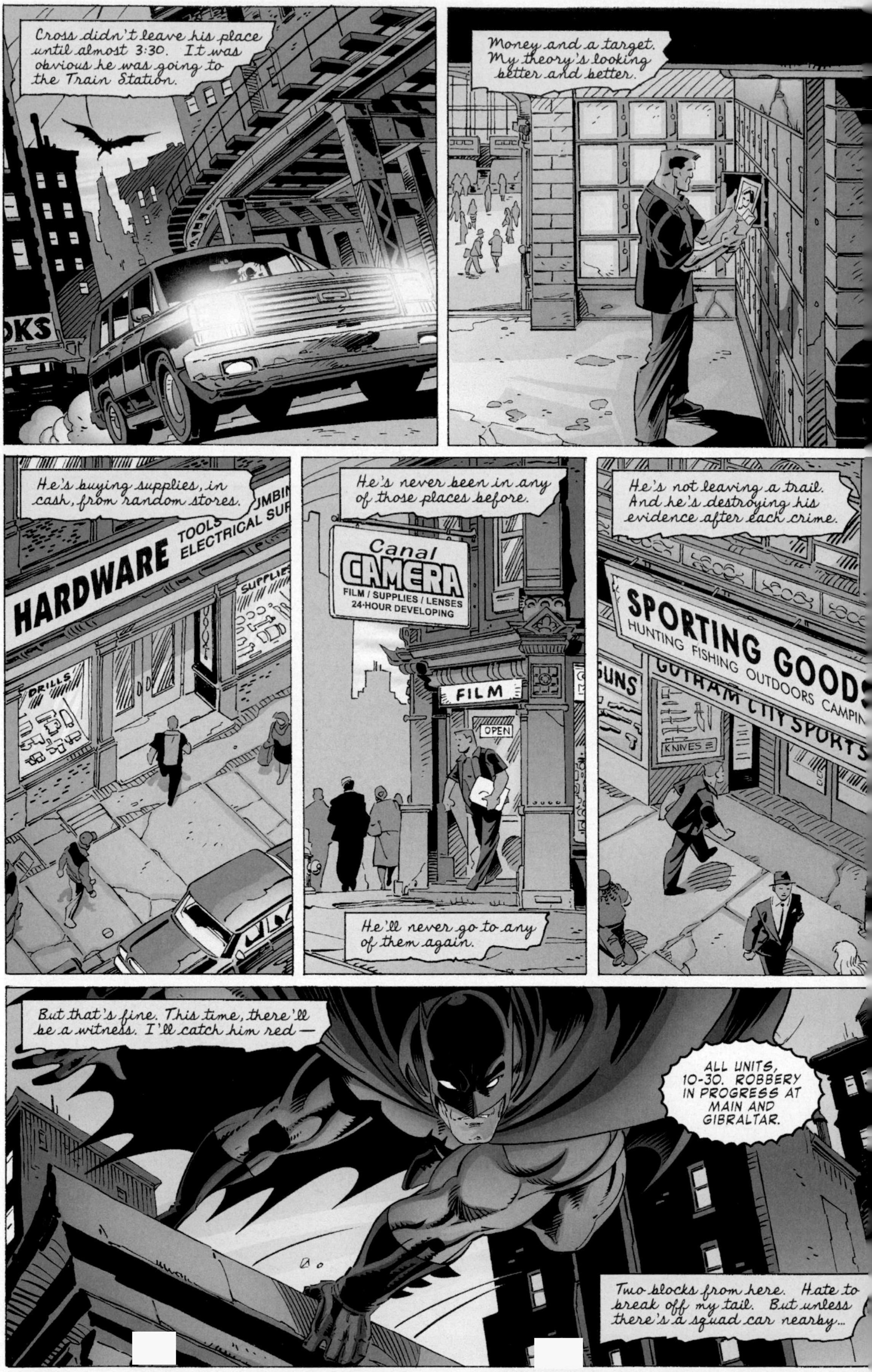
Cross didn't leave his place until almost 3:30. It was obvious he was going to the Train Station.
Money and a target. My theory's looking better and better.
He's buying supplies, in cash, from random stores.
HARDWARE TOOLS ELECTRICAL SU
DRILLS
He's never been in any of those places before.
Canal CAMERA FILM / SUPPLIES / LENSES 24-HOUR DEVELOPING
FILM
OPEN
He'll never go to any of them again.
He's not leaving a trail. And he's destroying his evidence after each crime.
SPORTING GOODS HUNTING FISHING OUTDOORS CAMPIN
GOTHAM CITY SPORTS
GUNS
KNIVES
But that's fine. This time, there'll be a witness. I'll catch him red—
ALL UNITS, 10-30. ROBBERY IN PROGRESS AT MAIN AND GIBRALTAR.
Two blocks from here. Hate to break off my tail. But unless there's a squad car nearby...

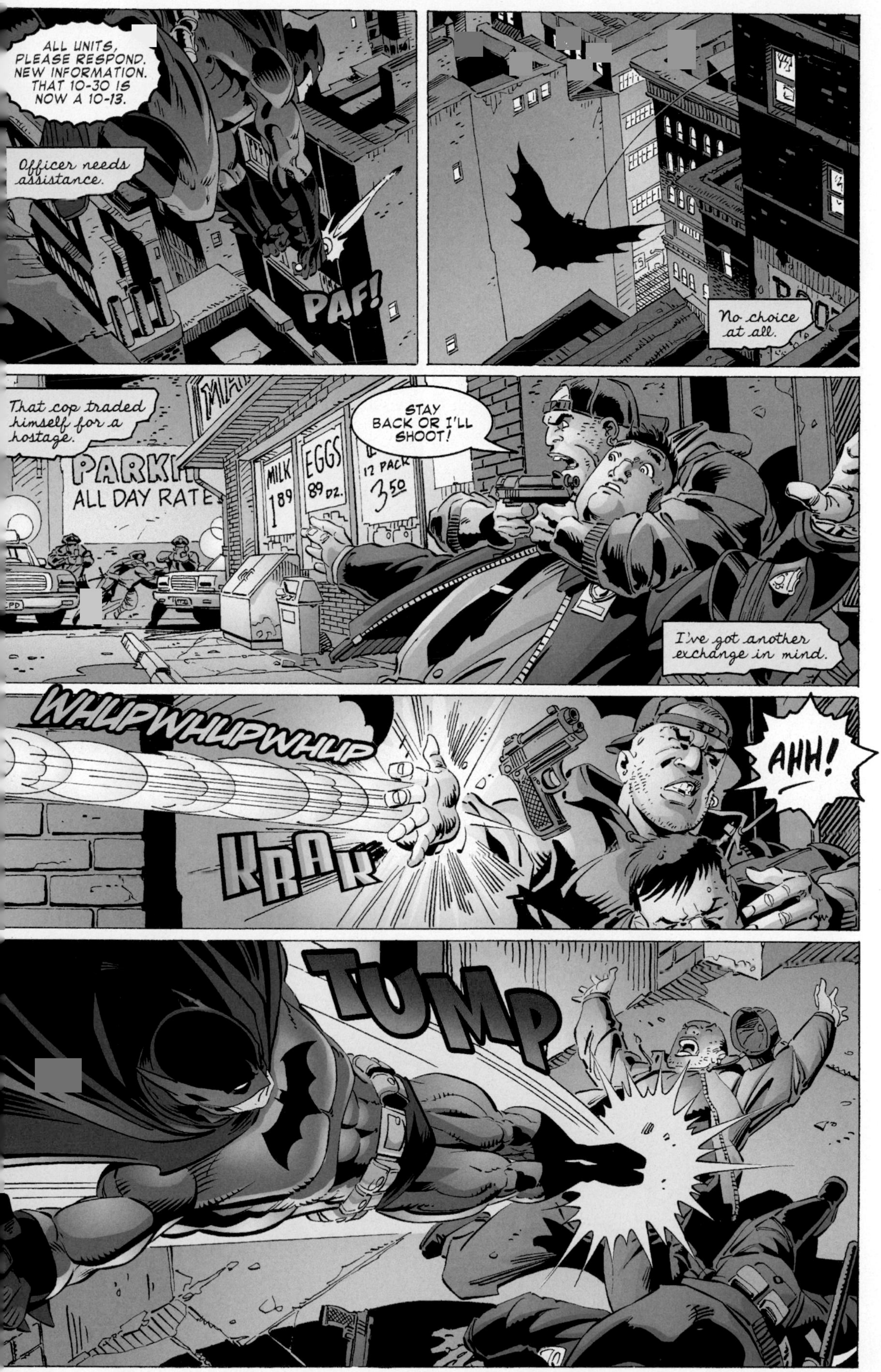
ALL UNITS, PLEASE RESPOND. NEW INFORMATION. THAT 10-30 IS NOW A 10-13.
Officer needs assistance.
PAF!
No choice at all.
That cop traded himself for a hostage.
PARKI
ALL DAY RATE
MILK 1.89
EGGS 89 DZ.
12 PACK 3.50
STAY BACK OR I'LL SHOOT!
I've got another exchange in mind.
WHUPWHUPWHUP
KRAAK
AHH!
TUMP

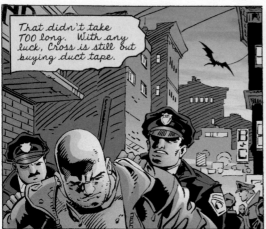

That didn't take TOO long. With any luck, Cross is still out buying duct tape.

I was off his trail for 20 minutes.

It took another 15 to track the G.P.S. transmitter I'd planted on him.

Plenty of time for him to put his plan in motion.

I'M GOING TO TAKE OFF YOUR GAG NOW. I WANT TO HEAR YOU SCREAM.

mnnnf!

But not NEARLY enough time for him to succeed.

PUT DOWN THE KNIFE.

WHAT--?

PUT DOWN THE KNIFE AND STEP AWAY FROM THE WOMAN.

STAY BACK! I'LL KILL YOU!

Another second and he'd be disarmed.

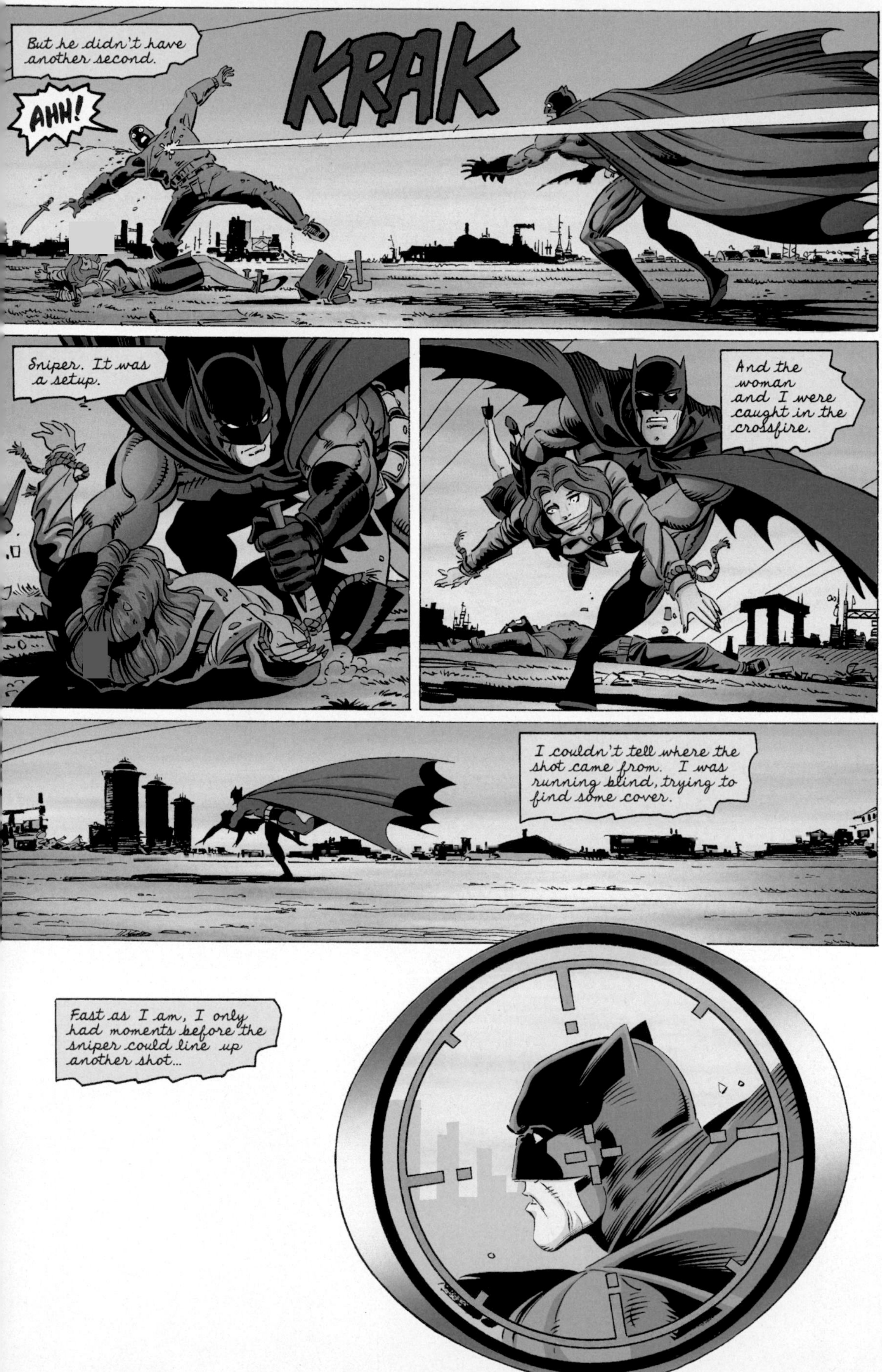
But he didn't have another second.
AHH!
KRAK
Sniper. It was a setup.
And the woman and I were caught in the crossfire.
I couldn't tell where the shot came from. I was running blind, trying to find some cover.
Fast as I am, I only had moments before the sniper could line up another shot...

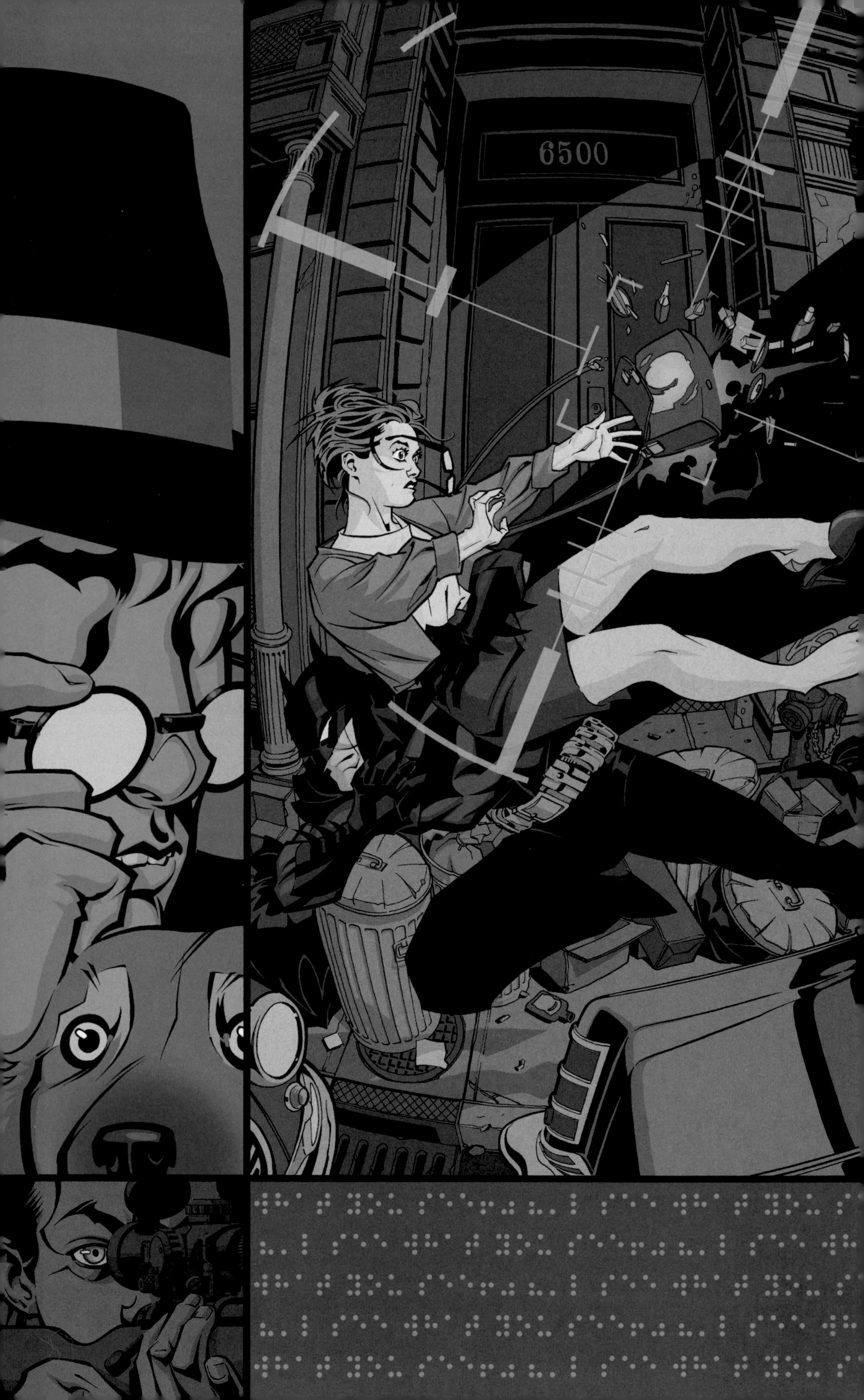
6500

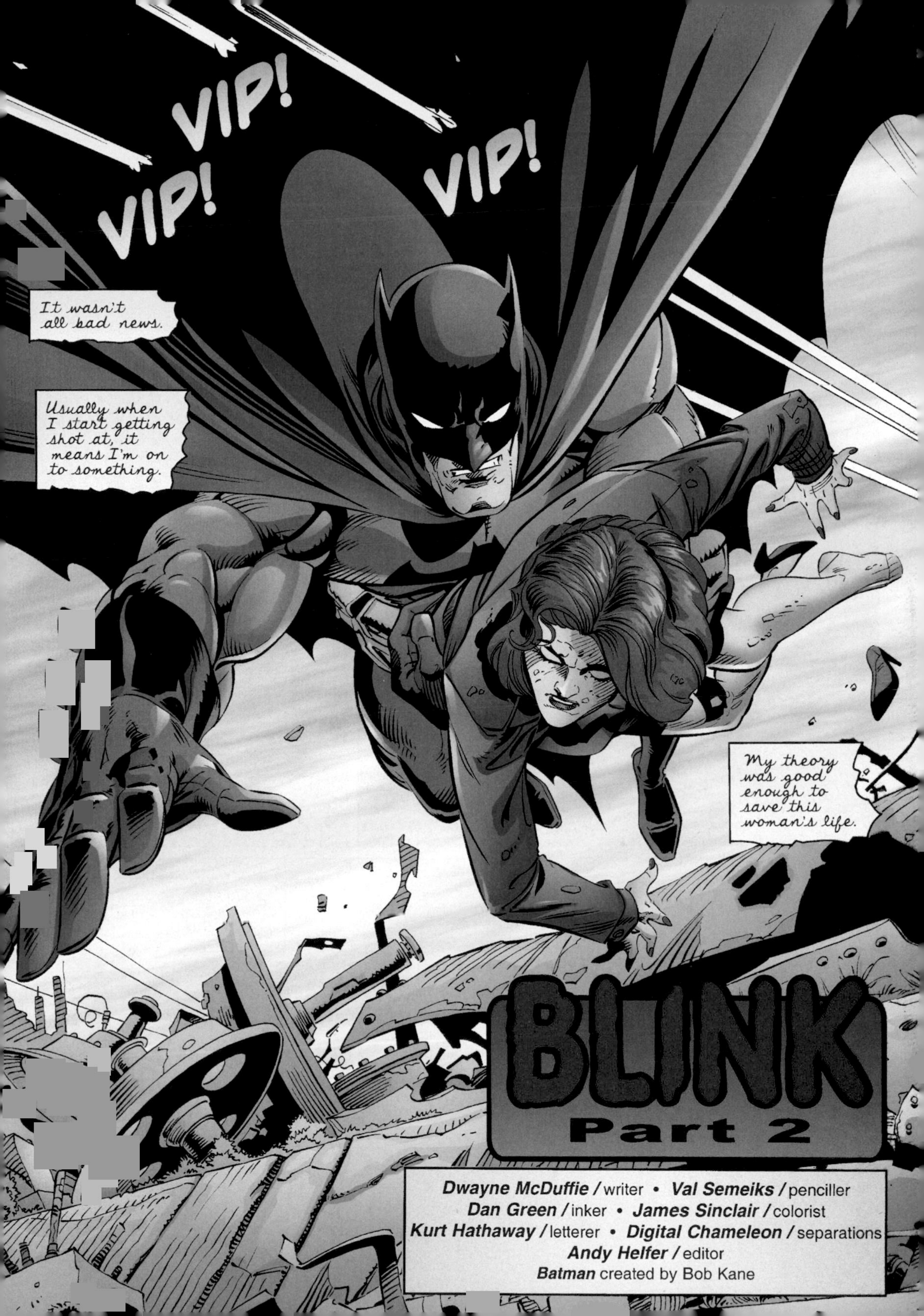
VIP!
VIP!
VIP!
It wasn't all bad news.
Usually when I start getting shot at, it means I'm on to something.
My theory was good enough to save this woman's life.
BLINK
Part 2
Dwayne McDuffie / writer • Val Semeiks / penciller
Dan Green / inker • James Sinclair / colorist
Kurt Hathaway / letterer • Digital Chameleon / separations
Andy Helfer / editor
Batman created by Bob Kane

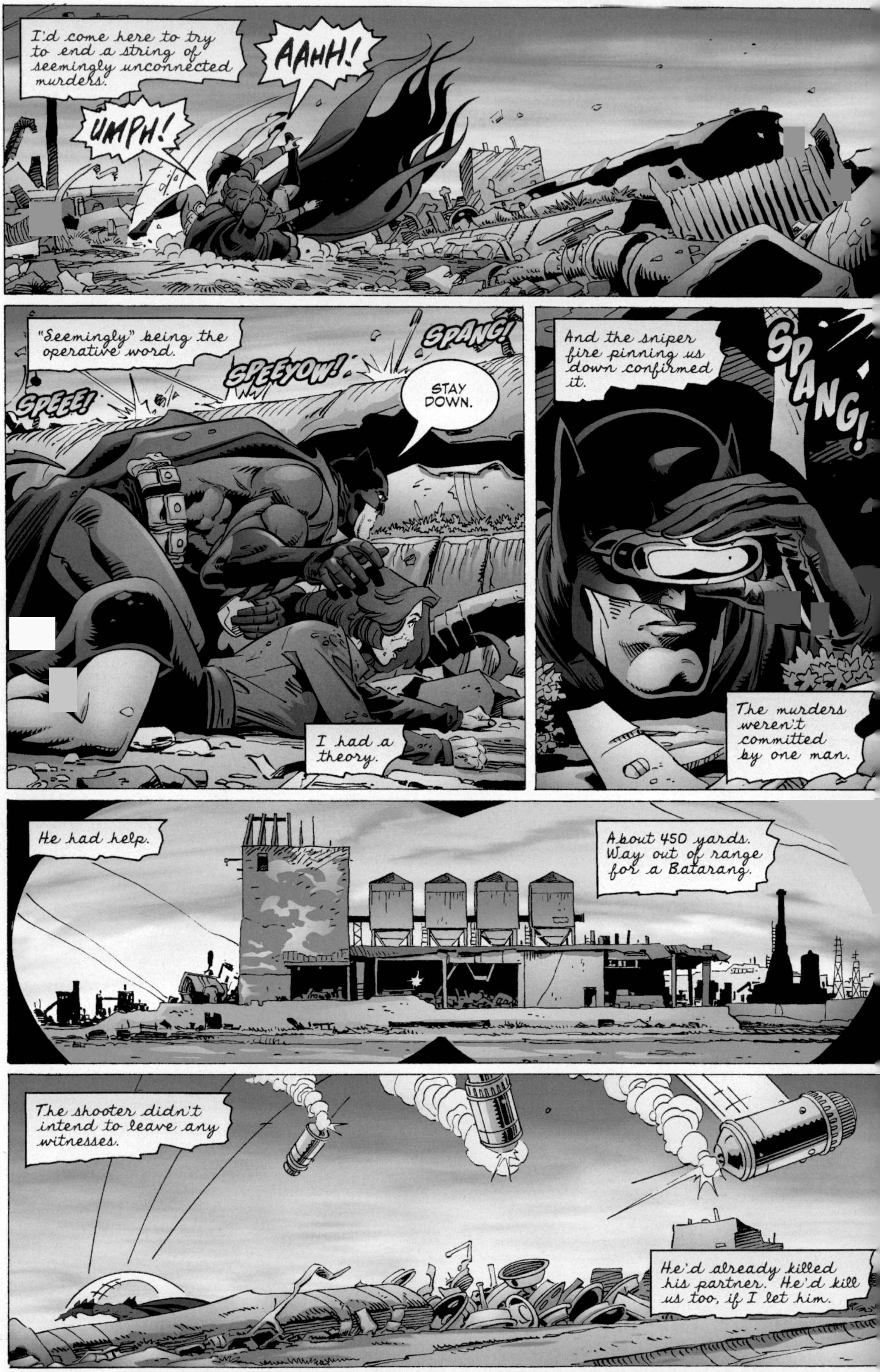

I'd come here to try to end a string of seemingly unconnected murders.
AAHH!
UMPH!
"Seemingly" being the operative word.
SPEEE!
SPEEYOW!
SPANG!
STAY DOWN.
I had a theory.
And the sniper fire pinning us down confirmed it.
SPANG!
The murders weren't committed by one man.
He had help.
About 450 yards. Way out of range for a Batarang.
The shooter didn't intend to leave any witnesses.
He'd already killed his partner. He'd kill us too, if I let him.

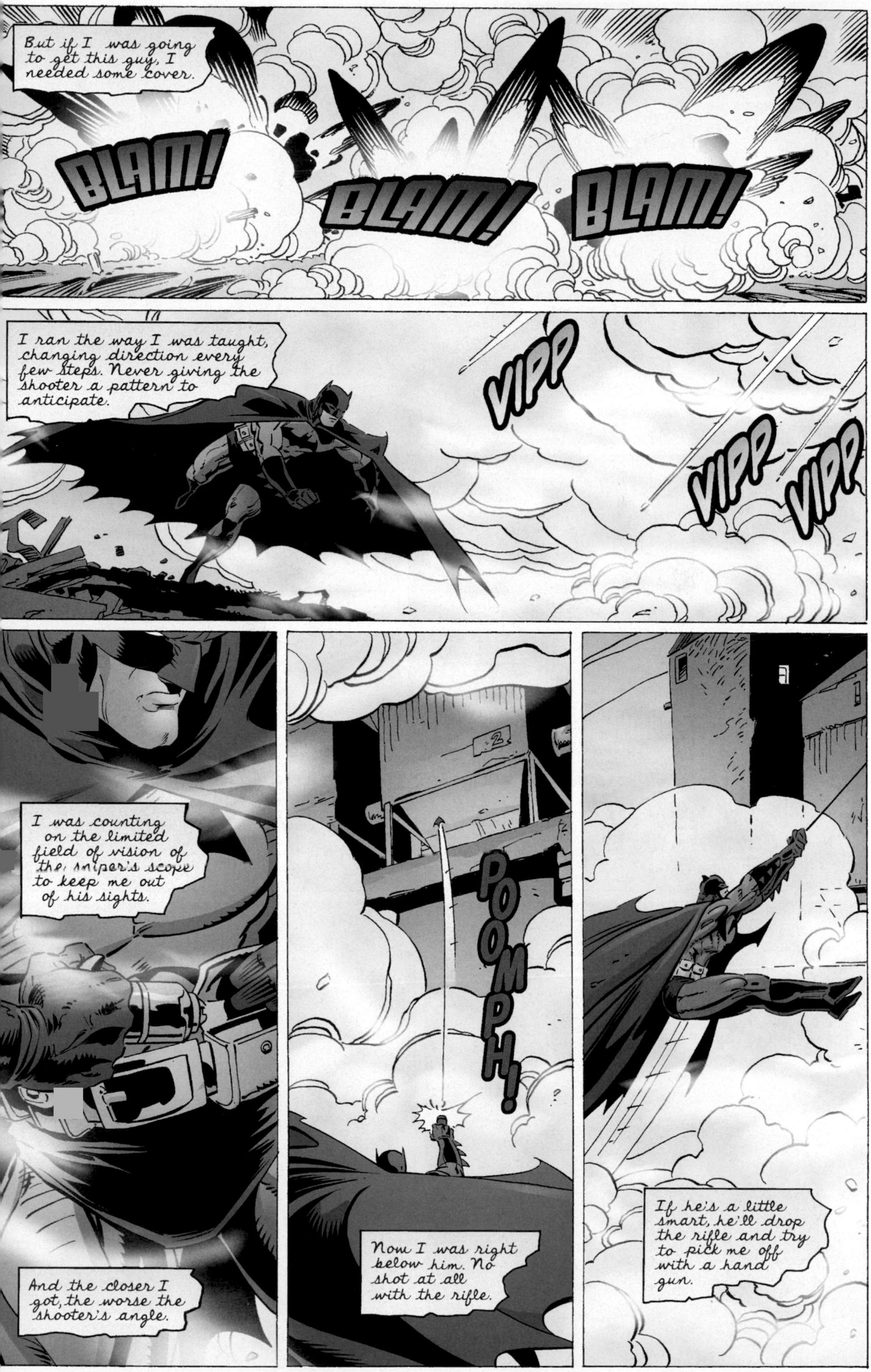
But if I was going to get this guy, I needed some cover.
BLAM!
BLAM!
BLAM!
I ran the way I was taught, changing direction every few steps. Never giving the shooter a pattern to anticipate.
VIPP
VIPP
VIPP
I was counting on the limited field of vision of the sniper's scope to keep me out of his sights.
And the closer I got, the worse the shooter's angle.
POOMPH!
Now I was right below him. No shot at all with the rifle.
If he's a little smart, he'll drop the rifle and try to pick me off with a hand gun.

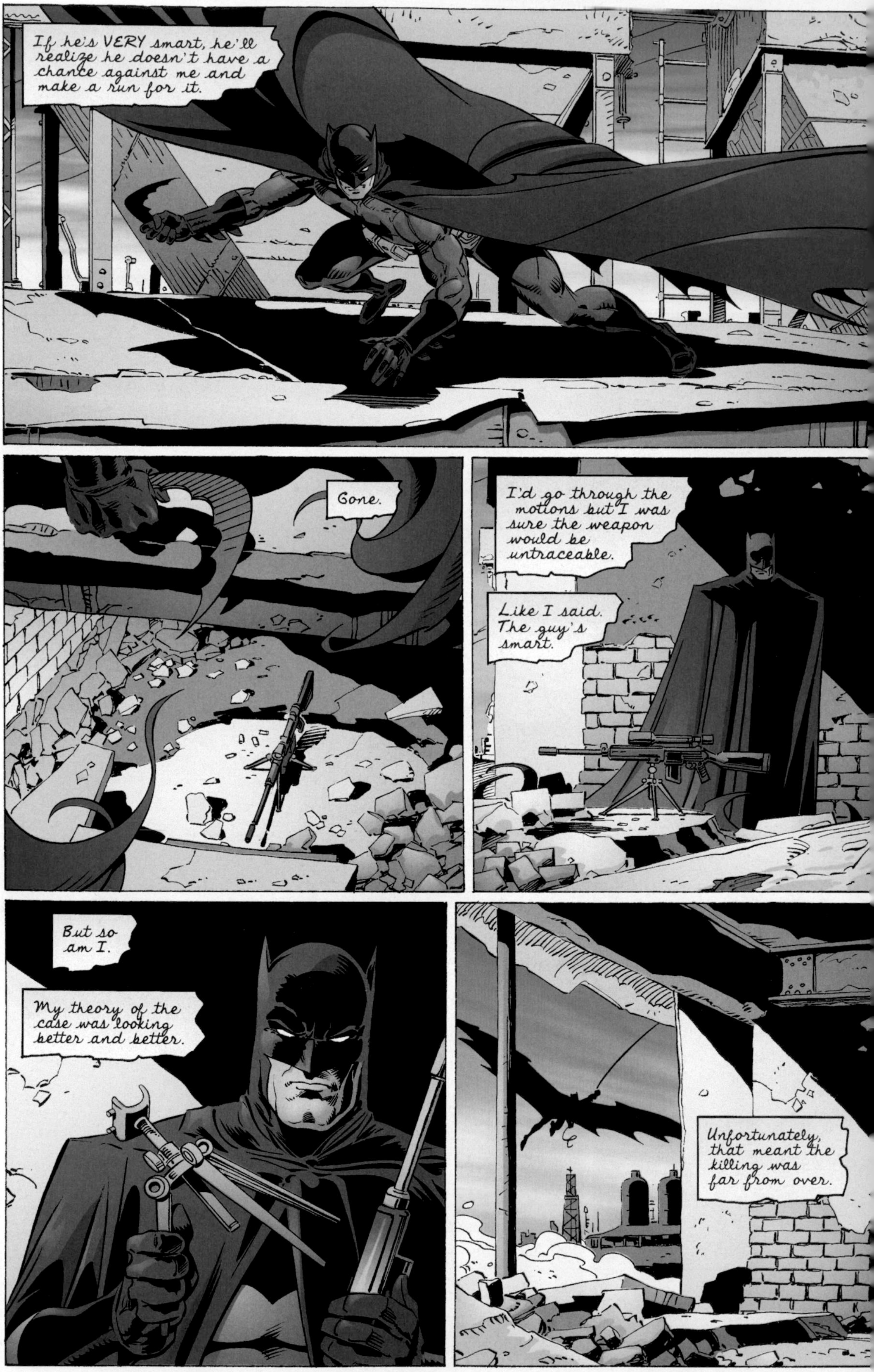

If he's VERY smart, he'll realize he doesn't have a chance against me and make a run for it.
Gone.
I'd go through the motions but I was sure the weapon would be untraceable.
Like I said. The guy's smart.
But so am I.
My theory of the case was looking better and better.
Unfortunately, that meant the killing was far from over.

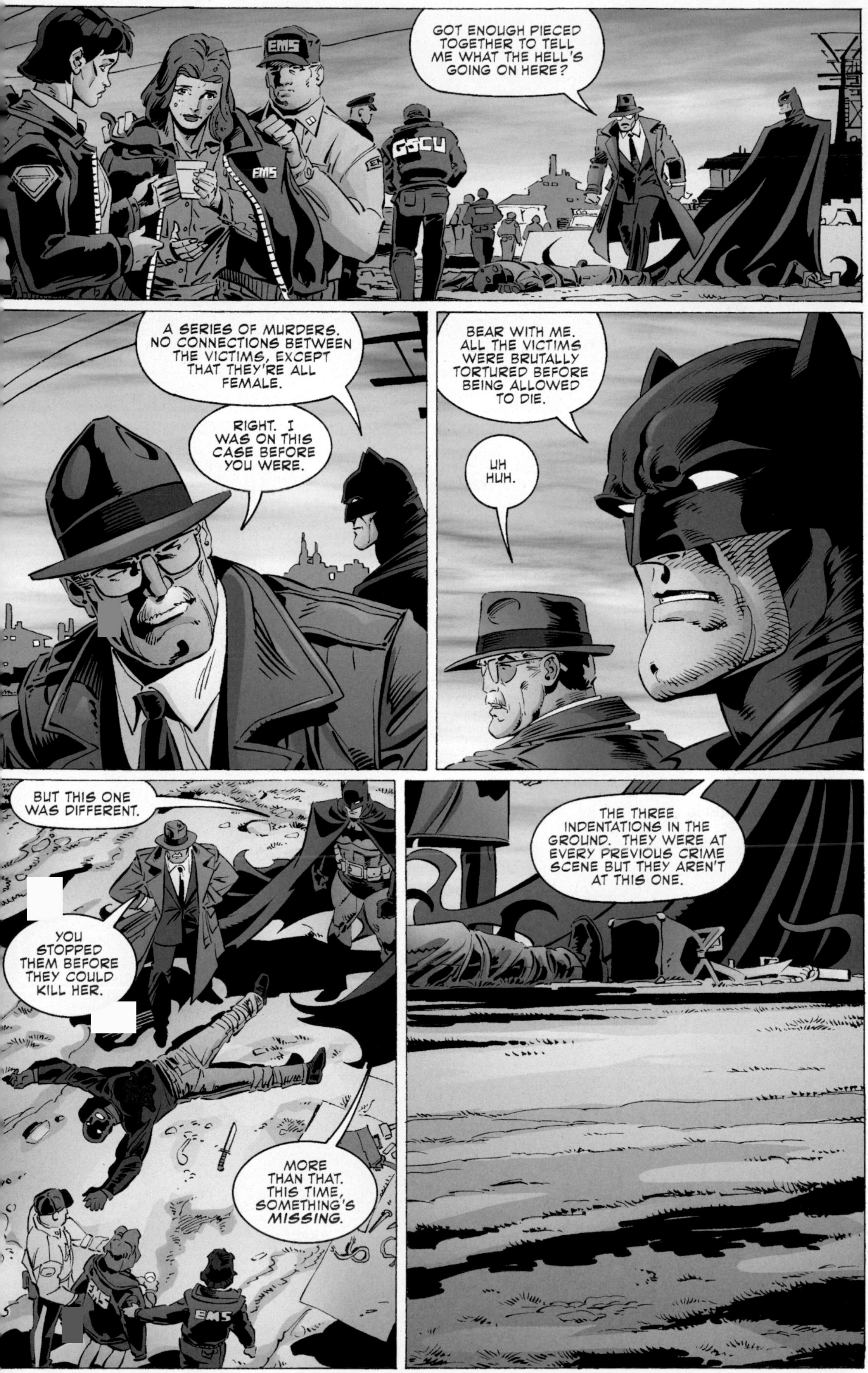

GOT ENOUGH PIECED TOGETHER TO TELL ME WHAT THE HELL'S GOING ON HERE?
A SERIES OF MURDERS. NO CONNECTIONS BETWEEN THE VICTIMS, EXCEPT THAT THEY'RE ALL FEMALE.
RIGHT. I WAS ON THIS CASE BEFORE YOU WERE.
BEAR WITH ME. ALL THE VICTIMS WERE BRUTALLY TORTURED BEFORE BEING ALLOWED TO DIE.
UH HUH.
BUT THIS ONE WAS DIFFERENT.
YOU STOPPED THEM BEFORE THEY COULD KILL HER.
MORE THAN THAT. THIS TIME, SOMETHING'S *MISSING*.
THE THREE INDENTATIONS IN THE GROUND. THEY WERE AT EVERY PREVIOUS CRIME SCENE BUT THEY AREN'T AT THIS ONE.

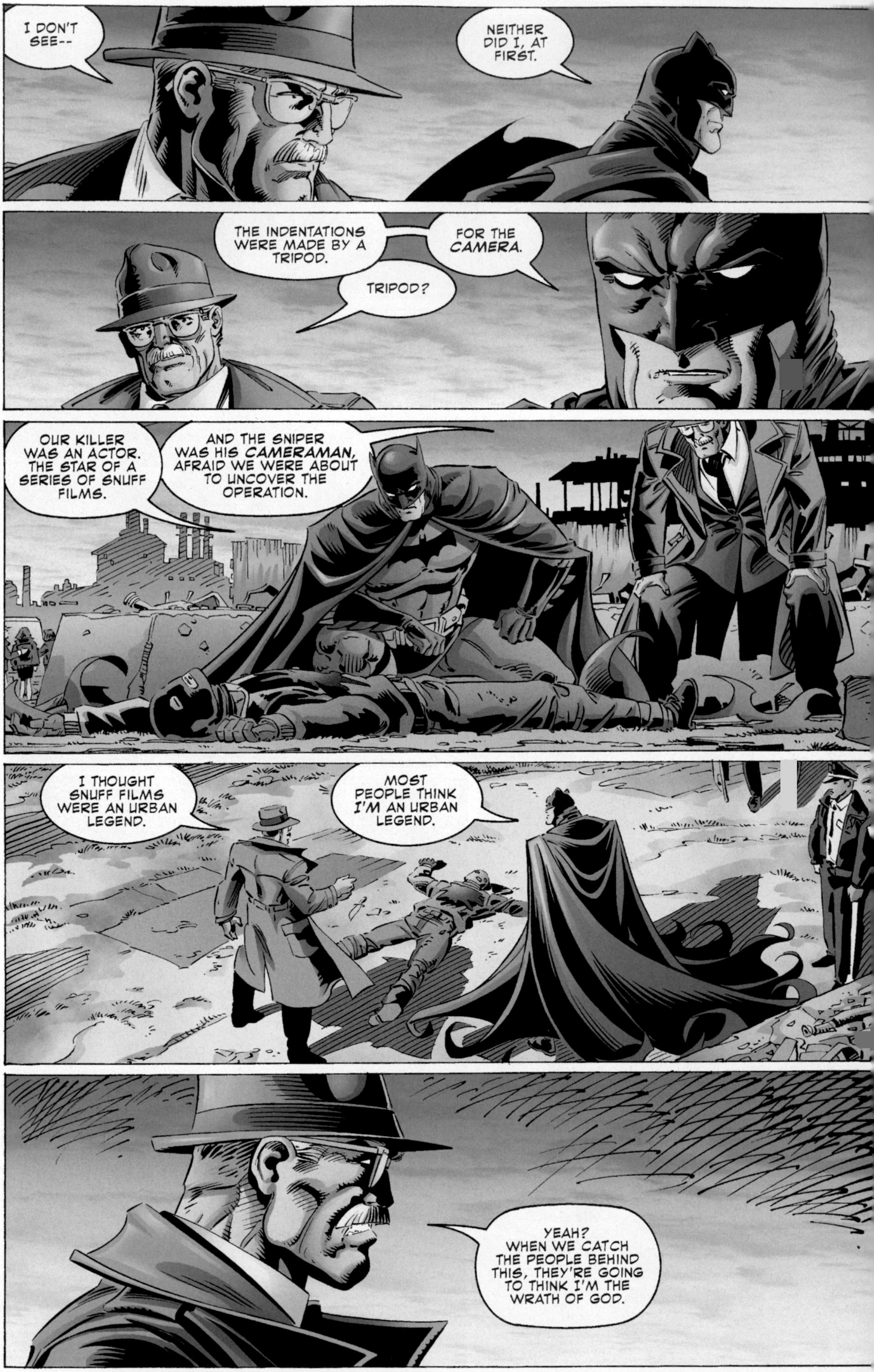
I DON'T SEE--
NEITHER DID I, AT FIRST.
THE INDENTATIONS WERE MADE BY A TRIPOD.
FOR THE CAMERA.
TRIPOD?
OUR KILLER WAS AN ACTOR. THE STAR OF A SERIES OF SNUFF FILMS.
AND THE SNIPER WAS HIS CAMERAMAN, AFRAID WE WERE ABOUT TO UNCOVER THE OPERATION.
I THOUGHT SNUFF FILMS WERE AN URBAN LEGEND.
MOST PEOPLE THINK I'M AN URBAN LEGEND.
YEAH? WHEN WE CATCH THE PEOPLE BEHIND THIS, THEY'RE GOING TO THINK I'M THE WRATH OF GOD.

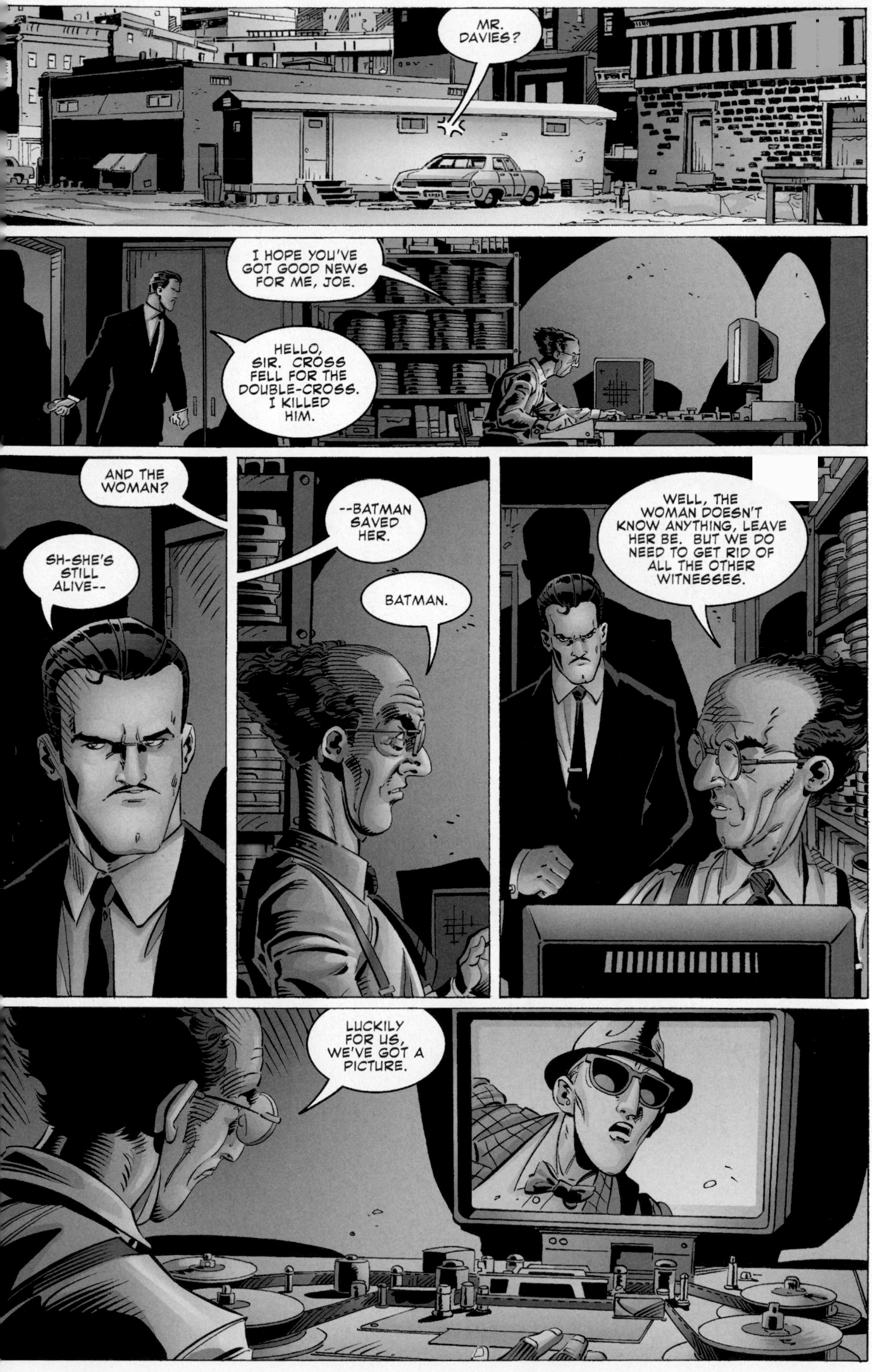
MR. DAVIES?
I HOPE YOU'VE GOT GOOD NEWS FOR ME, JOE.
HELLO, SIR. CROSS FELL FOR THE DOUBLE-CROSS. I KILLED HIM.
AND THE WOMAN?
SH-SHE'S STILL ALIVE--
--BATMAN SAVED HER.
BATMAN.
WELL, THE WOMAN DOESN'T KNOW ANYTHING, LEAVE HER BE. BUT WE DO NEED TO GET RID OF ALL THE OTHER WITNESSES.
LUCKILY FOR US, WE'VE GOT A PICTURE.

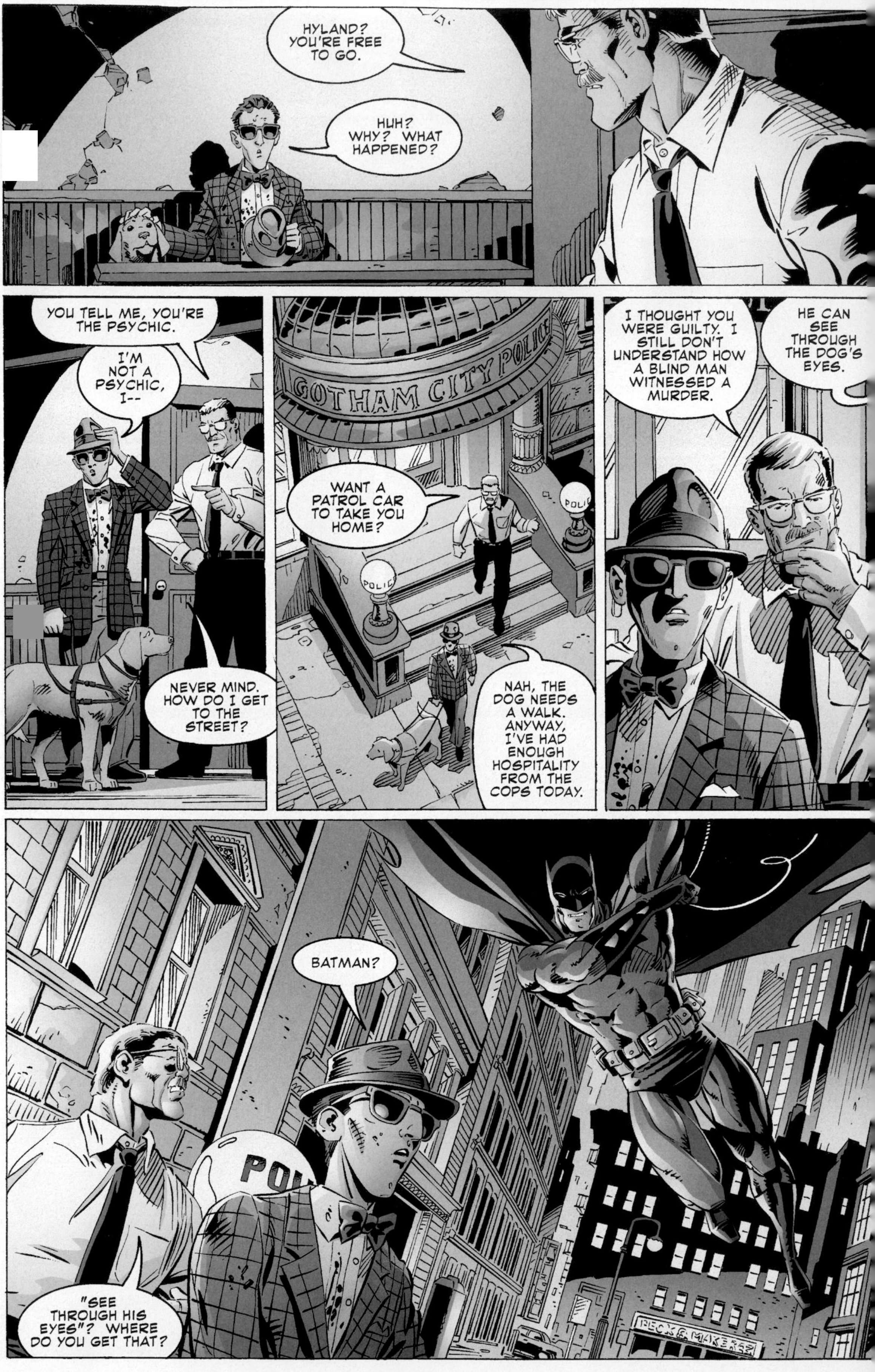
HYLAND? YOU'RE FREE TO GO.
HUH? WHY? WHAT HAPPENED?
YOU TELL ME, YOU'RE THE PSYCHIC.
I'M NOT A PSYCHIC, I--
NEVER MIND. HOW DO I GET TO THE STREET?
GOTHAM CITY POLICE
WANT A PATROL CAR TO TAKE YOU HOME?
NAH, THE DOG NEEDS A WALK. ANYWAY, I'VE HAD ENOUGH HOSPITALITY FROM THE COPS TODAY.
I THOUGHT YOU WERE GUILTY. I STILL DON'T UNDERSTAND HOW A BLIND MAN WITNESSED A MURDER.
HE CAN SEE THROUGH THE DOG'S EYES.
BATMAN?
"SEE THROUGH HIS EYES"? WHERE DO YOU GET THAT?

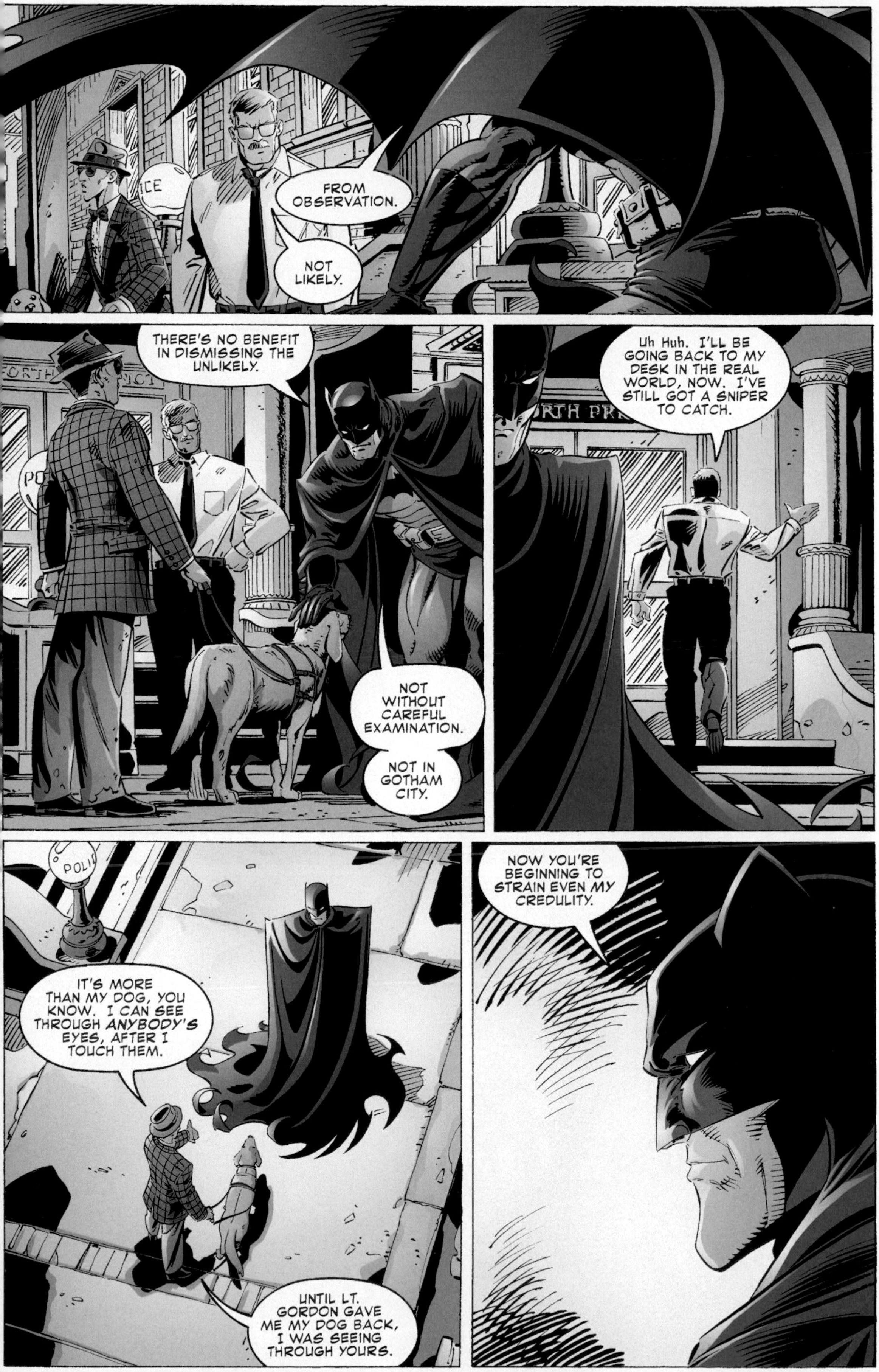
ICE
FROM OBSERVATION.
NOT LIKELY.
THERE'S NO BENEFIT IN DISMISSING THE UNLIKELY.
NOT WITHOUT CAREFUL EXAMINATION.
NOT IN GOTHAM CITY.
Uh Huh. I'LL BE GOING BACK TO MY DESK IN THE REAL WORLD, NOW. I'VE STILL GOT A SNIPER TO CATCH.
IT'S MORE THAN MY DOG, YOU KNOW. I CAN SEE THROUGH ANYBODY'S EYES, AFTER I TOUCH THEM.
UNTIL LT. GORDON GAVE ME MY DOG BACK, I WAS SEEING THROUGH YOURS.
NOW YOU'RE BEGINNING TO STRAIN EVEN MY CREDULITY.

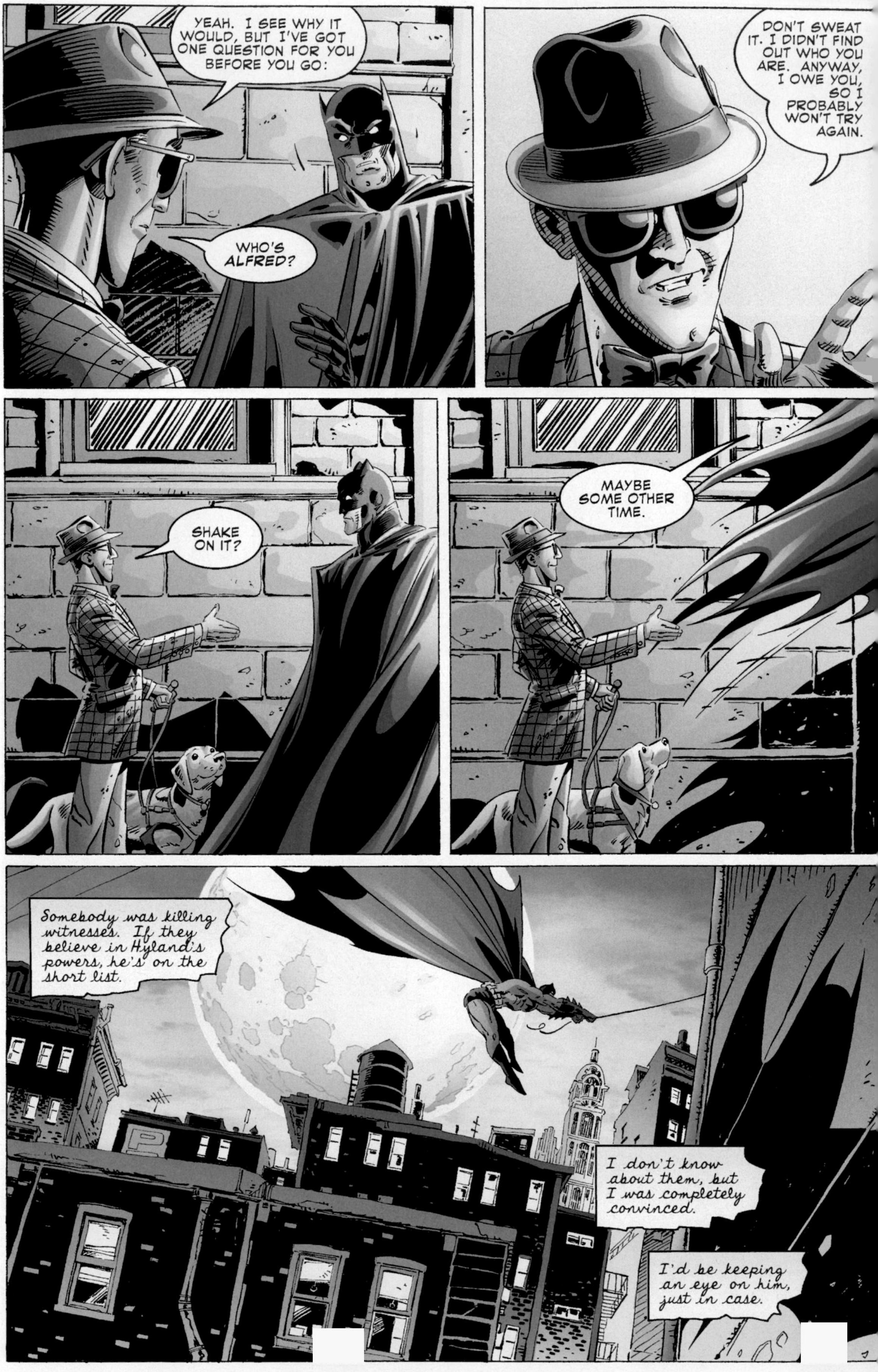
YEAH. I SEE WHY IT WOULD, BUT I'VE GOT ONE QUESTION FOR YOU BEFORE YOU GO:
WHO'S ALFRED?
DON'T SWEAT IT. I DIDN'T FIND OUT WHO YOU ARE. ANYWAY, I OWE YOU, SO I PROBABLY WON'T TRY AGAIN.
SHAKE ON IT?
MAYBE SOME OTHER TIME.
Somebody was killing witnesses. If they believe in Hyland's powers, he's on the short list.
I don't know about them, but I was completely convinced.
I'd be keeping an eye on him, just in case.

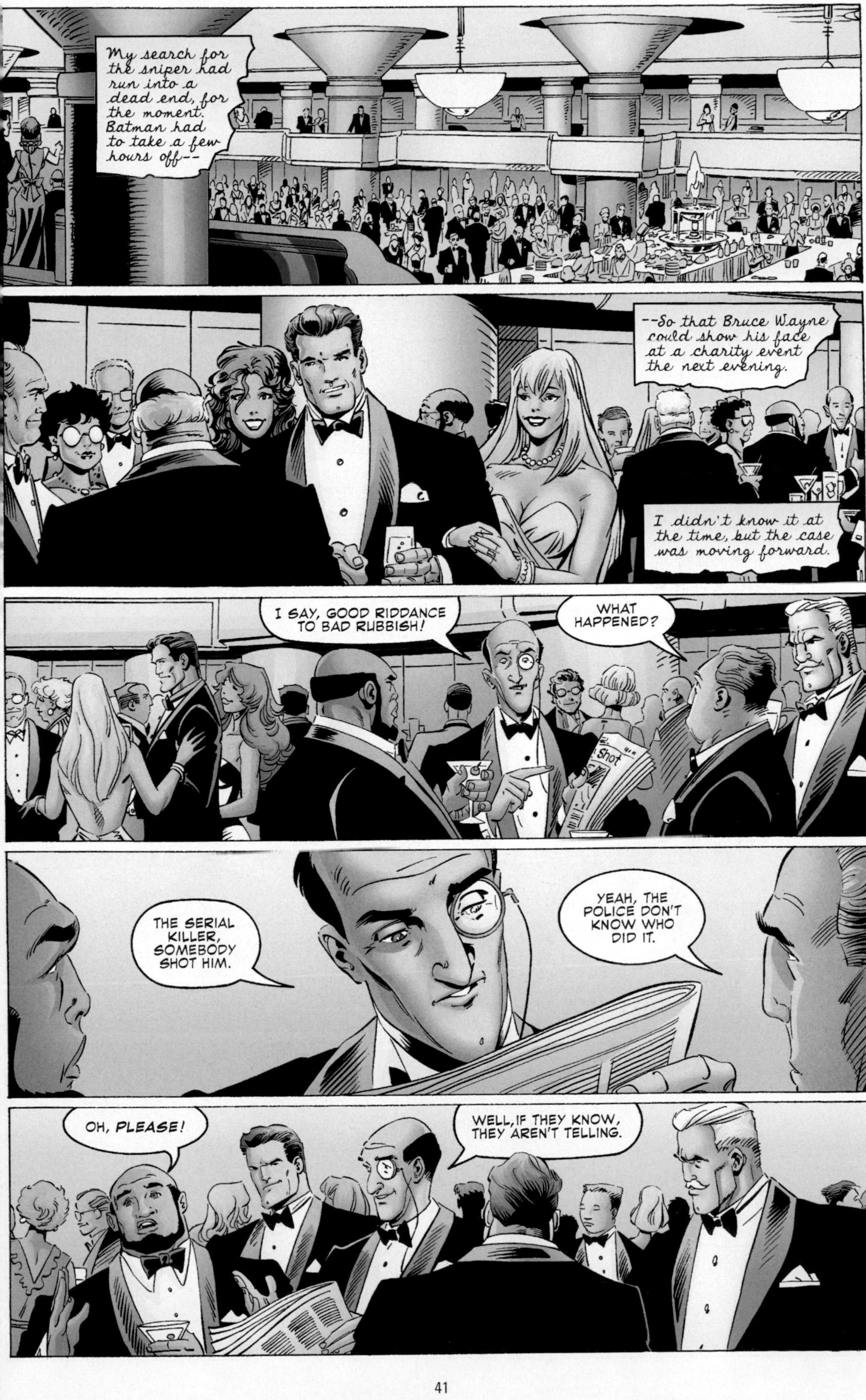
My search for the sniper had run into a dead end, for the moment. Batman had to take a few hours off--
--So that Bruce Wayne could show his face at a charity event the next evening.
I didn't know it at the time, but the case was moving forward.
I SAY, GOOD RIDDANCE TO BAD RUBBISH!
WHAT HAPPENED?
THE SERIAL KILLER, SOMEBODY SHOT HIM.
YEAH, THE POLICE DON'T KNOW WHO DID IT.
OH, PLEASE!
WELL, IF THEY KNOW, THEY AREN'T TELLING.

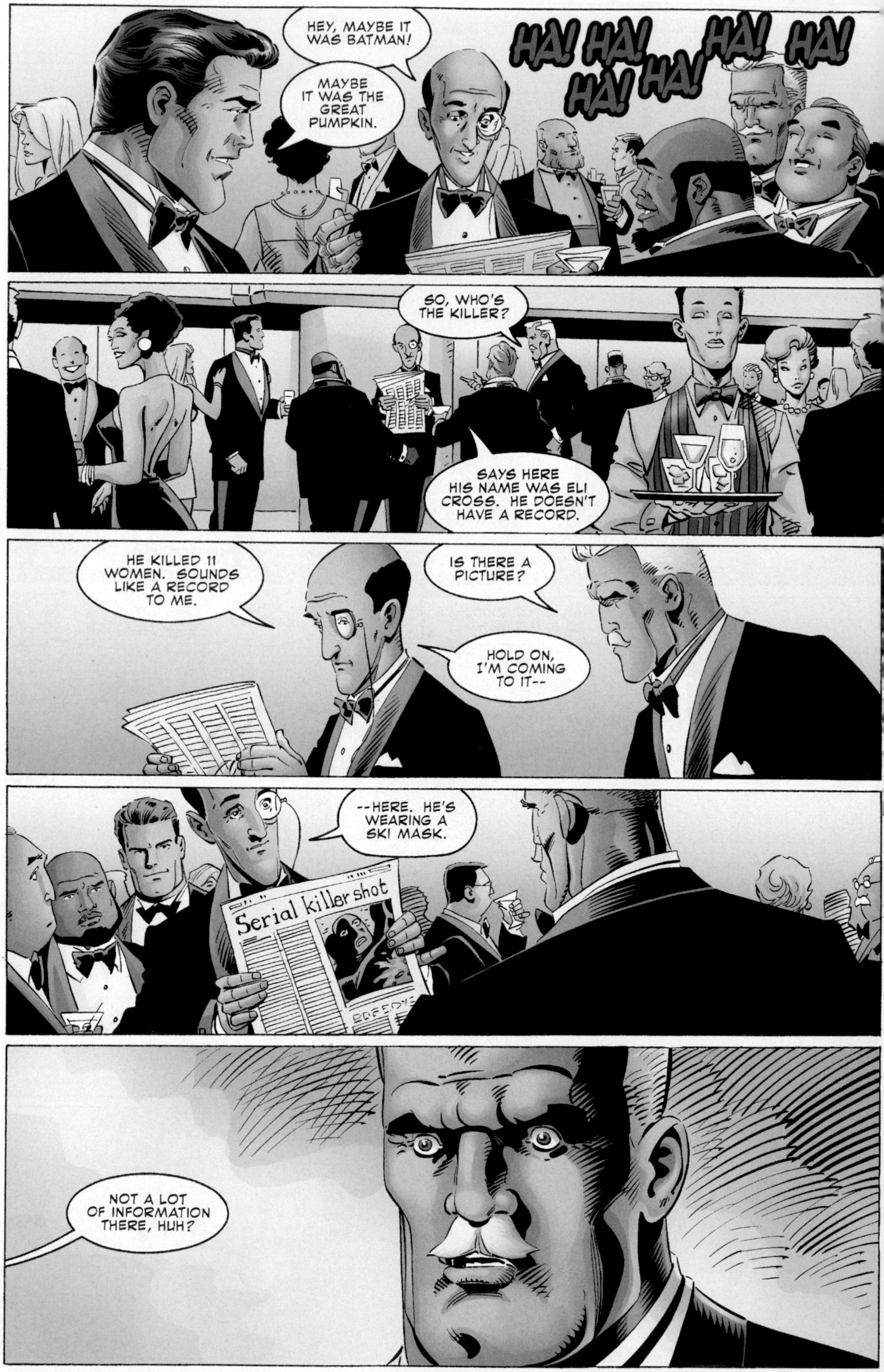
HEY, MAYBE IT WAS BATMAN!
MAYBE IT WAS THE GREAT PUMPKIN.
HA! HA! HA! HA! HA! HA!
SO, WHO'S THE KILLER?
SAYS HERE HIS NAME WAS ELI CROSS. HE DOESN'T HAVE A RECORD.
HE KILLED 11 WOMEN. SOUNDS LIKE A RECORD TO ME.
IS THERE A PICTURE?
HOLD ON, I'M COMING TO IT--
--HERE. HE'S WEARING A SKI MASK.
Serial killer shot
NOT A LOT OF INFORMATION THERE, HUH?

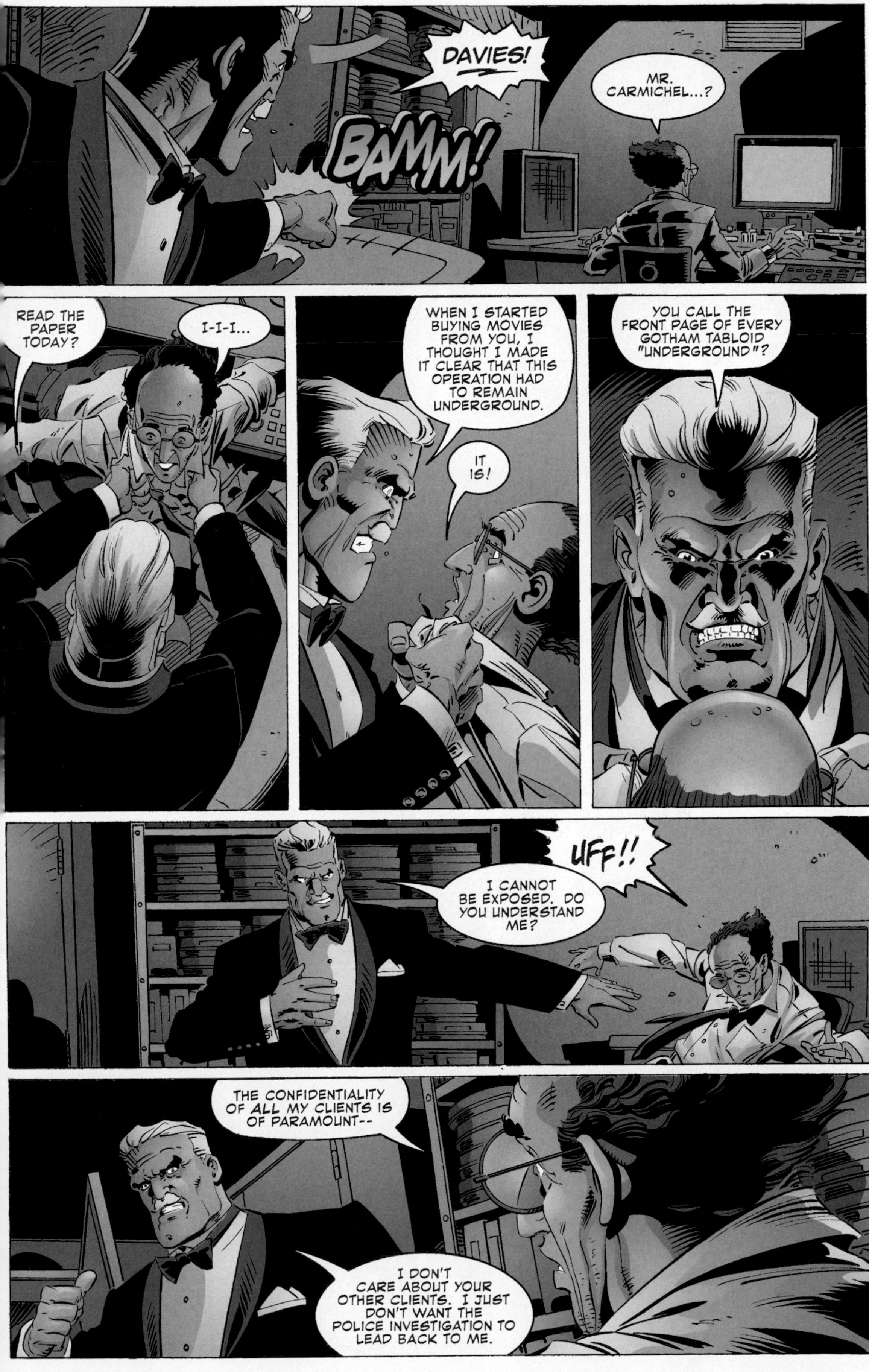
DAVIES!
BAMM!
MR. CARMICHEL...?
READ THE PAPER TODAY?
I-I-I...
WHEN I STARTED BUYING MOVIES FROM YOU, I THOUGHT I MADE IT CLEAR THAT THIS OPERATION HAD TO REMAIN UNDERGROUND.
IT IS!
YOU CALL THE FRONT PAGE OF EVERY GOTHAM TABLOID "UNDERGROUND"?
UFF!!
I CANNOT BE EXPOSED. DO YOU UNDERSTAND ME?
THE CONFIDENTIALITY OF ALL MY CLIENTS IS OF PARAMOUNT--
I DON'T CARE ABOUT YOUR OTHER CLIENTS. I JUST DON'T WANT THE POLICE INVESTIGATION TO LEAD BACK TO ME.

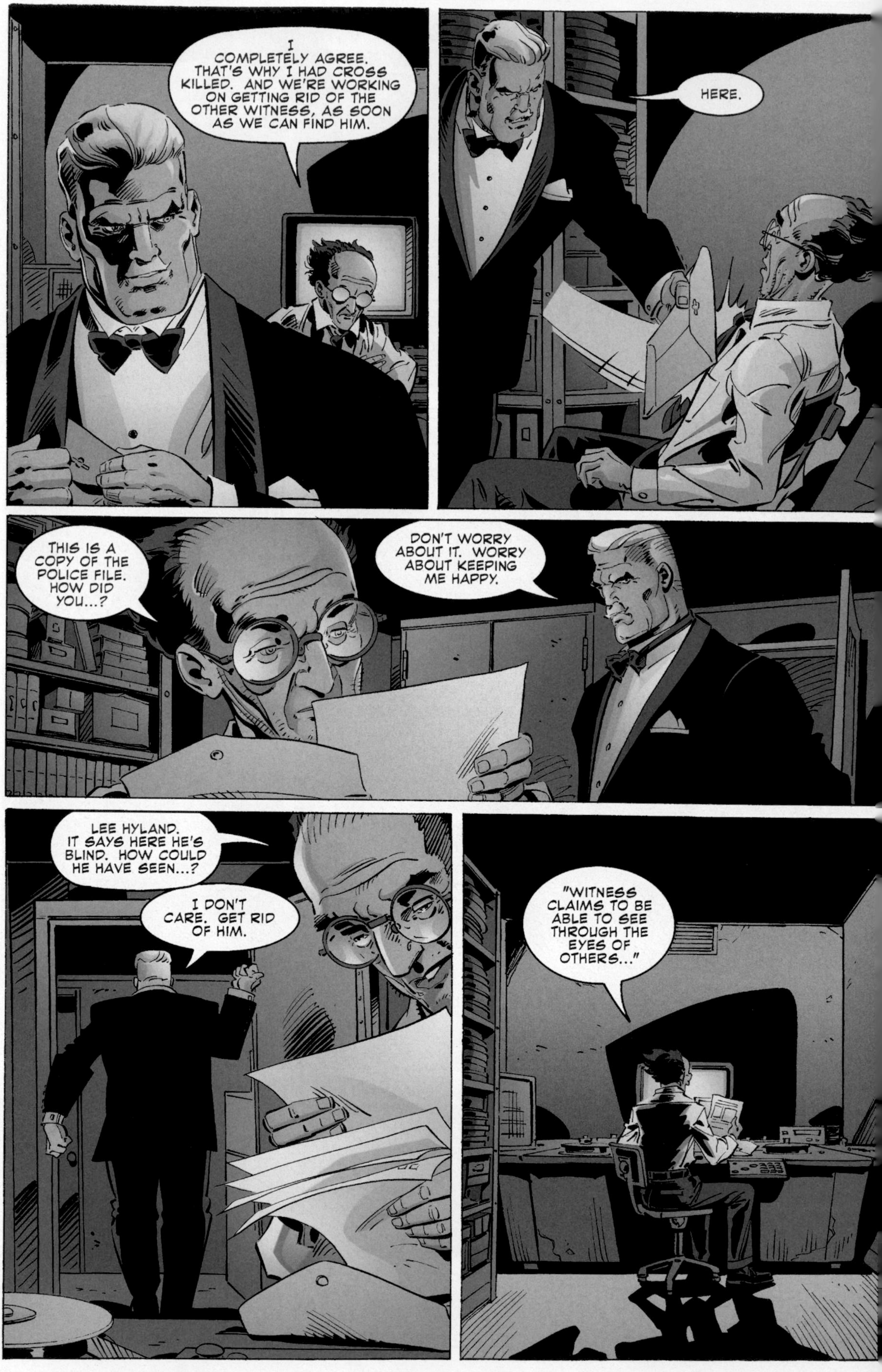
I COMPLETELY AGREE. THAT'S WHY I HAD CROSS KILLED. AND WE'RE WORKING ON GETTING RID OF THE OTHER WITNESS, AS SOON AS WE CAN FIND HIM.
HERE.
THIS IS A COPY OF THE POLICE FILE. HOW DID YOU...?
DON'T WORRY ABOUT IT. WORRY ABOUT KEEPING ME HAPPY.
LEE HYLAND. IT SAYS HERE HE'S BLIND. HOW COULD HE HAVE SEEN...?
I DON'T CARE. GET RID OF HIM.
"WITNESS CLAIMS TO BE ABLE TO SEE THROUGH THE EYES OF OTHERS..."

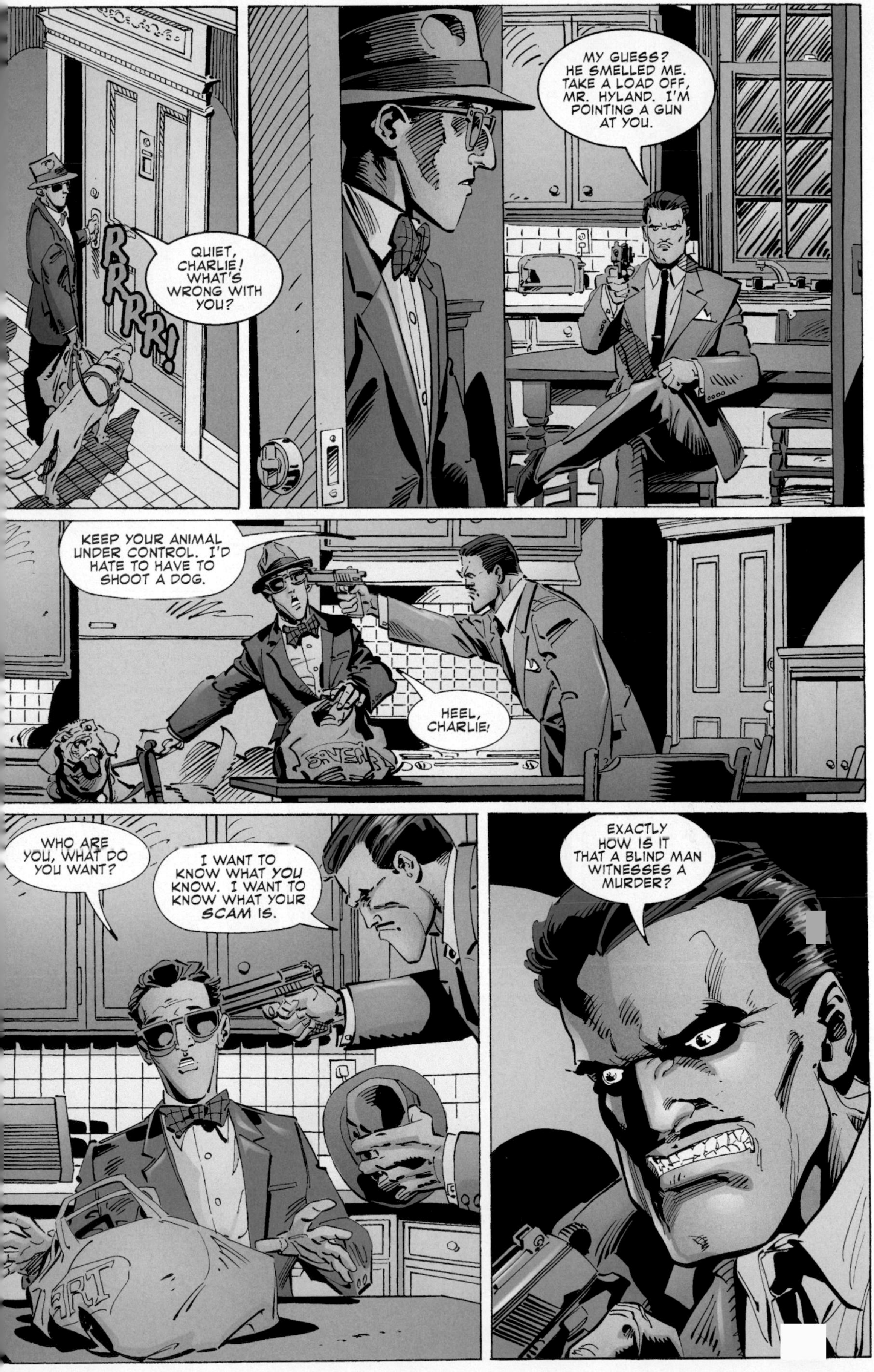
RRRRR!
QUIET, CHARLIE! WHAT'S WRONG WITH YOU?
MY GUESS? HE SMELLED ME. TAKE A LOAD OFF, MR. HYLAND. I'M POINTING A GUN AT YOU.
KEEP YOUR ANIMAL UNDER CONTROL. I'D HATE TO HAVE TO SHOOT A DOG.
HEEL, CHARLIE!
WHO ARE YOU, WHAT DO YOU WANT?
I WANT TO KNOW WHAT YOU KNOW. I WANT TO KNOW WHAT YOUR SCAM IS.
EXACTLY HOW IS IT THAT A BLIND MAN WITNESSES A MURDER?

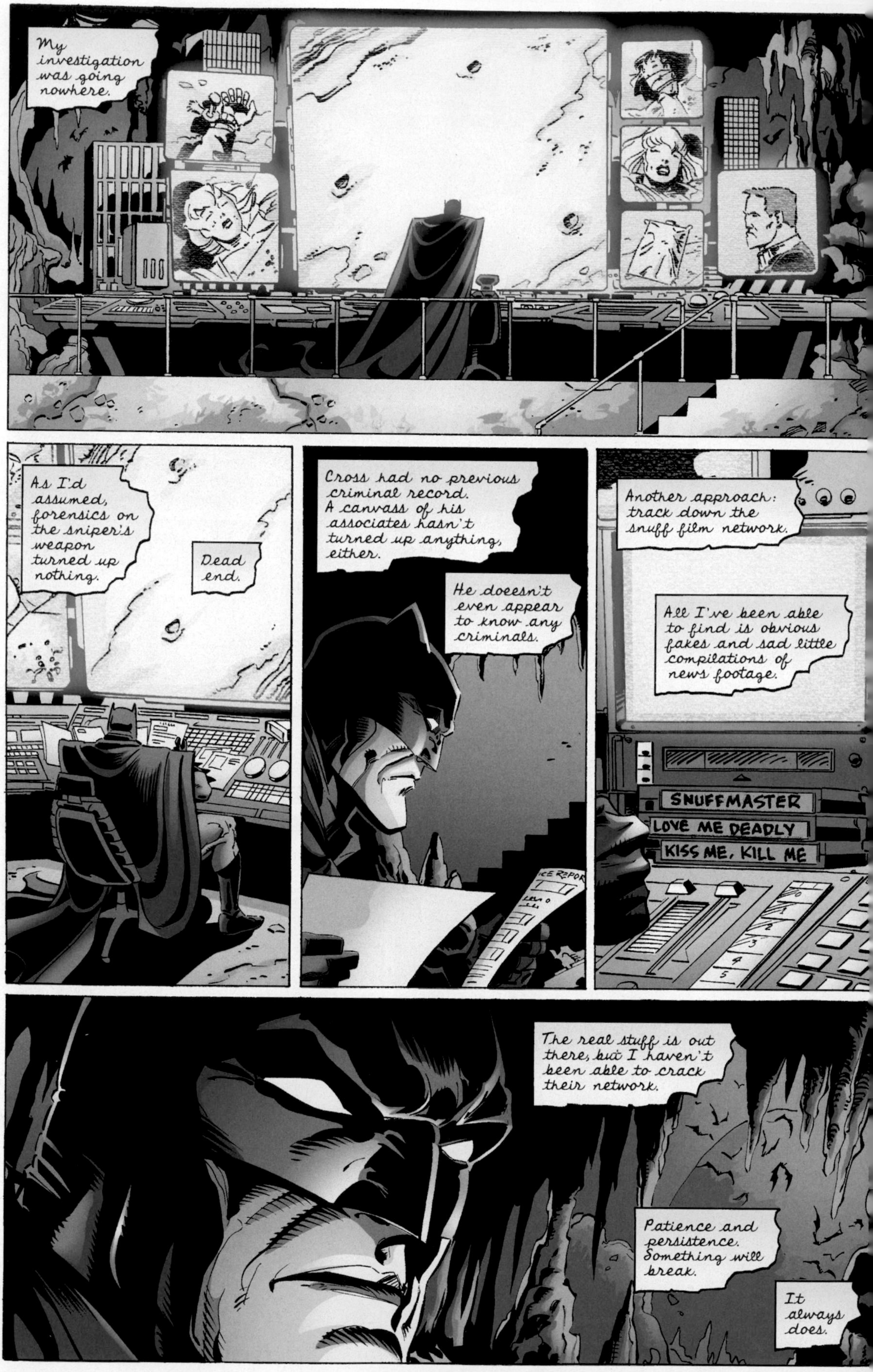
My investigation was going nowhere.
As I'd assumed, forensics on the sniper's weapon turned up nothing.
Dead end.
Cross had no previous criminal record. A canvass of his associates hasn't turned up anything, either.
He doesn't even appear to know any criminals.
Another approach: track down the snuff film network.
All I've been able to find is obvious fakes and sad little compilations of news footage.
SNUFFMASTER
LOVE ME DEADLY
KISS ME, KILL ME
The real stuff is out there, but I haven't been able to crack their network.
Patience and persistence. Something will break.
It always does.

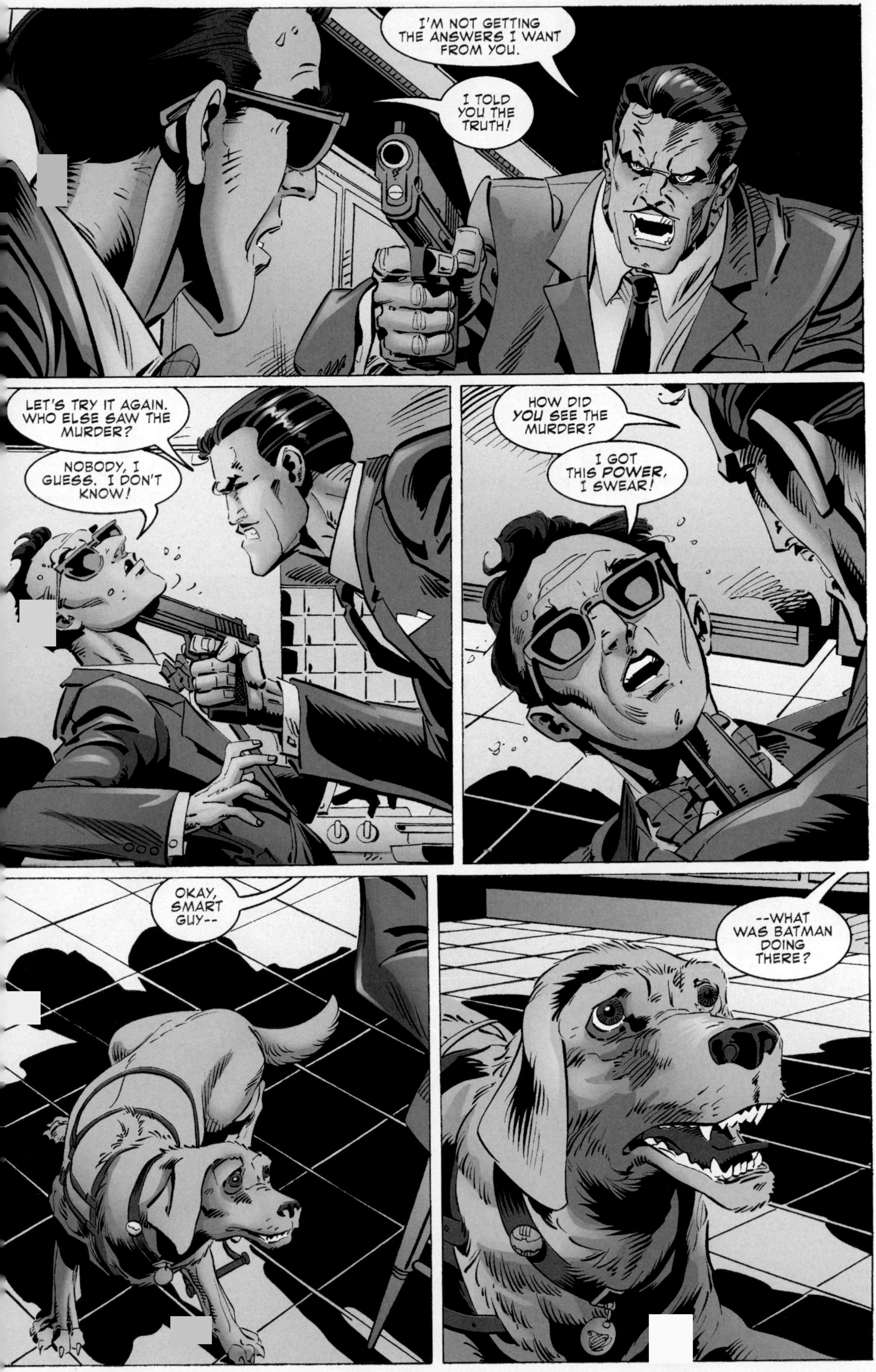
I'M NOT GETTING THE ANSWERS I WANT FROM YOU.
I TOLD YOU THE TRUTH!
LET'S TRY IT AGAIN. WHO ELSE SAW THE MURDER?
NOBODY, I GUESS. I DON'T KNOW!
HOW DID YOU SEE THE MURDER?
I GOT THIS POWER, I SWEAR!
OKAY, SMART GUY--
--WHAT WAS BATMAN DOING THERE?

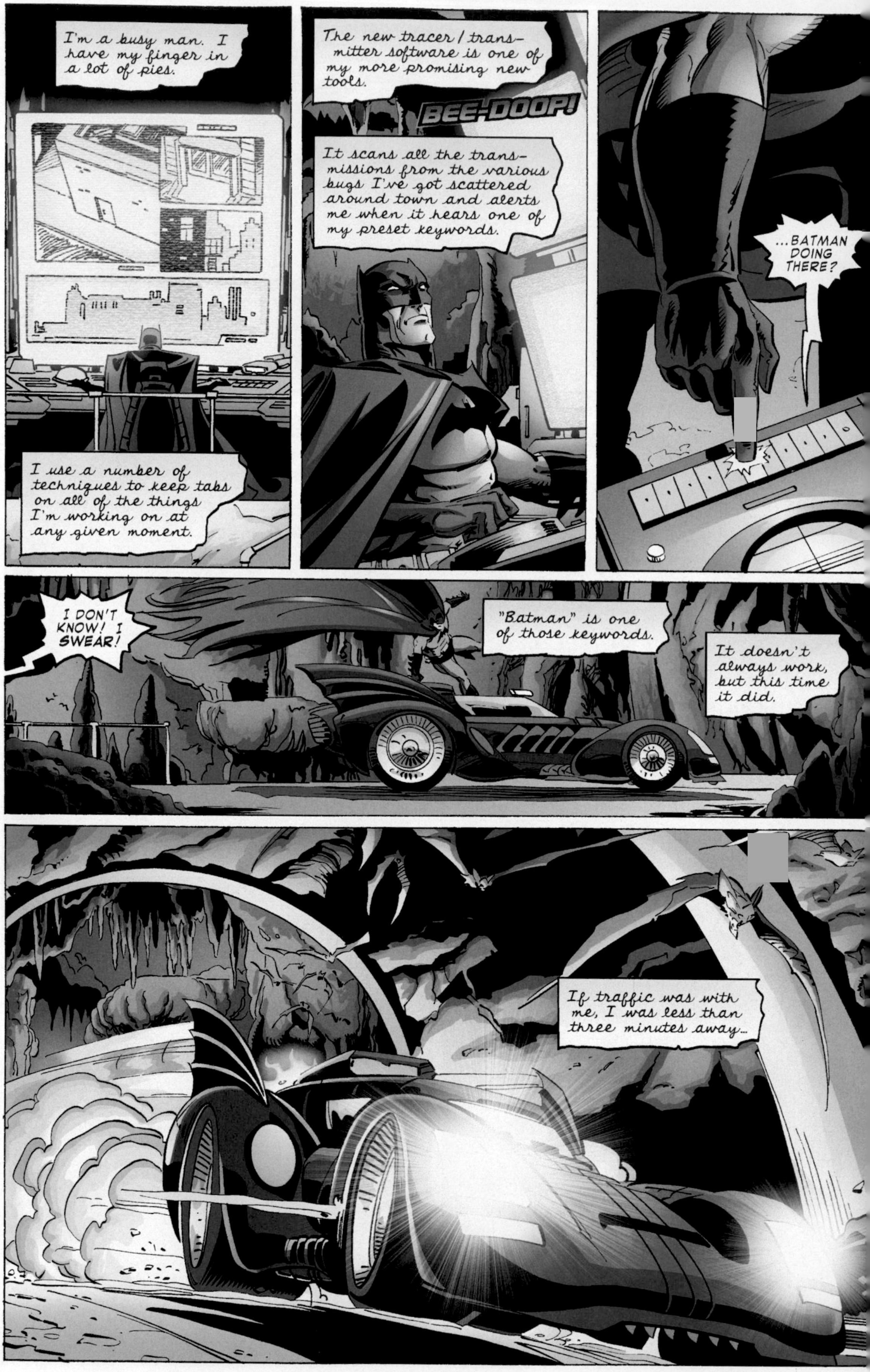

I'm a busy man. I have my finger in a lot of pies.
I use a number of techniques to keep tabs on all of the things I'm working on at any given moment.
The new tracer / transmitter software is one of my more promising new tools.
BEE-DOOP!
It scans all the transmissions from the various bugs I've got scattered around town and alerts me when it hears one of my preset keywords.
...BATMAN DOING THERE?
I DON'T KNOW! I SWEAR!
"Batman" is one of those keywords.
It doesn't always work, but this time it did.
If traffic was with me, I was less than three minutes away...

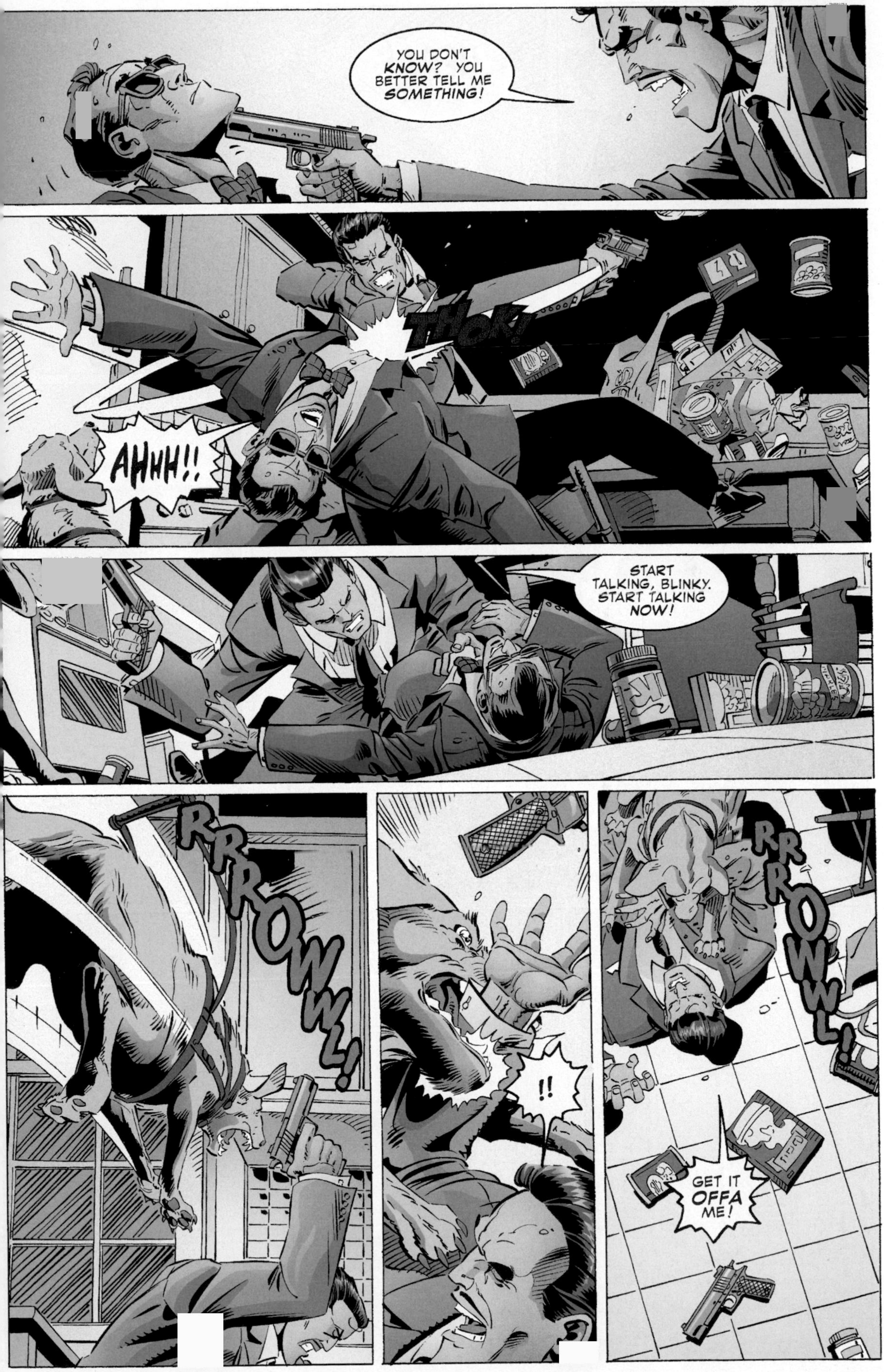
YOU DON'T KNOW? YOU BETTER TELL ME SOMETHING!
THOK!
AHHH!!
START TALKING, BLINKY. START TALKING NOW!
RRRROWWL!
!!
RRROWWL!
GET IT OFFA ME!

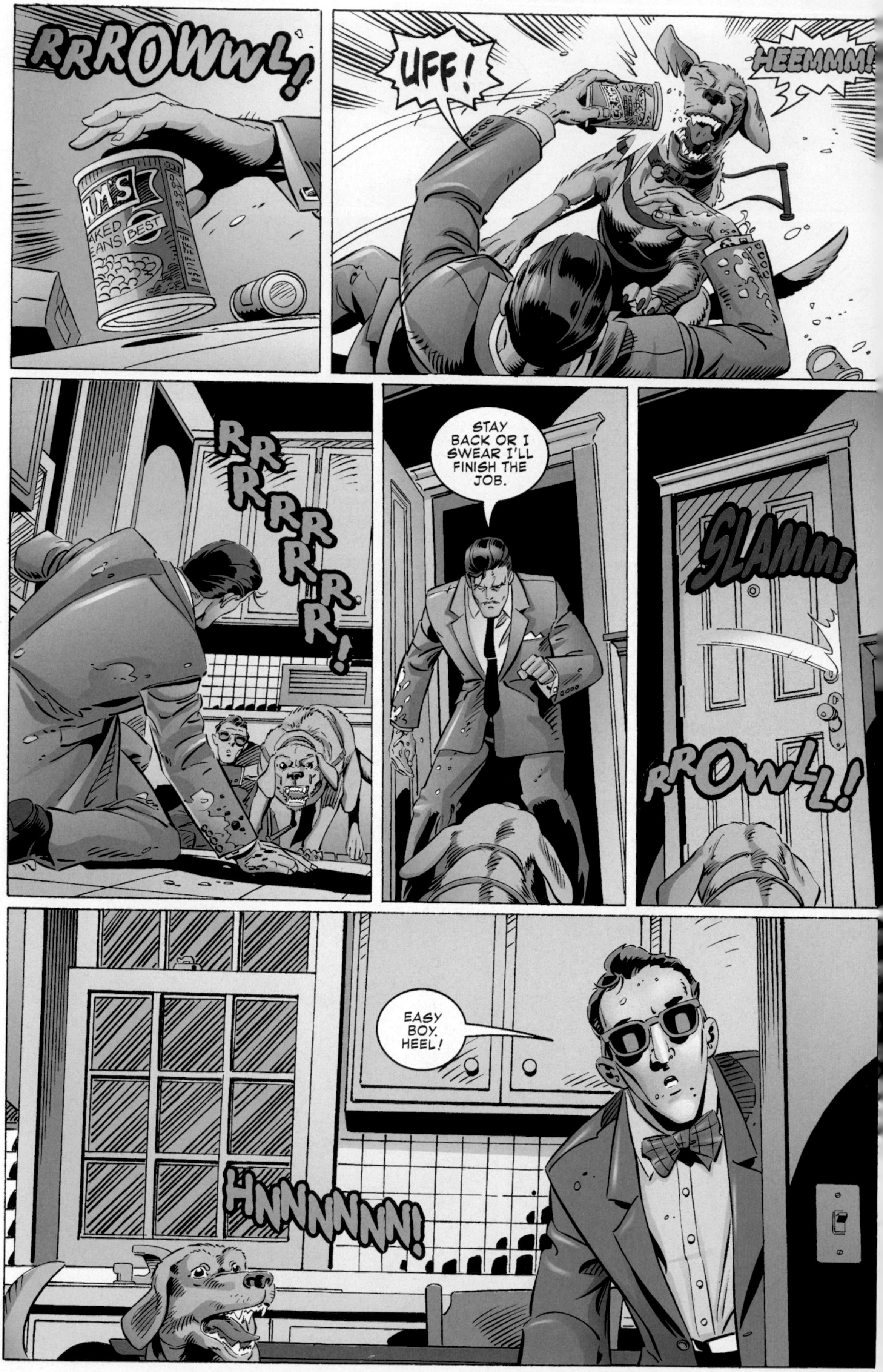
RRROWWL!
UFF!
HEEMMM!
RRRRRRRRR!
STAY BACK OR I SWEAR I'LL FINISH THE JOB.
SLAMM!
RROWLL!
EASY BOY. HEEL!
HNNNNNN!

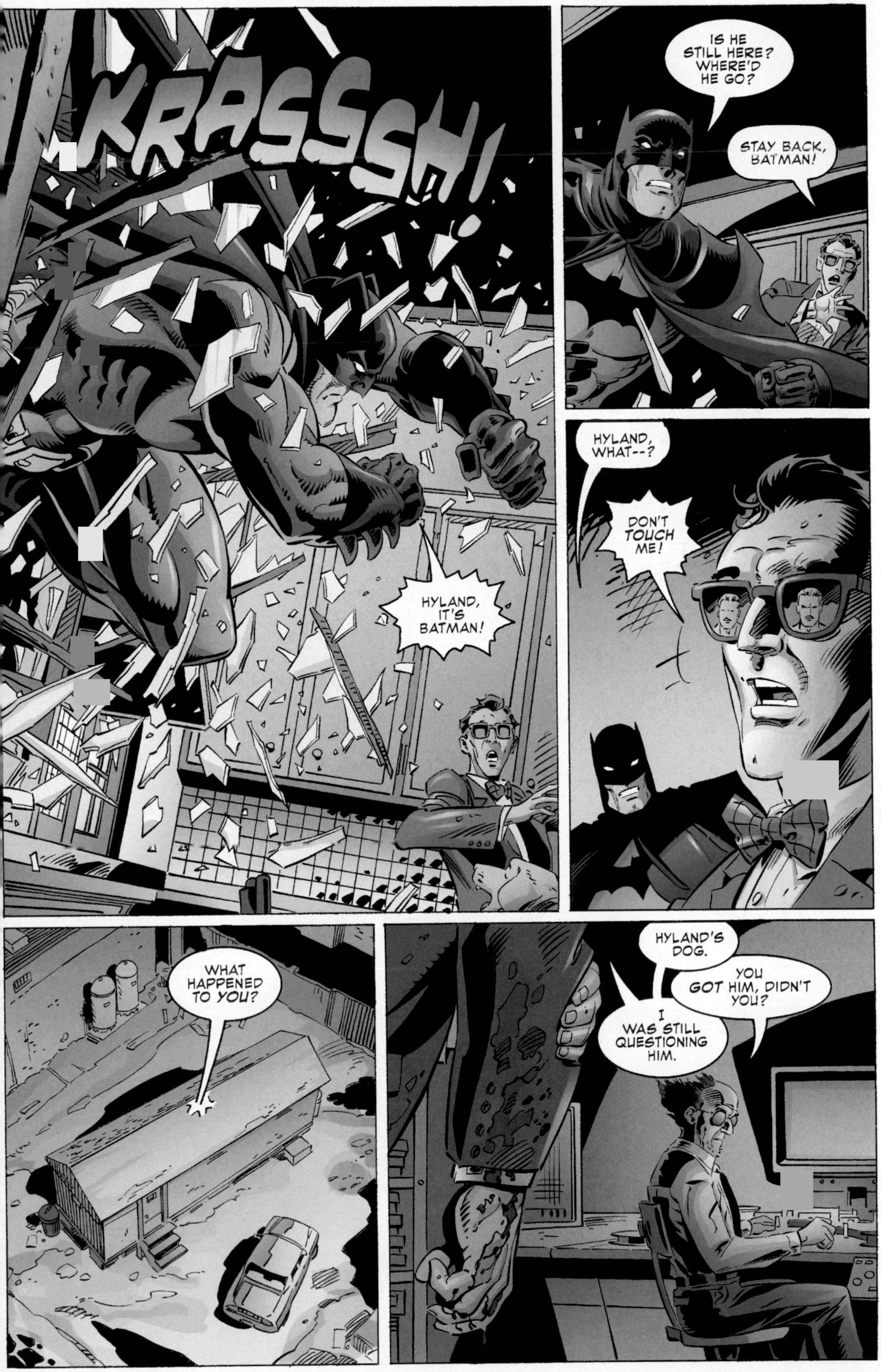
KRASSSH!
HYLAND, IT'S BATMAN!
IS HE STILL HERE? WHERE'D HE GO?
STAY BACK, BATMAN!
HYLAND, WHAT--?
DON'T TOUCH ME!
WHAT HAPPENED TO YOU?
HYLAND'S DOG.
YOU GOT HIM, DIDN'T YOU?
I WAS STILL QUESTIONING HIM.

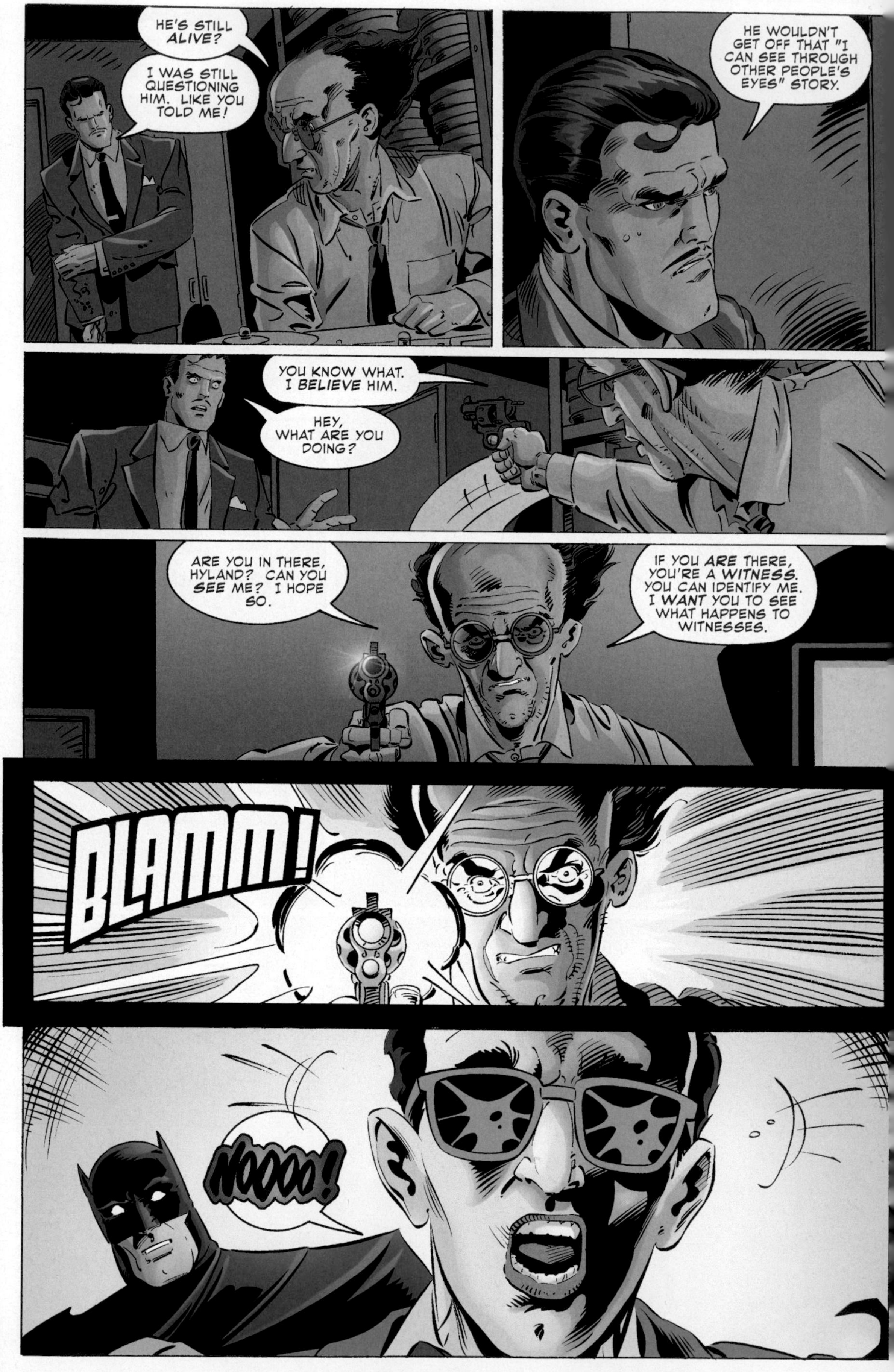
HE'S STILL ALIVE?
I WAS STILL QUESTIONING HIM. LIKE YOU TOLD ME!
HE WOULDN'T GET OFF THAT "I CAN SEE THROUGH OTHER PEOPLE'S EYES" STORY.
YOU KNOW WHAT. I BELIEVE HIM.
HEY, WHAT ARE YOU DOING?
ARE YOU IN THERE, HYLAND? CAN YOU SEE ME? I HOPE SO.
IF YOU ARE THERE, YOU'RE A WITNESS. YOU CAN IDENTIFY ME. I WANT YOU TO SEE WHAT HAPPENS TO WITNESSES.
BLAMM!
NOOOO!

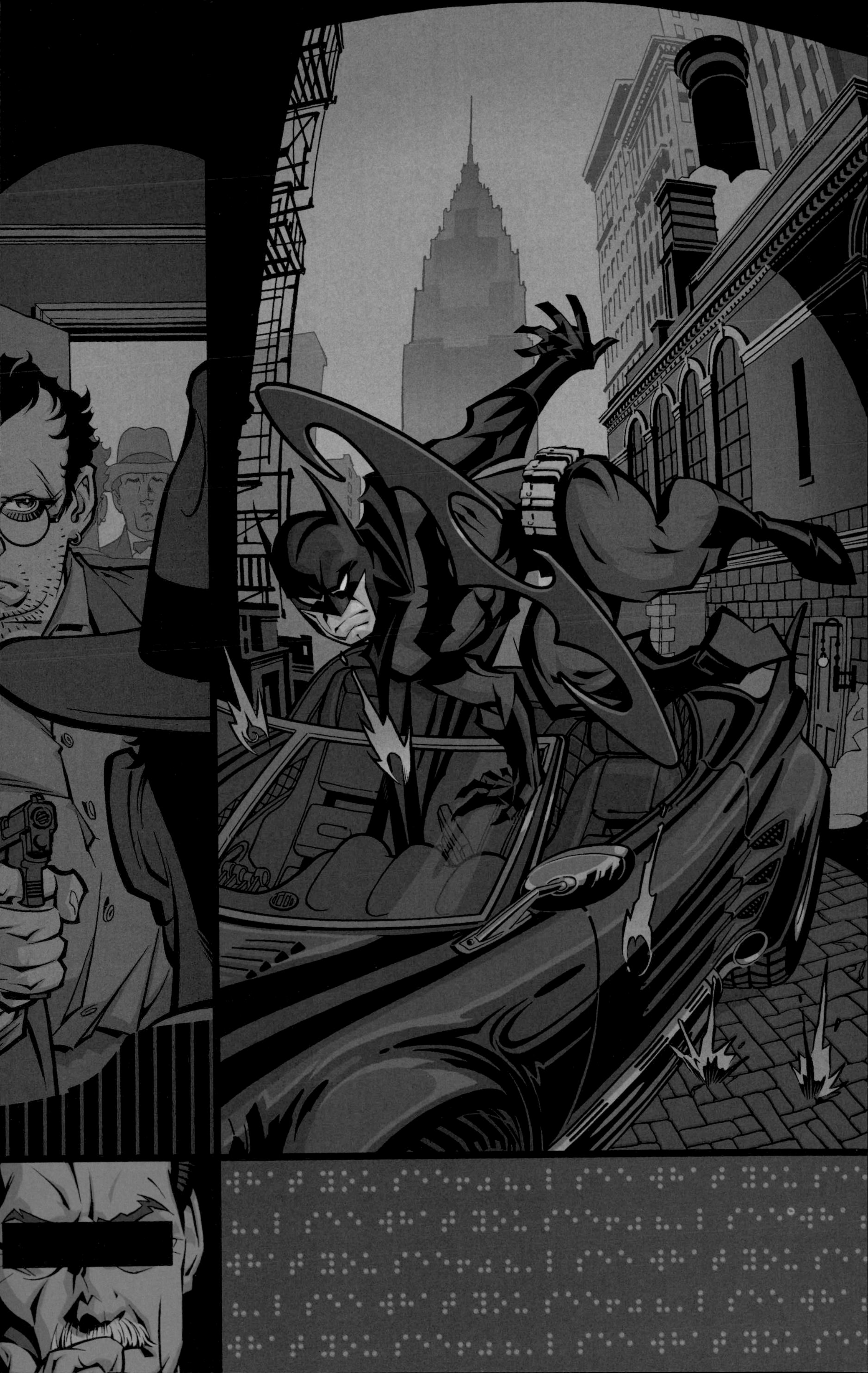

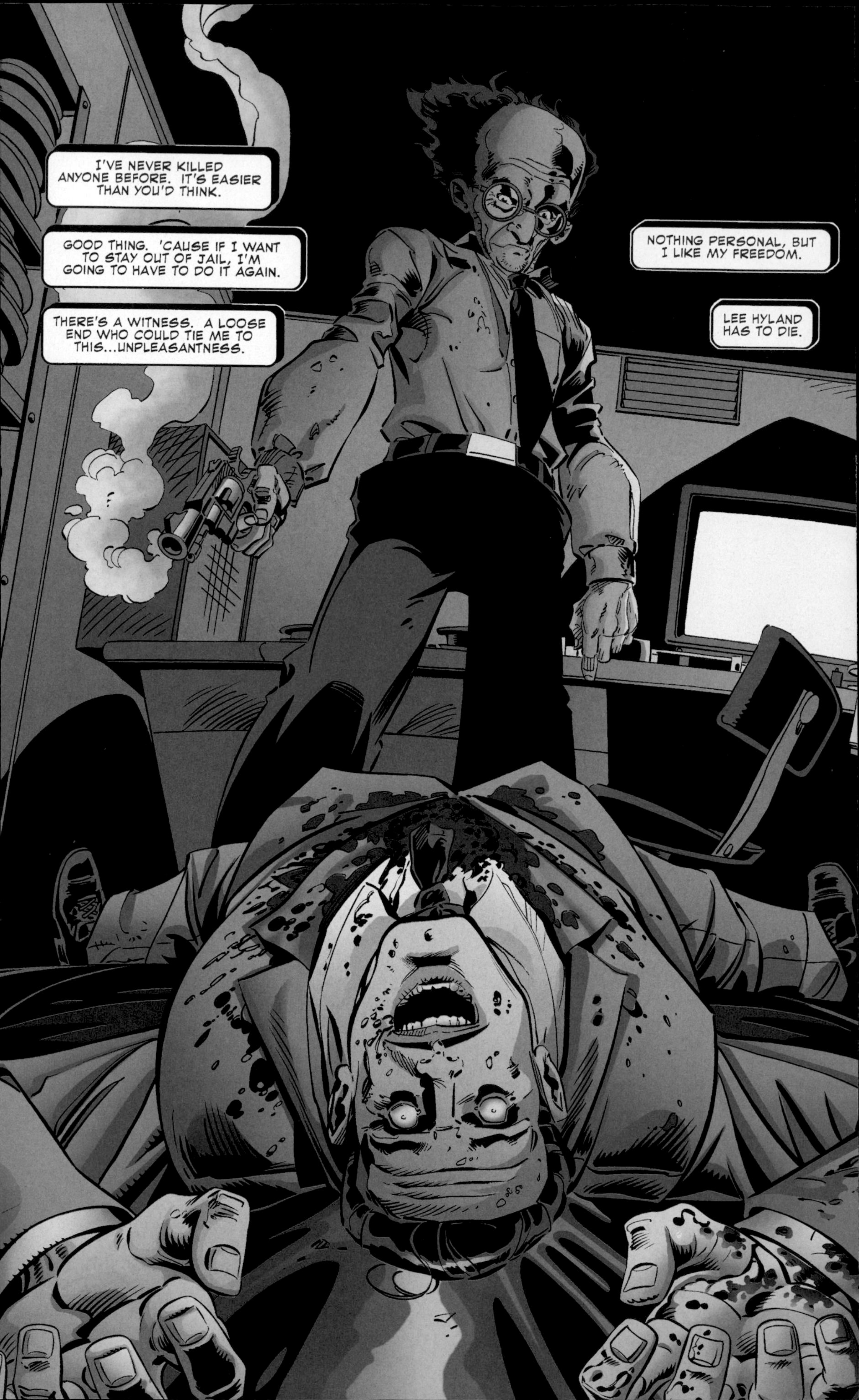
I'VE NEVER KILLED ANYONE BEFORE. IT'S EASIER THAN YOU'D THINK.
GOOD THING. 'CAUSE IF I WANT TO STAY OUT OF JAIL, I'M GOING TO HAVE TO DO IT AGAIN.
THERE'S A WITNESS. A LOOSE END WHO COULD TIE ME TO THIS...UNPLEASANTNESS.
NOTHING PERSONAL, BUT I LIKE MY FREEDOM.
LEE HYLAND HAS TO DIE.

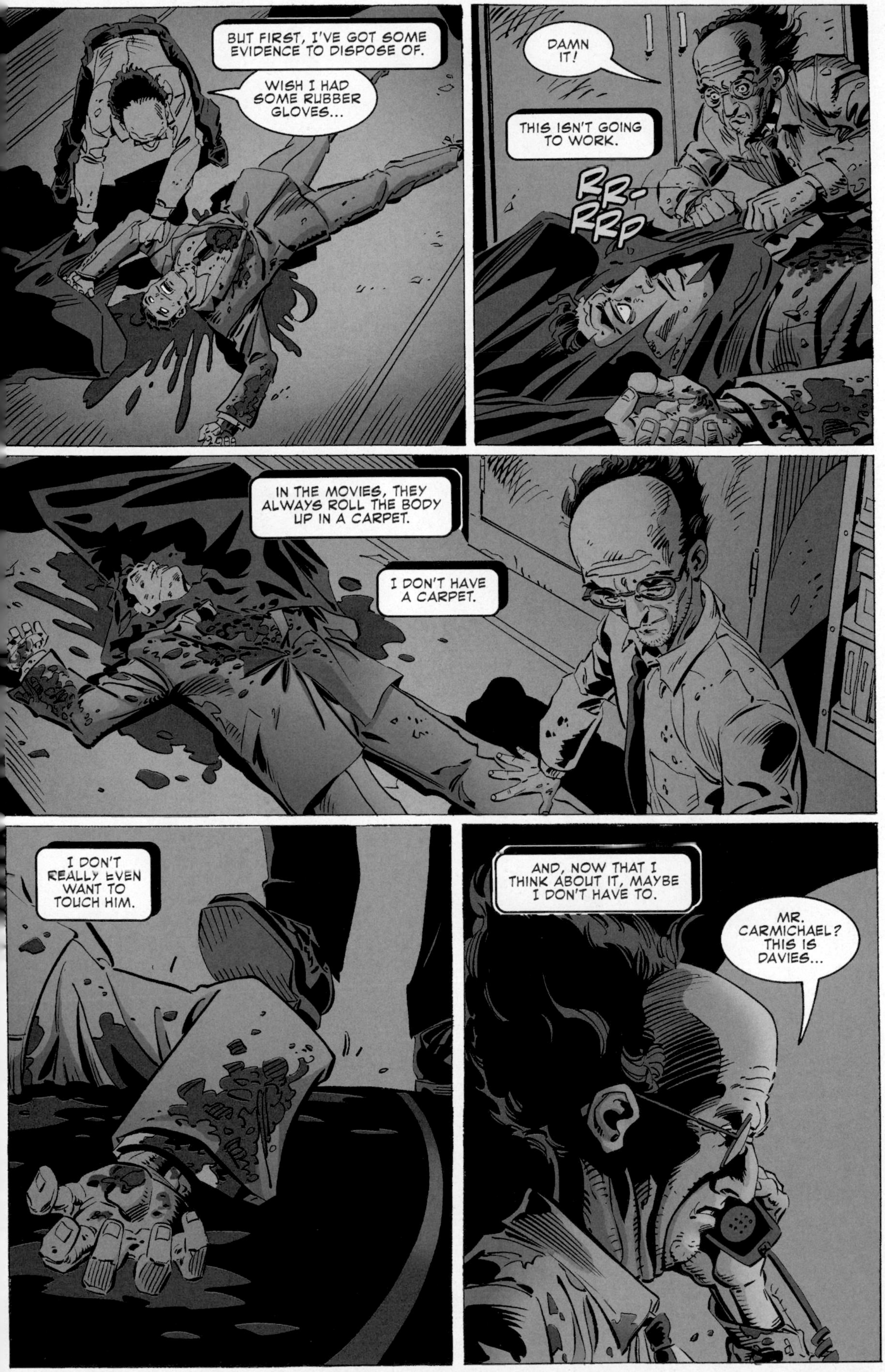
BUT FIRST, I'VE GOT SOME EVIDENCE TO DISPOSE OF.
WISH I HAD SOME RUBBER GLOVES...
DAMN IT!
THIS ISN'T GOING TO WORK.
RR-RRP
IN THE MOVIES, THEY ALWAYS ROLL THE BODY UP IN A CARPET.
I DON'T HAVE A CARPET.
I DON'T REALLY EVEN WANT TO TOUCH HIM.
AND, NOW THAT I THINK ABOUT IT, MAYBE I DON'T HAVE TO.
MR. CARMICHAEL? THIS IS DAVIES...

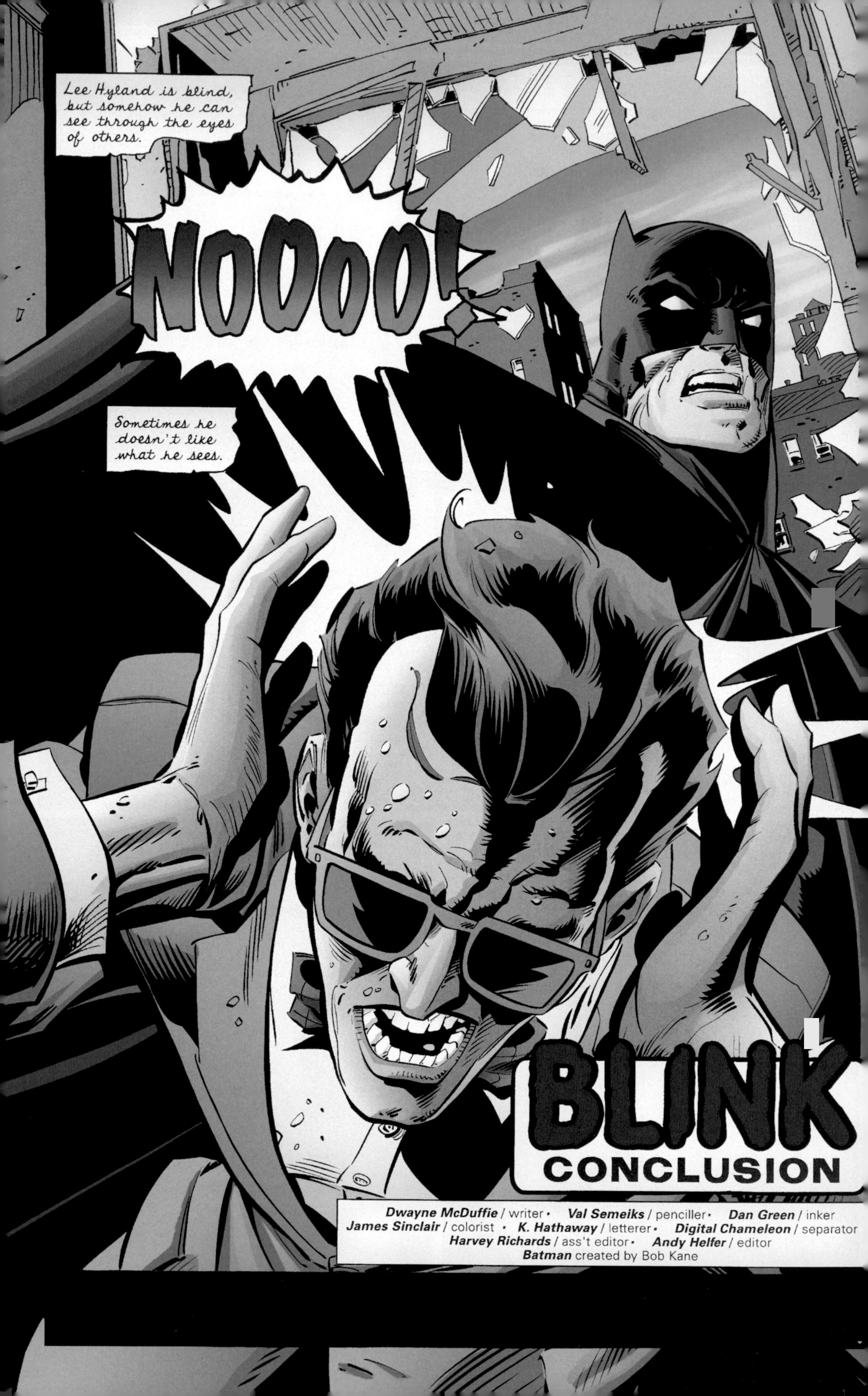
Lee Hyland is blind, but somehow he can see through the eyes of others.
NOOOO!
Sometimes he doesn't like what he sees.
BLINK
CONCLUSION
Dwayne McDuffie / writer • Val Semeiks / penciller • Dan Green / inker
James Sinclair / colorist • K. Hathaway / letterer • Digital Chameleon / separator
Harvey Richards / ass't editor • Andy Helfer / editor
Batman created by Bob Kane

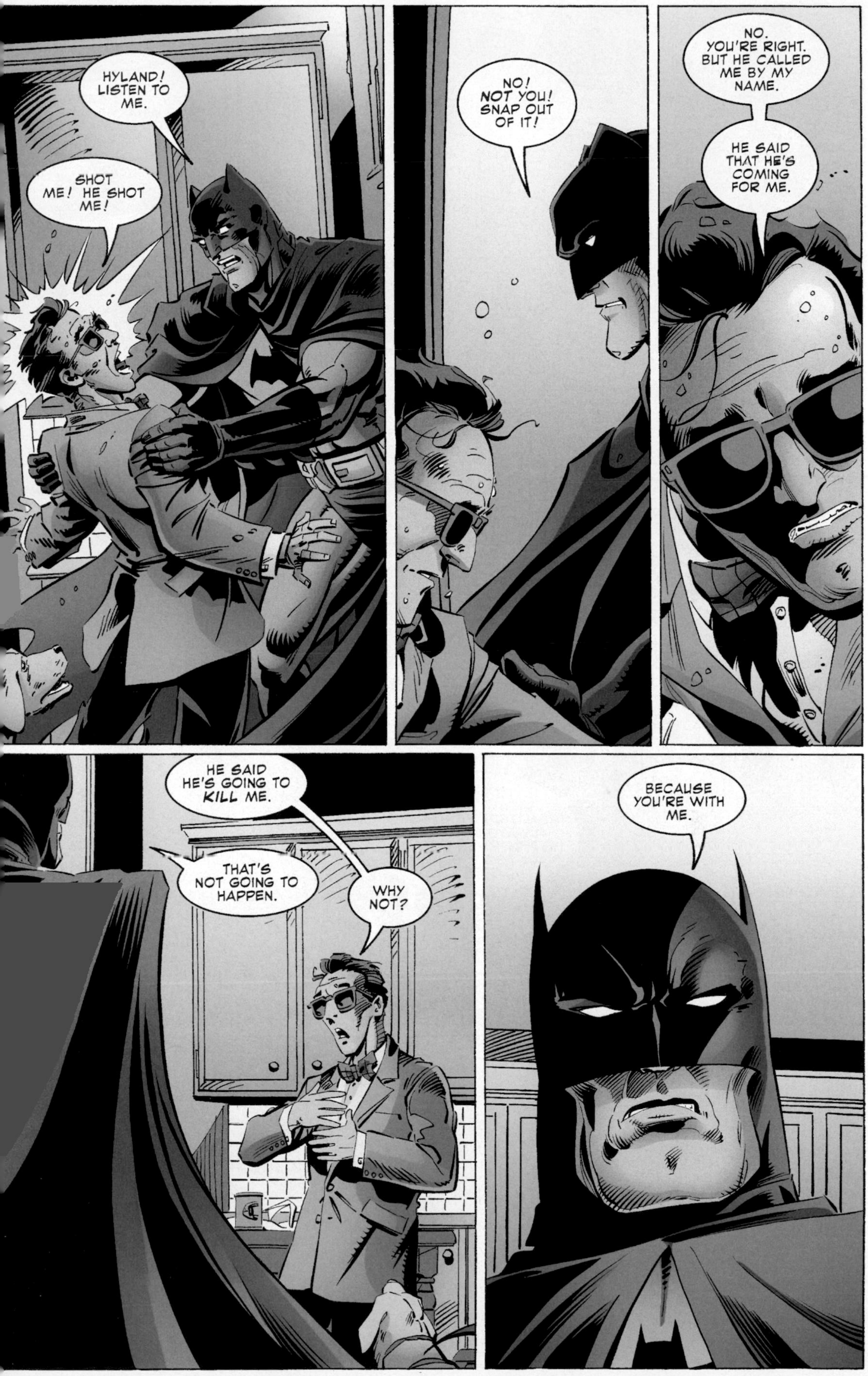
HYLAND! LISTEN TO ME.
SHOT ME! HE SHOT ME!
NO! NOT YOU! SNAP OUT OF IT!
NO. YOU'RE RIGHT. BUT HE CALLED ME BY MY NAME.
HE SAID THAT HE'S COMING FOR ME.
HE SAID HE'S GOING TO KILL ME.
THAT'S NOT GOING TO HAPPEN.
WHY NOT?
BECAUSE YOU'RE WITH ME.

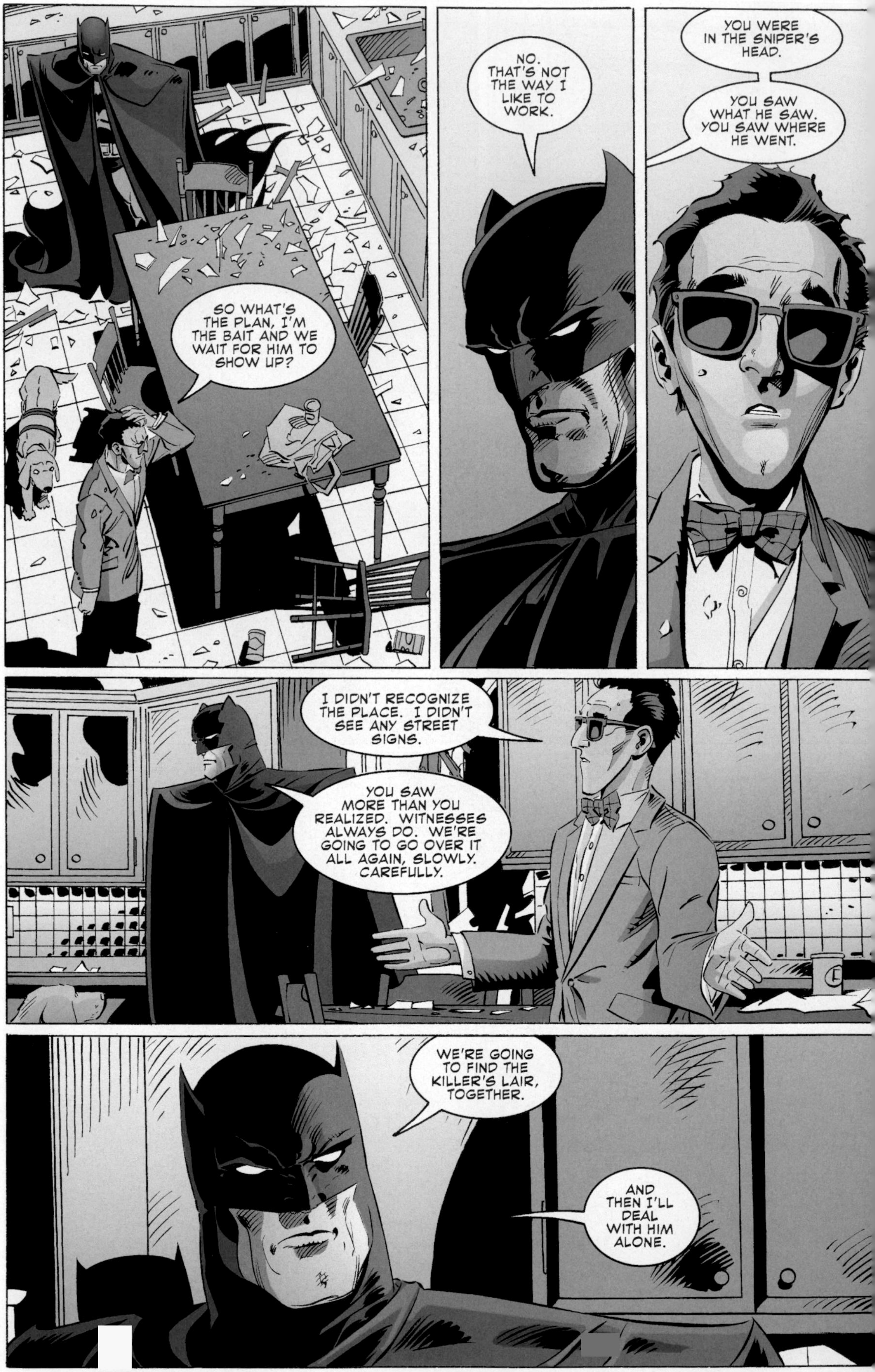
SO WHAT'S THE PLAN, I'M THE BAIT AND WE WAIT FOR HIM TO SHOW UP?
NO. THAT'S NOT THE WAY I LIKE TO WORK.
YOU WERE IN THE SNIPER'S HEAD.
YOU SAW WHAT HE SAW. YOU SAW WHERE HE WENT.
I DIDN'T RECOGNIZE THE PLACE. I DIDN'T SEE ANY STREET SIGNS.
YOU SAW MORE THAN YOU REALIZED. WITNESSES ALWAYS DO. WE'RE GOING TO GO OVER IT ALL AGAIN, SLOWLY. CAREFULLY.
WE'RE GOING TO FIND THE KILLER'S LAIR, TOGETHER.
AND THEN I'LL DEAL WITH HIM ALONE.

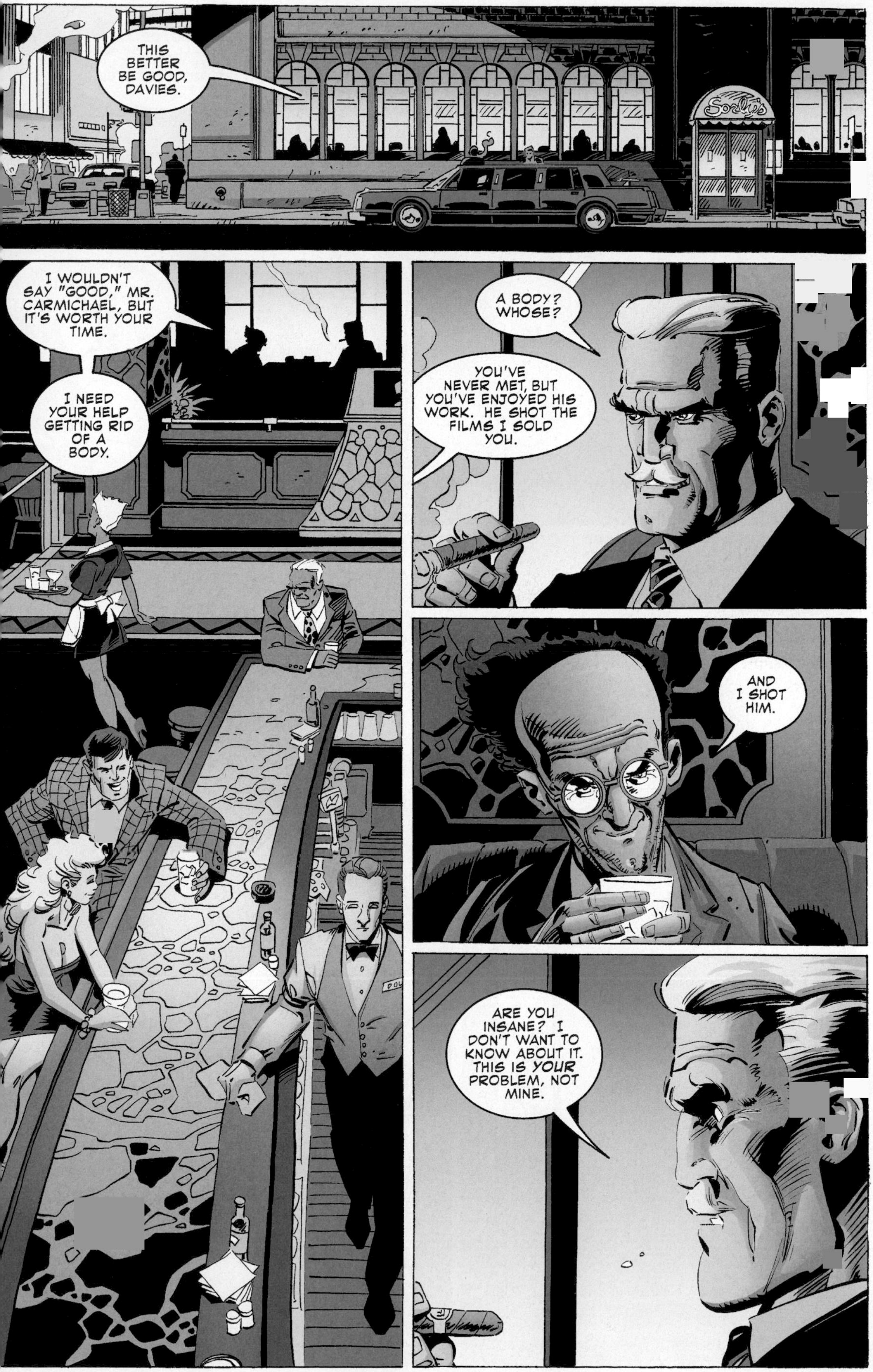
THIS BETTER BE GOOD, DAVIES.
I WOULDN'T SAY "GOOD," MR. CARMICHAEL, BUT IT'S WORTH YOUR TIME.
I NEED YOUR HELP GETTING RID OF A BODY.
A BODY? WHOSE?
YOU'VE NEVER MET, BUT YOU'VE ENJOYED HIS WORK. HE SHOT THE FILMS I SOLD YOU.
AND I SHOT HIM.
ARE YOU INSANE? I DON'T WANT TO KNOW ABOUT IT. THIS IS *YOUR* PROBLEM, NOT MINE.

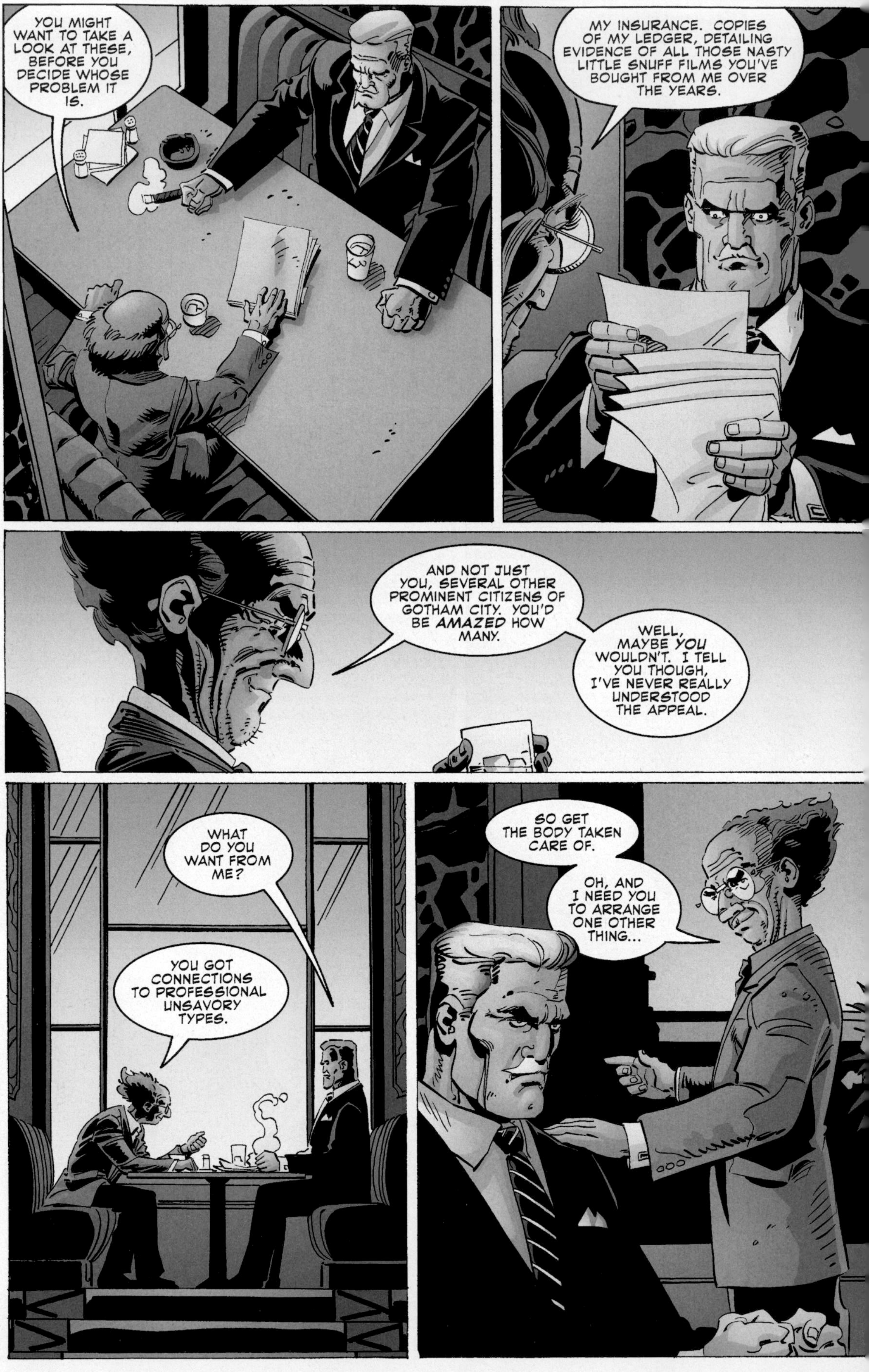
YOU MIGHT WANT TO TAKE A LOOK AT THESE, BEFORE YOU DECIDE WHOSE PROBLEM IT IS.
MY INSURANCE. COPIES OF MY LEDGER, DETAILING EVIDENCE OF ALL THOSE NASTY LITTLE SNUFF FILMS YOU'VE BOUGHT FROM ME OVER THE YEARS.
AND NOT JUST YOU, SEVERAL OTHER PROMINENT CITIZENS OF GOTHAM CITY. YOU'D BE AMAZED HOW MANY.
WELL, MAYBE YOU WOULDN'T. I TELL YOU THOUGH, I'VE NEVER REALLY UNDERSTOOD THE APPEAL.
WHAT DO YOU WANT FROM ME?
YOU GOT CONNECTIONS TO PROFESSIONAL UNSAVORY TYPES.
SO GET THE BODY TAKEN CARE OF.
OH, AND I NEED YOU TO ARRANGE ONE OTHER THING...

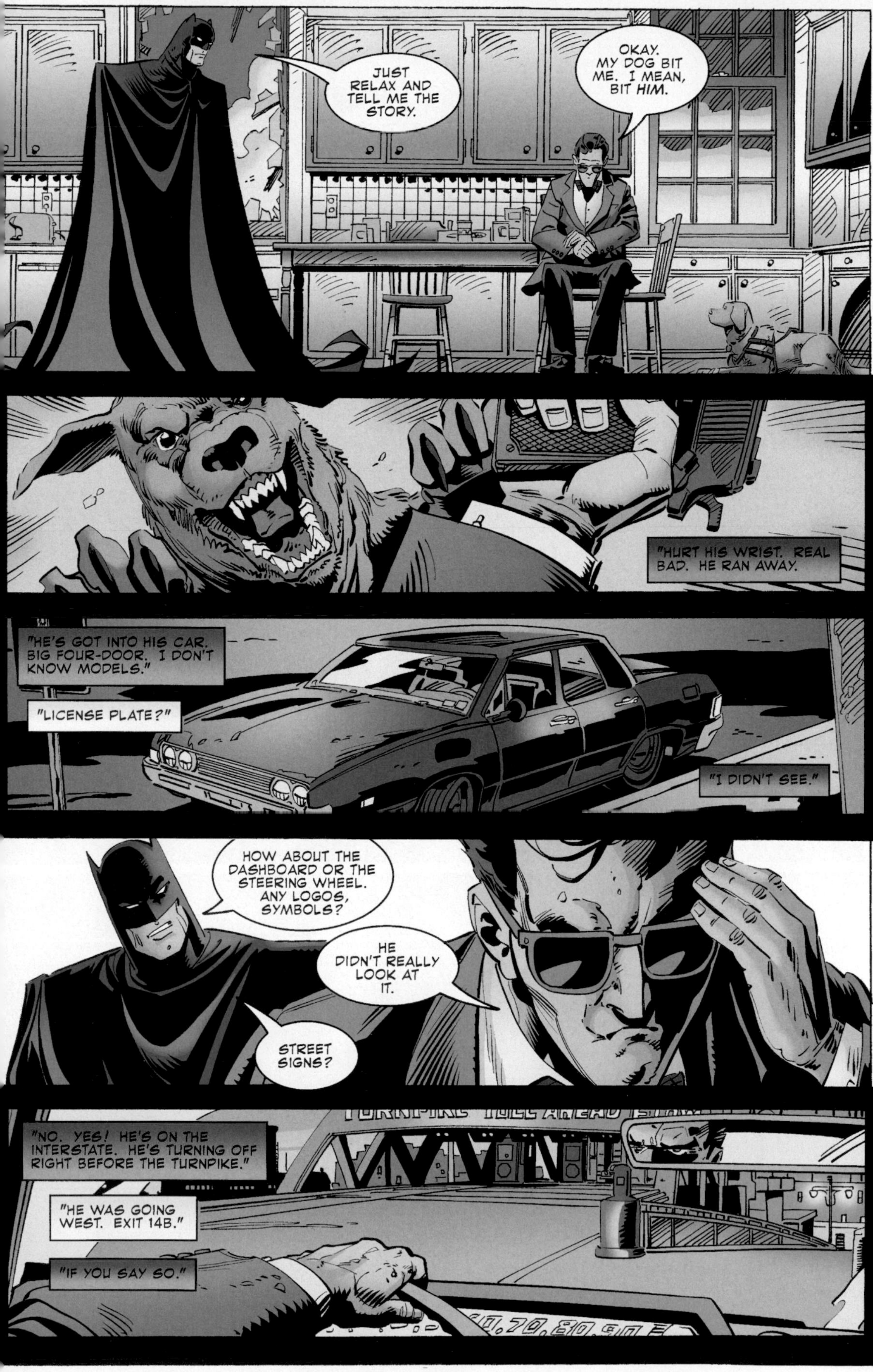
JUST RELAX AND TELL ME THE STORY.
OKAY. MY DOG BIT ME. I MEAN, BIT *HIM*.
"HURT HIS WRIST. REAL BAD. HE RAN AWAY.
"HE'S GOT INTO HIS CAR. BIG FOUR-DOOR. I DON'T KNOW MODELS."
"LICENSE PLATE?"
"I DIDN'T SEE."
HOW ABOUT THE DASHBOARD OR THE STEERING WHEEL. ANY LOGOS, SYMBOLS?
HE DIDN'T REALLY LOOK AT IT.
STREET SIGNS?
"NO. YES! HE'S ON THE INTERSTATE. HE'S TURNING OFF RIGHT BEFORE THE TURNPIKE."
"HE WAS GOING WEST. EXIT 14B."
"IF YOU SAY SO."

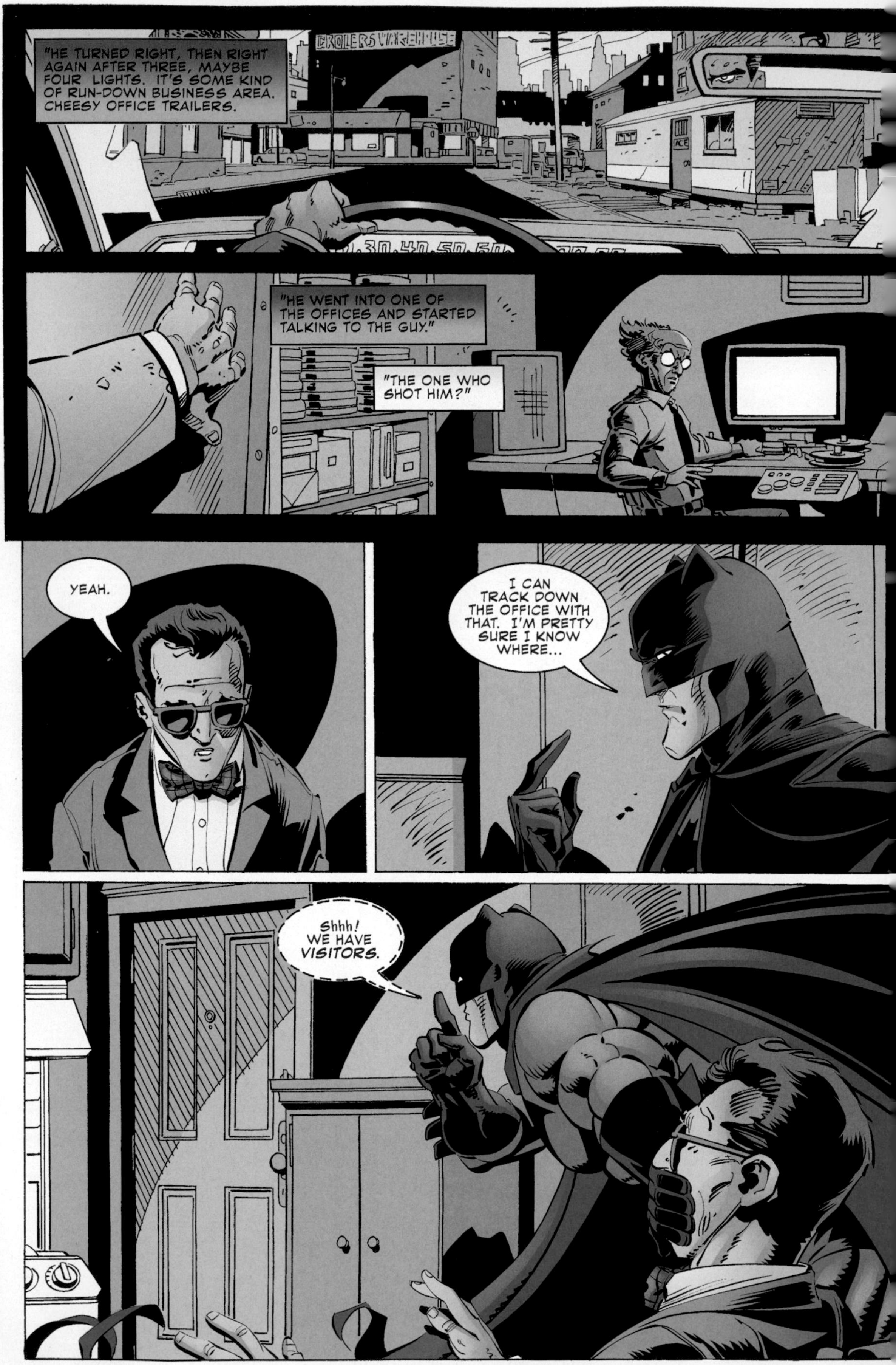
"HE TURNED RIGHT, THEN RIGHT AGAIN AFTER THREE, MAYBE FOUR LIGHTS. IT'S SOME KIND OF RUN-DOWN BUSINESS AREA. CHEESY OFFICE TRAILERS.
"HE WENT INTO ONE OF THE OFFICES AND STARTED TALKING TO THE GUY."
"THE ONE WHO SHOT HIM?"
YEAH.
I CAN TRACK DOWN THE OFFICE WITH THAT. I'M PRETTY SURE I KNOW WHERE...
Shhh! WE HAVE VISITORS.

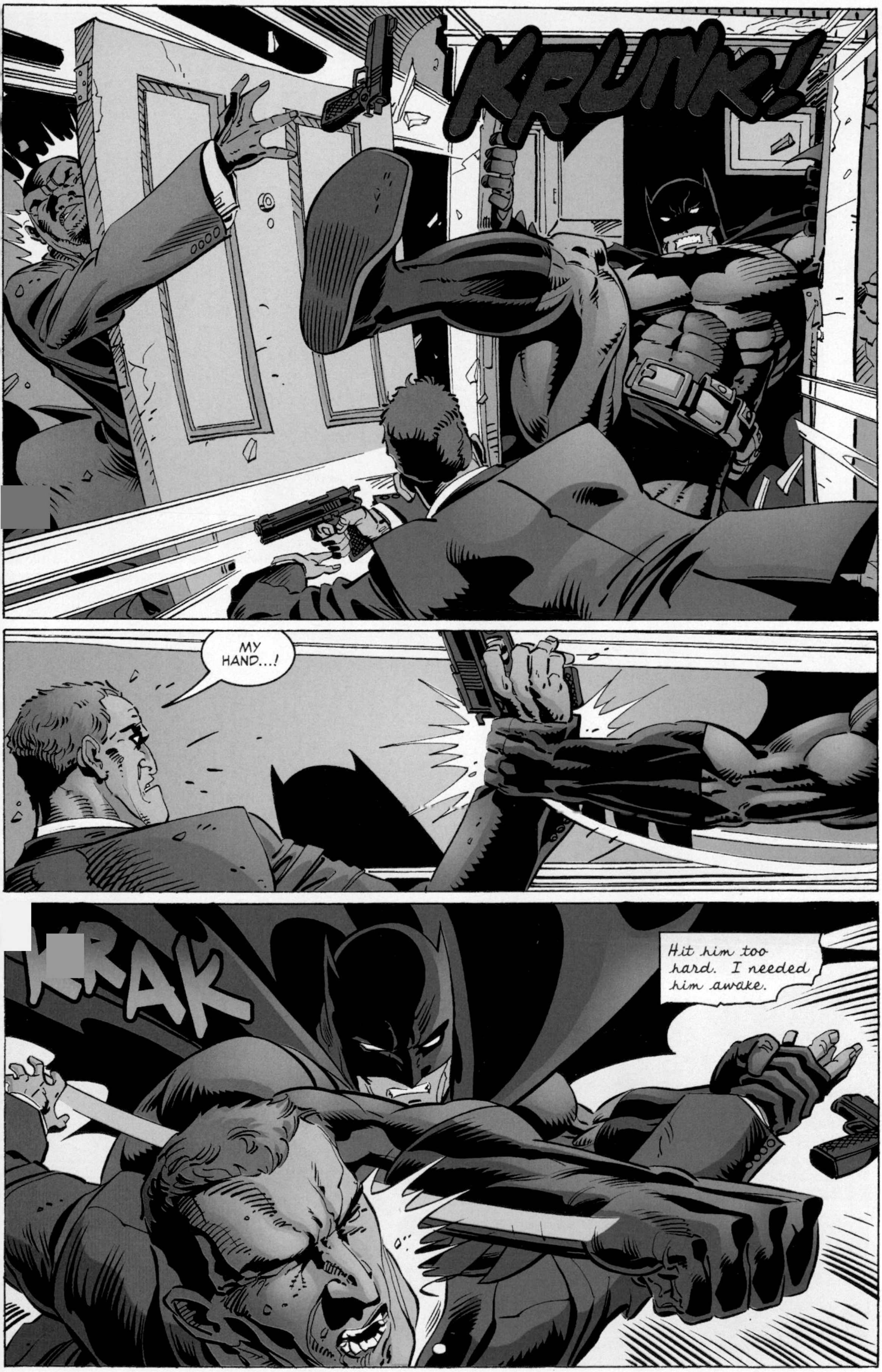
KRUNK!
MY HAND...!
RAK
Hit him too hard. I needed him awake.

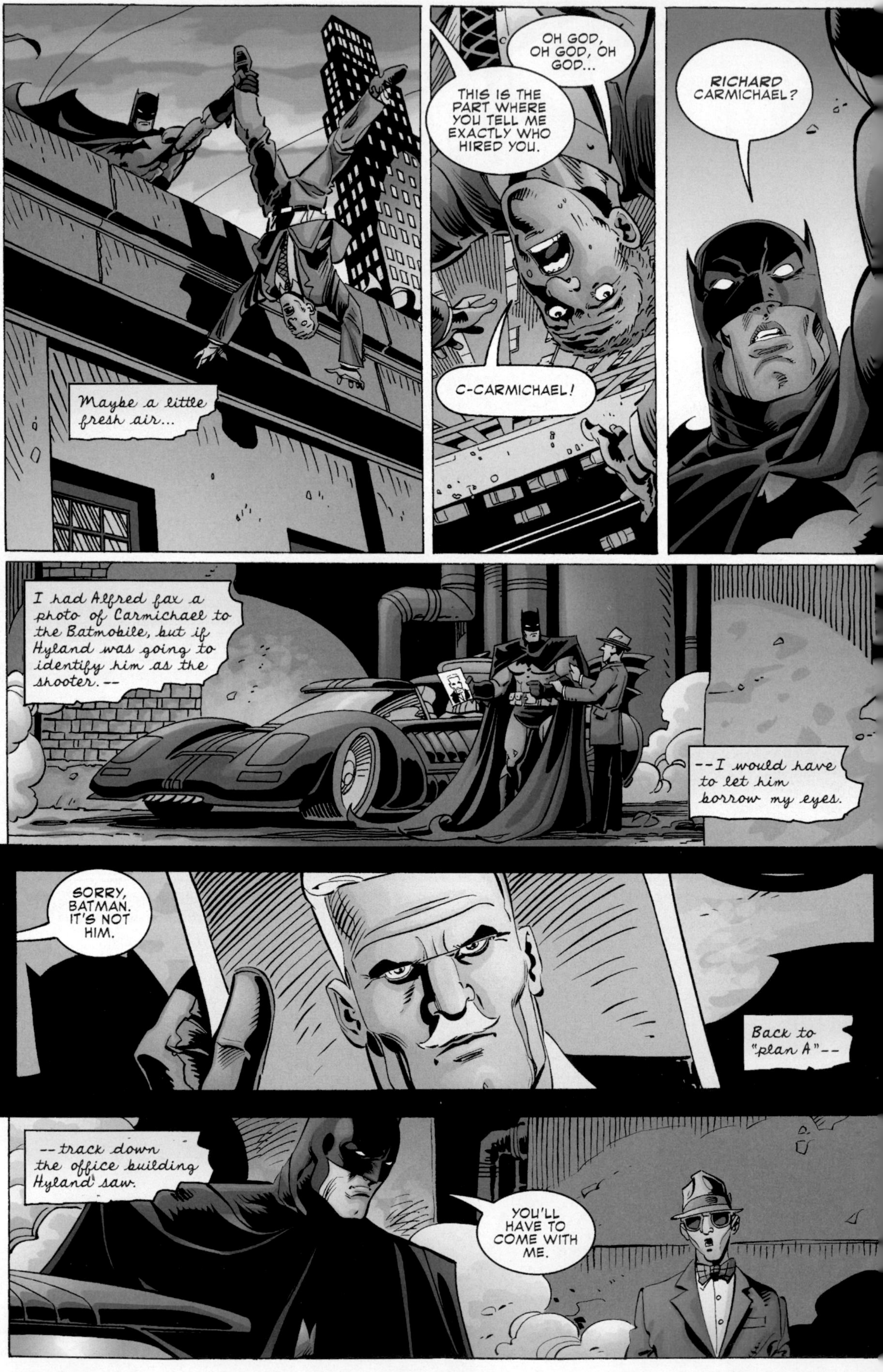
Maybe a little fresh air...
OH GOD, OH GOD, OH GOD...
THIS IS THE PART WHERE YOU TELL ME EXACTLY WHO HIRED YOU.
C-CARMICHAEL!
RICHARD CARMICHAEL?
I had Alfred fax a photo of Carmichael to the Batmobile, but if Hyland was going to identify him as the shooter.--
--I would have to let him borrow my eyes.
SORRY, BATMAN. IT'S NOT HIM.
Back to "plan A"--
--track down the office building Hyland saw.
YOU'LL HAVE TO COME WITH ME.

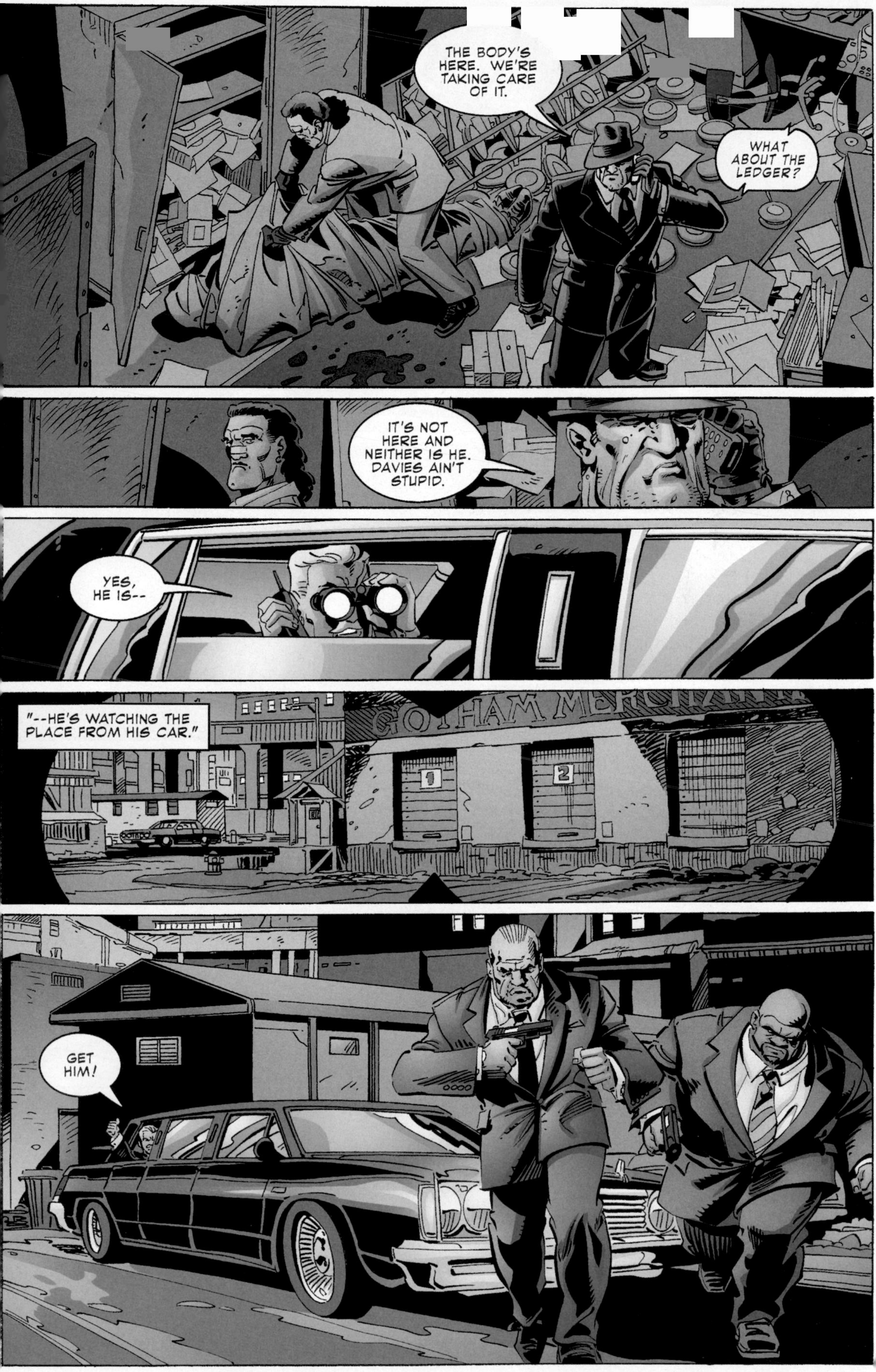
THE BODY'S HERE. WE'RE TAKING CARE OF IT.
WHAT ABOUT THE LEDGER?
IT'S NOT HERE AND NEITHER IS HE. DAVIES AIN'T STUPID.
YES, HE IS--
"--HE'S WATCHING THE PLACE FROM HIS CAR."
GET HIM!

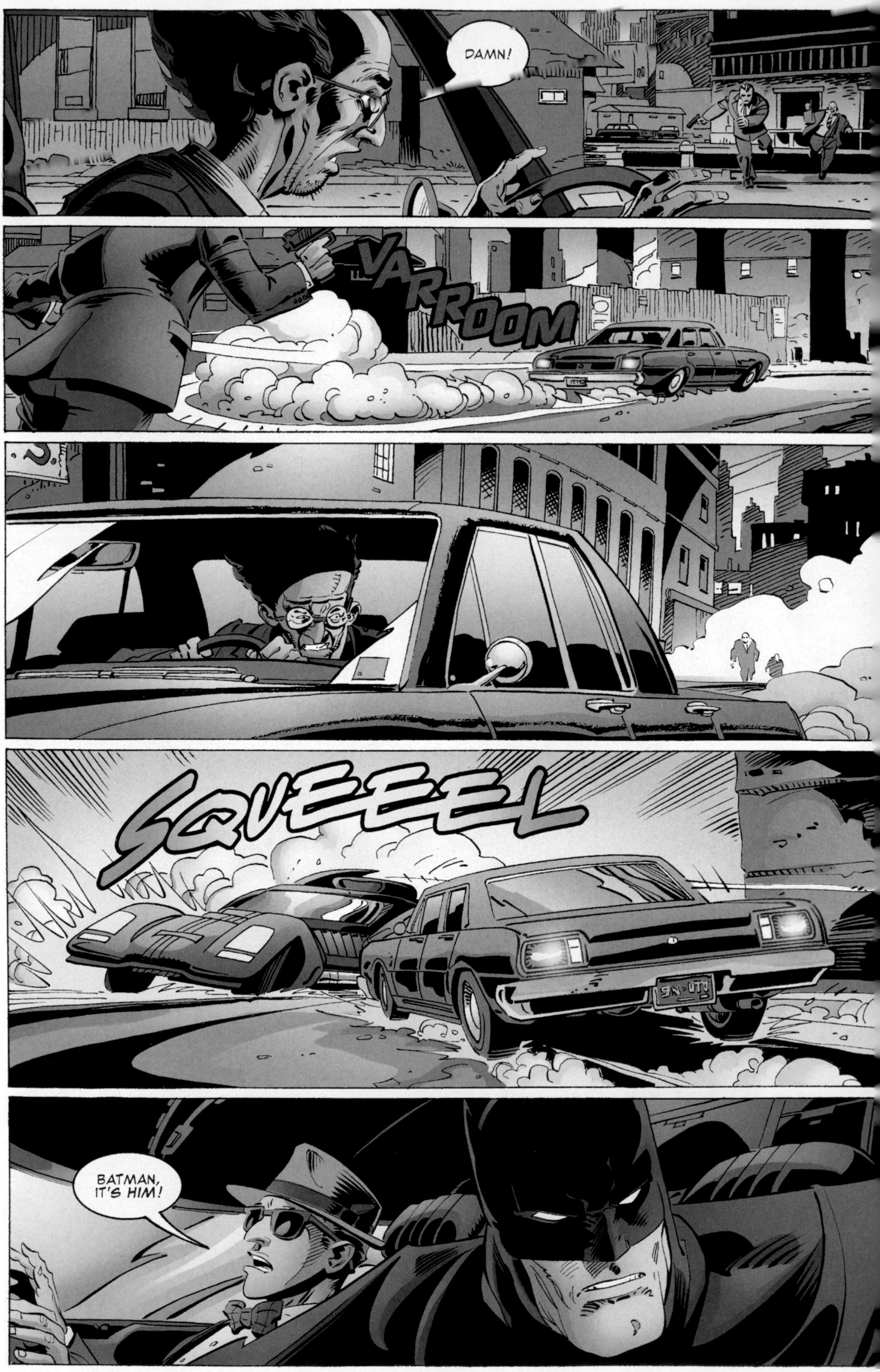
DAMN!
VARROOM
SQUEEEL
BATMAN, IT'S HIM!

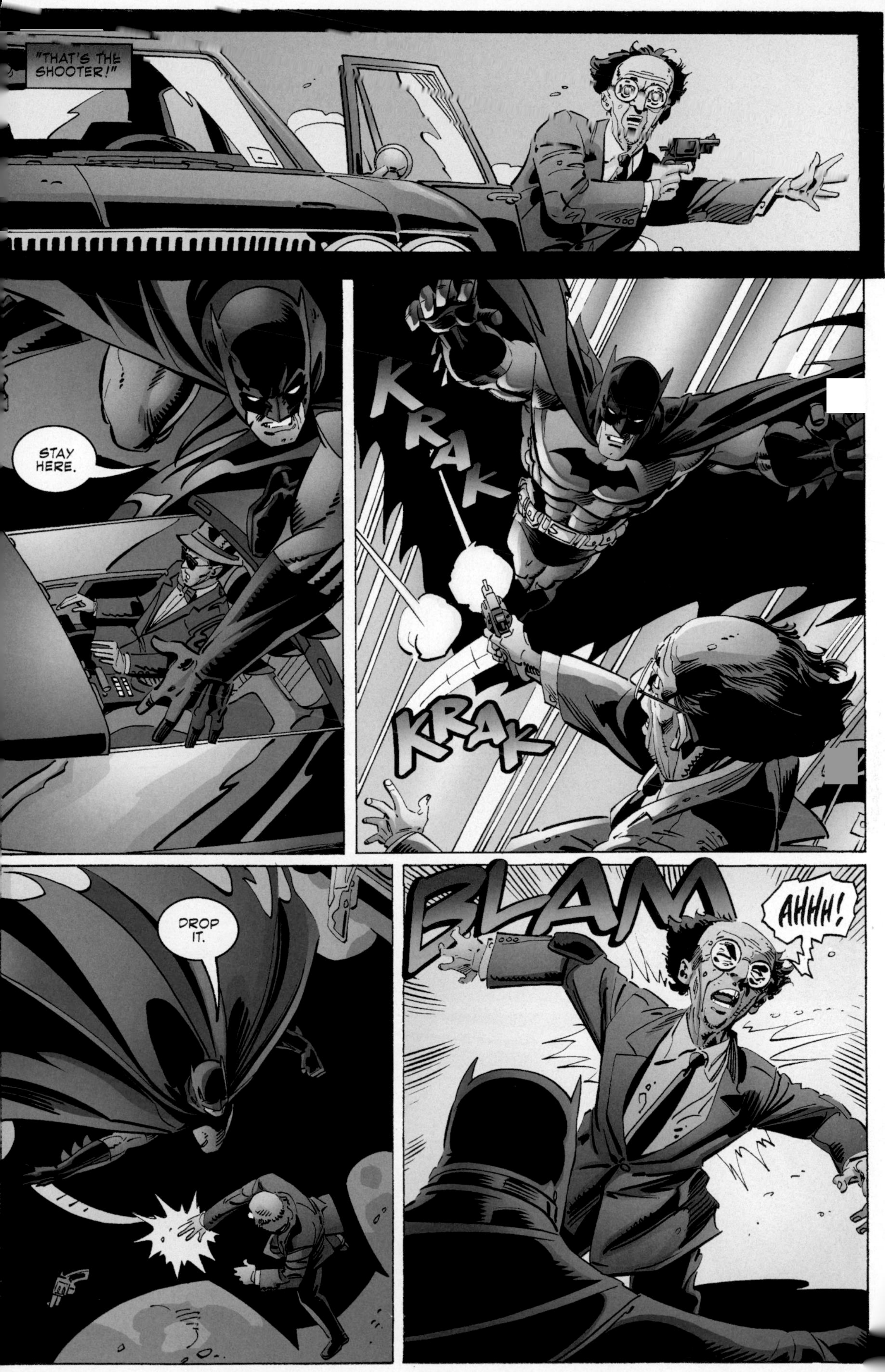
"THAT'S THE SHOOTER!"
STAY HERE.
KRAK
KRAK
DROP IT.
BLAM
AHHH!

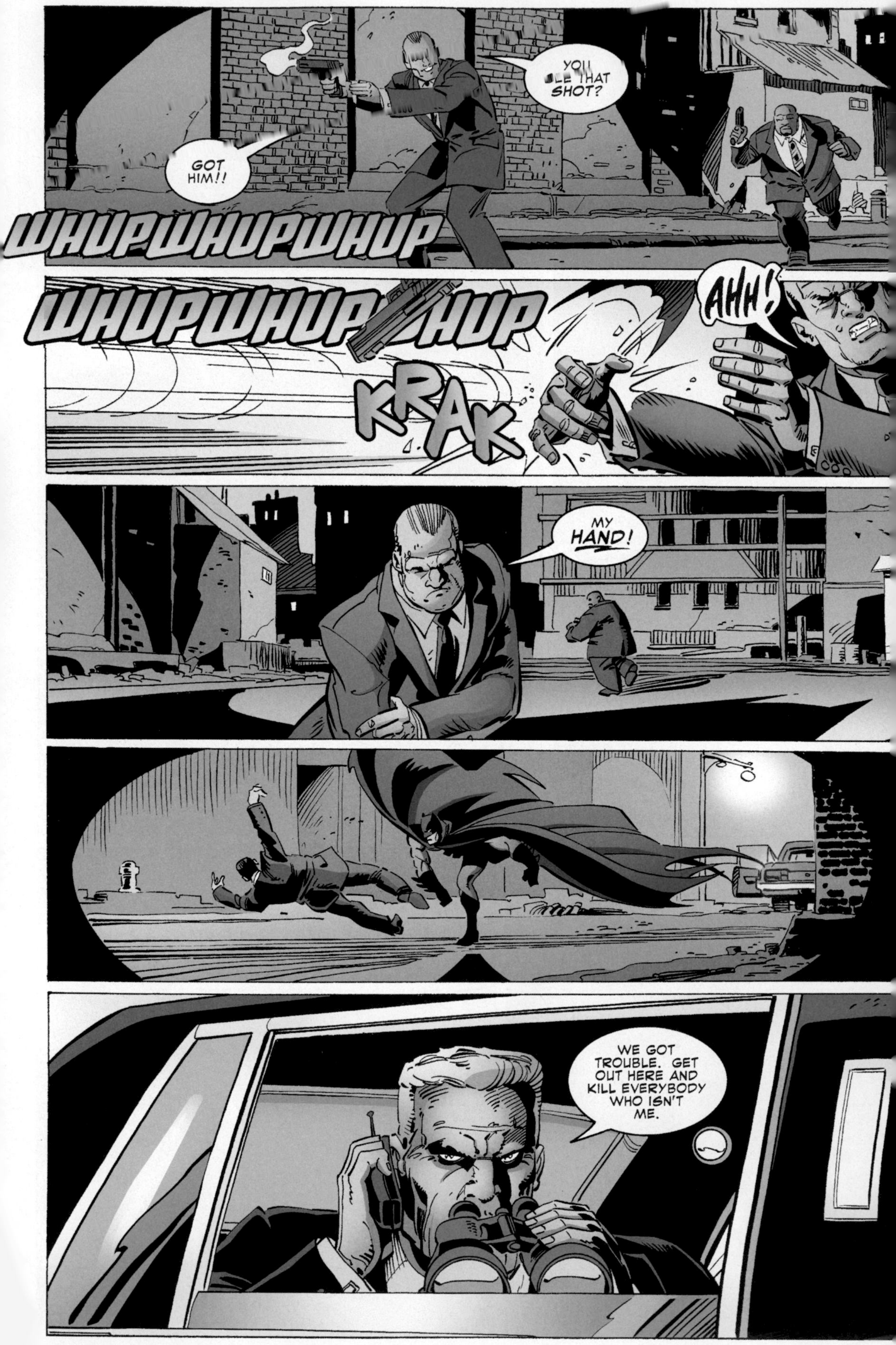
YOU ... THAT SHOT?
GOT HIM!!
WHUPWHUPWHUP
WHUPWHUPWHUP
AHH!
KRAK
MY HAND!
WE GOT TROUBLE. GET OUT HERE AND KILL EVERYBODY WHO ISN'T ME.

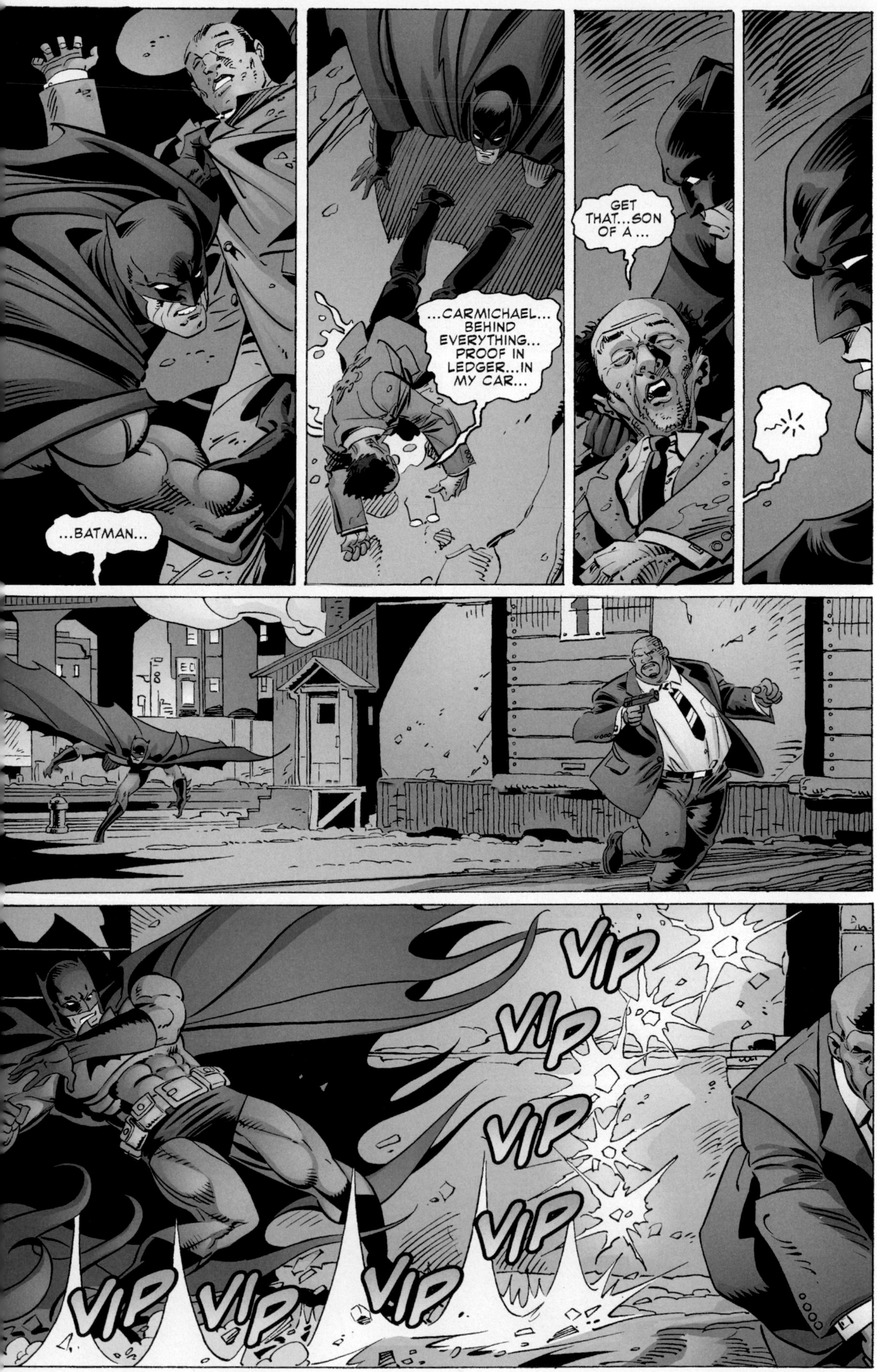

...BATMAN...
...CARMICHAEL... BEHIND EVERYTHING... PROOF IN LEDGER...IN MY CAR...
GET THAT...SON OF A...
VIP
VIP
VIP
VIP
VIP
VIP
VIP

BUDDABUDDABUDDA

I GOT HIM! I GOT--

--HIIIMMM!

BUDDABUDDABUDDA

ARGH!

HOLD FIRE! HOLD FIRE!

WE HIT MIKE!

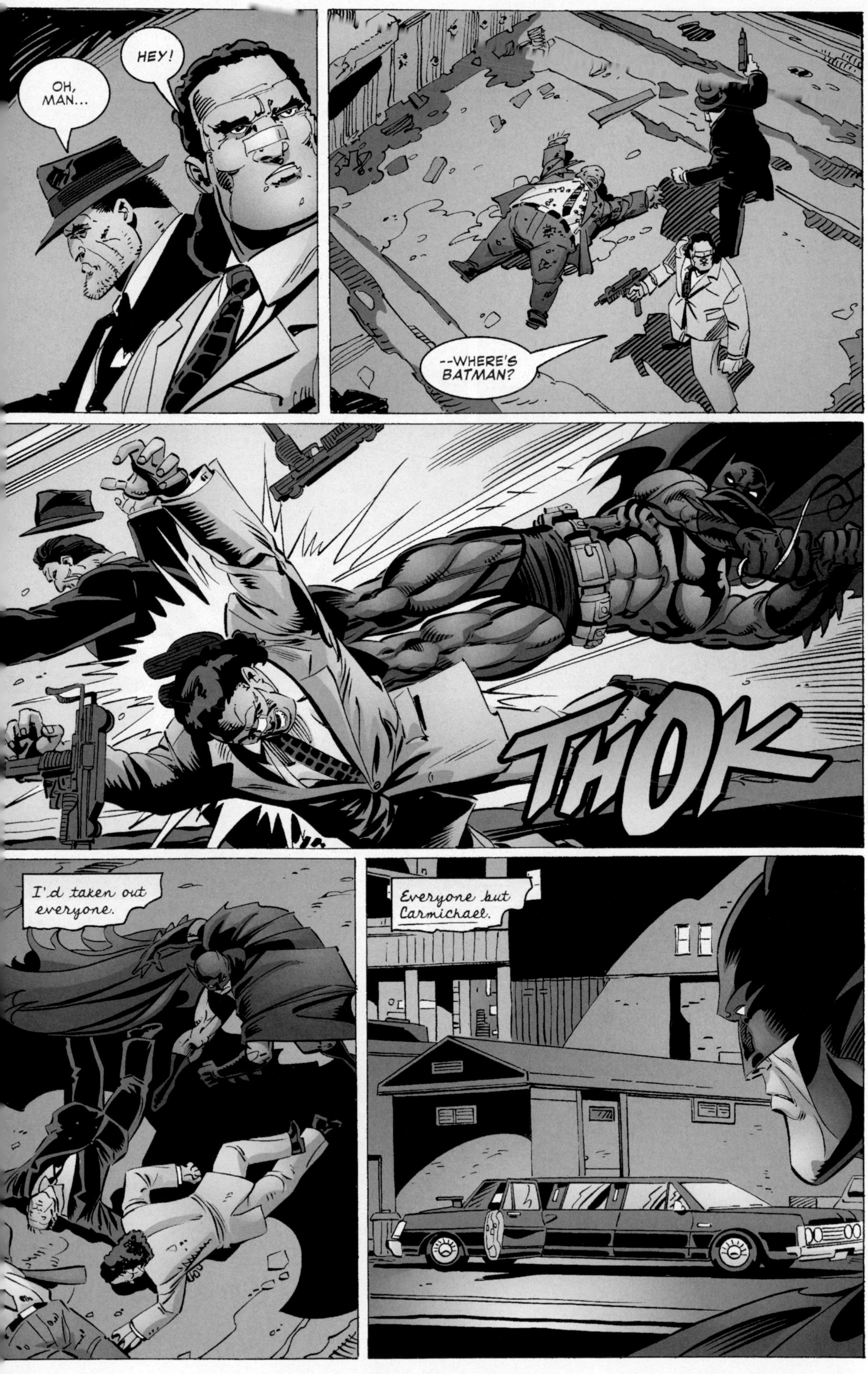
OH, MAN...
HEY!
--WHERE'S BATMAN?
THOK
I'd taken out everyone.
Everyone but Carmichael.

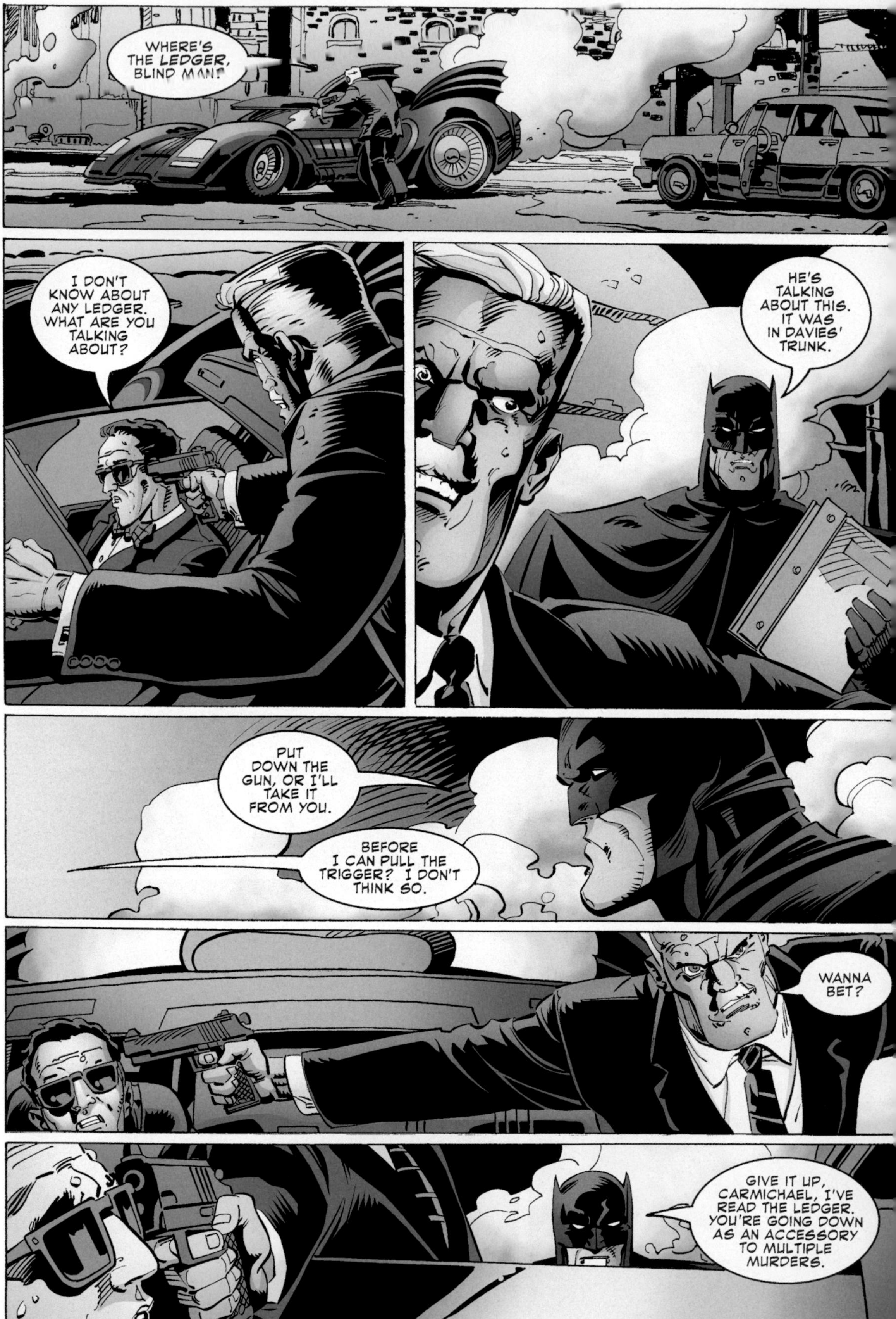

WHERE'S THE LEDGER, BLIND MAN?
I DON'T KNOW ABOUT ANY LEDGER. WHAT ARE YOU TALKING ABOUT?
HE'S TALKING ABOUT THIS. IT WAS IN DAVIES' TRUNK.
PUT DOWN THE GUN, OR I'LL TAKE IT FROM YOU.
BEFORE I CAN PULL THE TRIGGER? I DON'T THINK SO.
WANNA BET?
GIVE IT UP, CARMICHAEL, I'VE READ THE LEDGER. YOU'RE GOING DOWN AS AN ACCESSORY TO MULTIPLE MURDERS.

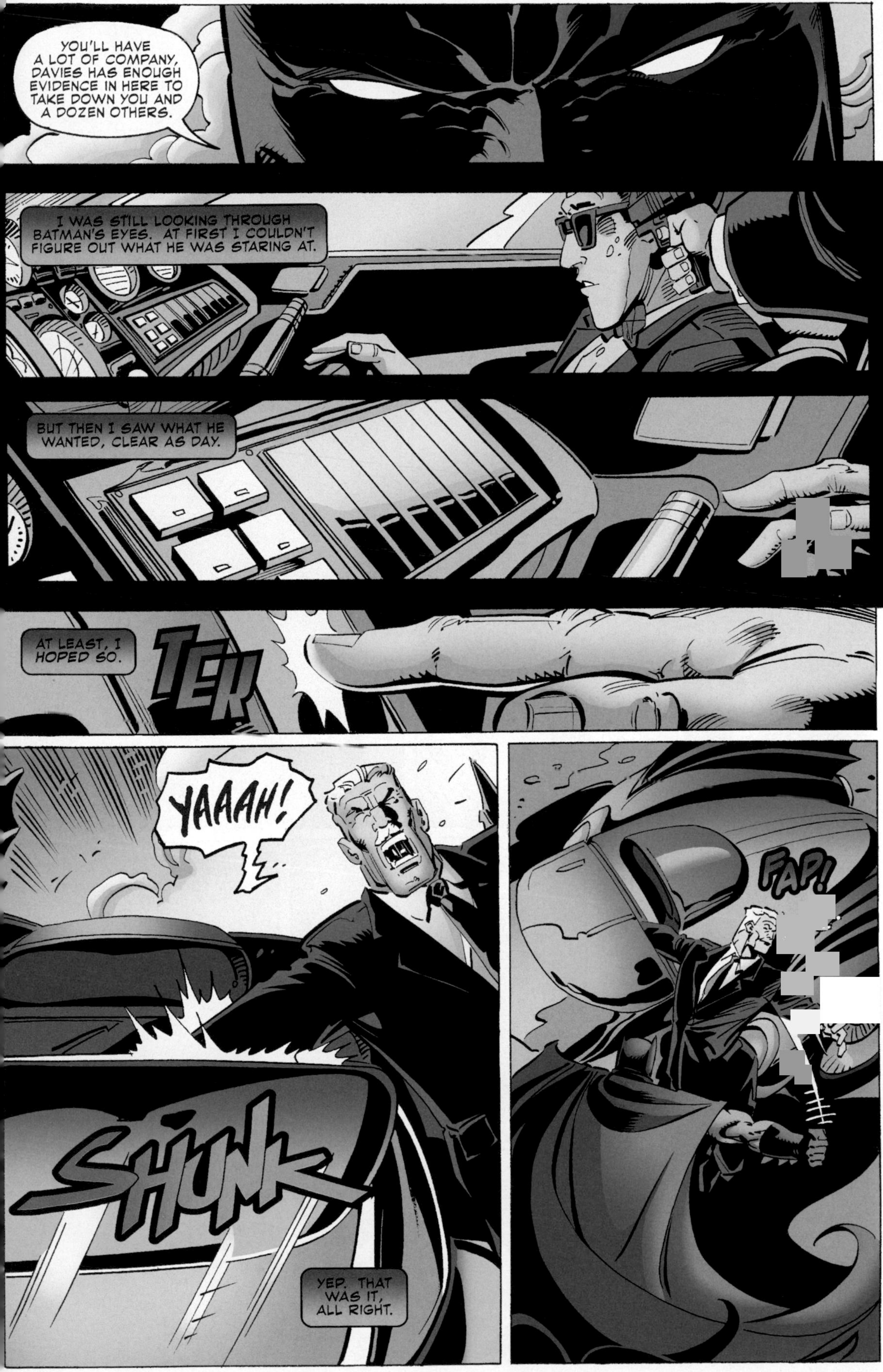
YOU'LL HAVE A LOT OF COMPANY. DAVIES HAS ENOUGH EVIDENCE IN HERE TO TAKE DOWN YOU AND A DOZEN OTHERS.
I WAS STILL LOOKING THROUGH BATMAN'S EYES. AT FIRST I COULDN'T FIGURE OUT WHAT HE WAS STARING AT.
BUT THEN I SAW WHAT HE WANTED, CLEAR AS DAY.
AT LEAST, I HOPED SO.
TEK
YAAAH!
SHUNK
YEP. THAT WAS IT, ALL RIGHT.
FAP!

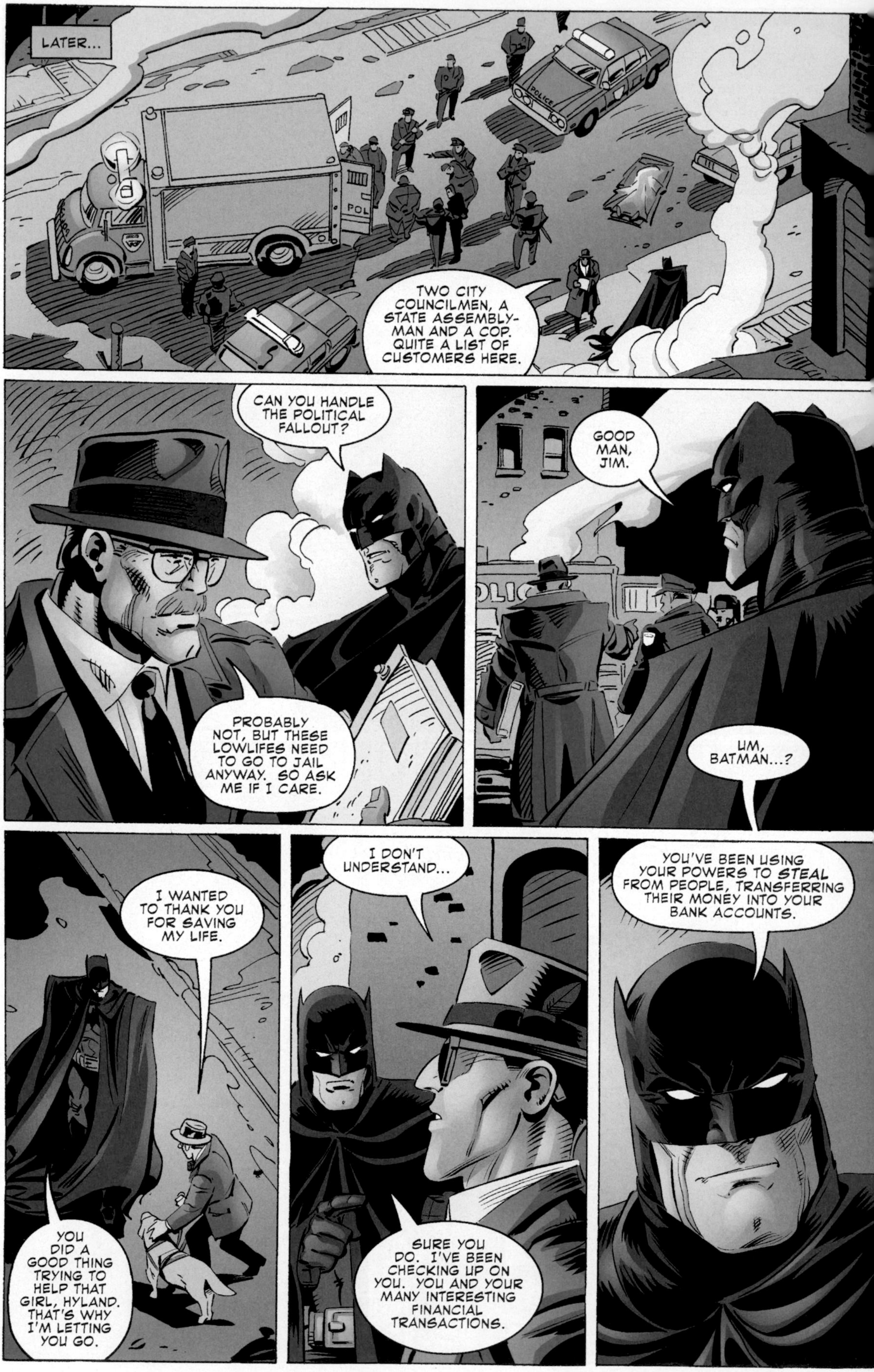
LATER...
TWO CITY COUNCILMEN, A STATE ASSEMBLY-MAN AND A COP. QUITE A LIST OF CUSTOMERS HERE.
CAN YOU HANDLE THE POLITICAL FALLOUT?
PROBABLY NOT, BUT THESE LOWLIFES NEED TO GO TO JAIL ANYWAY. SO ASK ME IF I CARE.
GOOD MAN, JIM.
UM, BATMAN...?
I WANTED TO THANK YOU FOR SAVING MY LIFE.
YOU DID A GOOD THING TRYING TO HELP THAT GIRL, HYLAND. THAT'S WHY I'M LETTING YOU GO.
I DON'T UNDERSTAND...
SURE YOU DO. I'VE BEEN CHECKING UP ON YOU. YOU AND YOUR MANY INTERESTING FINANCIAL TRANSACTIONS.
YOU'VE BEEN USING YOUR POWERS TO STEAL FROM PEOPLE, TRANSFERRING THEIR MONEY INTO YOUR BANK ACCOUNTS.

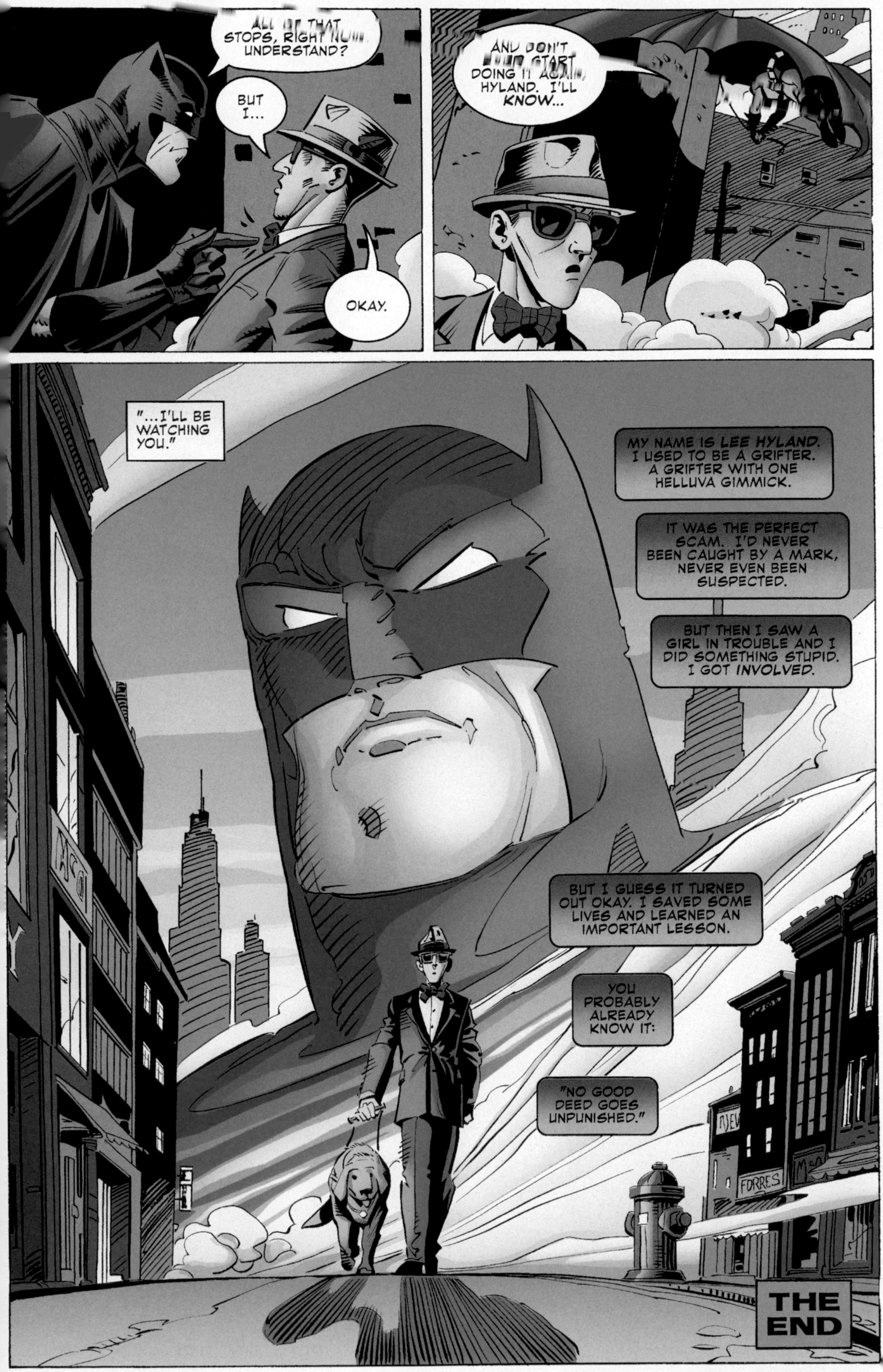
ALL OF THAT STOPS, RIGHT NOW, UNDERSTAND?
BUT I...
OKAY.
AND DON'T START DOING IT AGAIN, HYLAND. I'LL KNOW...
"...I'LL BE WATCHING YOU."
MY NAME IS LEE HYLAND. I USED TO BE A GRIFTER. A GRIFTER WITH ONE HELLUVA GIMMICK.
IT WAS THE PERFECT SCAM. I'D NEVER BEEN CAUGHT BY A MARK, NEVER EVEN BEEN SUSPECTED.
BUT THEN I SAW A GIRL IN TROUBLE AND I DID SOMETHING STUPID. I GOT INVOLVED.
BUT I GUESS IT TURNED OUT OKAY. I SAVED SOME LIVES AND LEARNED AN IMPORTANT LESSON.
YOU PROBABLY ALREADY KNOW IT:
"NO GOOD DEED GOES UNPUNISHED."
FORRES
THE END

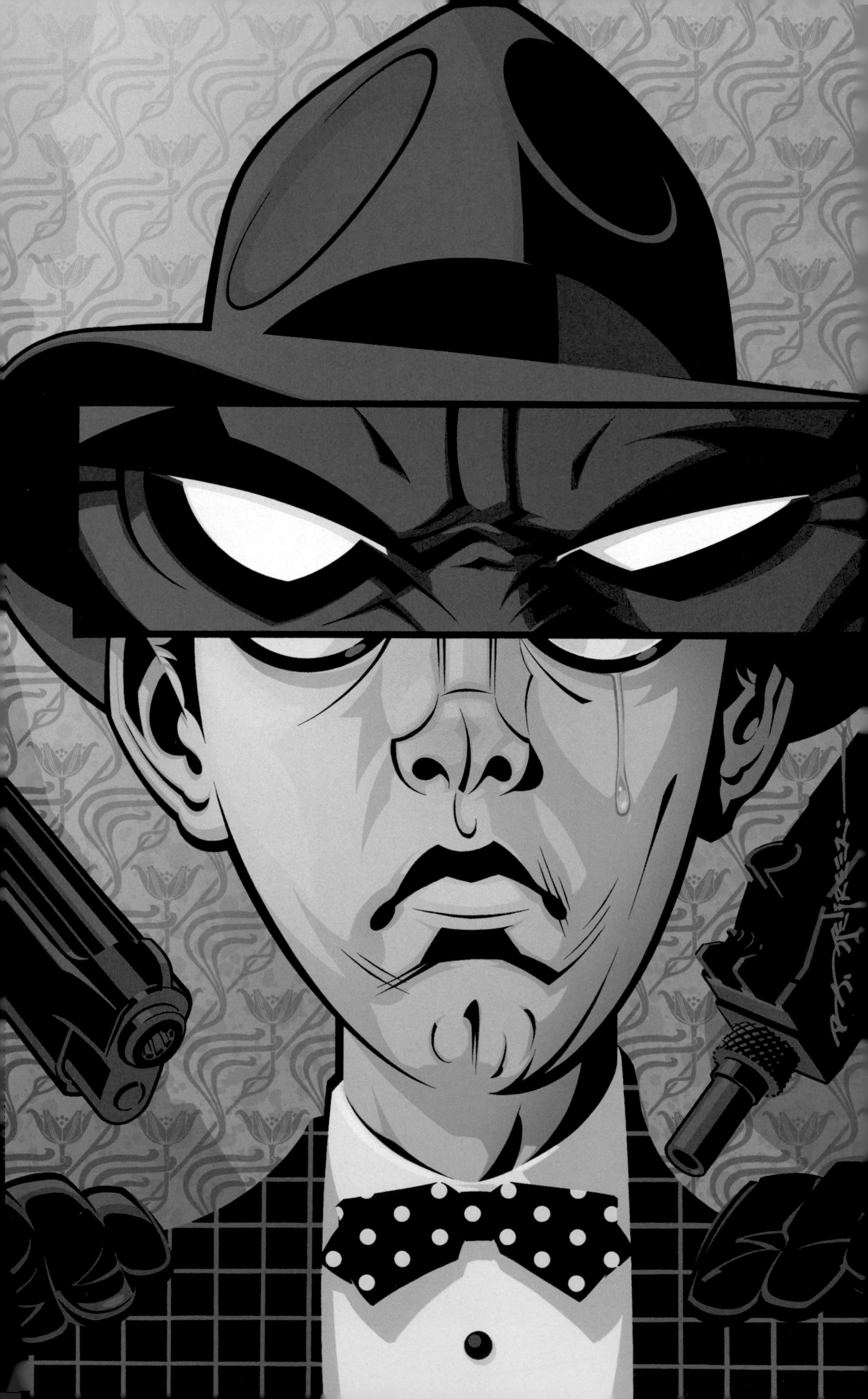

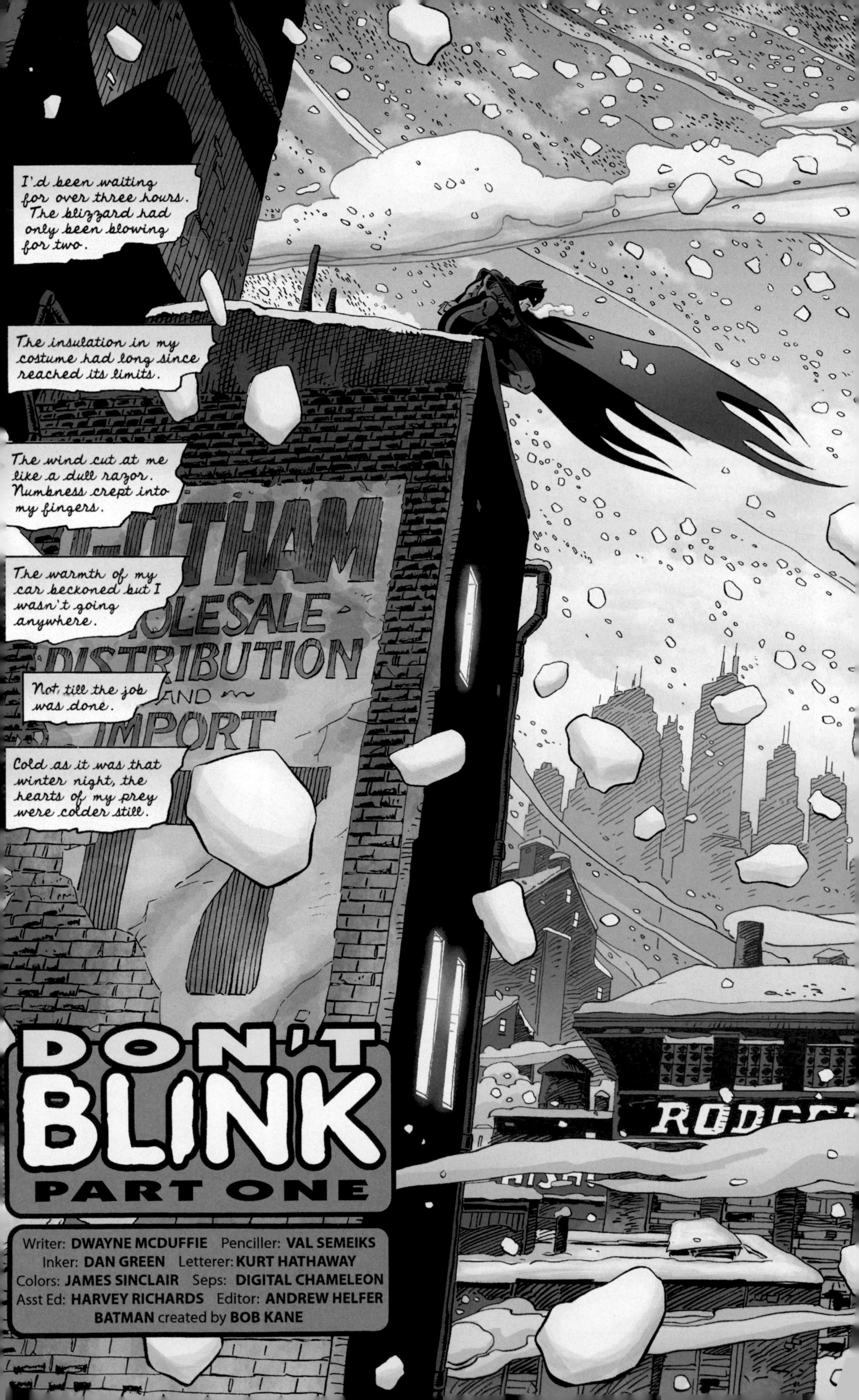
I'd been waiting for over three hours. The blizzard had only been blowing for two.
The insulation in my costume had long since reached its limits.
The wind cut at me like a dull razor. Numbness crept into my fingers.
The warmth of my car beckoned but I wasn't going anywhere.
Not till the job was done.
Cold as it was that winter night, the hearts of my prey were colder still.
THAM
OLESALE
DISTRIBUTION
AND
IMPORT
RODG
DON'T BLINK
PART ONE
Writer: DWAYNE MCDUFFIE Penciller: VAL SEMEIKS
Inker: DAN GREEN Letterer: KURT HATHAWAY
Colors: JAMES SINCLAIR Seps: DIGITAL CHAMELEON
Asst Ed: HARVEY RICHARDS Editor: ANDREW HELFER
BATMAN created by BOB KANE

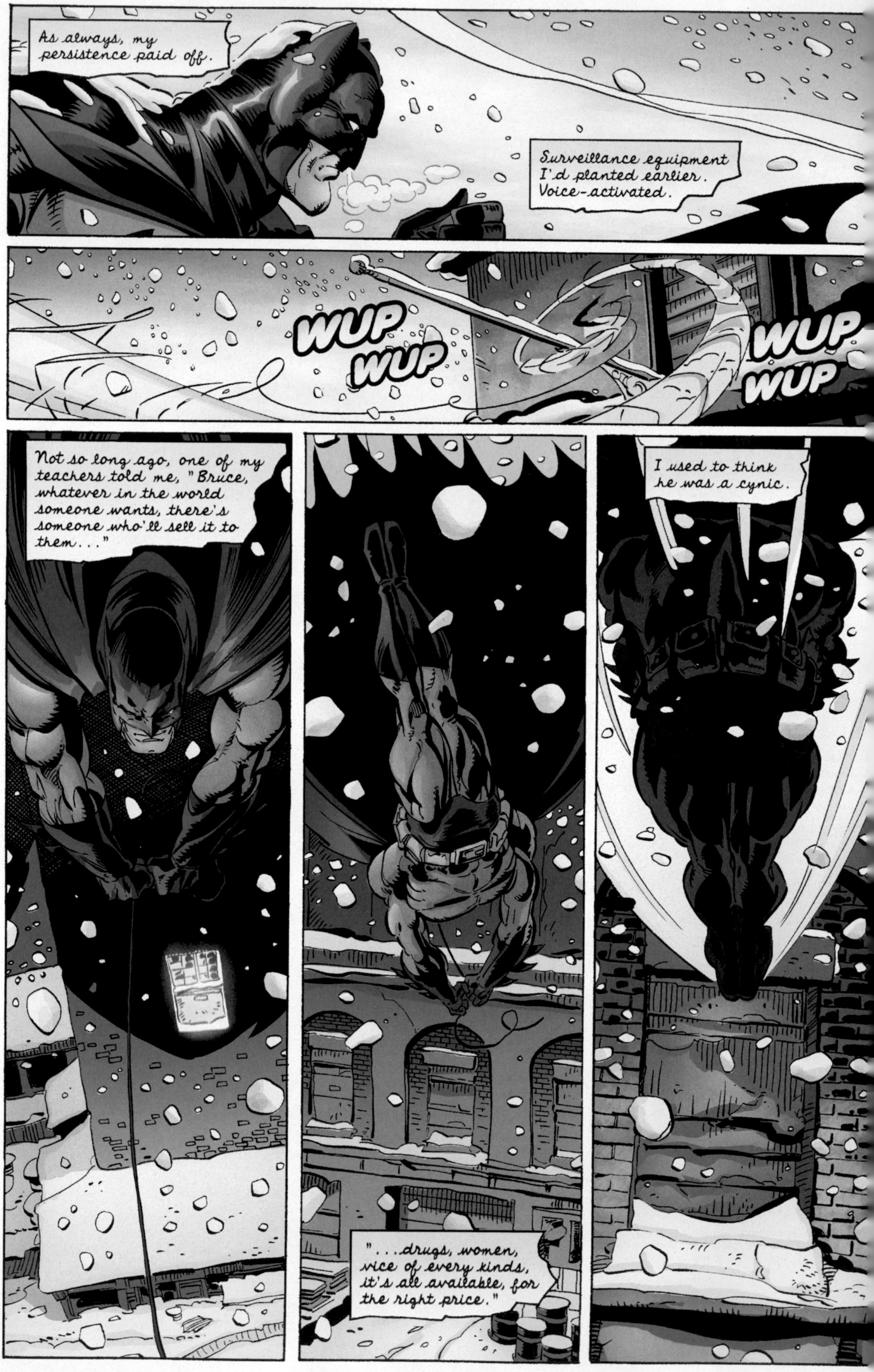
As always, my persistence paid off.
Surveillance equipment I'd planted earlier. Voice-activated.
WUP WUP
WUP WUP
Not so long ago, one of my teachers told me, "Bruce, whatever in the world someone wants, there's someone who'll sell it to them..."
"...drugs, women, vice of every kinds, it's all available, for the right price."
I used to think he was a cynic.

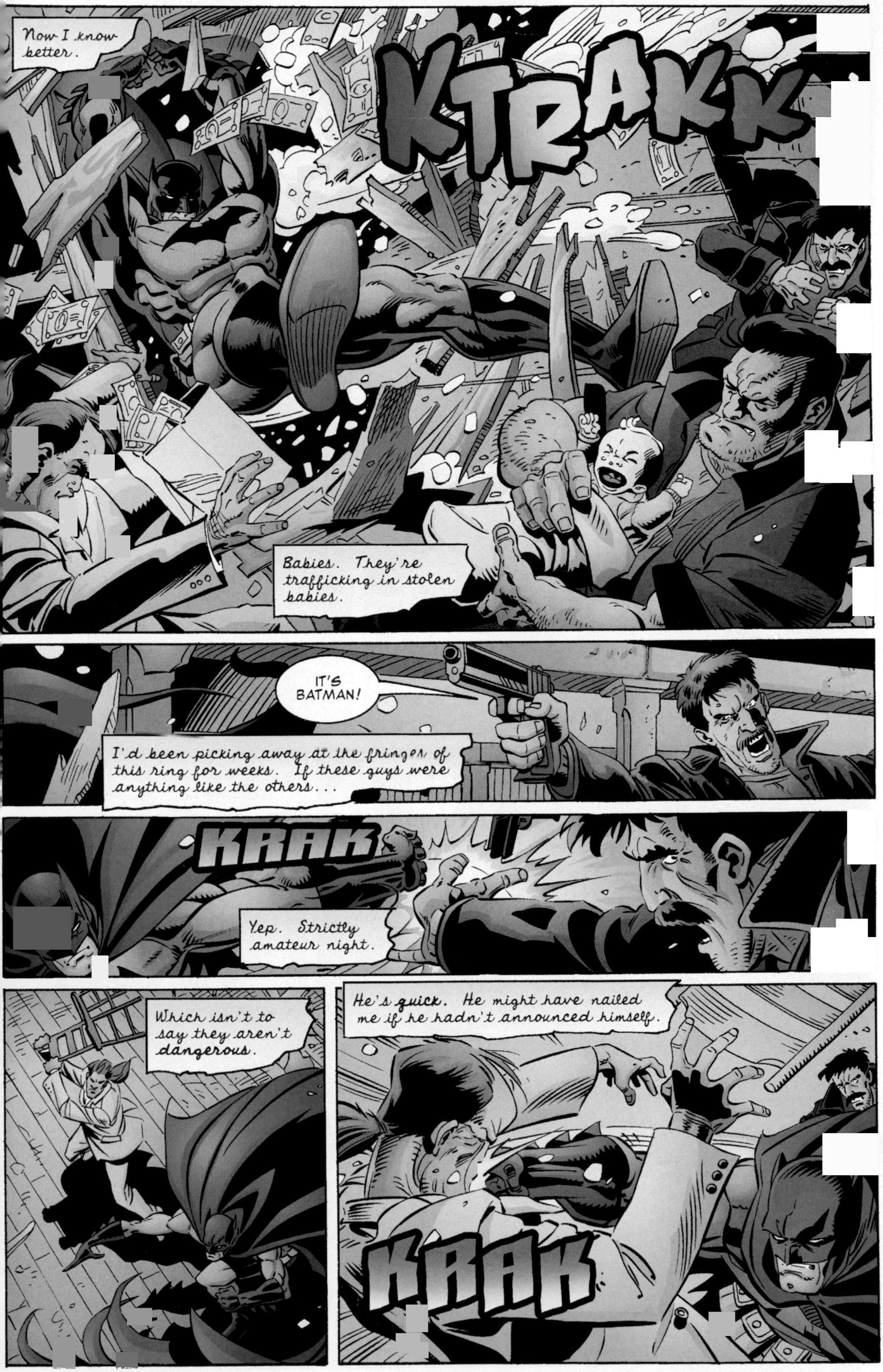
Now I know better.
KTRAKK
Babies. They're trafficking in stolen babies.
IT'S BATMAN!
I'd been picking away at the fringes of this ring for weeks. If these guys were anything like the others...
KRAK
Yep. Strictly amateur night.
Which isn't to say they aren't dangerous.
He's quick. He might have nailed me if he hadn't announced himself.
KRAK

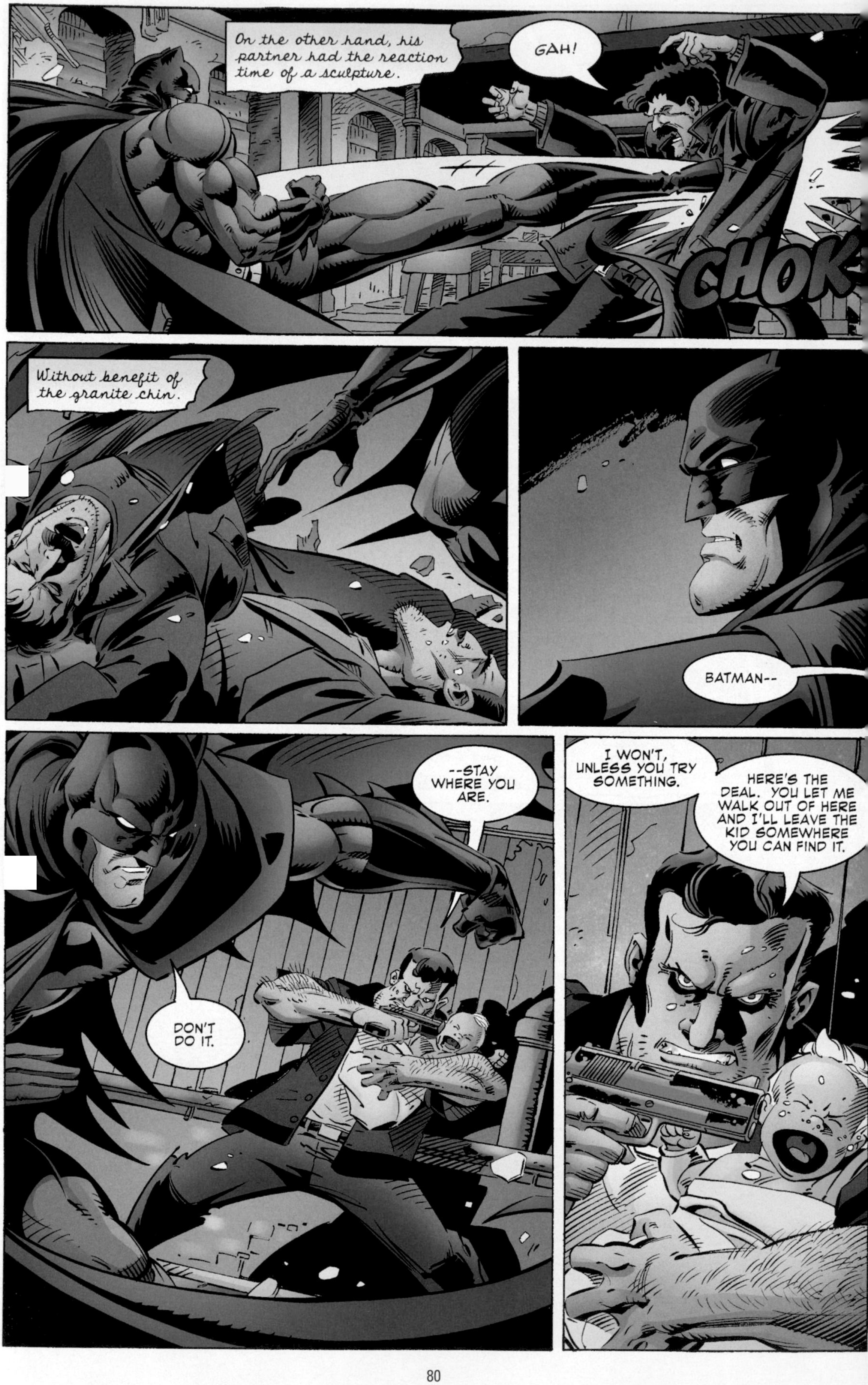
On the other hand, his partner had the reaction time of a sculpture.
GAH!
CHOK
Without benefit of the granite chin.
BATMAN--
--STAY WHERE YOU ARE.
DON'T DO IT.
I WON'T, UNLESS YOU TRY SOMETHING.
HERE'S THE DEAL. YOU LET ME WALK OUT OF HERE AND I'LL LEAVE THE KID SOMEWHERE YOU CAN FIND IT.

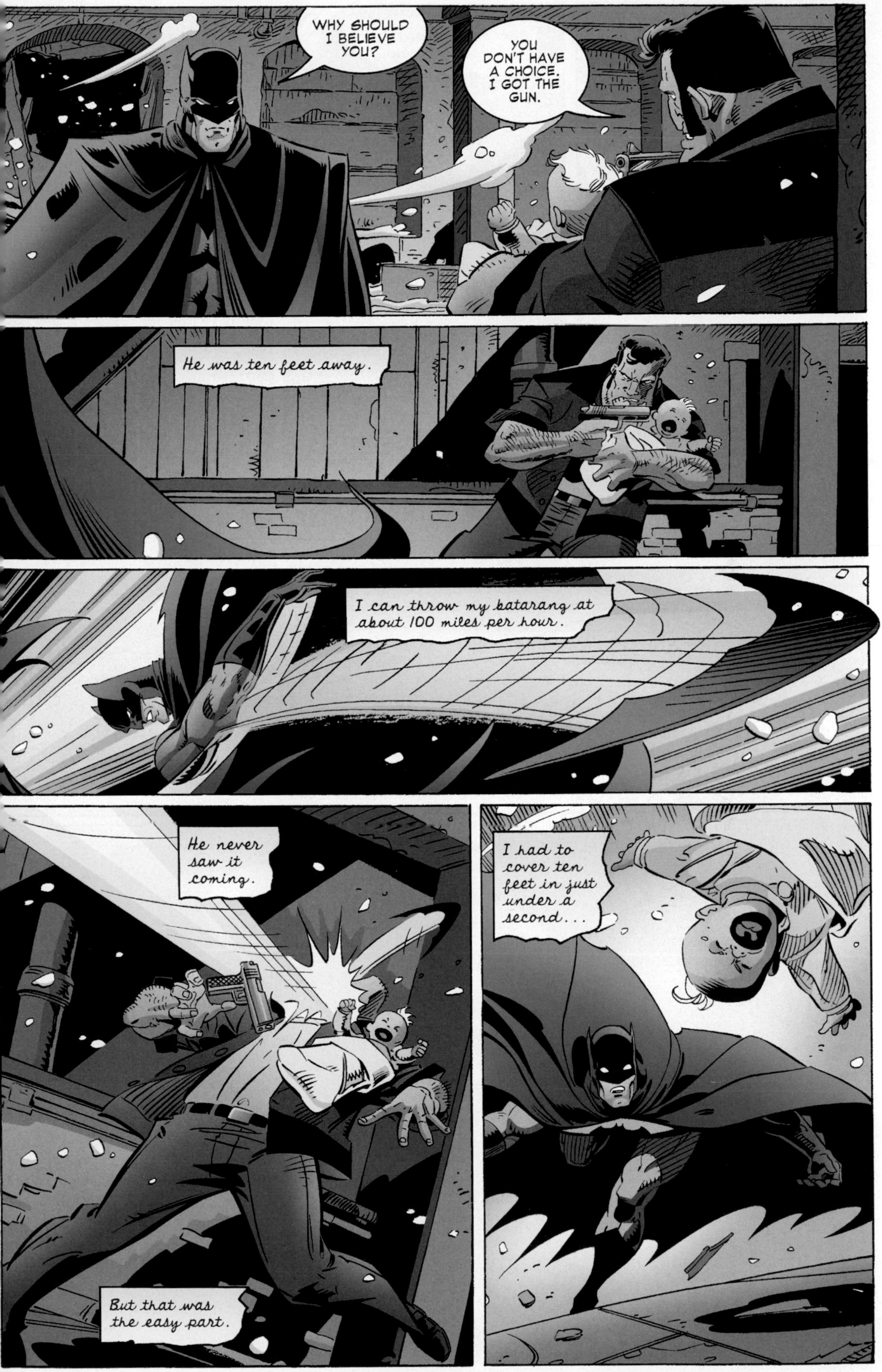
WHY SHOULD I BELIEVE YOU?
YOU DON'T HAVE A CHOICE. I GOT THE GUN.
He was ten feet away.
I can throw my batarang at about 100 miles per hour.
He never saw it coming.
But that was the easy part.
I had to cover ten feet in just under a second...

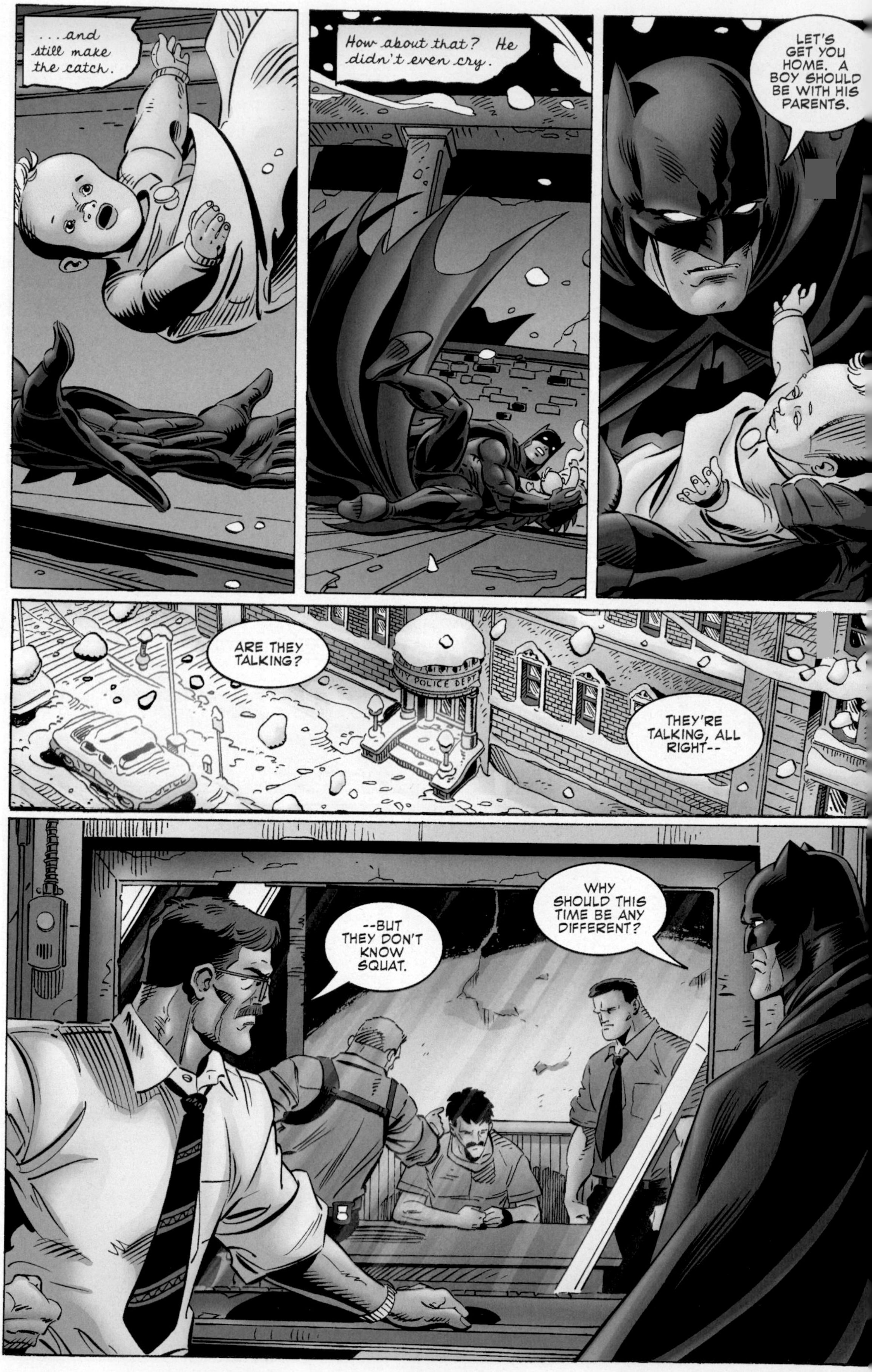
...and still make the catch.
How about that? He didn't even cry.
LET'S GET YOU HOME. A BOY SHOULD BE WITH HIS PARENTS.
ARE THEY TALKING?
POLICE DEPT
THEY'RE TALKING, ALL RIGHT--
--BUT THEY DON'T KNOW SQUAT.
WHY SHOULD THIS TIME BE ANY DIFFERENT?

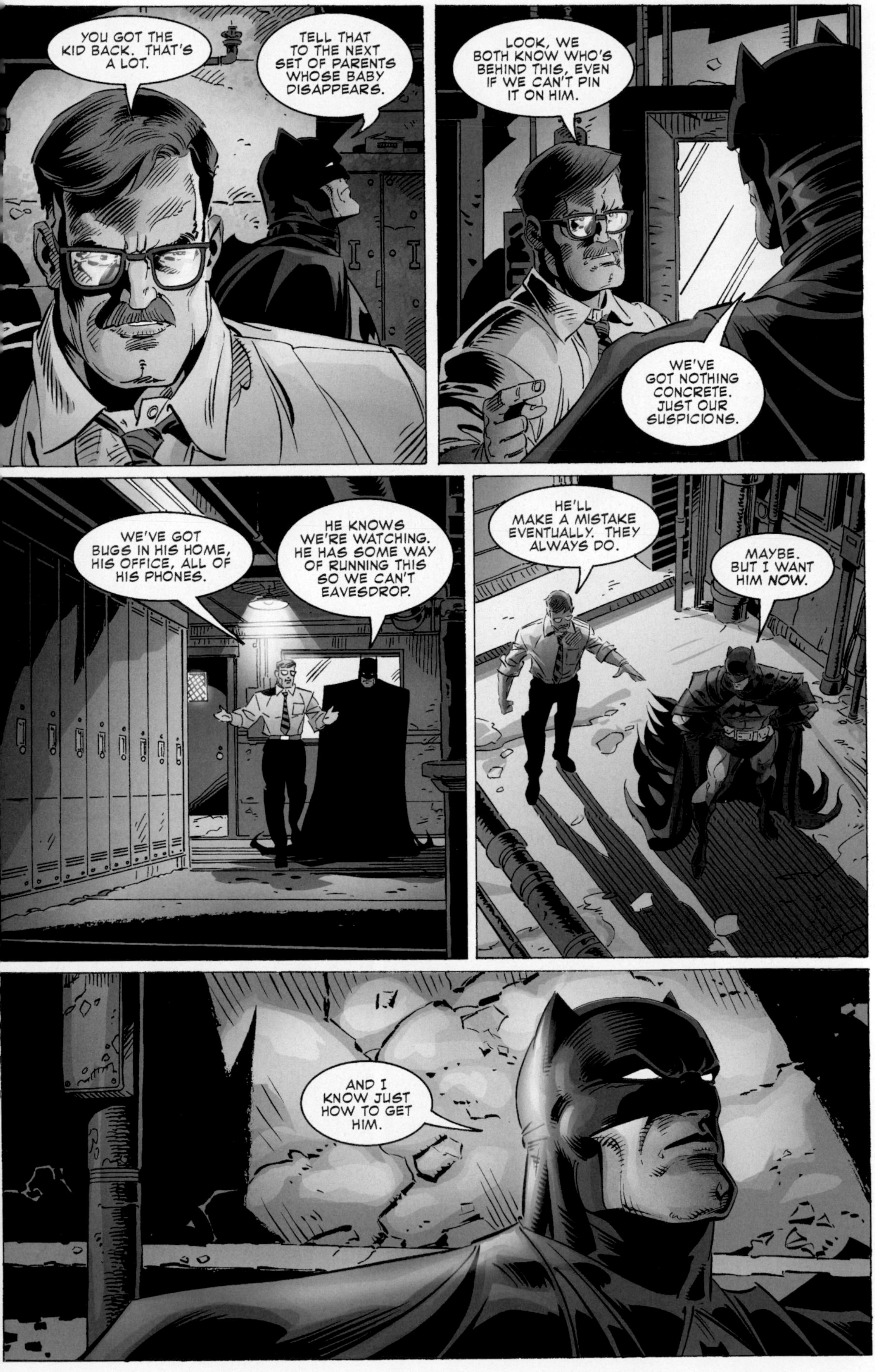
YOU GOT THE KID BACK. THAT'S A LOT.
TELL THAT TO THE NEXT SET OF PARENTS WHOSE BABY DISAPPEARS.
LOOK, WE BOTH KNOW WHO'S BEHIND THIS, EVEN IF WE CAN'T PIN IT ON HIM.
WE'VE GOT NOTHING CONCRETE. JUST OUR SUSPICIONS.
WE'VE GOT BUGS IN HIS HOME, HIS OFFICE, ALL OF HIS PHONES.
HE KNOWS WE'RE WATCHING. HE HAS SOME WAY OF RUNNING THIS SO WE CAN'T EAVESDROP.
HE'LL MAKE A MISTAKE EVENTUALLY. THEY ALWAYS DO.
MAYBE. BUT I WANT HIM **NOW**.
AND I KNOW JUST HOW TO GET HIM.

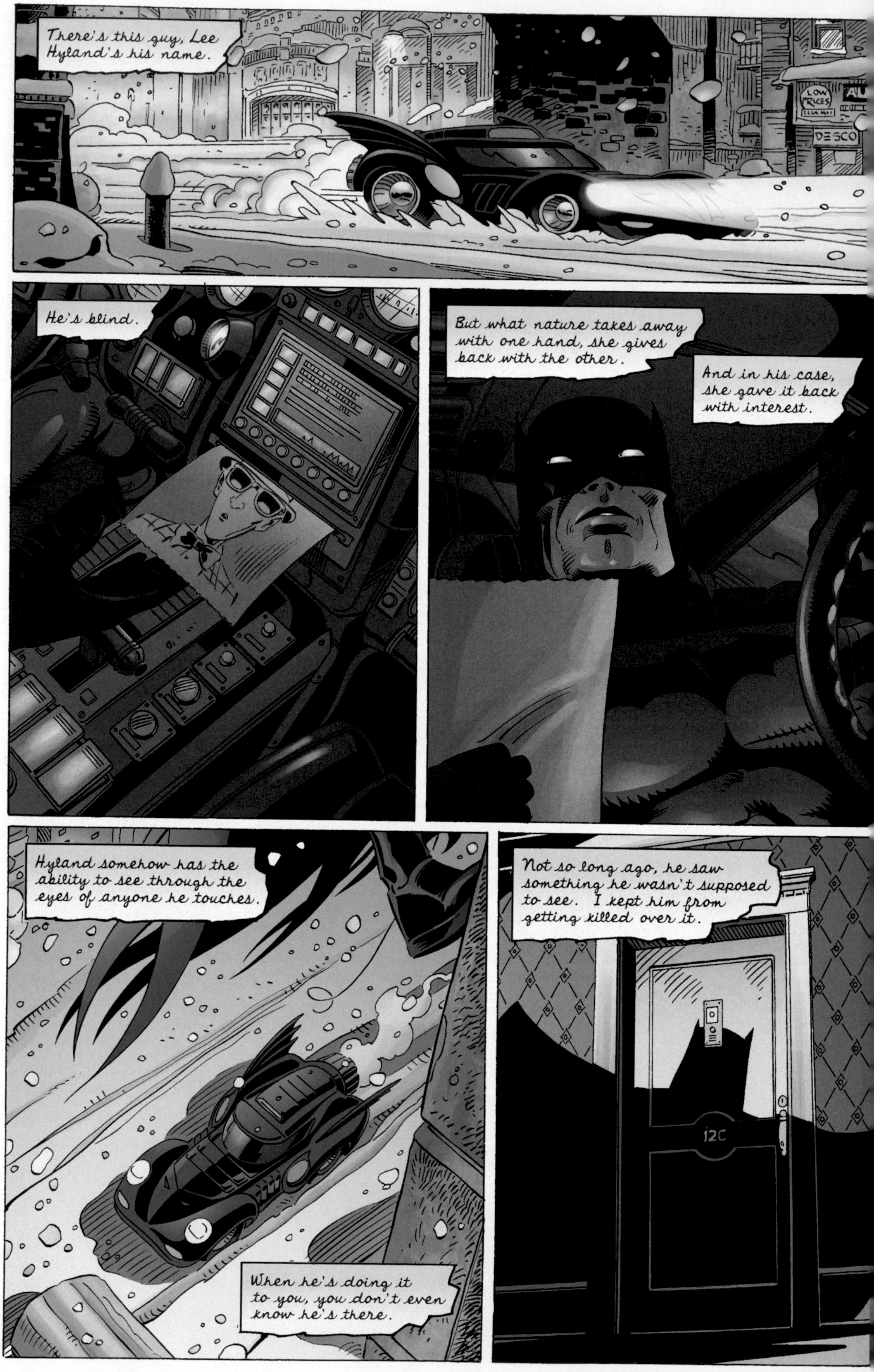
There's this guy, Lee Hyland's his name.
LOW PRICES
DESCO
He's blind.
But what nature takes away with one hand, she gives back with the other.
And in his case, she gave it back with interest.
Hyland somehow has the ability to see through the eyes of anyone he touches.
When he's doing it to you, you don't even know he's there.
Not so long ago, he saw something he wasn't supposed to see. I kept him from getting killed over it.
12C

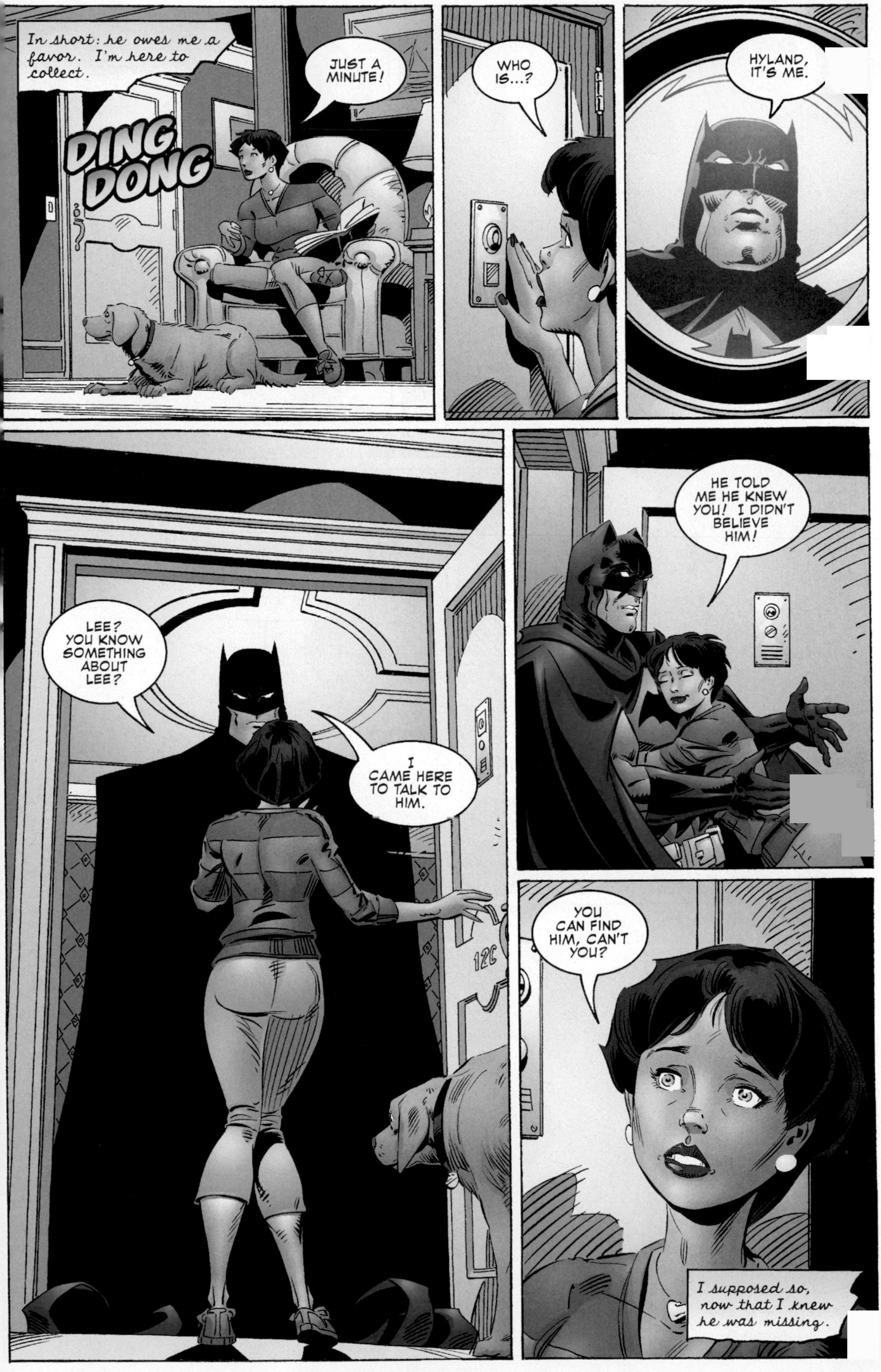
In short: he owes me a favor. I'm here to collect.
JUST A MINUTE!
DING DONG
WHO IS...?
HYLAND, IT'S ME.
LEE? YOU KNOW SOMETHING ABOUT LEE?
I CAME HERE TO TALK TO HIM.
12C
HE TOLD ME HE KNEW YOU! I DIDN'T BELIEVE HIM!
YOU CAN FIND HIM, CAN'T YOU?
I supposed so, now that I knew he was missing.

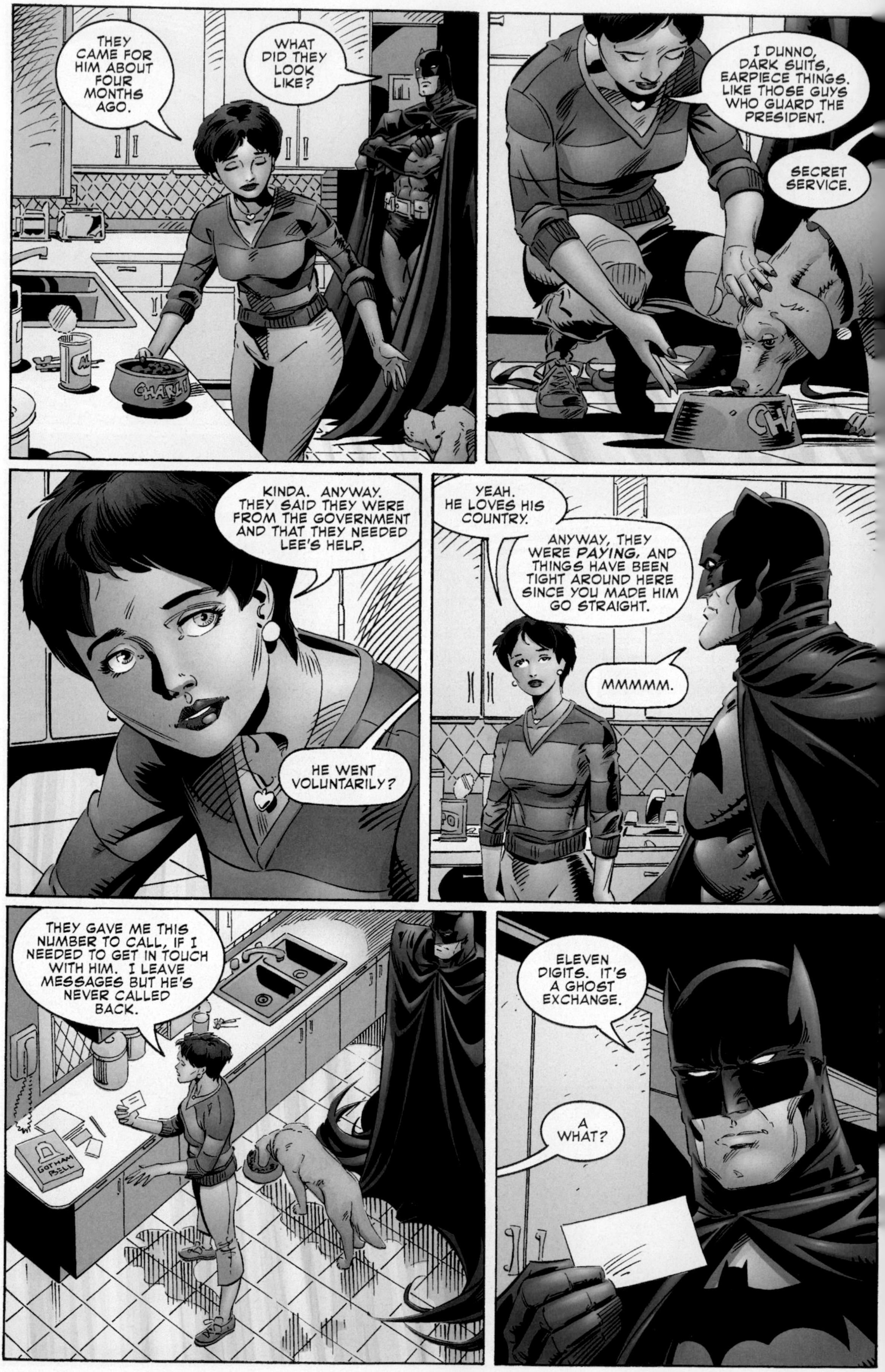
THEY CAME FOR HIM ABOUT FOUR MONTHS AGO.
WHAT DID THEY LOOK LIKE?
I DUNNO, DARK SUITS, EARPIECE THINGS. LIKE THOSE GUYS WHO GUARD THE PRESIDENT.
SECRET SERVICE.
KINDA. ANYWAY. THEY SAID THEY WERE FROM THE GOVERNMENT AND THAT THEY NEEDED LEE'S HELP.
HE WENT VOLUNTARILY?
YEAH. HE LOVES HIS COUNTRY.
ANYWAY, THEY WERE *PAYING*, AND THINGS HAVE BEEN TIGHT AROUND HERE SINCE YOU MADE HIM GO STRAIGHT.
MMMMM.
THEY GAVE ME THIS NUMBER TO CALL, IF I NEEDED TO GET IN TOUCH WITH HIM. I LEAVE MESSAGES BUT HE'S NEVER CALLED BACK.
ELEVEN DIGITS. IT'S A GHOST EXCHANGE.
A WHAT?

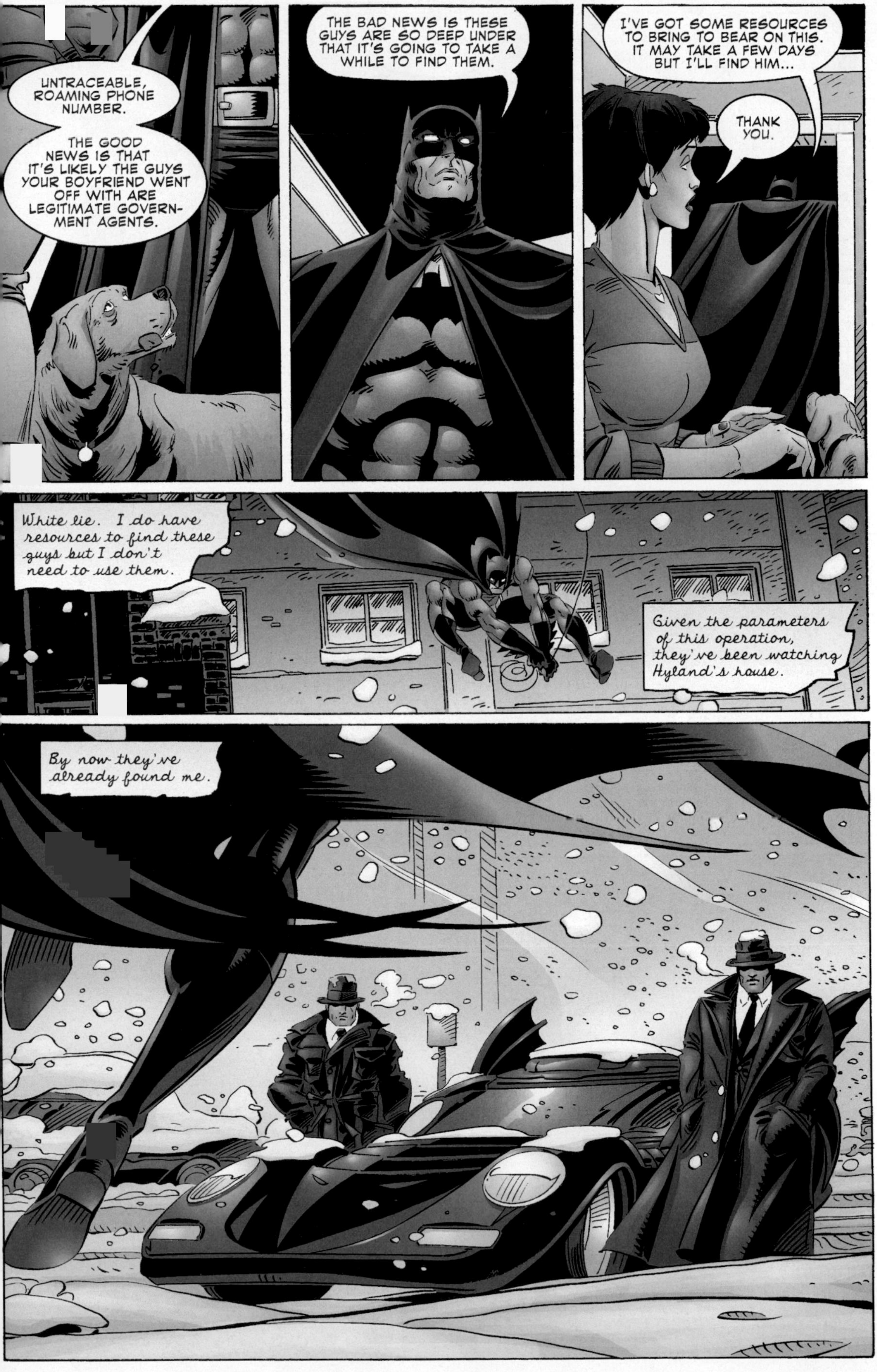
UNTRACEABLE, ROAMING PHONE NUMBER.
THE GOOD NEWS IS THAT IT'S LIKELY THE GUYS YOUR BOYFRIEND WENT OFF WITH ARE LEGITIMATE GOVERNMENT AGENTS.
THE BAD NEWS IS THESE GUYS ARE SO DEEP UNDER THAT IT'S GOING TO TAKE A WHILE TO FIND THEM.
I'VE GOT SOME RESOURCES TO BRING TO BEAR ON THIS. IT MAY TAKE A FEW DAYS BUT I'LL FIND HIM...
THANK YOU.
White lie. I do have resources to find these guys but I don't need to use them.
Given the parameters of this operation, they've been watching Hyland's house.
By now they've already found me.

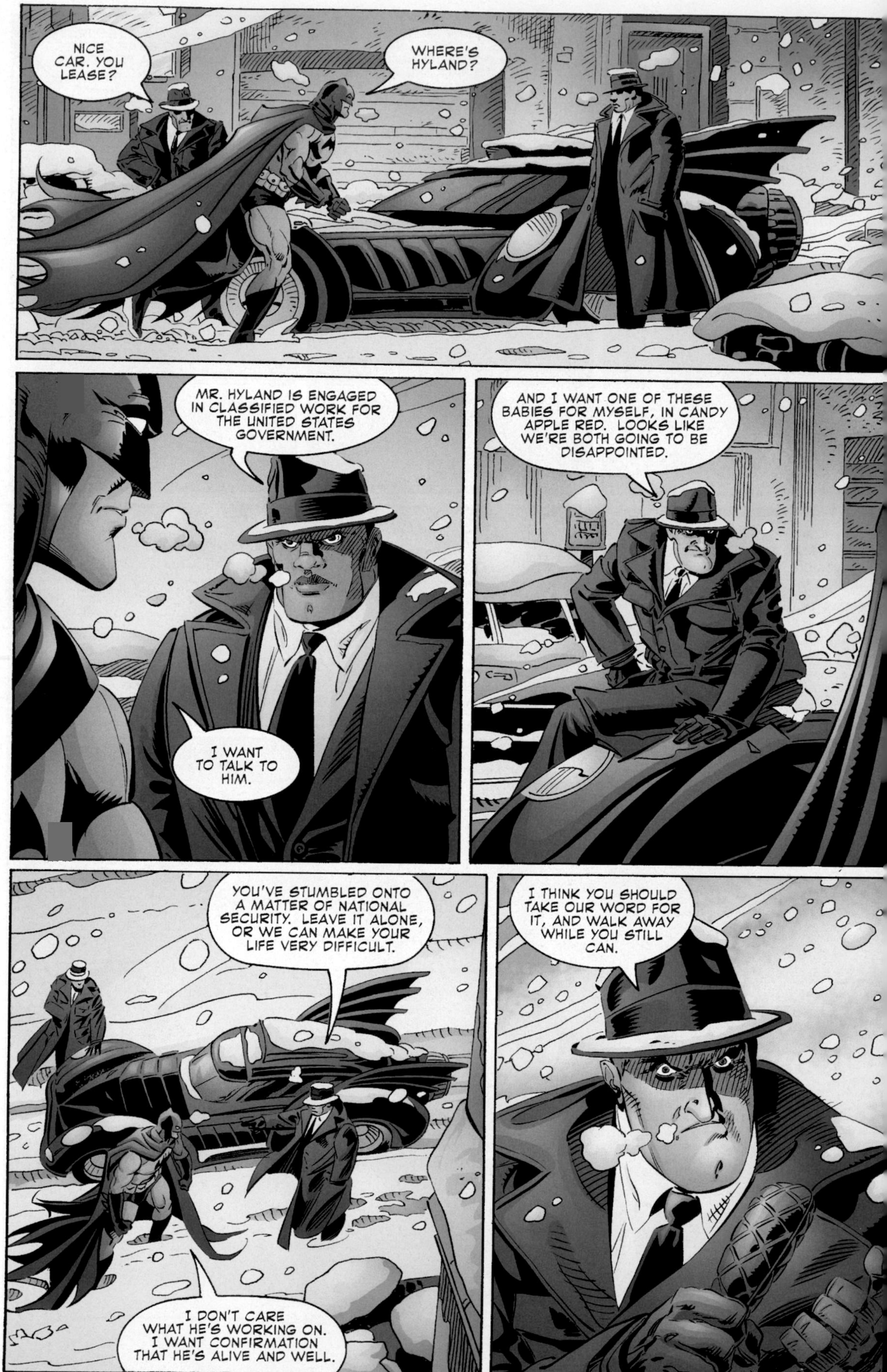
NICE CAR. YOU LEASE?
WHERE'S HYLAND?
MR. HYLAND IS ENGAGED IN CLASSIFIED WORK FOR THE UNITED STATES GOVERNMENT.
I WANT TO TALK TO HIM.
AND I WANT ONE OF THESE BABIES FOR MYSELF, IN CANDY APPLE RED. LOOKS LIKE WE'RE BOTH GOING TO BE DISAPPOINTED.
YOU'VE STUMBLED ONTO A MATTER OF NATIONAL SECURITY. LEAVE IT ALONE, OR WE CAN MAKE YOUR LIFE VERY DIFFICULT.
I DON'T CARE WHAT HE'S WORKING ON. I WANT CONFIRMATION THAT HE'S ALIVE AND WELL.
I THINK YOU SHOULD TAKE OUR WORD FOR IT, AND WALK AWAY WHILE YOU STILL CAN.

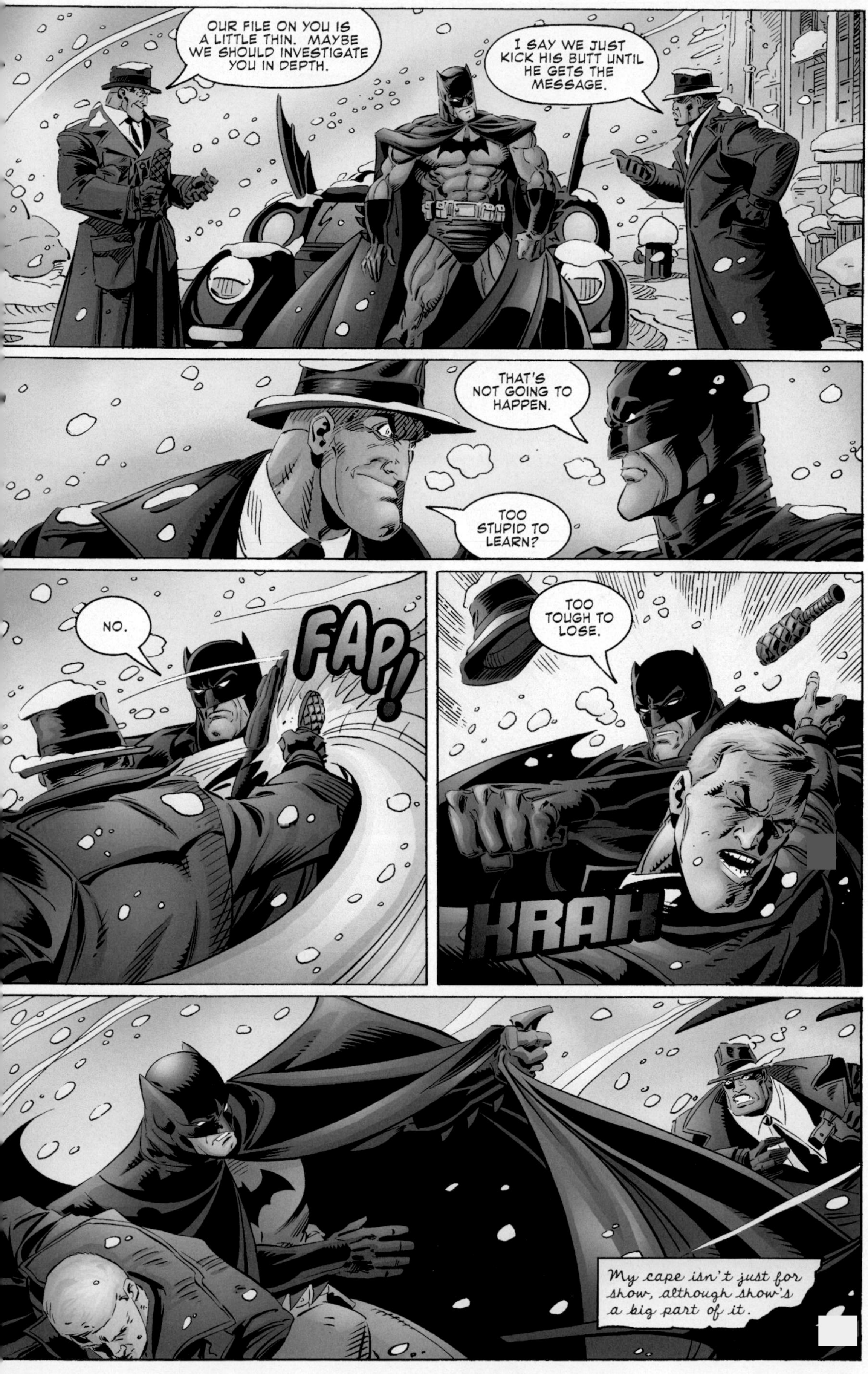
OUR FILE ON YOU IS A LITTLE THIN. MAYBE WE SHOULD INVESTIGATE YOU IN DEPTH.
I SAY WE JUST KICK HIS BUTT UNTIL HE GETS THE MESSAGE.
THAT'S NOT GOING TO HAPPEN.
TOO STUPID TO LEARN?
NO.
FAP!
TOO TOUGH TO LOSE.
KRAK
My cape isn't just for show, although show's a big part of it.

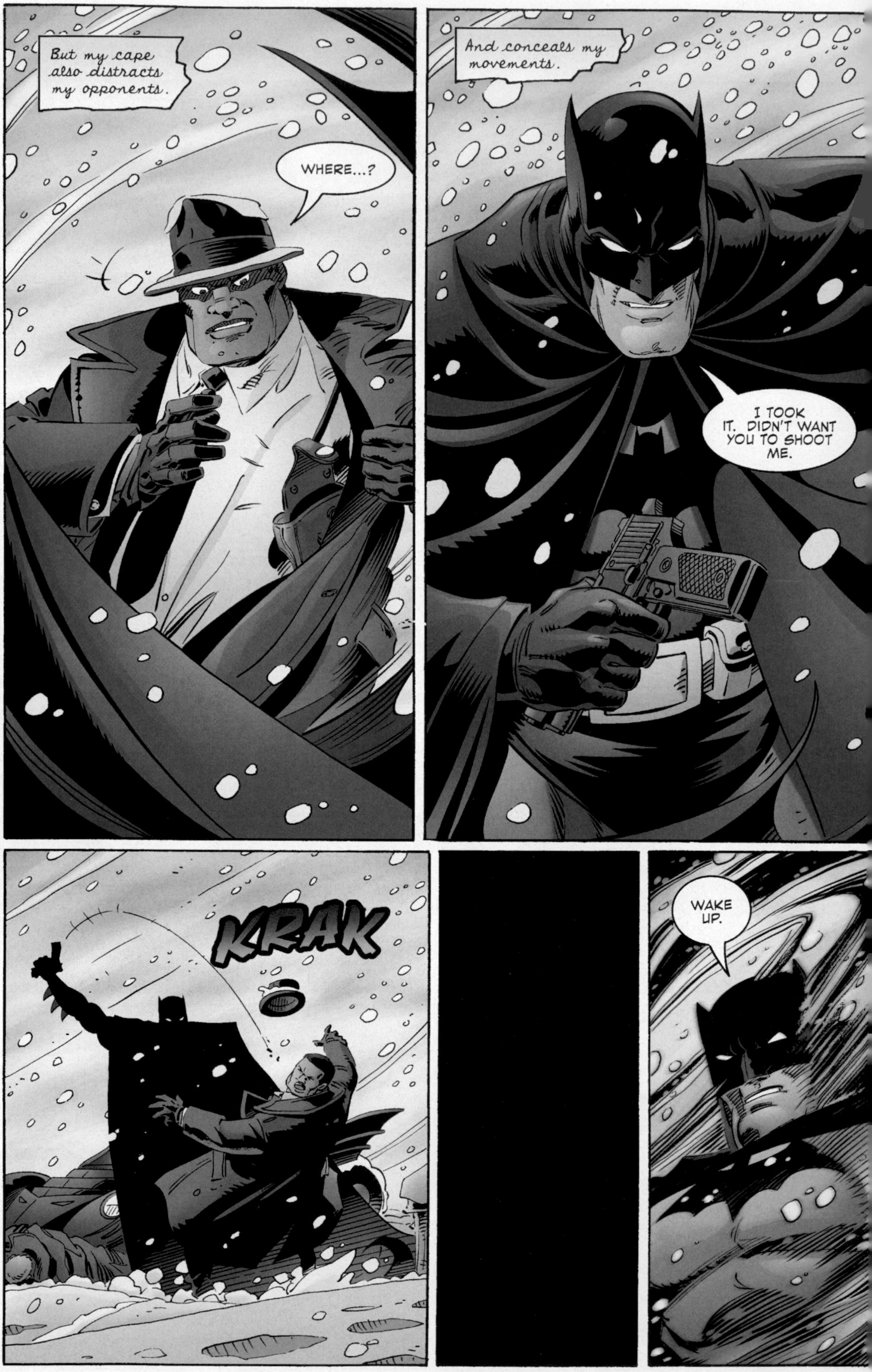
But my cape also distracts my opponents.
WHERE...?
And conceals my movements.
I TOOK IT. DIDN'T WANT YOU TO SHOOT ME.
KRAK
WAKE UP.

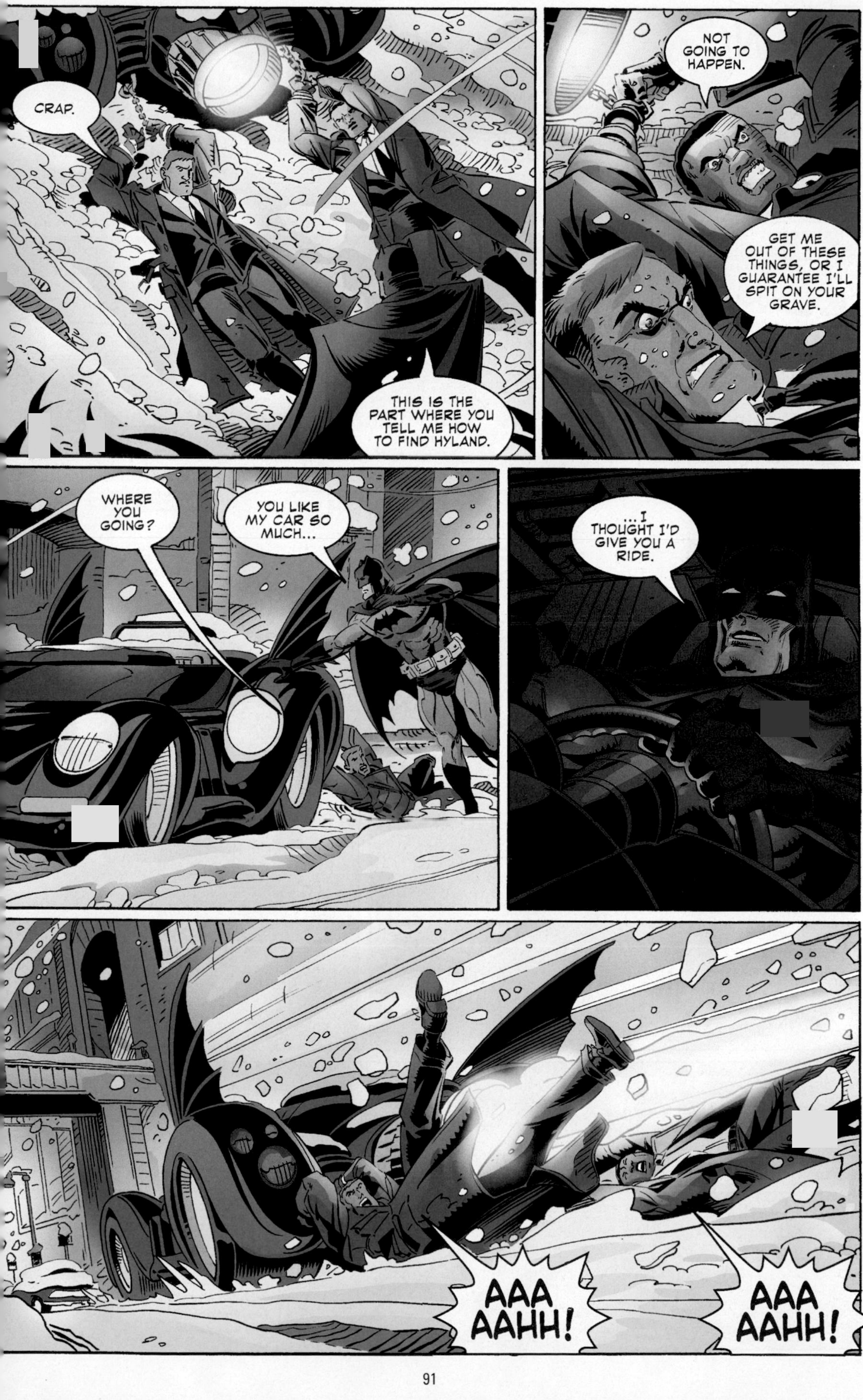
CRAP.
THIS IS THE PART WHERE YOU TELL ME HOW TO FIND HYLAND.
NOT GOING TO HAPPEN.
GET ME OUT OF THESE THINGS, OR I GUARANTEE I'LL SPIT ON YOUR GRAVE.
WHERE YOU GOING?
YOU LIKE MY CAR SO MUCH...
...I THOUGHT I'D GIVE YOU A RIDE.
AAAAAHH!
AAAAAHH!

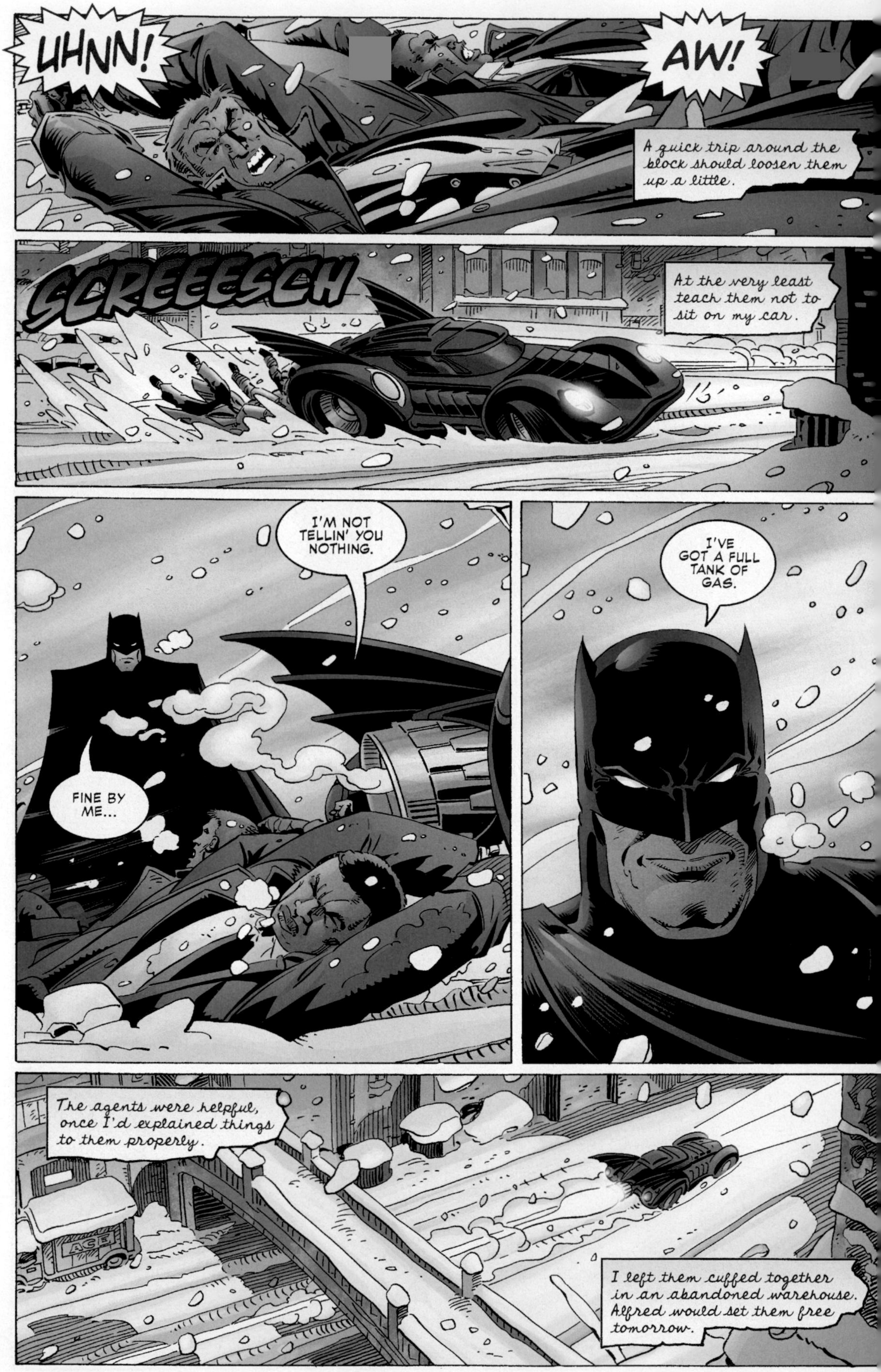
UHNN!
AW!
A quick trip around the block should loosen them up a little.
SCREEESCH
At the very least teach them not to sit on my car.
I'M NOT TELLIN' YOU NOTHING.
FINE BY ME...
I'VE GOT A FULL TANK OF GAS.
The agents were helpful, once I'd explained things to them properly.
ACE
I left them cuffed together in an abandoned warehouse. Alfred would set them free tomorrow.

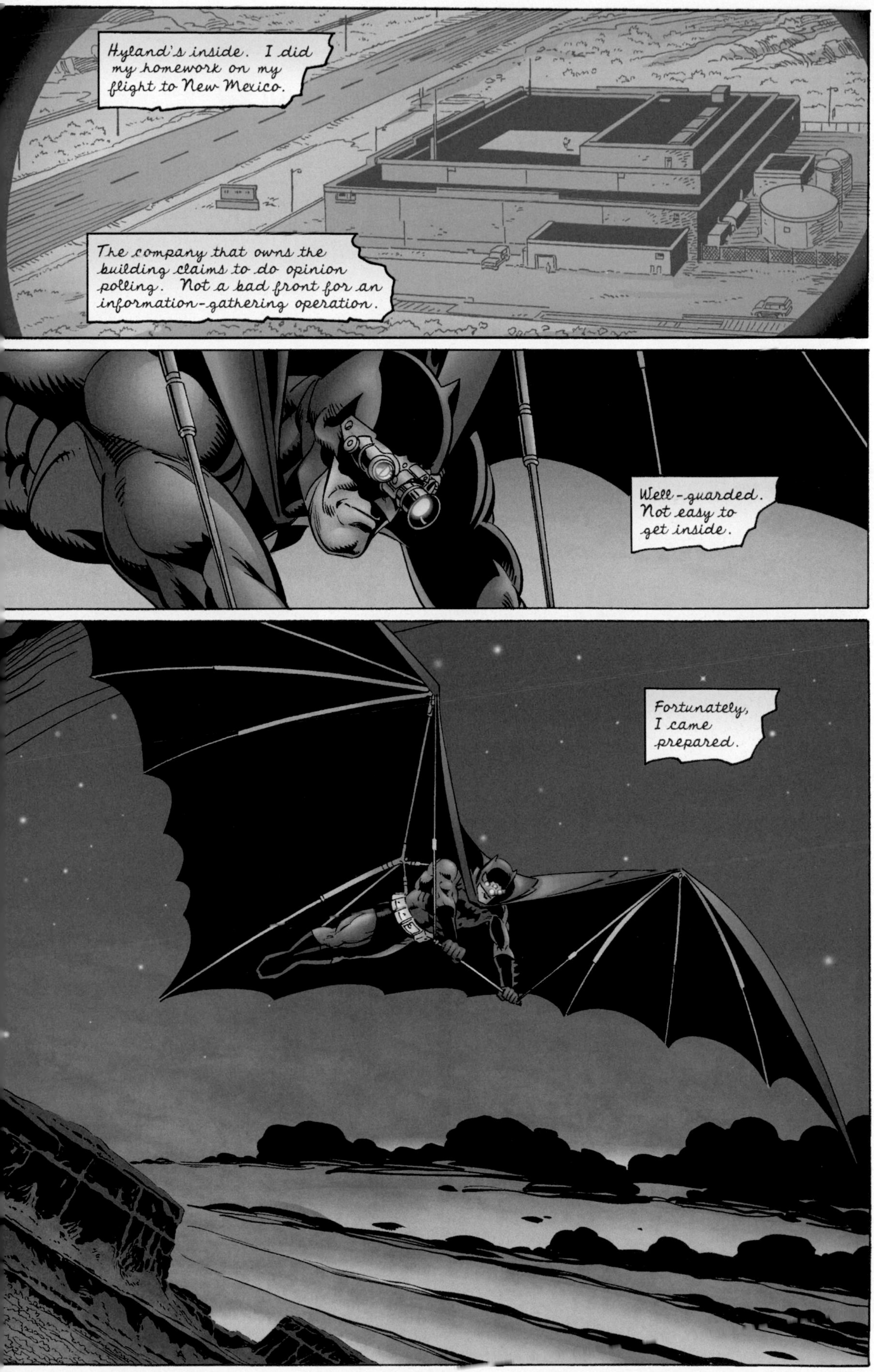
Hyland's inside. I did my homework on my flight to New Mexico.
The company that owns the building claims to do opinion polling. Not a bad front for an information-gathering operation.
Well-guarded. Not easy to get inside.
Fortunately, I came prepared.

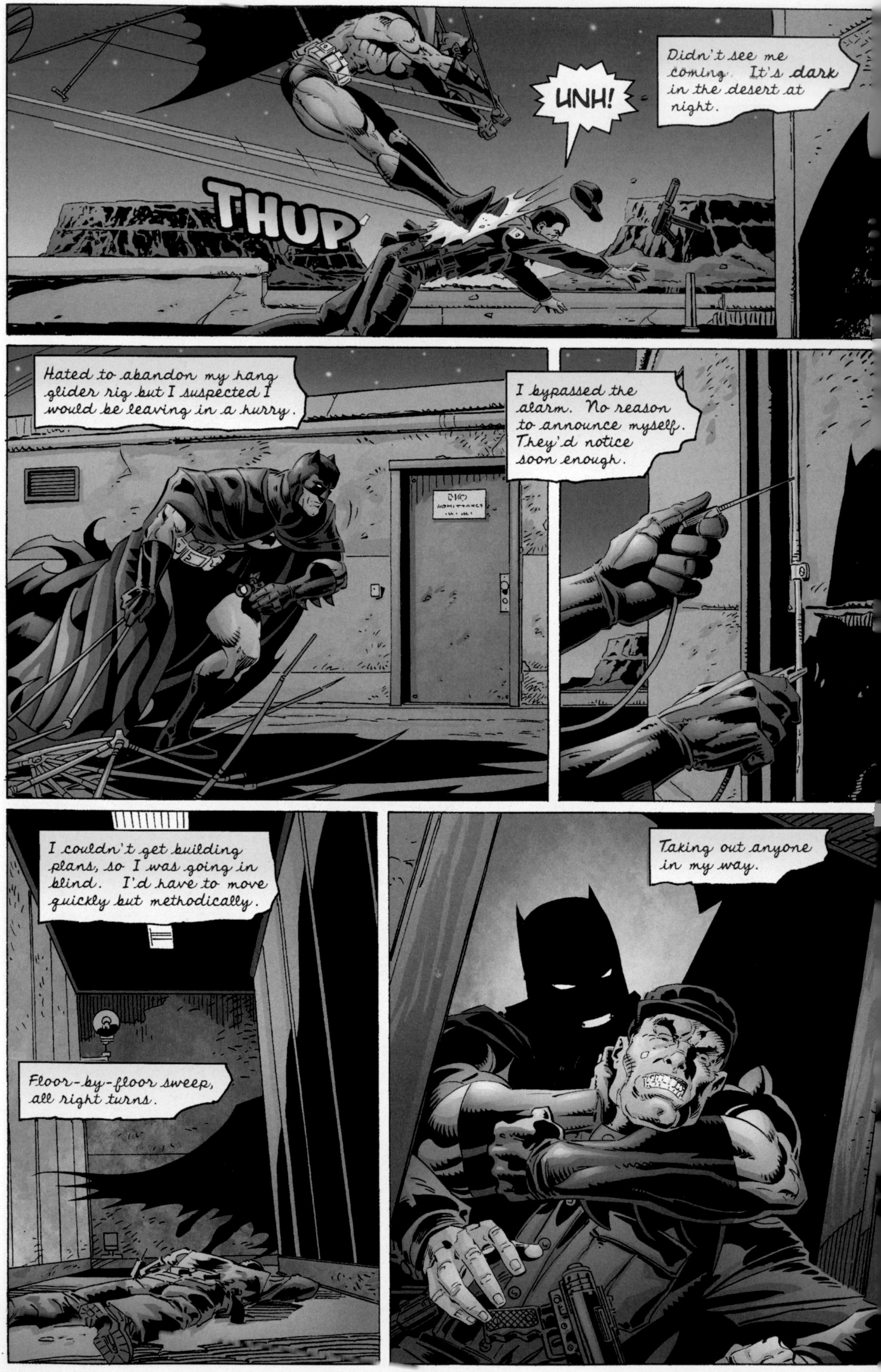
UNH!
Didn't see me coming. It's dark in the desert at night.
THUP
Hated to abandon my hang glider rig but I suspected I would be leaving in a hurry.
I bypassed the alarm. No reason to announce myself. They'd notice soon enough.
I couldn't get building plans, so I was going in blind. I'd have to move quickly but methodically.
Floor-by-floor sweep, all right turns.
Taking out anyone in my way.

The more men I had to take down, the more likely I was to set off a general alarm.

KRAK

Still, it couldn't be helped.

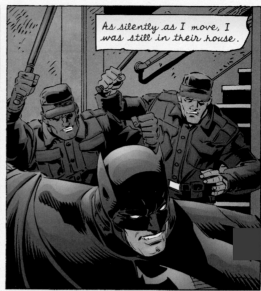

As silently as I move, I was still in their house.

CHOK

It was only a matter of time before someone spotted me or some of the men I took out.

Fortunately, time was on my side.

RESTRICTED AREA
AUTHORIZED PERSONNEL
BLUE CLEARANCE ONLY

I'd found what I'd been looking for.

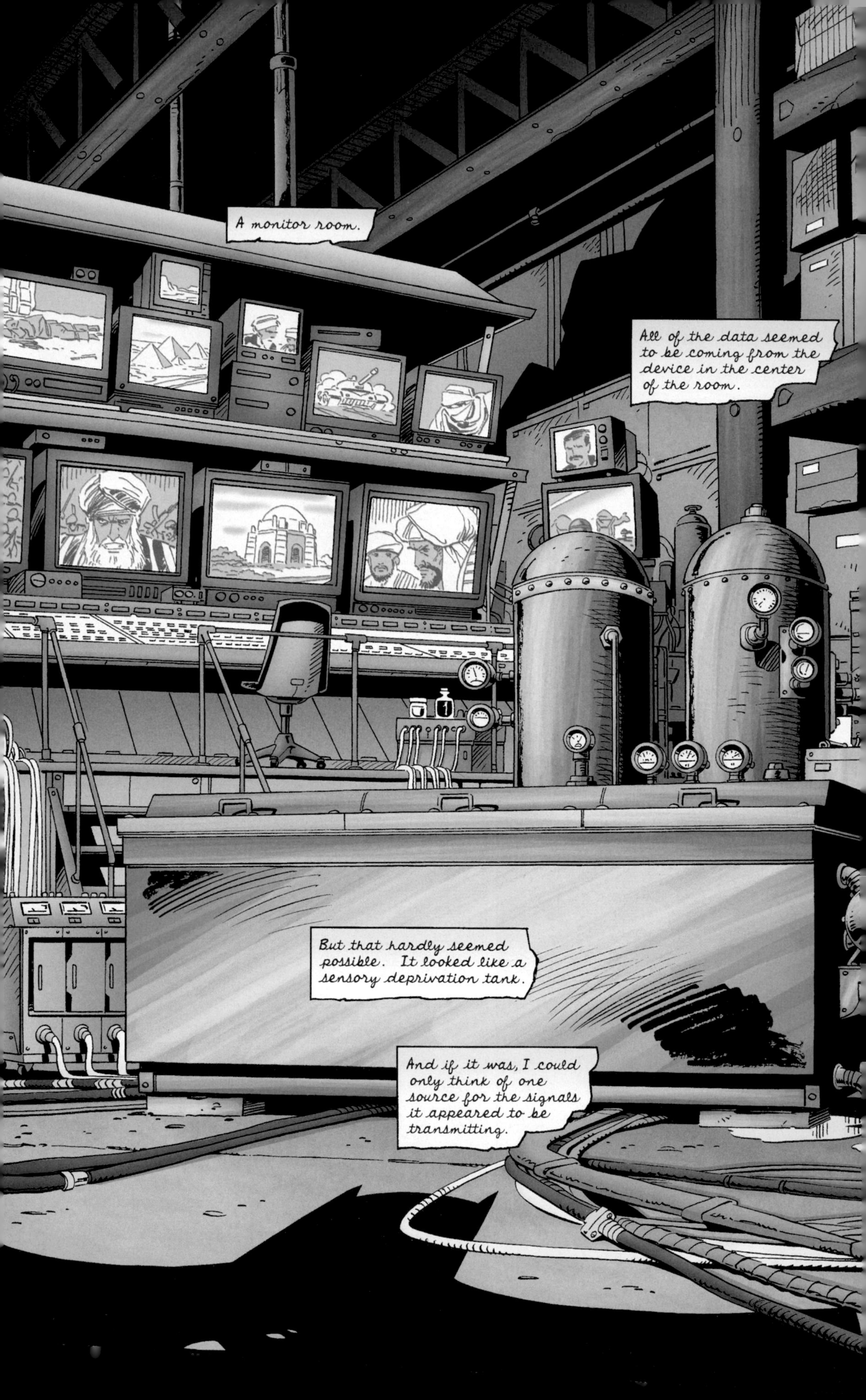
A monitor room.
All of the data seemed to be coming from the device in the center of the room.
But that hardly seemed possible. It looked like a sensory deprivation tank.
And if it was, I could only think of one source for the signals it appeared to be transmitting.

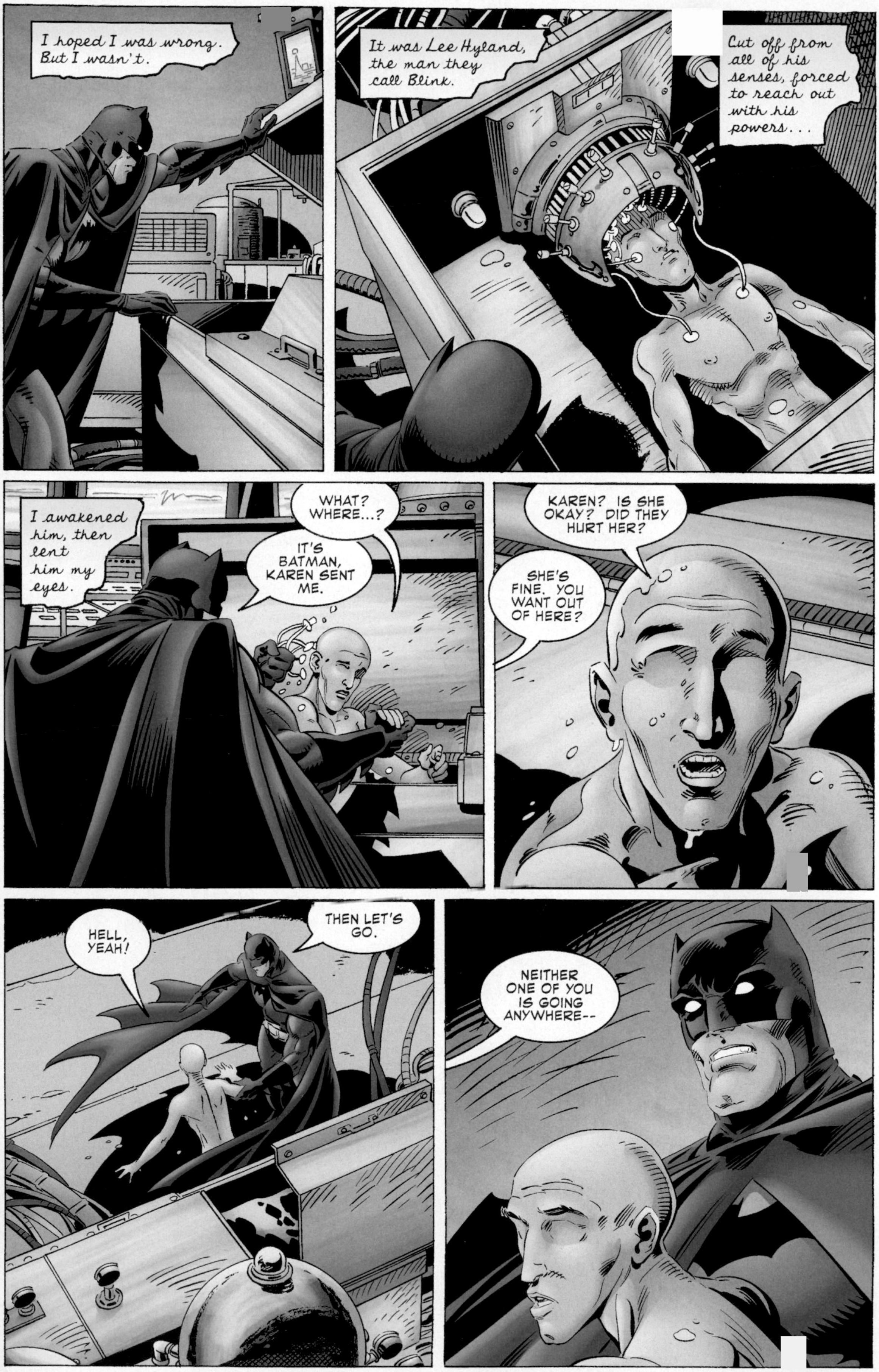
I hoped I was wrong. But I wasn't.
It was Lee Hyland, the man they call Blink.
Cut off from all of his senses, forced to reach out with his powers...
I awakened him, then lent him my eyes.
WHAT? WHERE...?
IT'S BATMAN, KAREN SENT ME.
KAREN? IS SHE OKAY? DID THEY HURT HER?
SHE'S FINE. YOU WANT OUT OF HERE?
HELL, YEAH!
THEN LET'S GO.
NEITHER ONE OF YOU IS GOING ANYWHERE--

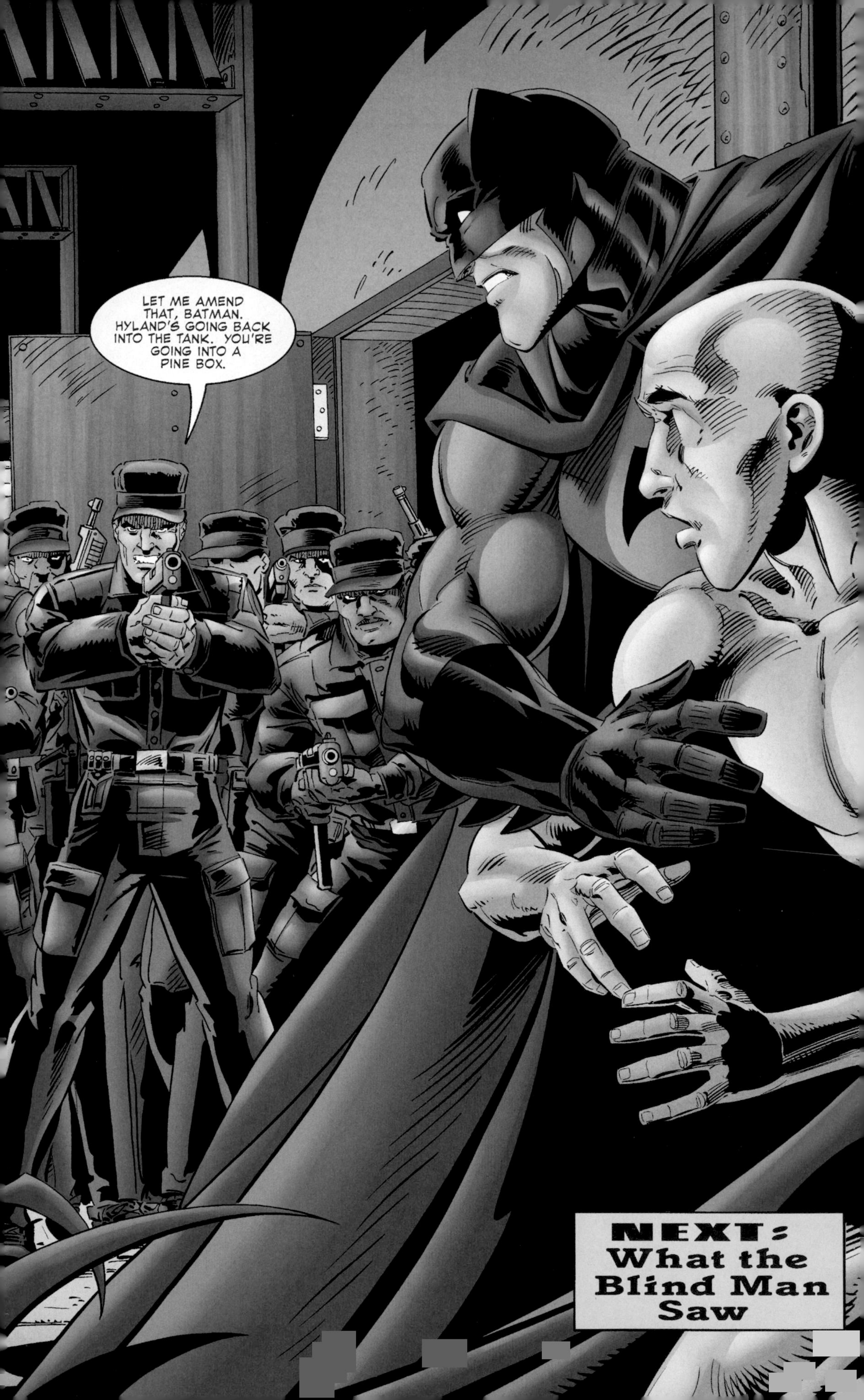
LET ME AMEND THAT, BATMAN. HYLAND'S GOING BACK INTO THE TANK. YOU'RE GOING INTO A PINE BOX.
NEXT: What the Blind Man Saw

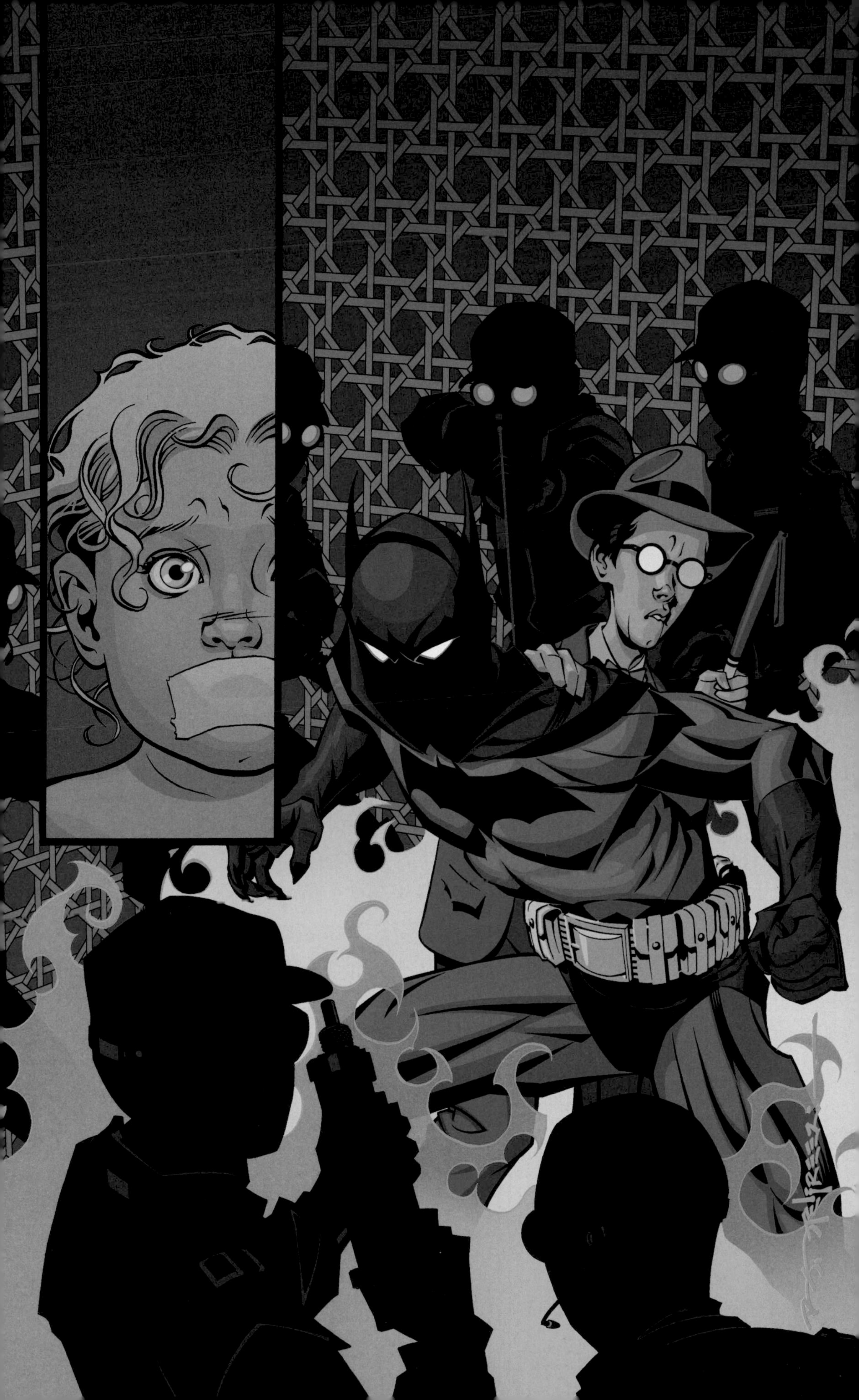

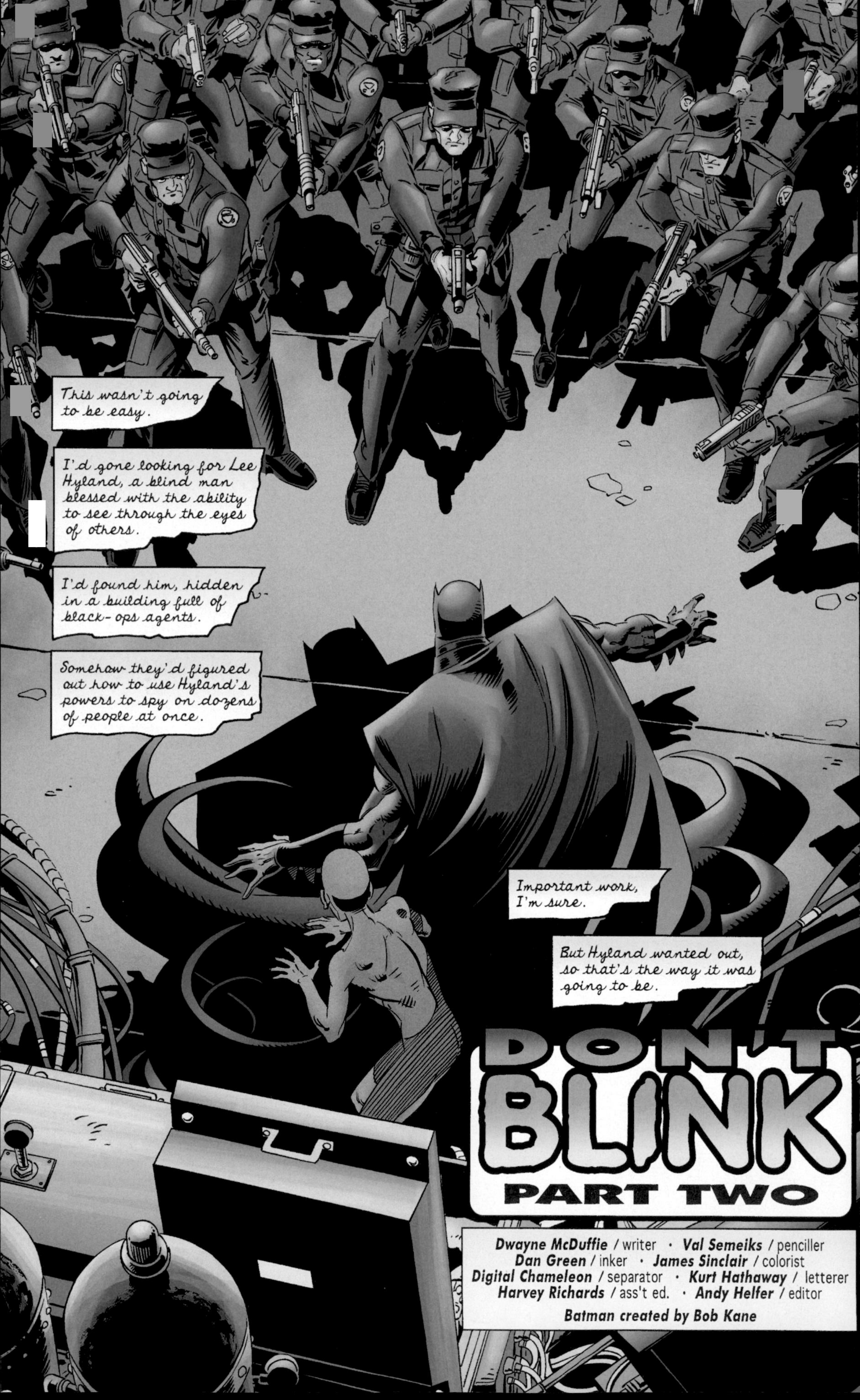
This wasn't going to be easy.
I'd gone looking for Lee Hyland, a blind man blessed with the ability to see through the eyes of others.
I'd found him, hidden in a building full of black-ops agents.
Somehow they'd figured out how to use Hyland's powers to spy on dozens of people at once.
Important work, I'm sure.
But Hyland wanted out, so that's the way it was going to be.
DON'T BLINK
PART TWO
Dwayne McDuffie / writer · Val Semeiks / penciller
Dan Green / inker · James Sinclair / colorist
Digital Chameleon / separator · Kurt Hathaway / letterer
Harvey Richards / ass't ed. · Andy Helfer / editor
Batman created by Bob Kane

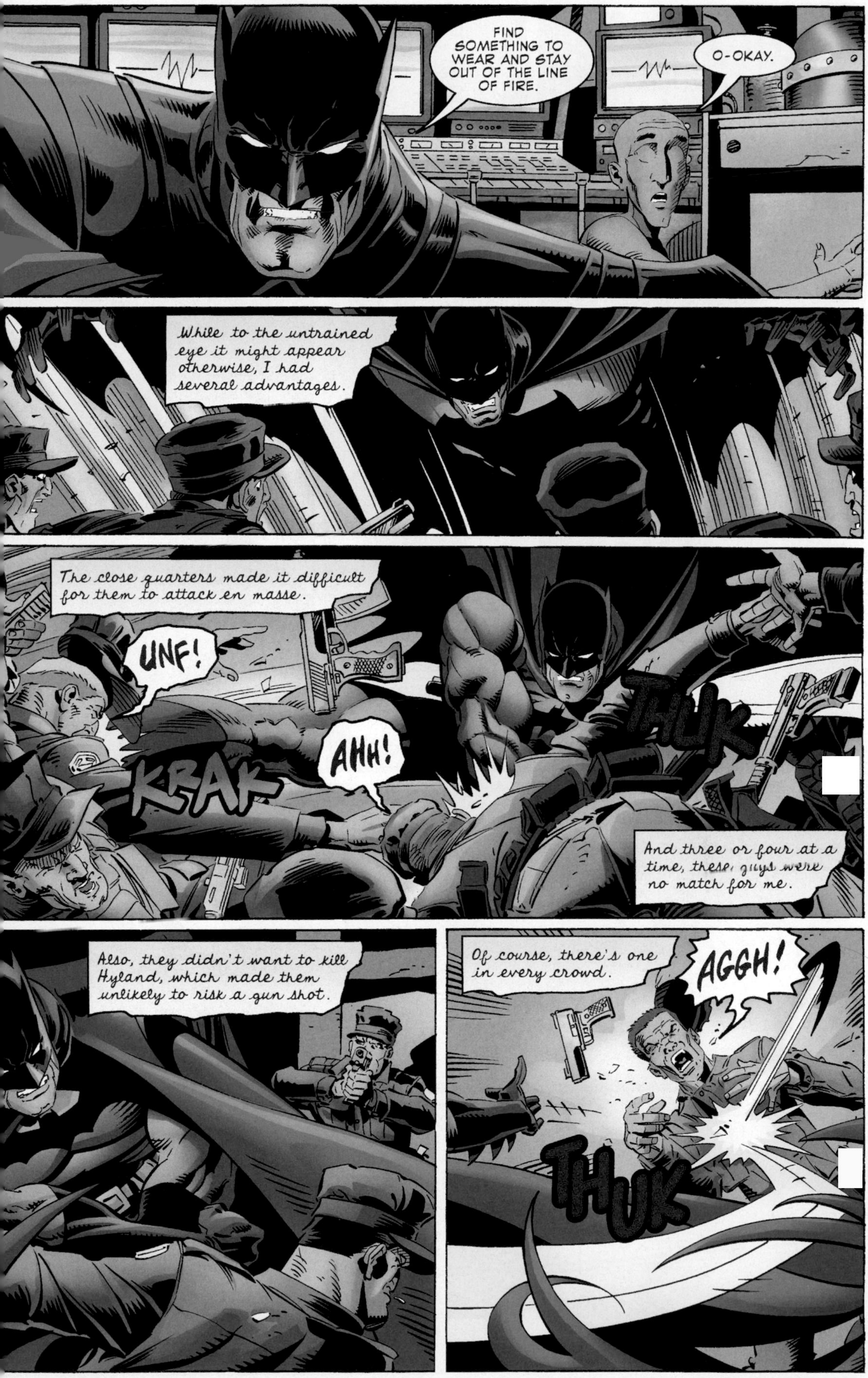
FIND SOMETHING TO WEAR AND STAY OUT OF THE LINE OF FIRE.
O-OKAY.
While to the untrained eye it might appear otherwise, I had several advantages.
The close quarters made it difficult for them to attack en masse.
UNF!
KRAK
AHH!
THUK
And three or four at a time, these guys were no match for me.
Also, they didn't want to kill Hyland, which made them unlikely to risk a gun shot.
Of course, there's one in every crowd.
AGGH!
THUK

BLAM BLAM BLAM

VIP VIP VIP

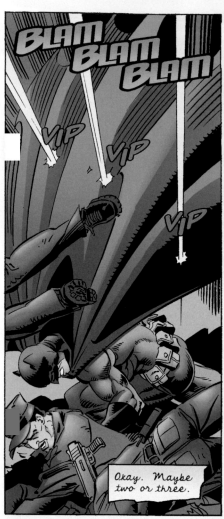

Okay. Maybe two or three.

POOMPH!

I was going to have to give these guys something else to think about.

First, I moved to the high ground, then I gave them the goods.

Flash-bang grenades. Relatively harmless concussive charges that produce a lot of light and noise.

Also smoke.

LOOK OUT!

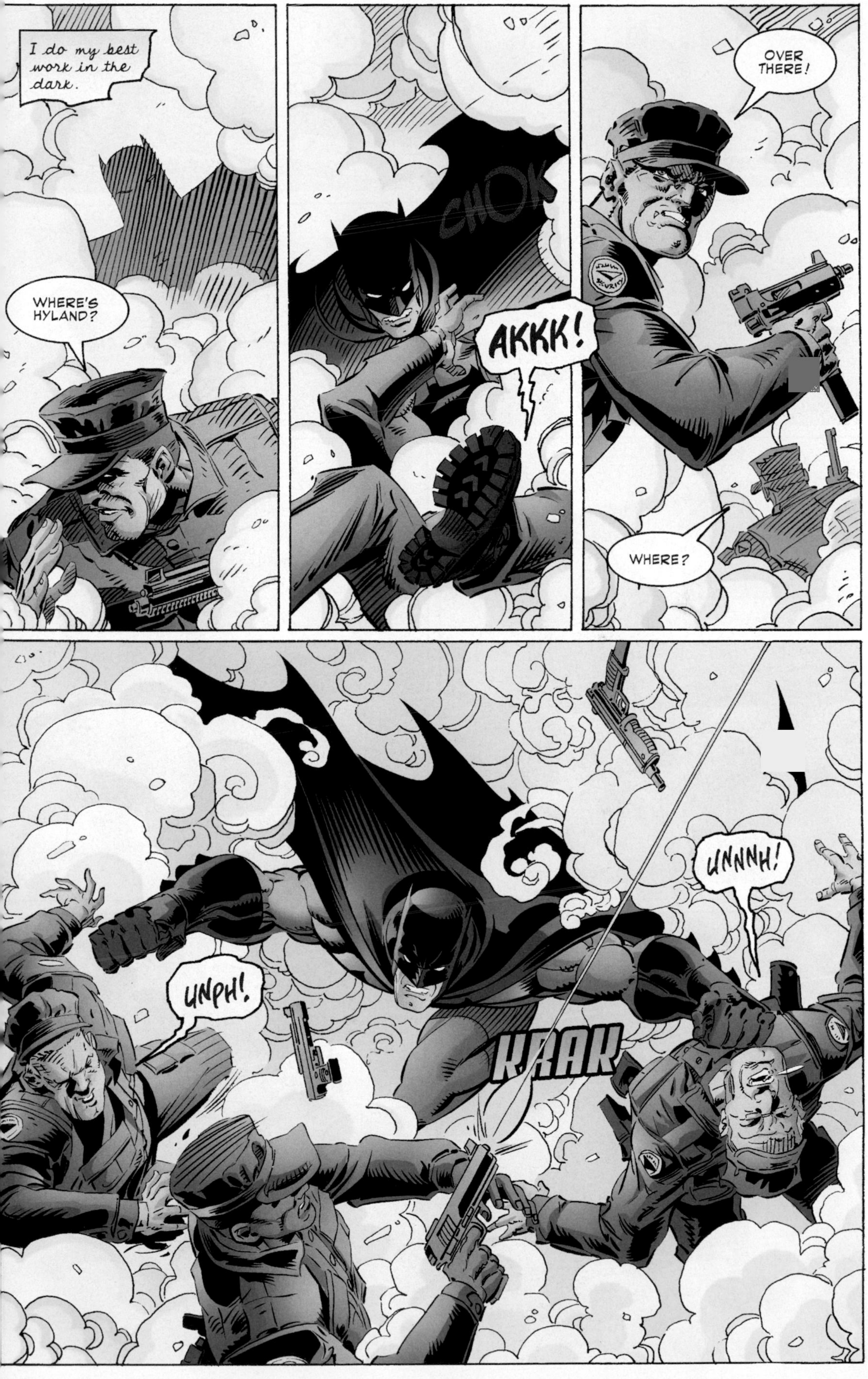
I do my best work in the dark.
WHERE'S HYLAND?
CHOK
AKKK!
OVER THERE!
WHERE?
UNNNH!
UNPH!
KRAK

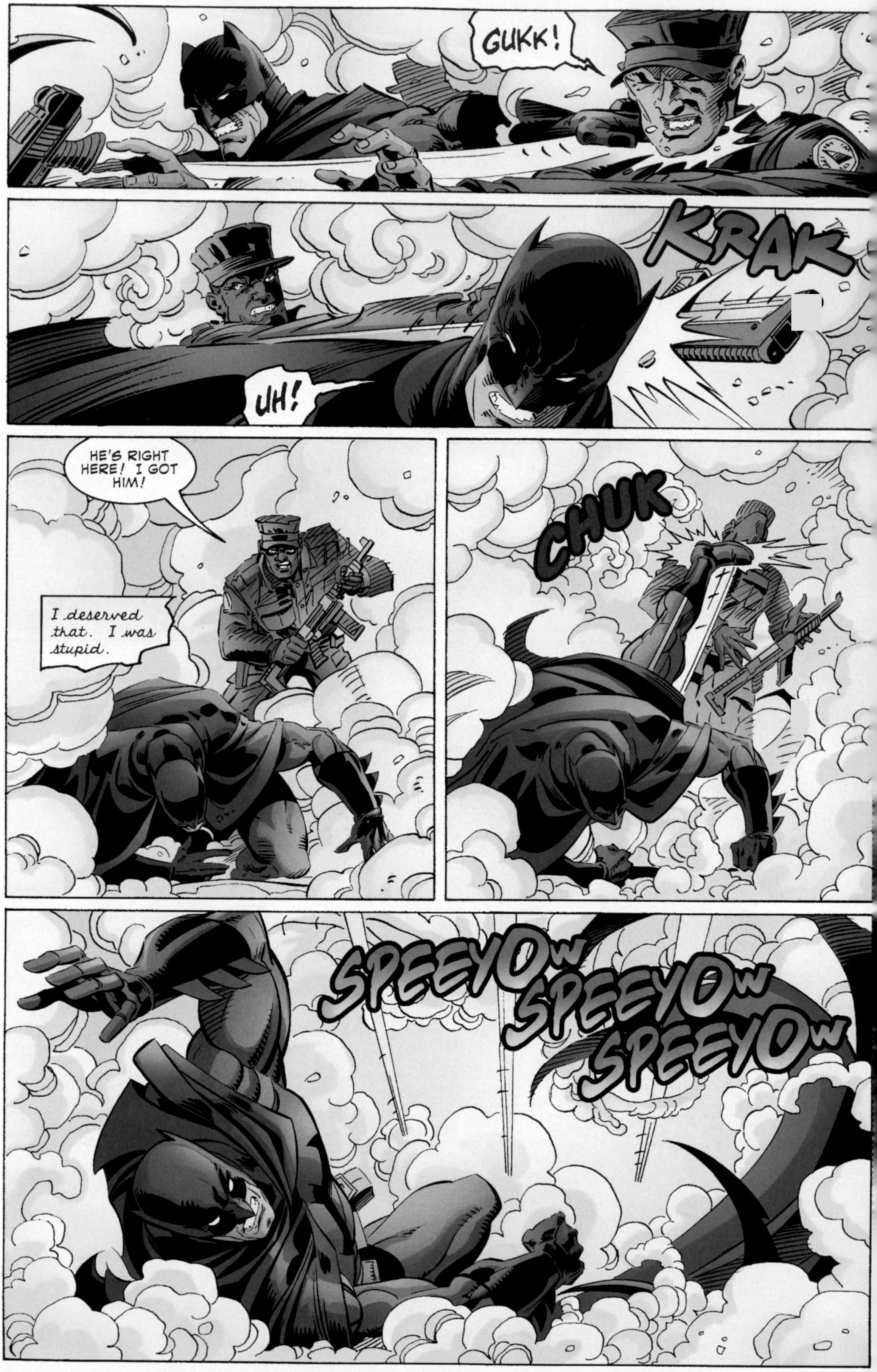
GUKK!
KRAK
UH!
HE'S RIGHT HERE! I GOT HIM!
I deserved that. I was stupid.
CHUK
SPEEYOw
SPEEYOw
SPEEYOw

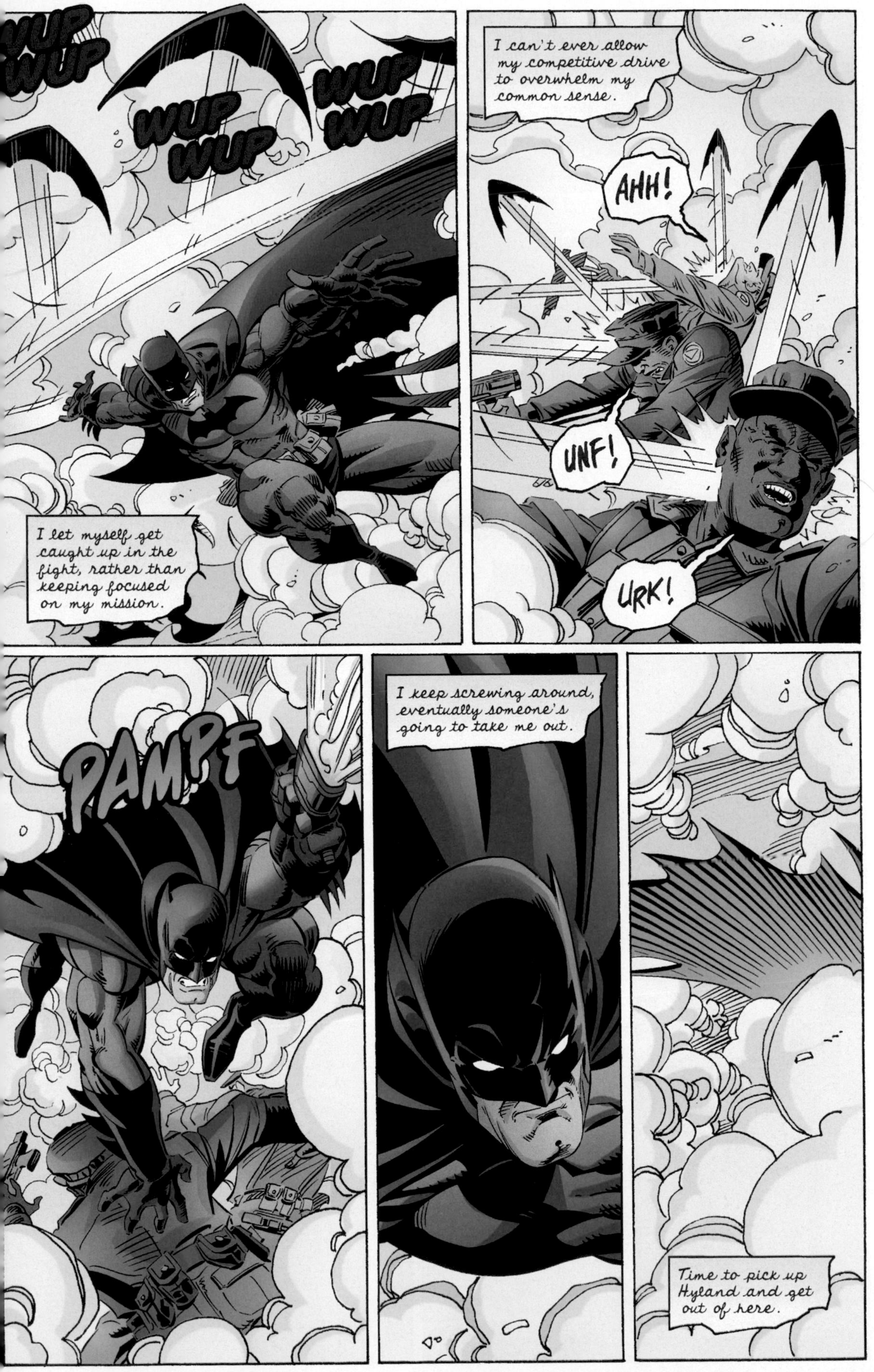
WUP WUP
WUP WUP
WUP WUP
I let myself get caught up in the fight, rather than keeping focused on my mission.
I can't ever allow my competitive drive to overwhelm my common sense.
AHH!
UNF!
URK!
PAMPF
I keep screwing around, eventually someone's going to take me out.
Time to pick up Hyland and get out of here.

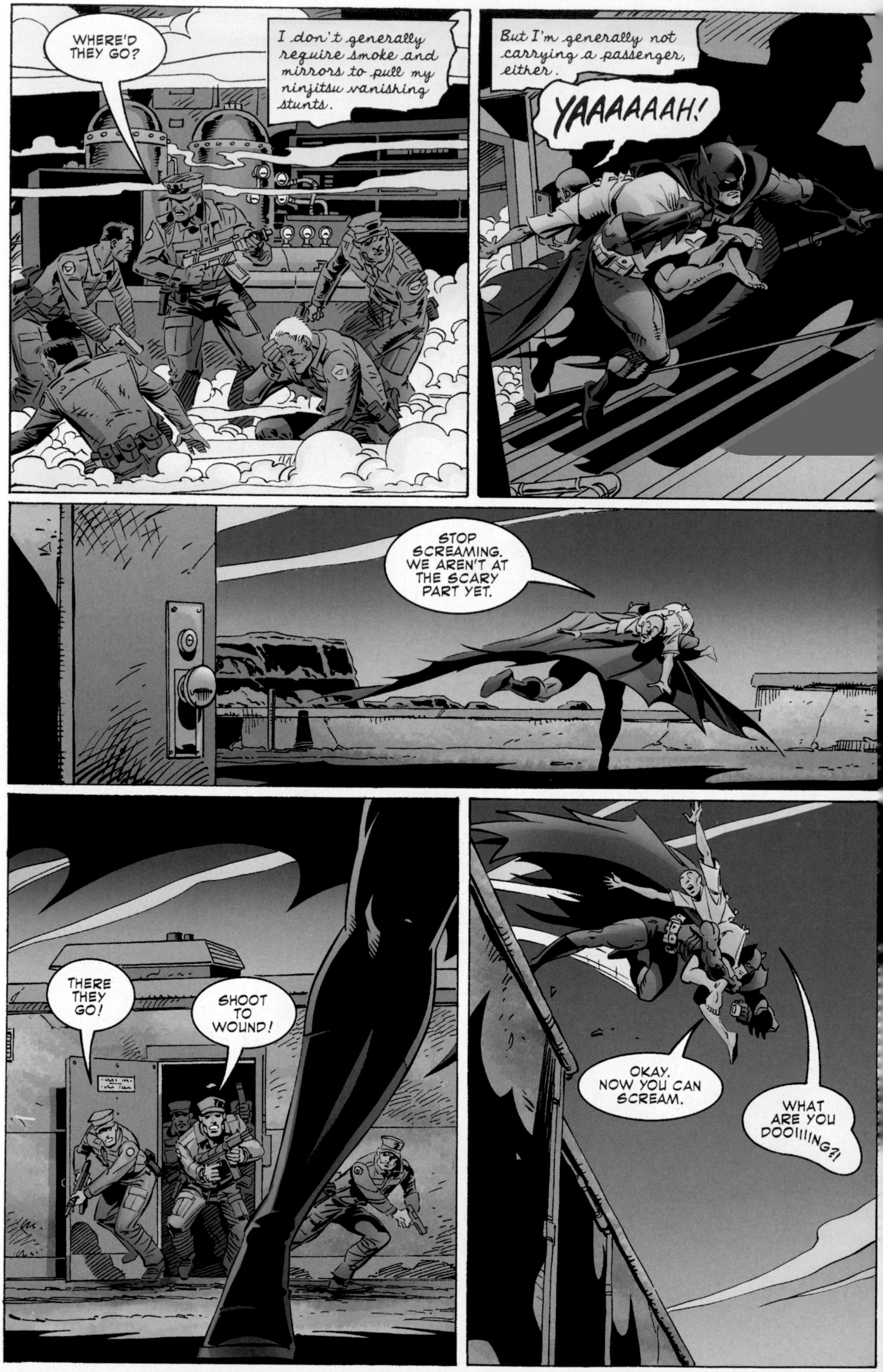
WHERE'D THEY GO?
I don't generally require smoke and mirrors to pull my ninjitsu vanishing stunts.
But I'm generally not carrying a passenger, either.
YAAAAAAH!
STOP SCREAMING. WE AREN'T AT THE SCARY PART YET.
THERE THEY GO!
SHOOT TO WOUND!
OKAY. NOW YOU CAN SCREAM.
WHAT ARE YOU DOO!!!!ING?!

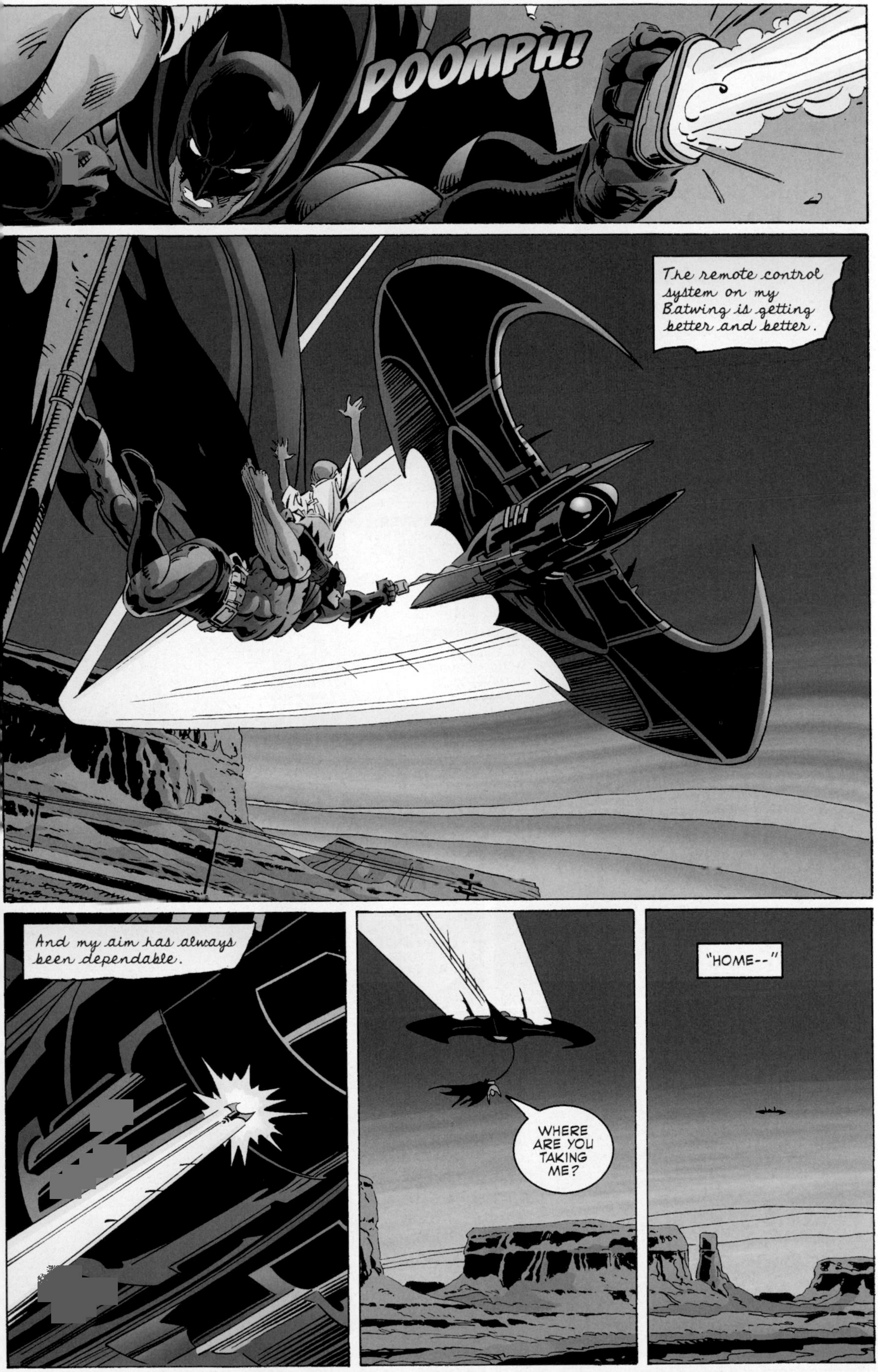
POOMPH!
The remote control system on my Batwing is getting better and better.
And my aim has always been dependable.
WHERE ARE YOU TAKING ME?
"HOME--"

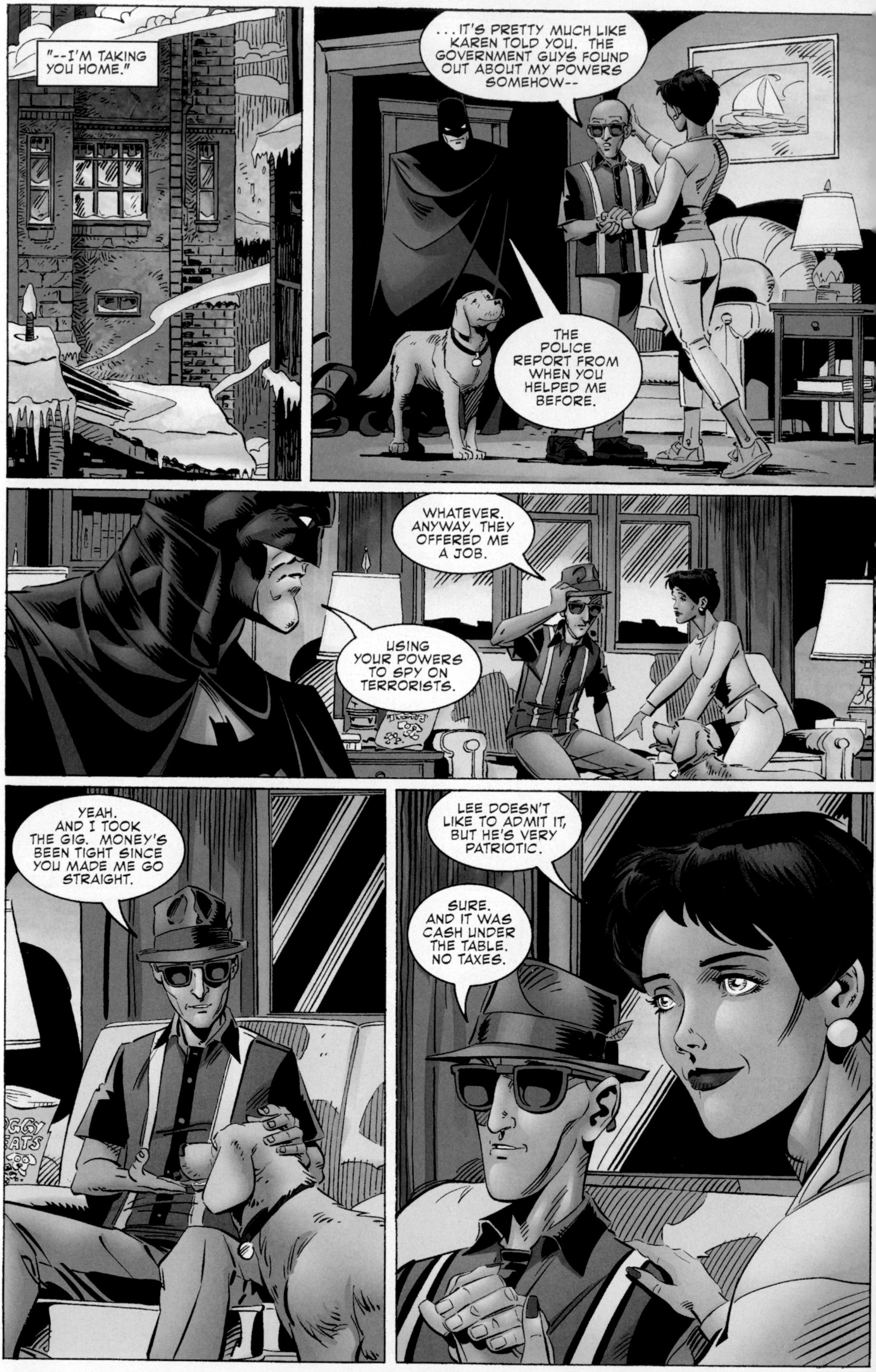
"--I'M TAKING YOU HOME."
...IT'S PRETTY MUCH LIKE KAREN TOLD YOU. THE GOVERNMENT GUYS FOUND OUT ABOUT MY POWERS SOMEHOW--
THE POLICE REPORT FROM WHEN YOU HELPED ME BEFORE.
WHATEVER. ANYWAY, THEY OFFERED ME A JOB.
USING YOUR POWERS TO SPY ON TERRORISTS.
YEAH. AND I TOOK THE GIG. MONEY'S BEEN TIGHT SINCE YOU MADE ME GO STRAIGHT.
LEE DOESN'T LIKE TO ADMIT IT, BUT HE'S VERY PATRIOTIC.
SURE. AND IT WAS CASH UNDER THE TABLE. NO TAXES.

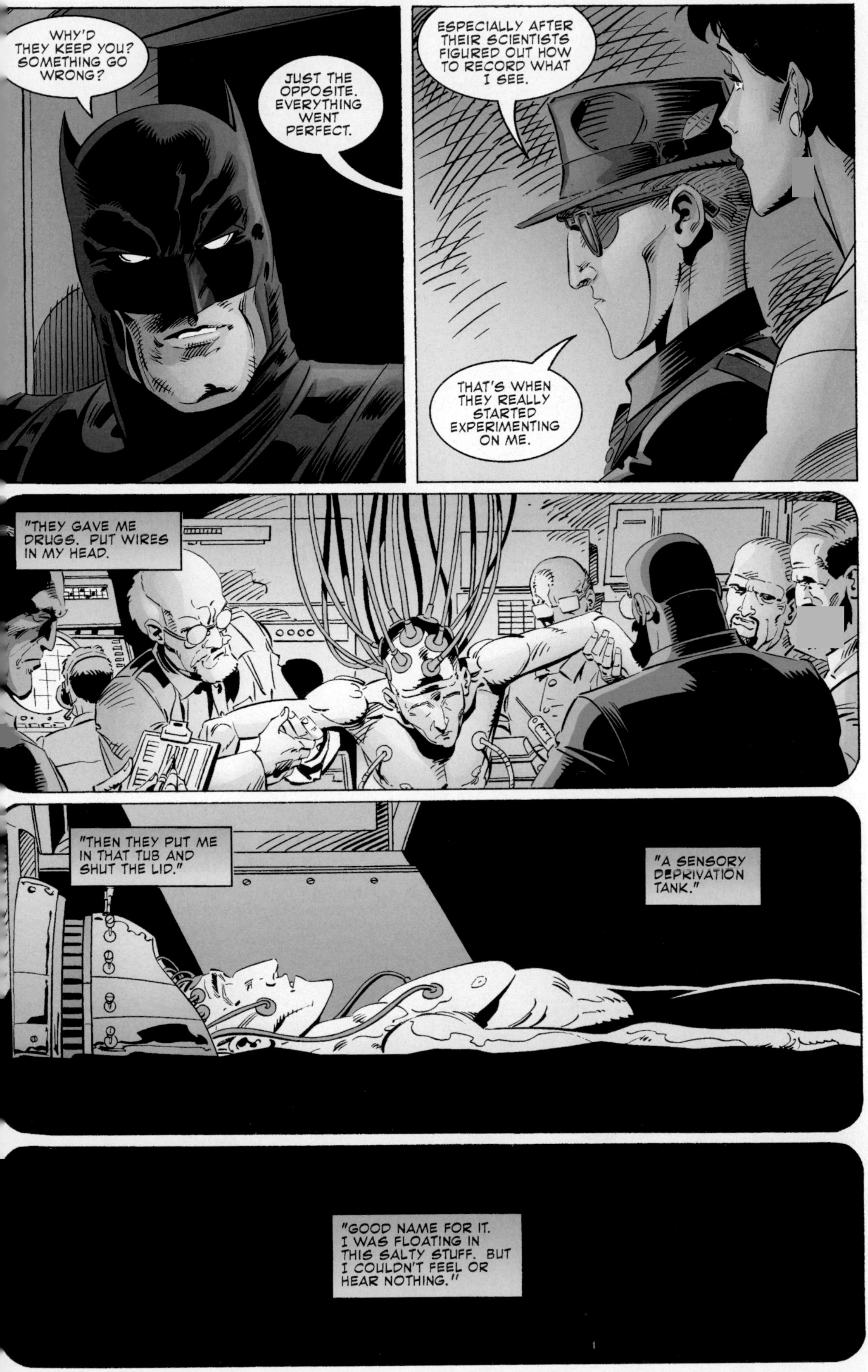
WHY'D THEY KEEP YOU? SOMETHING GO WRONG?
JUST THE OPPOSITE. EVERYTHING WENT PERFECT.
ESPECIALLY AFTER THEIR SCIENTISTS FIGURED OUT HOW TO RECORD WHAT I SEE.
THAT'S WHEN THEY REALLY STARTED EXPERIMENTING ON ME.
"THEY GAVE ME DRUGS. PUT WIRES IN MY HEAD.
"THEN THEY PUT ME IN THAT TUB AND SHUT THE LID."
"A SENSORY DEPRIVATION TANK."
"GOOD NAME FOR IT. I WAS FLOATING IN THIS SALTY STUFF. BUT I COULDN'T FEEL OR HEAR NOTHING."

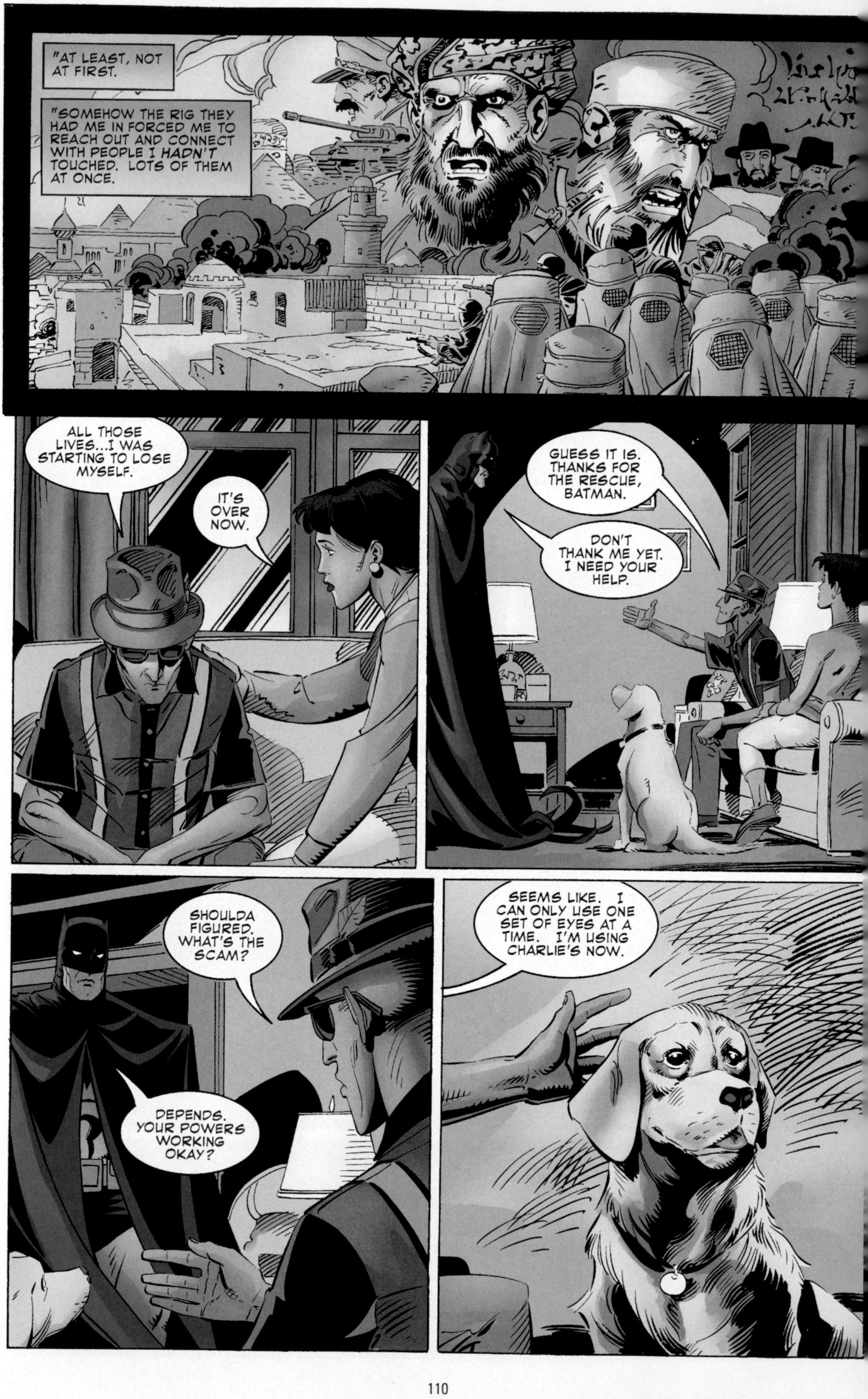

"AT LEAST, NOT AT FIRST.
"SOMEHOW THE RIG THEY HAD ME IN FORCED ME TO REACH OUT AND CONNECT WITH PEOPLE I *HADN'T* TOUCHED. LOTS OF THEM AT ONCE.
ALL THOSE LIVES...I WAS STARTING TO LOSE MYSELF.
IT'S OVER NOW.
GUESS IT IS. THANKS FOR THE RESCUE, BATMAN.
DON'T THANK ME YET. I NEED YOUR HELP.
SHOULDA FIGURED. WHAT'S THE SCAM?
DEPENDS. YOUR POWERS WORKING OKAY?
SEEMS LIKE. I CAN ONLY USE ONE SET OF EYES AT A TIME. I'M USING CHARLIE'S NOW.

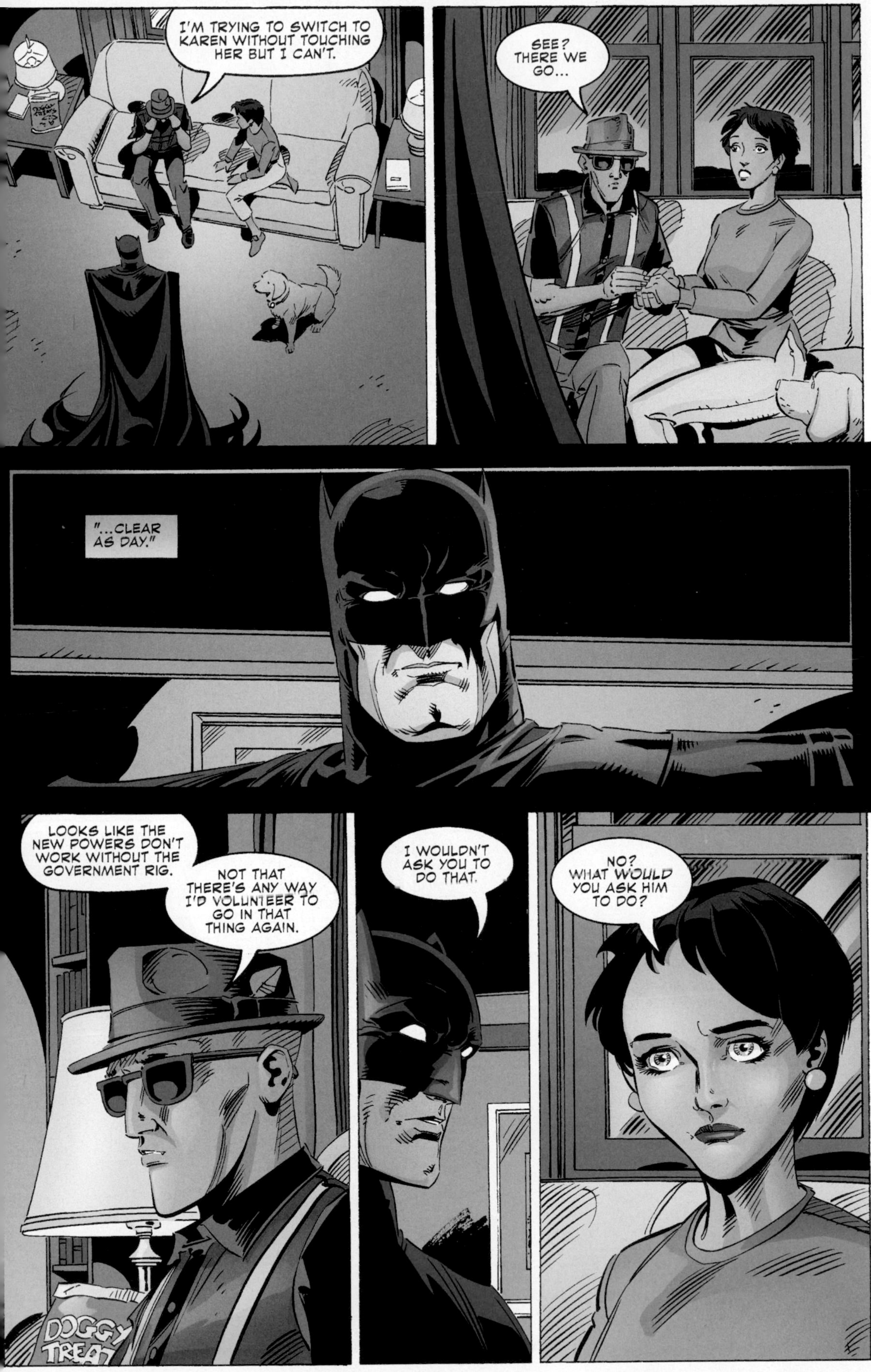
I'M TRYING TO SWITCH TO KAREN WITHOUT TOUCHING HER BUT I CAN'T.
SEE? THERE WE GO...
"...CLEAR AS DAY."
LOOKS LIKE THE NEW POWERS DON'T WORK WITHOUT THE GOVERNMENT RIG.
NOT THAT THERE'S ANY WAY I'D VOLUNTEER TO GO IN THAT THING AGAIN.
I WOULDN'T ASK YOU TO DO THAT.
NO? WHAT WOULD YOU ASK HIM TO DO?
DOGGY TREAT

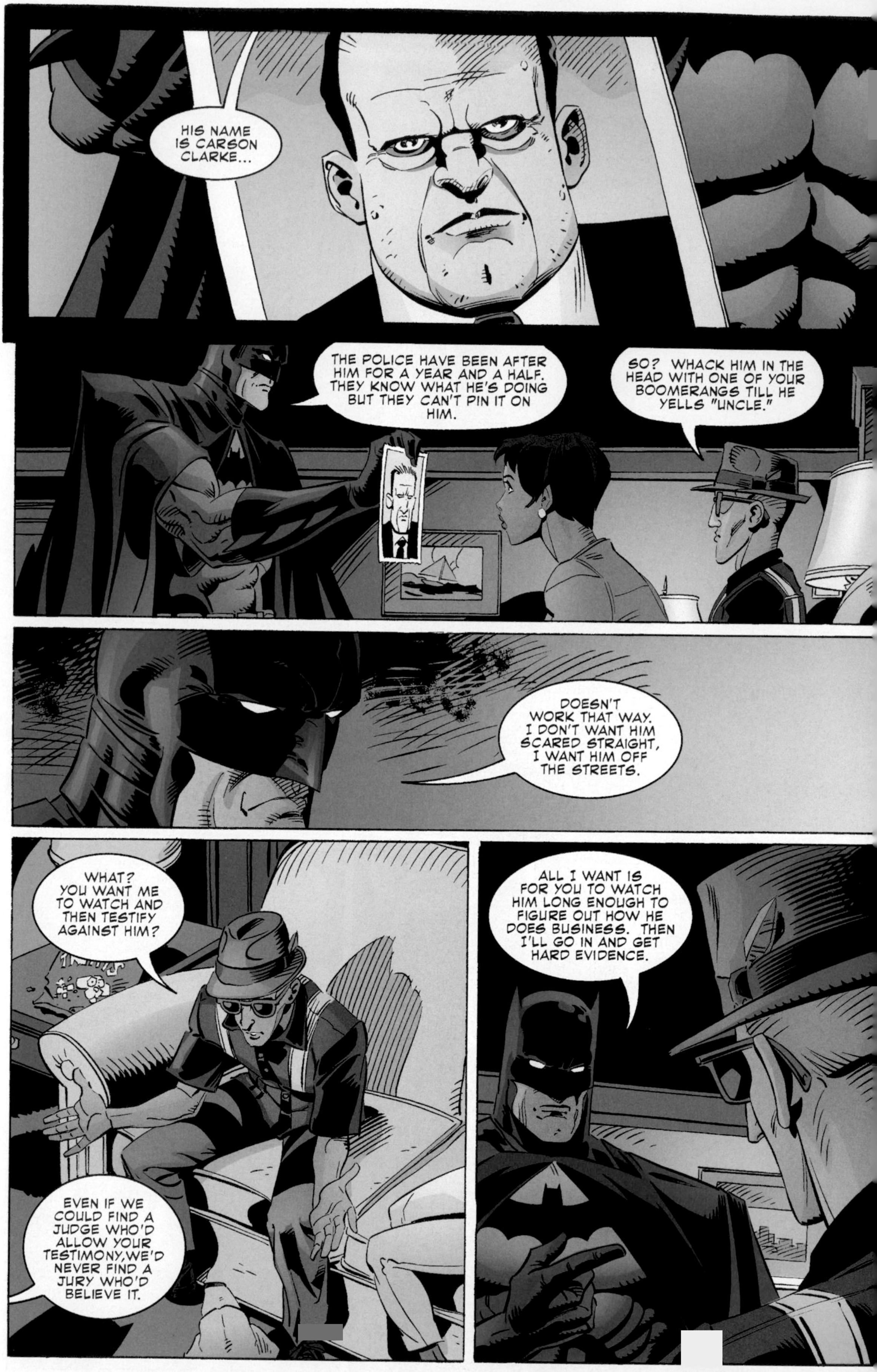
HIS NAME IS CARSON CLARKE...
THE POLICE HAVE BEEN AFTER HIM FOR A YEAR AND A HALF. THEY KNOW WHAT HE'S DOING BUT THEY CAN'T PIN IT ON HIM.
SO? WHACK HIM IN THE HEAD WITH ONE OF YOUR BOOMERANGS TILL HE YELLS "UNCLE."
DOESN'T WORK THAT WAY. I DON'T WANT HIM SCARED STRAIGHT, I WANT HIM OFF THE STREETS.
WHAT? YOU WANT ME TO WATCH AND THEN TESTIFY AGAINST HIM?
EVEN IF WE COULD FIND A JUDGE WHO'D ALLOW YOUR TESTIMONY, WE'D NEVER FIND A JURY WHO'D BELIEVE IT.
ALL I WANT IS FOR YOU TO WATCH HIM LONG ENOUGH TO FIGURE OUT HOW HE DOES BUSINESS. THEN I'LL GO IN AND GET HARD EVIDENCE.

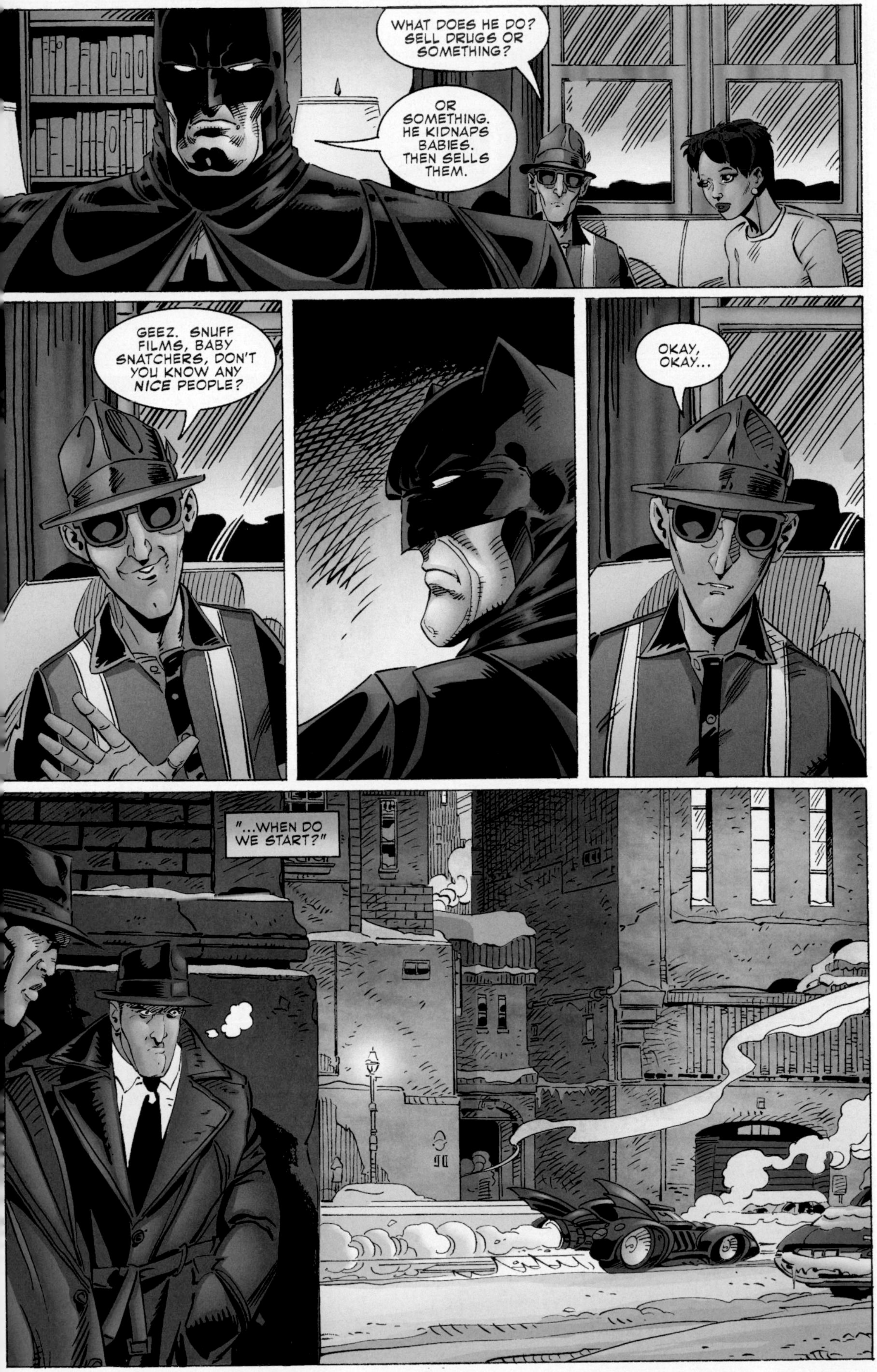
WHAT DOES HE DO? SELL DRUGS OR SOMETHING?
OR SOMETHING. HE KIDNAPS BABIES. THEN SELLS THEM.
GEEZ. SNUFF FILMS, BABY SNATCHERS, DON'T YOU KNOW ANY NICE PEOPLE?
OKAY, OKAY...
"...WHEN DO WE START?"

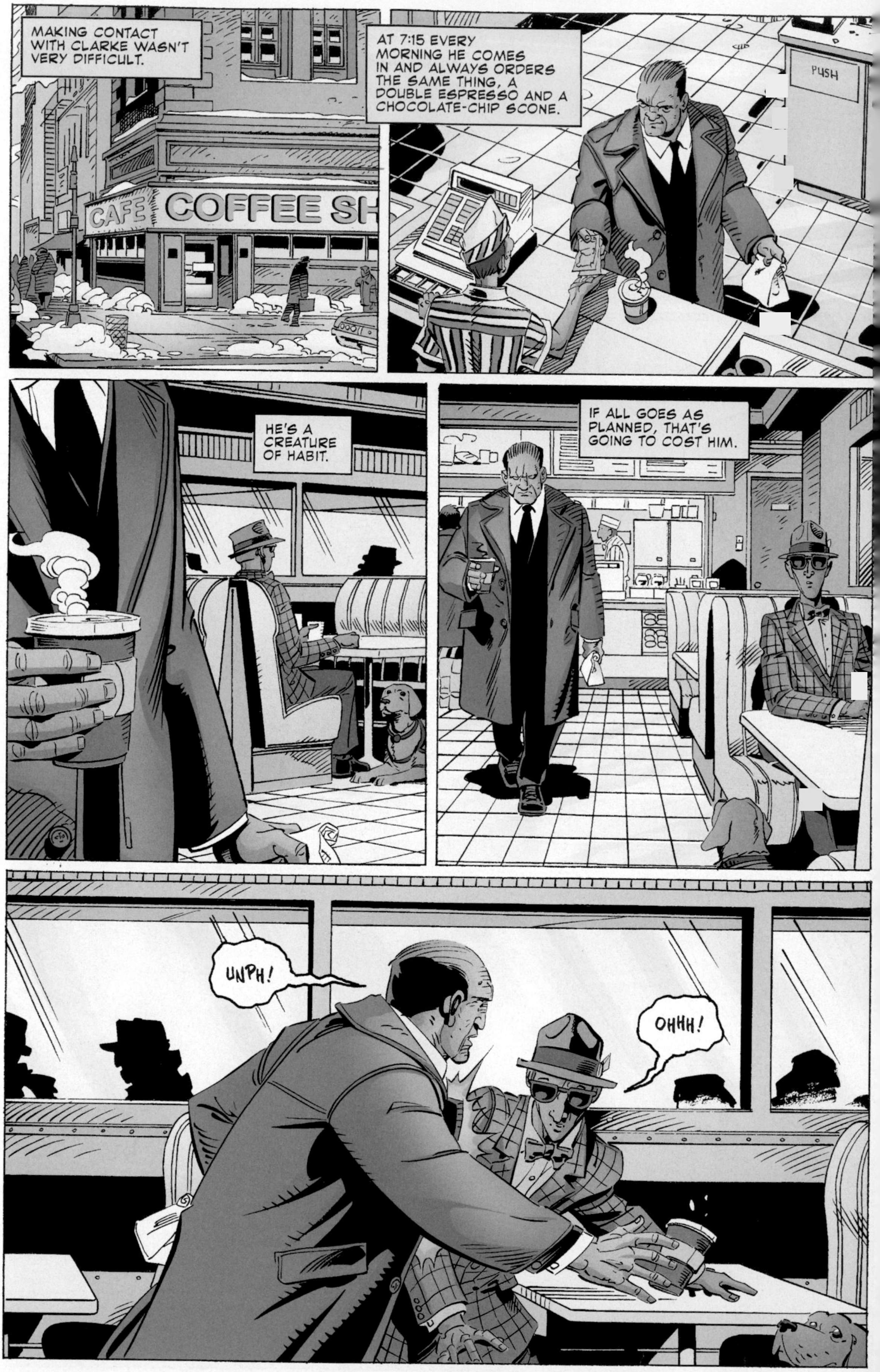
MAKING CONTACT WITH CLARKE WASN'T VERY DIFFICULT.
CAFE
COFFEE SH
AT 7:15 EVERY MORNING HE COMES IN AND ALWAYS ORDERS THE SAME THING, A DOUBLE ESPRESSO AND A CHOCOLATE-CHIP SCONE.
PUSH
HE'S A CREATURE OF HABIT.
IF ALL GOES AS PLANNED, THAT'S GOING TO COST HIM.
UNPH!
OHHH!

SORRY! I'M SO SORRY! THAT WAS COMPLETELY MY FAULT.

NEVER CEASES TO AMAZE ME. THE GUY'S IN THE BUSINESS OF SELLIN' KIDS AND HE'S APOLOGIZING FOR A LITTLE BUMP.

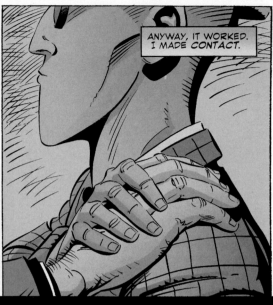

ANYWAY, IT WORKED. I MADE *CONTACT*.

NOW I WAS IN HIS HEAD, SEEING THE WORLD THROUGH HIS EYES.

AND HE DIDN'T HAVE A CLUE.

YOU SURE YOU OKAY?

JUST FINE, MISTER. THANKS.

MY DOG LED ME BACK TO WHERE BATMAN WAS WAITING FOR ME. I ONLY HAD EYES FOR CLARKE.

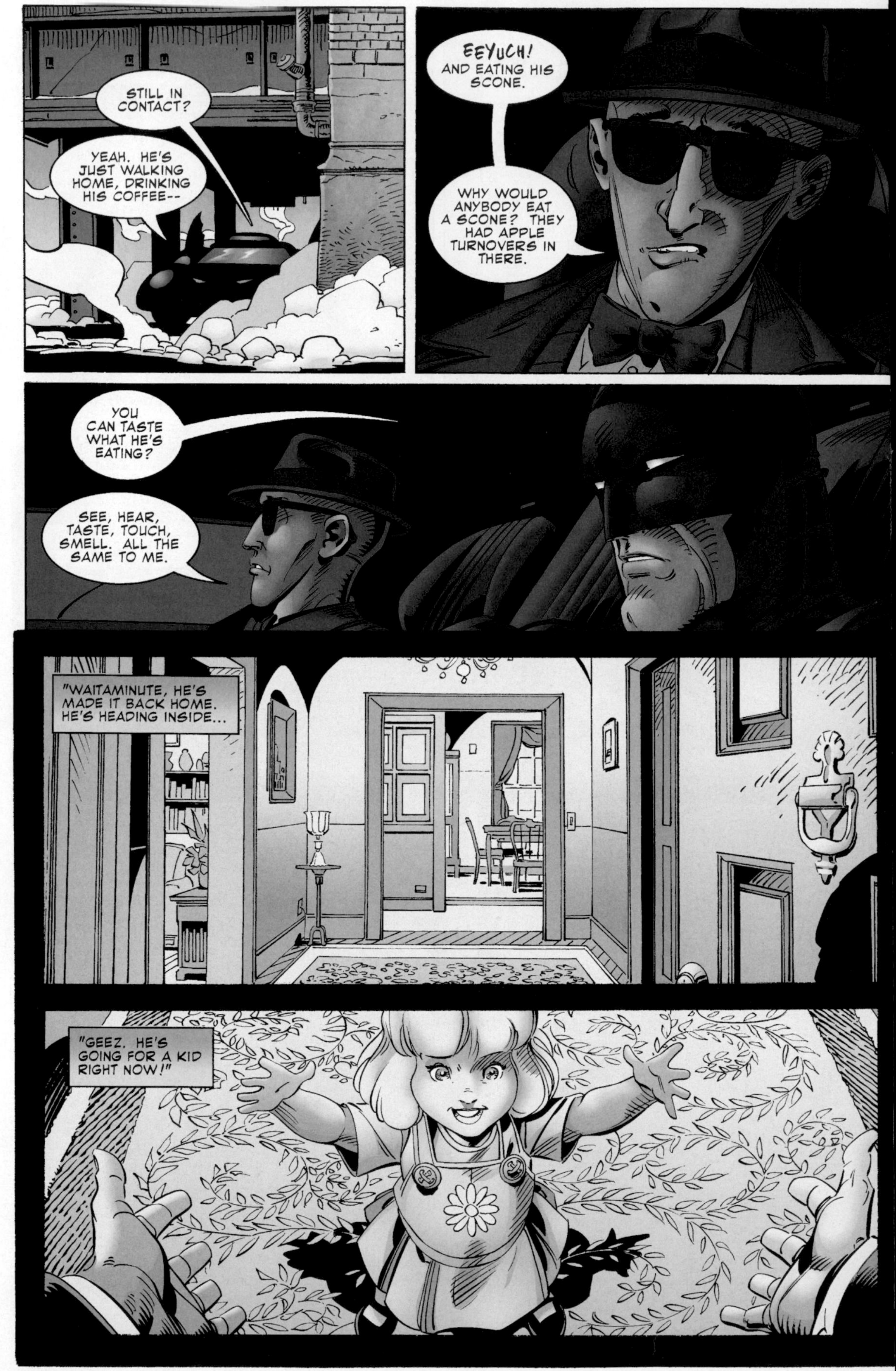
STILL IN CONTACT?
YEAH. HE'S JUST WALKING HOME, DRINKING HIS COFFEE--
EEYUCH! AND EATING HIS SCONE.
WHY WOULD ANYBODY EAT A SCONE? THEY HAD APPLE TURNOVERS IN THERE.
YOU CAN TASTE WHAT HE'S EATING?
SEE, HEAR, TASTE, TOUCH, SMELL. ALL THE SAME TO ME.
"WAITAMINUTE, HE'S MADE IT BACK HOME. HE'S HEADING INSIDE...
"GEEZ. HE'S GOING FOR A KID RIGHT NOW!"

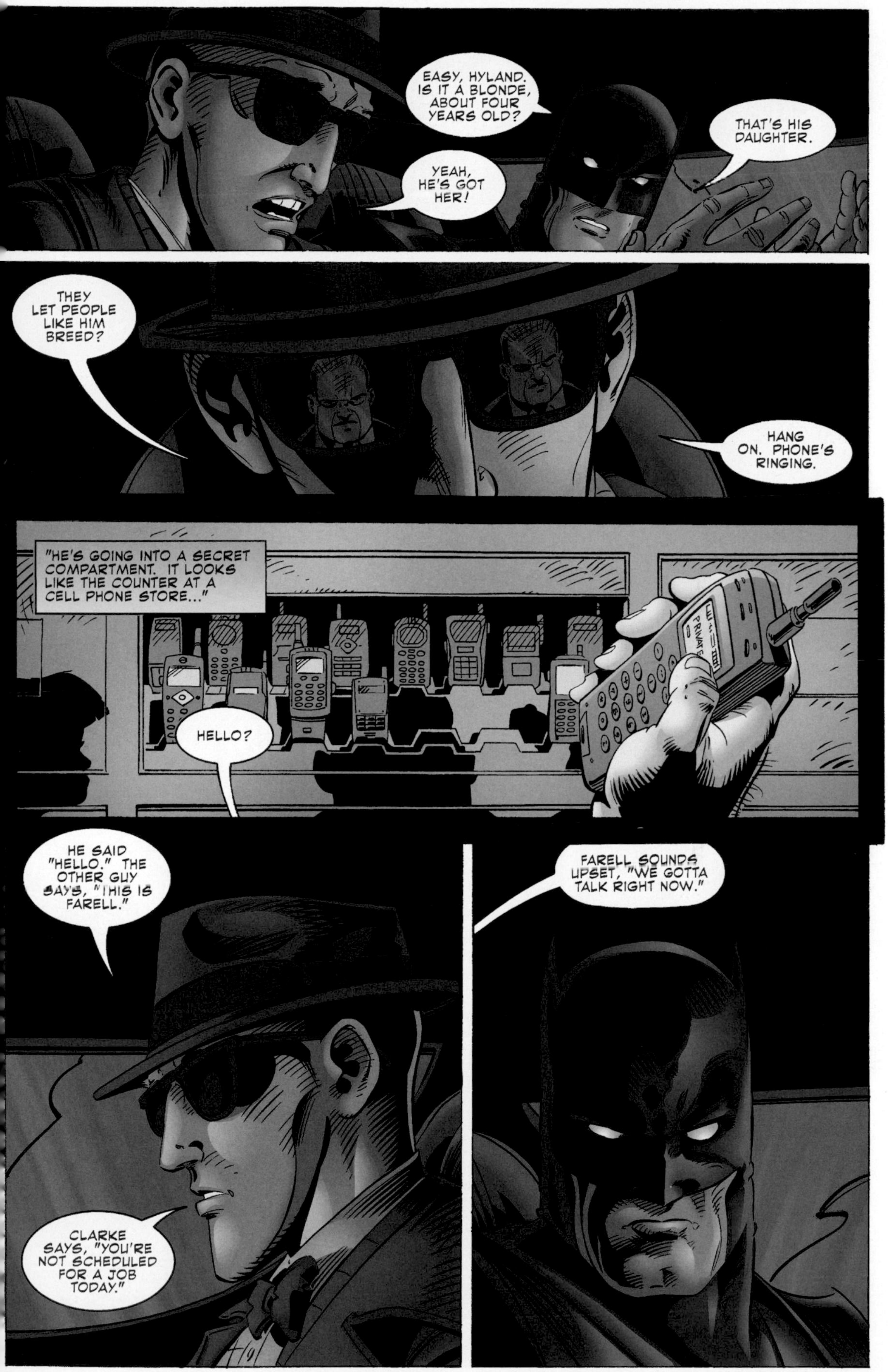
EASY, HYLAND. IS IT A BLONDE, ABOUT FOUR YEARS OLD?
YEAH, HE'S GOT HER!
THAT'S HIS DAUGHTER.
THEY LET PEOPLE LIKE HIM BREED?
HANG ON. PHONE'S RINGING.
"HE'S GOING INTO A SECRET COMPARTMENT. IT LOOKS LIKE THE COUNTER AT A CELL PHONE STORE..."
HELLO?
HE SAID "HELLO." THE OTHER GUY SAYS, "THIS IS FARELL."
CLARKE SAYS, "YOU'RE NOT SCHEDULED FOR A JOB TODAY."
FARELL SOUNDS UPSET, "WE GOTTA TALK RIGHT NOW."

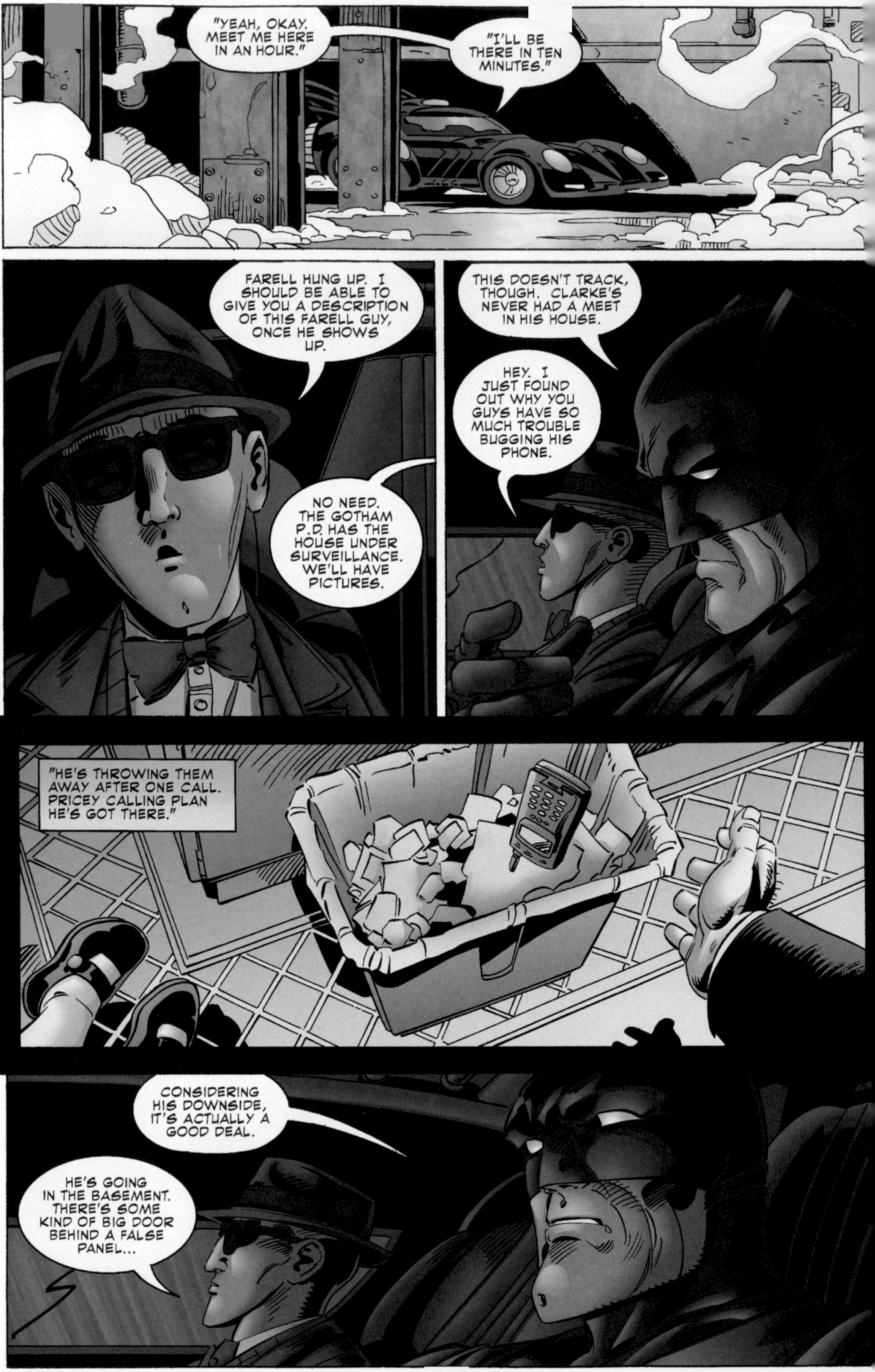
"YEAH, OKAY. MEET ME HERE IN AN HOUR."
"I'LL BE THERE IN TEN MINUTES."
FARELL HUNG UP. I SHOULD BE ABLE TO GIVE YOU A DESCRIPTION OF THIS FARELL GUY, ONCE HE SHOWS UP.
NO NEED. THE GOTHAM P.D. HAS THE HOUSE UNDER SURVEILLANCE. WE'LL HAVE PICTURES.
THIS DOESN'T TRACK, THOUGH. CLARKE'S NEVER HAD A MEET IN HIS HOUSE.
HEY. I JUST FOUND OUT WHY YOU GUYS HAVE SO MUCH TROUBLE BUGGING HIS PHONE.
"HE'S THROWING THEM AWAY AFTER ONE CALL. PRICEY CALLING PLAN HE'S GOT THERE."
CONSIDERING HIS DOWNSIDE, IT'S ACTUALLY A GOOD DEAL.
HE'S GOING IN THE BASEMENT. THERE'S SOME KIND OF BIG DOOR BEHIND A FALSE PANEL...

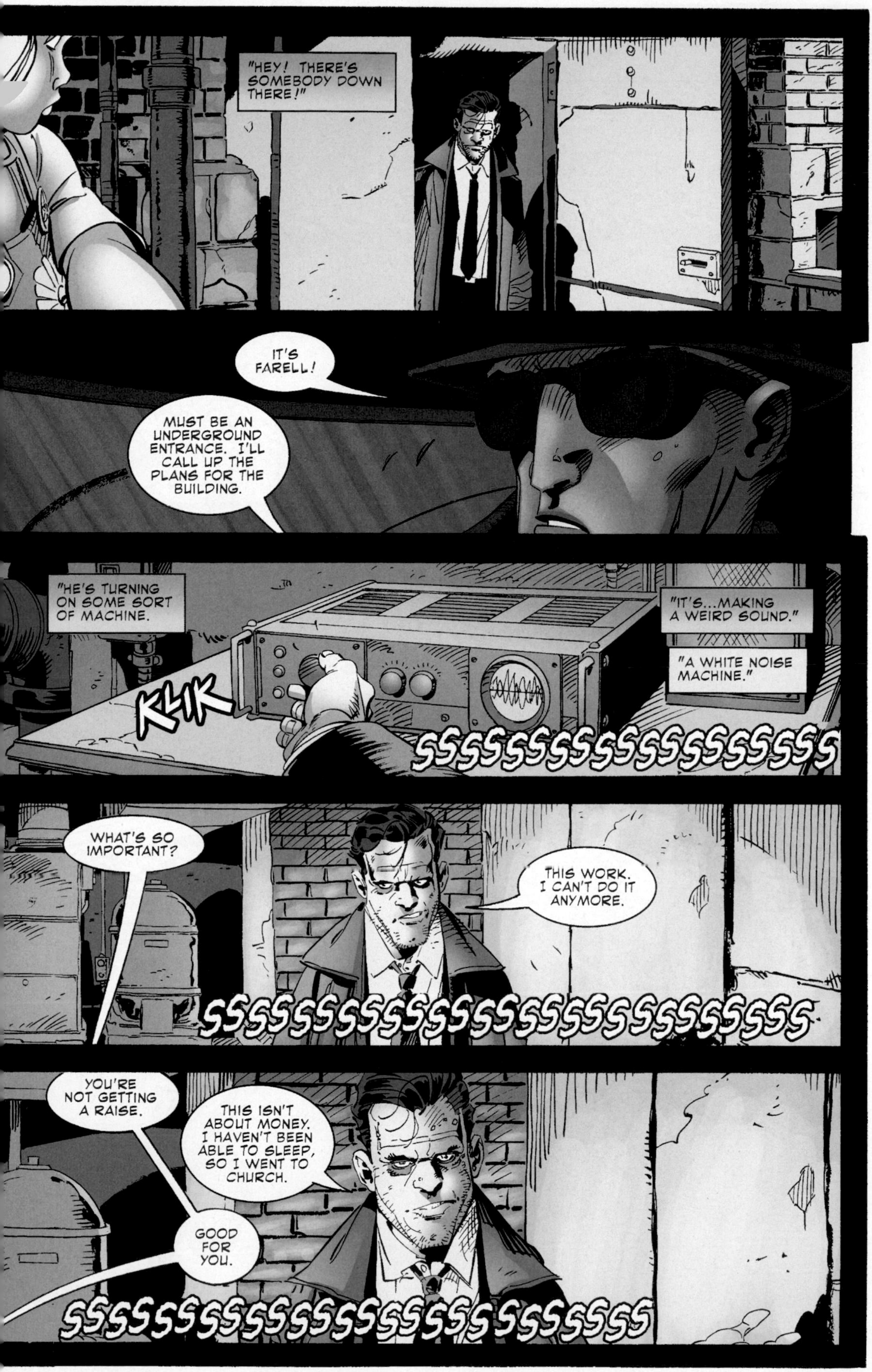
"HEY! THERE'S SOMEBODY DOWN THERE!"
IT'S FARELL!
MUST BE AN UNDERGROUND ENTRANCE. I'LL CALL UP THE PLANS FOR THE BUILDING.
"HE'S TURNING ON SOME SORT OF MACHINE.
KLIK
"IT'S...MAKING A WEIRD SOUND."
"A WHITE NOISE MACHINE."
SSSSSSSSSSSSSSSSSSSS
WHAT'S SO IMPORTANT?
THIS WORK. I CAN'T DO IT ANYMORE.
SSSSSSSSSSSSSSSSSSSSSSSSSSS
YOU'RE NOT GETTING A RAISE.
THIS ISN'T ABOUT MONEY. I HAVEN'T BEEN ABLE TO SLEEP, SO I WENT TO CHURCH.
GOOD FOR YOU.
SSSSSSSSSSSSSSSSSSSSSSSSSSSS

SSSSSSSSSSSSSSSSSSSSSSSSSSSSSSSSSSSSSSSSS

SSSSSSSSSSSSSSSSSSSSSSSSSSSSSSSSSSSSSSSSS

SSSSSSSSSSSSSSSSSSSSSSSSSSSSSSSSSSSSSSSSS

SSSSSSSSSSSSSSSSSSSSSSSSSSSSSSSSSSSSSSSSS

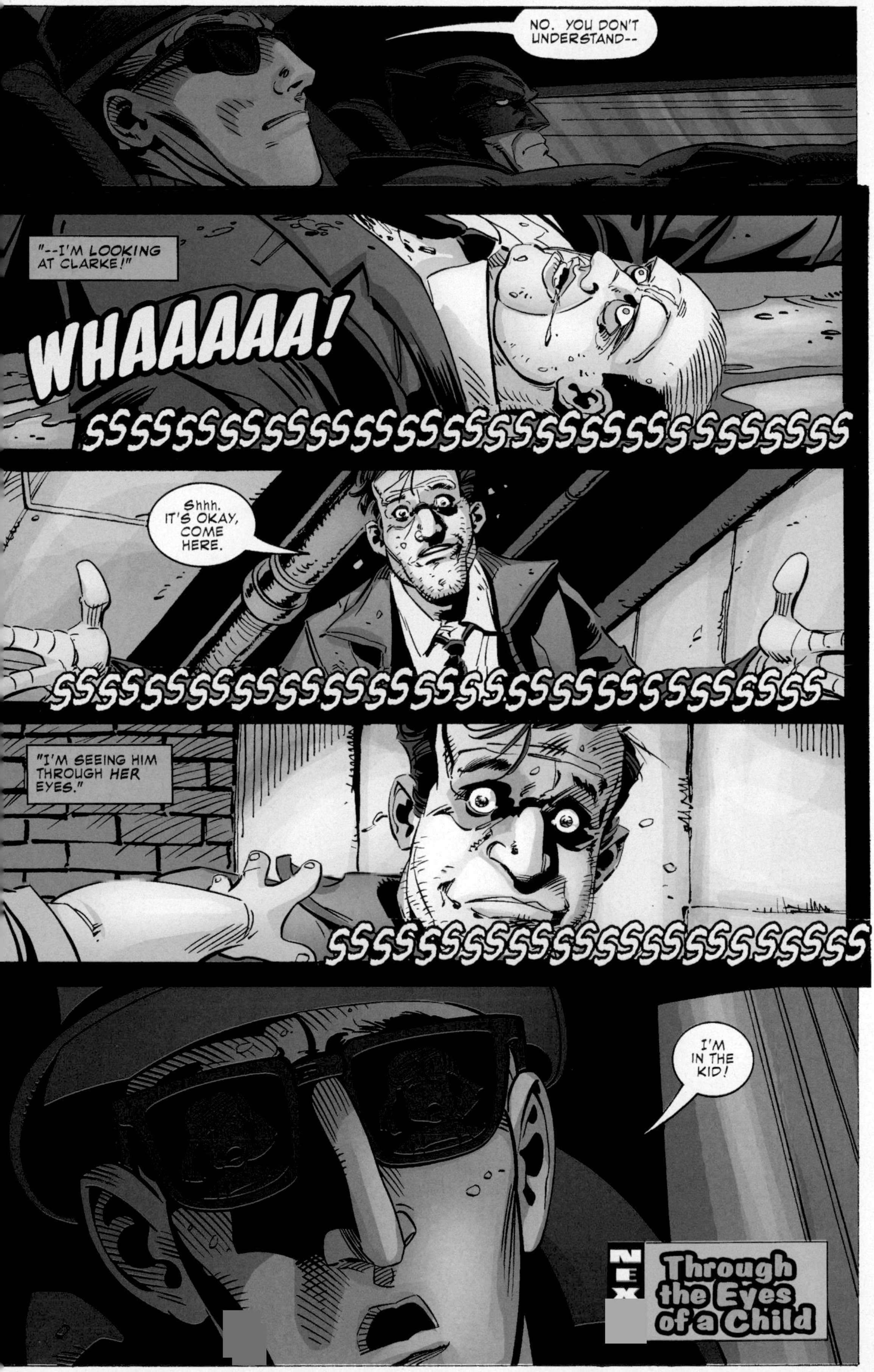
NO. YOU DON'T UNDERSTAND--
"--I'M LOOKING AT CLARKE!"
WHAAAAA!
SSSSSSSSSSSSSSSSSSSSSSSSSSSSSSS
Shhh. IT'S OKAY, COME HERE.
SSSSSSSSSSSSSSSSSSSSSSSSSSSSSSSS
"I'M SEEING HIM THROUGH HER EYES."
SSSSSSSSSSSSSSSSSSSSSSSSSSSS
I'M IN THE KID!
NEX
Through the Eyes of a Child

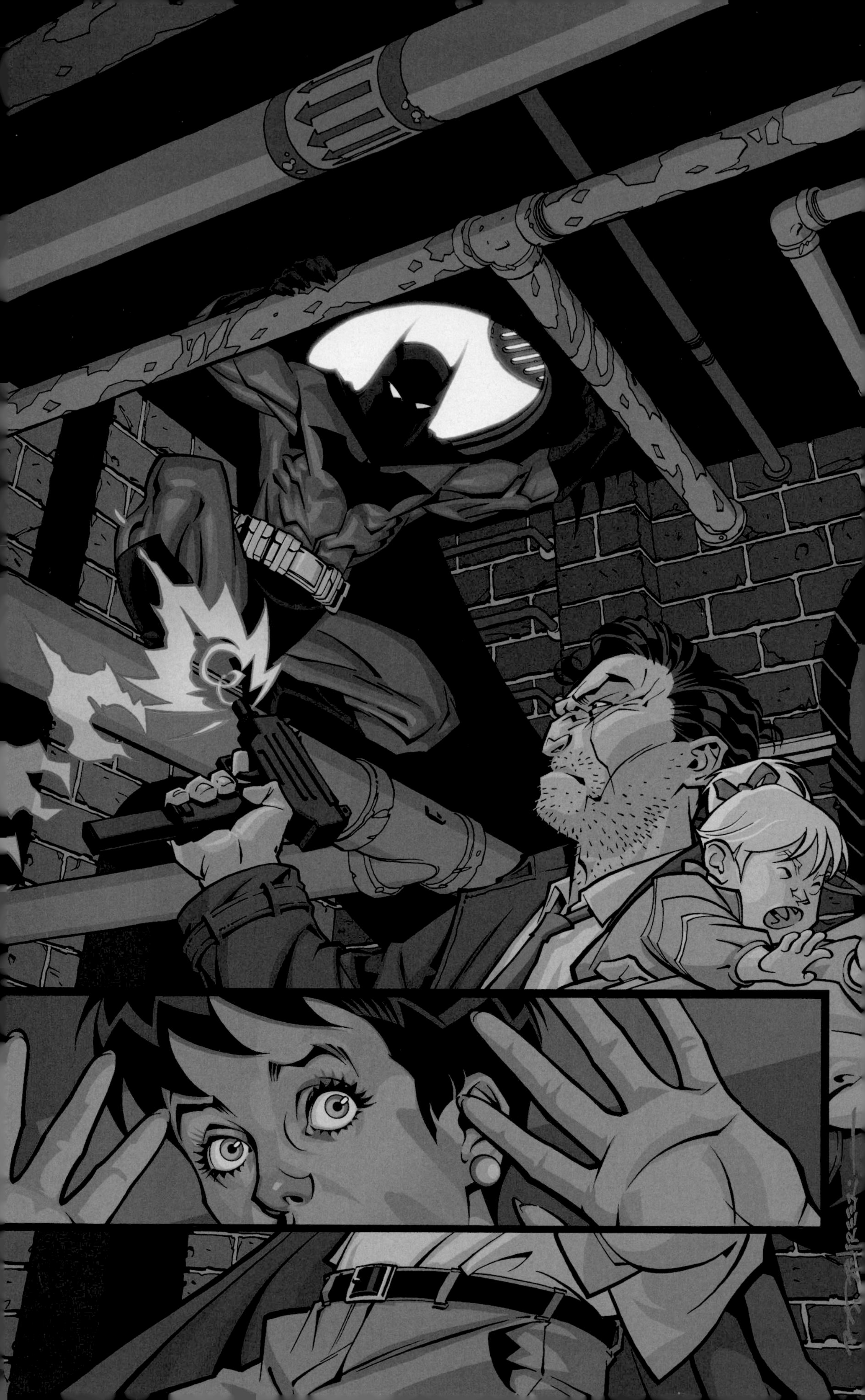

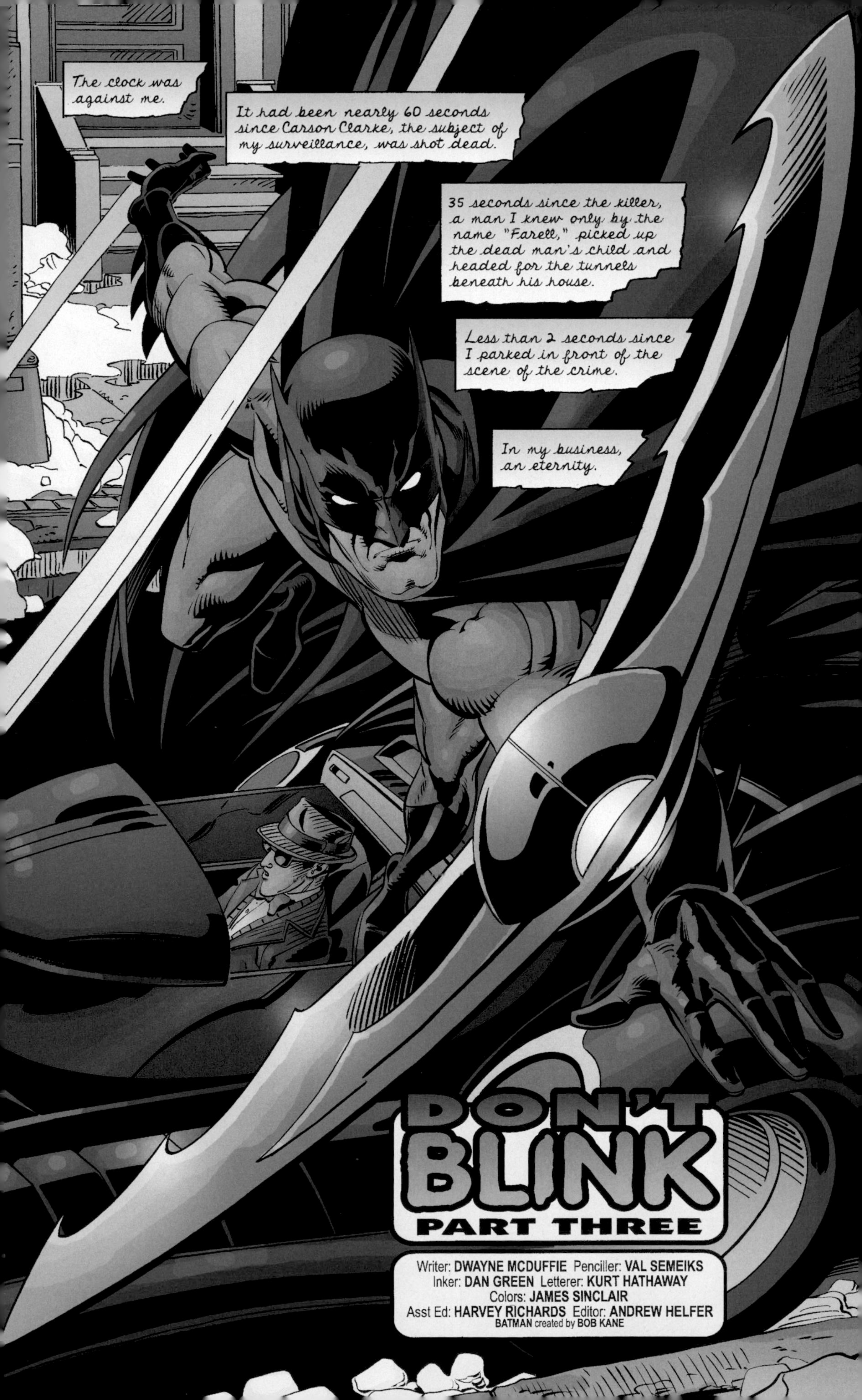

The clock was against me.
It had been nearly 60 seconds since Carson Clarke, the subject of my surveillance, was shot dead.
35 seconds since the killer, a man I knew only by the name "Farell," picked up the dead man's child and headed for the tunnels beneath his house.
Less than 2 seconds since I parked in front of the scene of the crime.
In my business, an eternity.
DON'T BLINK
PART THREE
Writer: DWAYNE MCDUFFIE Penciller: VAL SEMEIKS
Inker: DAN GREEN Letterer: KURT HATHAWAY
Colors: JAMES SINCLAIR
Asst Ed: HARVEY RICHARDS Editor: ANDREW HELFER
BATMAN created by BOB KANE

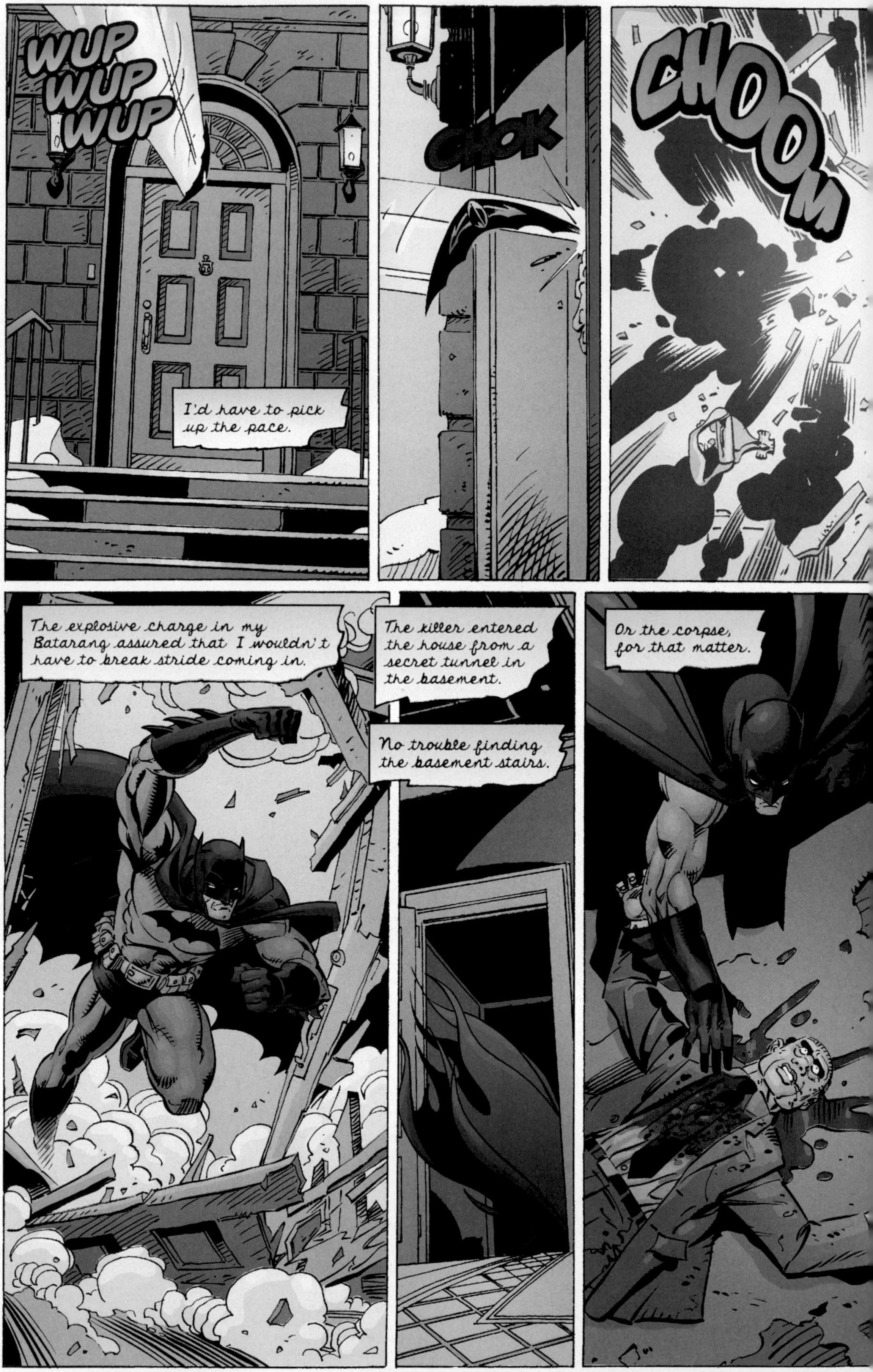
WUP
WUP
WUP
I'd have to pick up the pace.
CHOK
CHOOM
The explosive charge in my Batarang assured that I wouldn't have to break stride coming in.
The killer entered the house from a secret tunnel in the basement.
No trouble finding the basement stairs.
Or the corpse, for that matter.

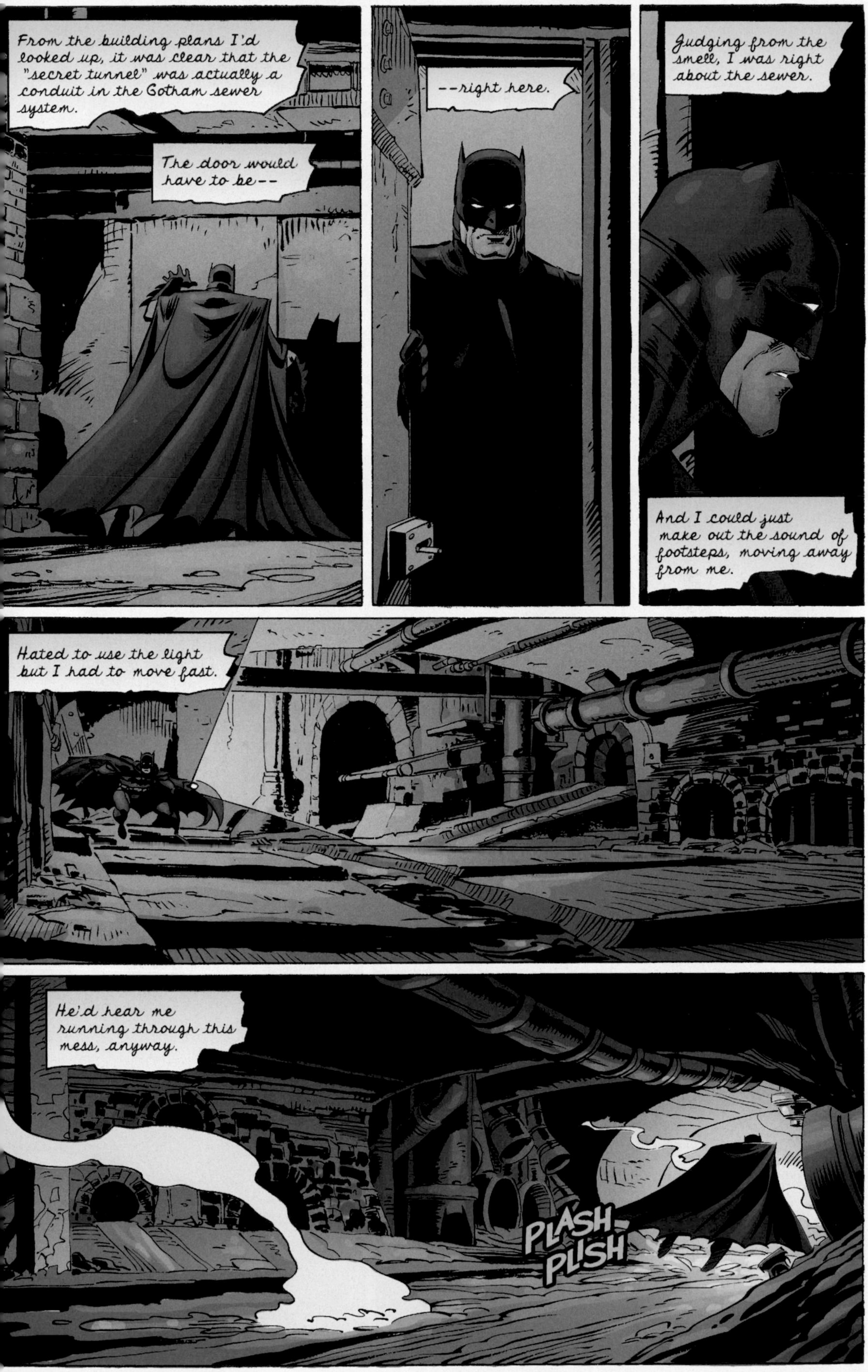
From the building plans I'd looked up, it was clear that the "secret tunnel" was actually a conduit in the Gotham sewer system.
The door would have to be--
--right here.
Judging from the smell, I was right about the sewer.
And I could just make out the sound of footsteps, moving away from me.
Hated to use the light but I had to move fast.
He'd hear me running through this mess, anyway.
PLASH
PLISH

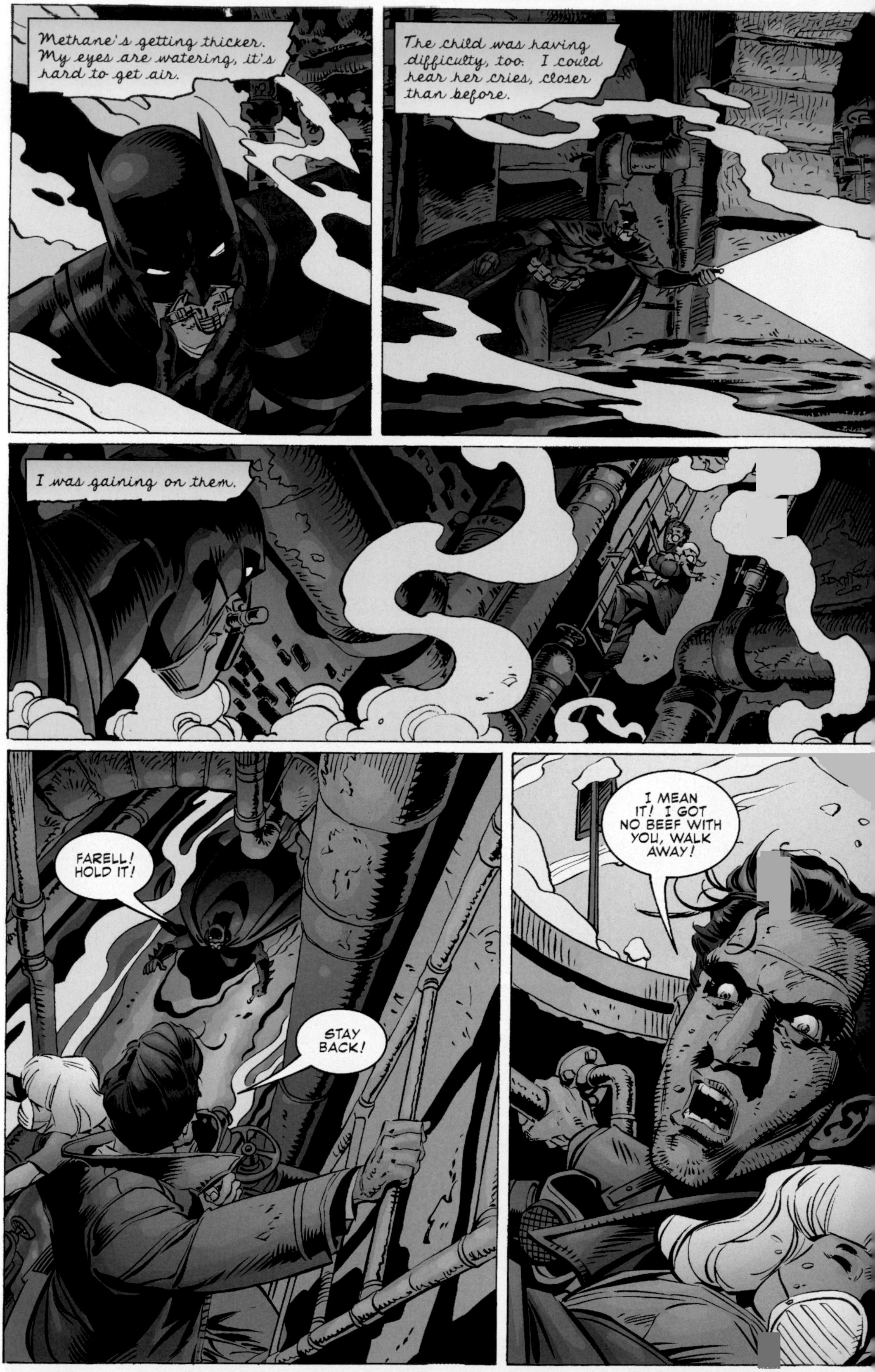

Methane's getting thicker. My eyes are watering, it's hard to get air.
The child was having difficulty, too. I could hear her cries, closer than before.
I was gaining on them.
FARELL! HOLD IT!
STAY BACK!
I MEAN IT! I GOT NO BEEF WITH YOU, WALK AWAY!

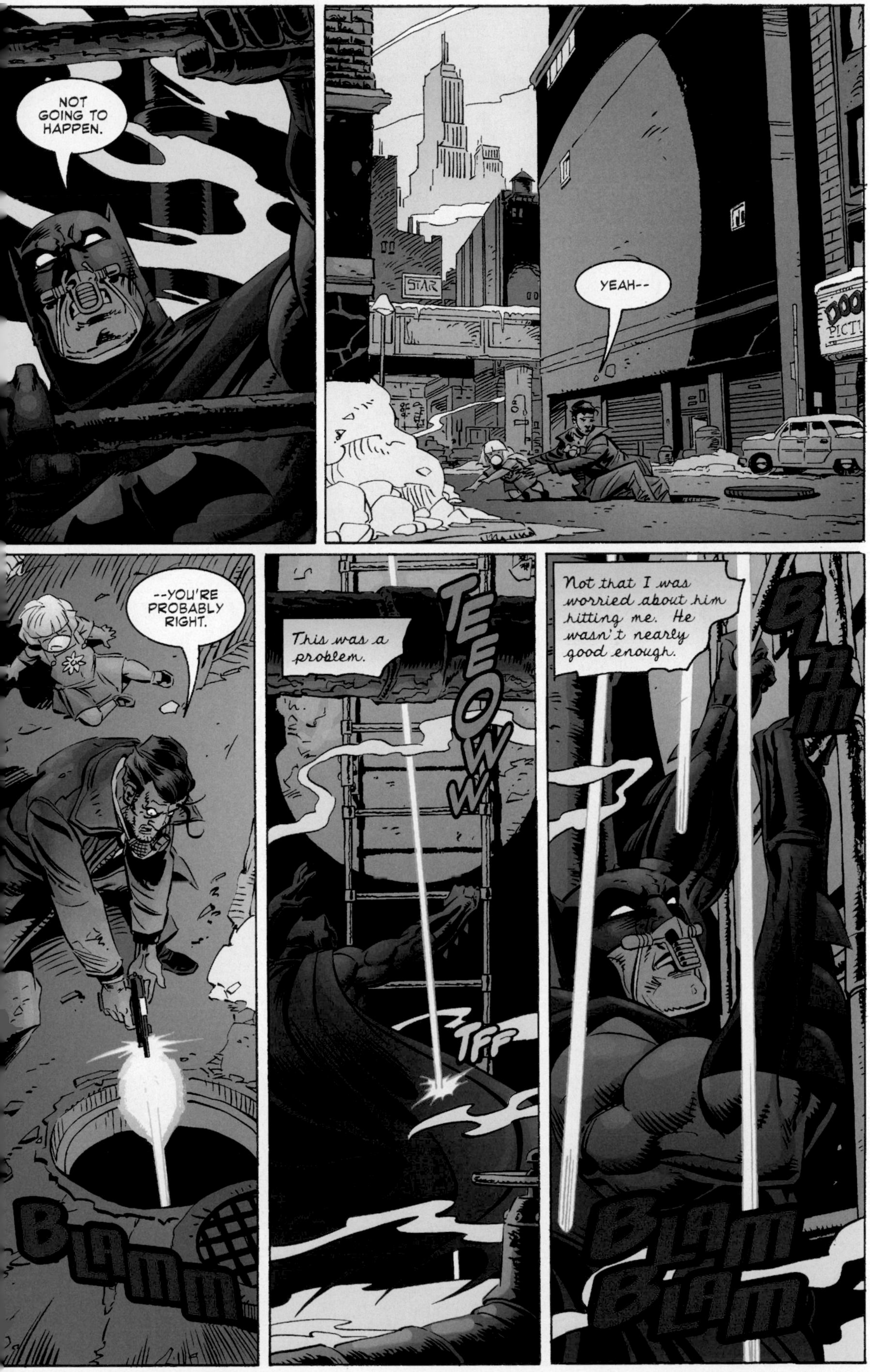

NOT GOING TO HAPPEN.
STAR
YEAH--
--YOU'RE PROBABLY RIGHT.
BLAMMM
This was a problem.
TEEOWW
TFF
Not that I was worried about him hitting me. He wasn't nearly good enough.
BLAM
BLAM BLAM

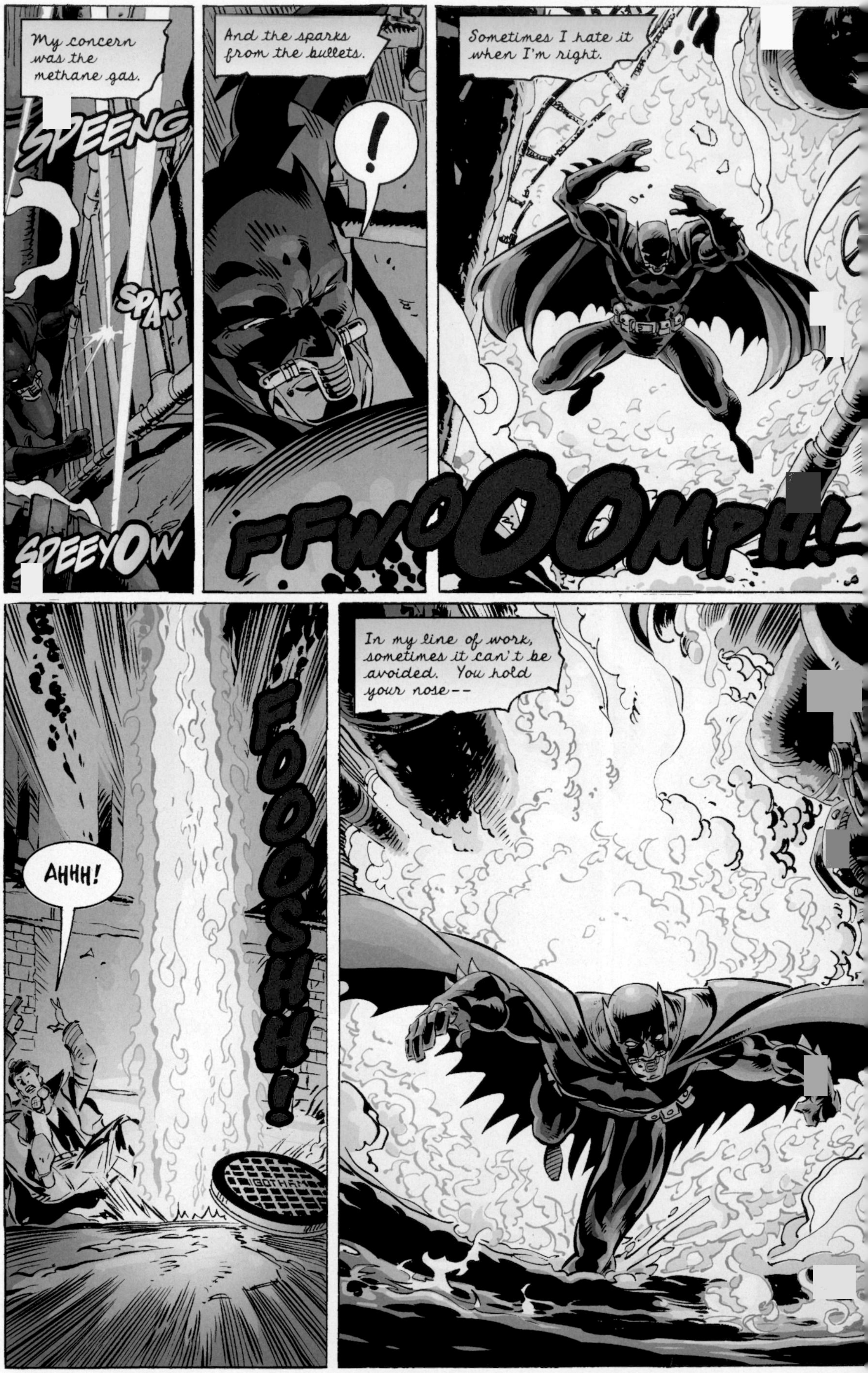

My concern was the methane gas.
SPEENG
SPAK
SPEEYOW
And the sparks from the bullets.
!
Sometimes I hate it when I'm right.
FFWOOOOMPH!
AHHH!
FOOOOSHH!
GOTHAM
In my line of work, sometimes it can't be avoided. You hold your nose--

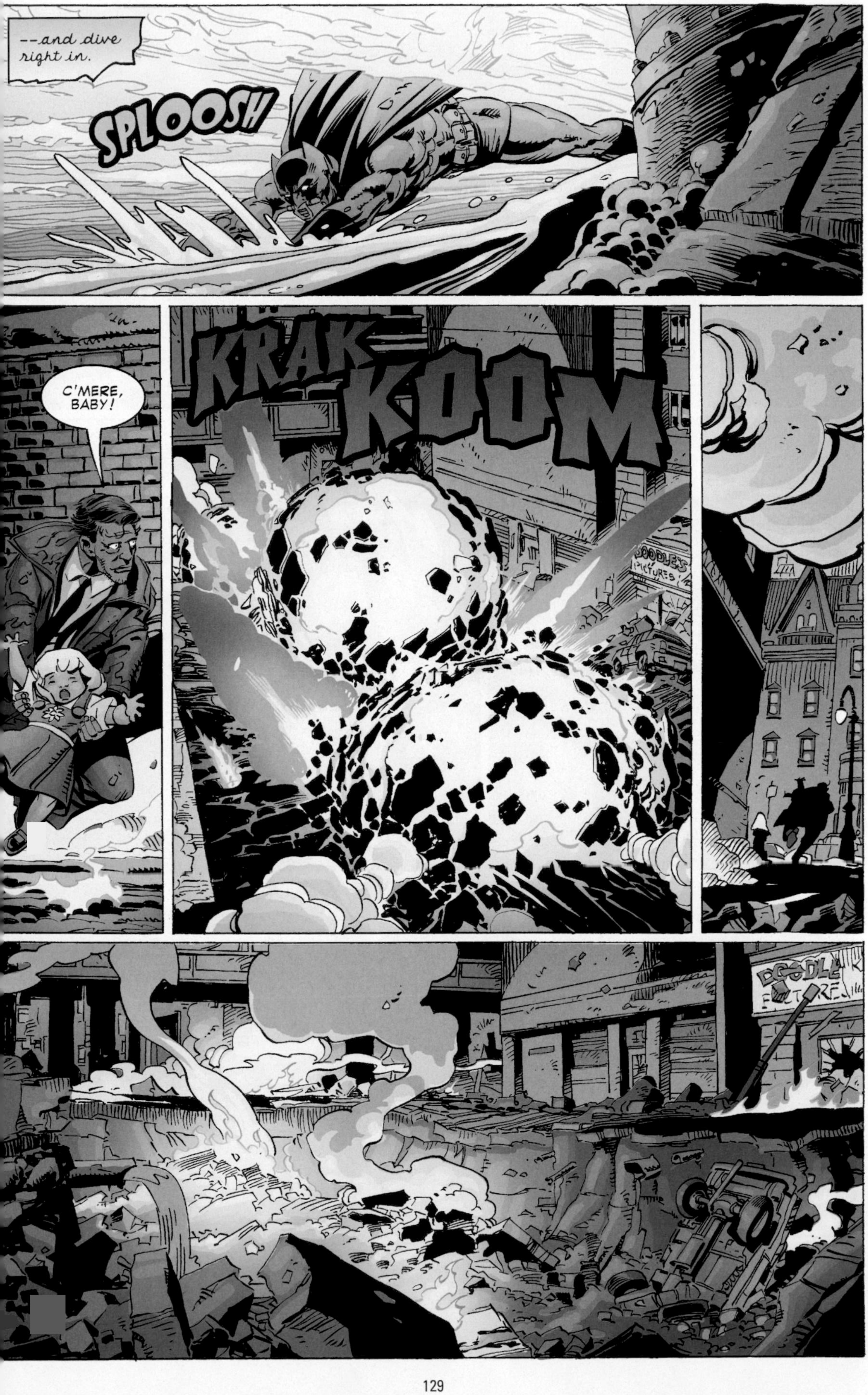
--and dive right in.
SPLOOSH
C'MERE, BABY!
KRAK
KOOM
DOODLE'S PICTURES

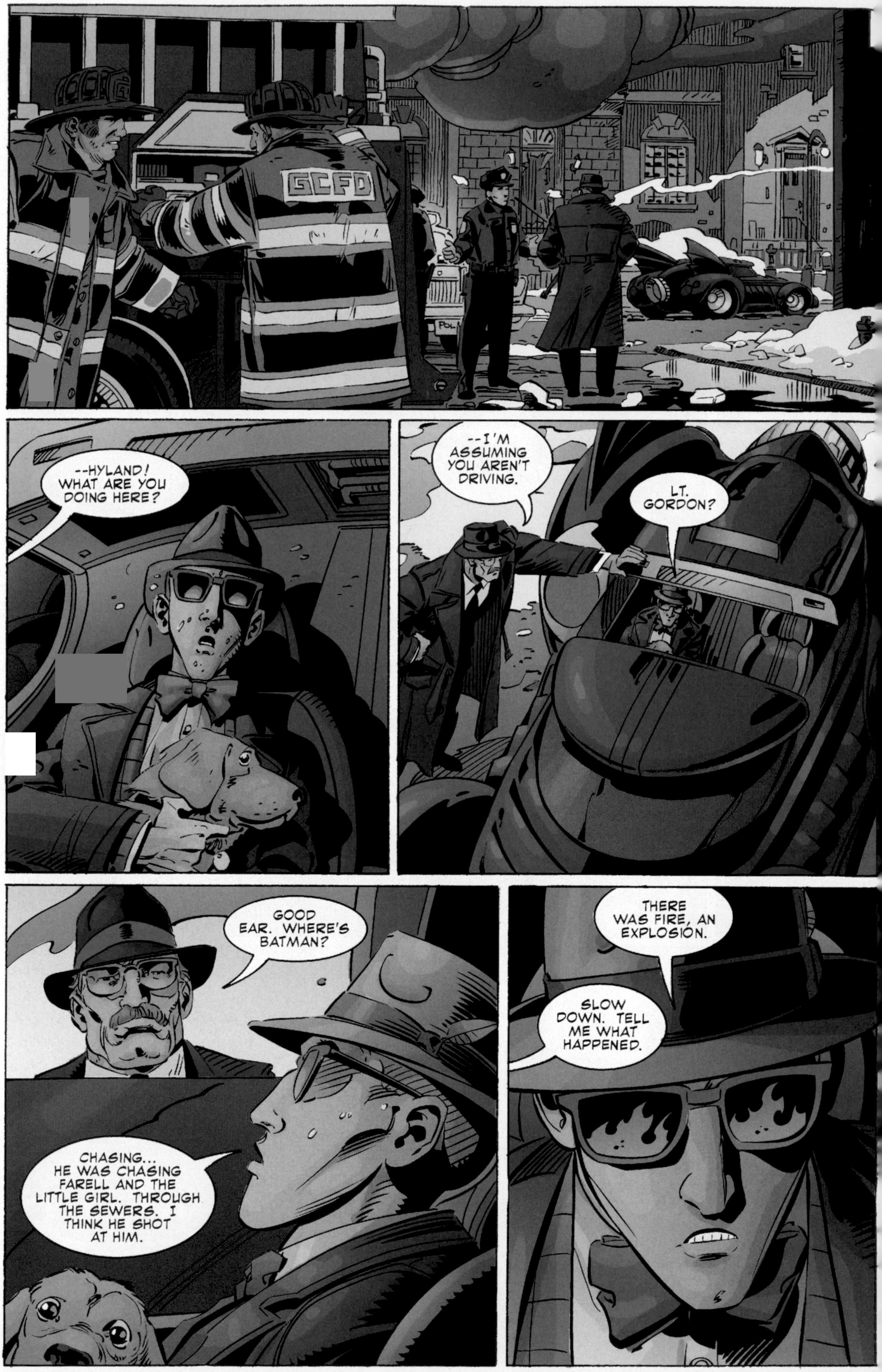
--HYLAND! WHAT ARE YOU DOING HERE?
--I'M ASSUMING YOU AREN'T DRIVING.
LT. GORDON?
GOOD EAR. WHERE'S BATMAN?
CHASING... HE WAS CHASING FARELL AND THE LITTLE GIRL. THROUGH THE SEWERS. I THINK HE SHOT AT HIM.
THERE WAS FIRE, AN EXPLOSION.
SLOW DOWN. TELL ME WHAT HAPPENED.

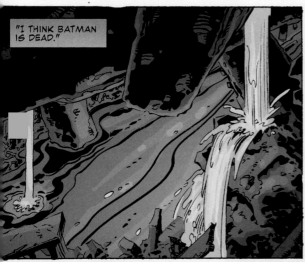

"I THINK BATMAN IS DEAD."

Not this time.

Surface of the water deflected most of the force of the explosion.

Not much of the heat, though.

If there had been much more gas down there, I would have been boiled alive.

It took me nearly three hours to dig my way out.

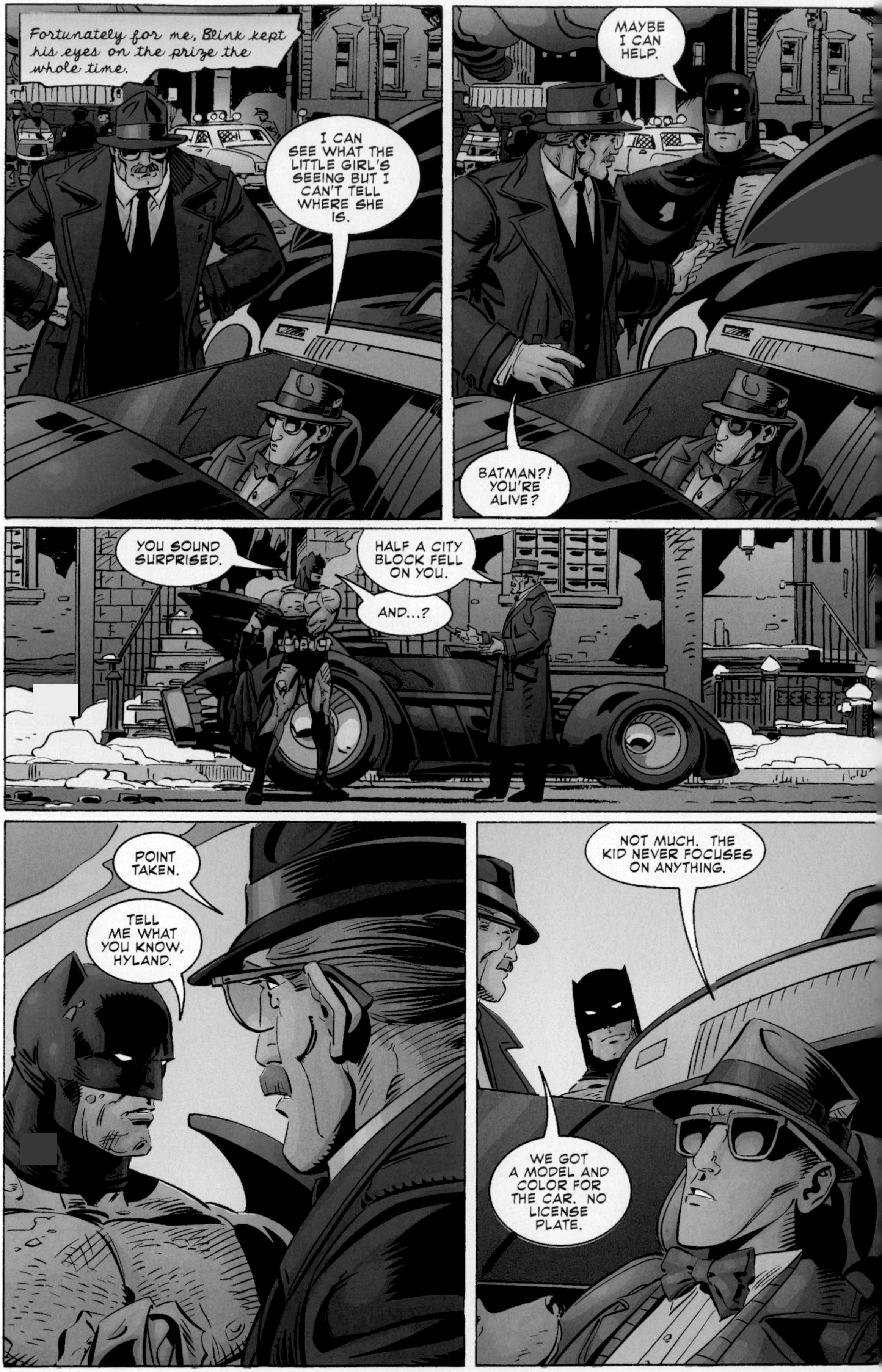
Fortunately for me, Blink kept his eyes on the prize the whole time.
I CAN SEE WHAT THE LITTLE GIRL'S SEEING BUT I CAN'T TELL WHERE SHE IS.
MAYBE I CAN HELP.
BATMAN?! YOU'RE ALIVE?
YOU SOUND SURPRISED.
HALF A CITY BLOCK FELL ON YOU.
AND...?
POINT TAKEN.
TELL ME WHAT YOU KNOW, HYLAND.
NOT MUCH. THE KID NEVER FOCUSES ON ANYTHING.
WE GOT A MODEL AND COLOR FOR THE CAR. NO LICENSE PLATE.

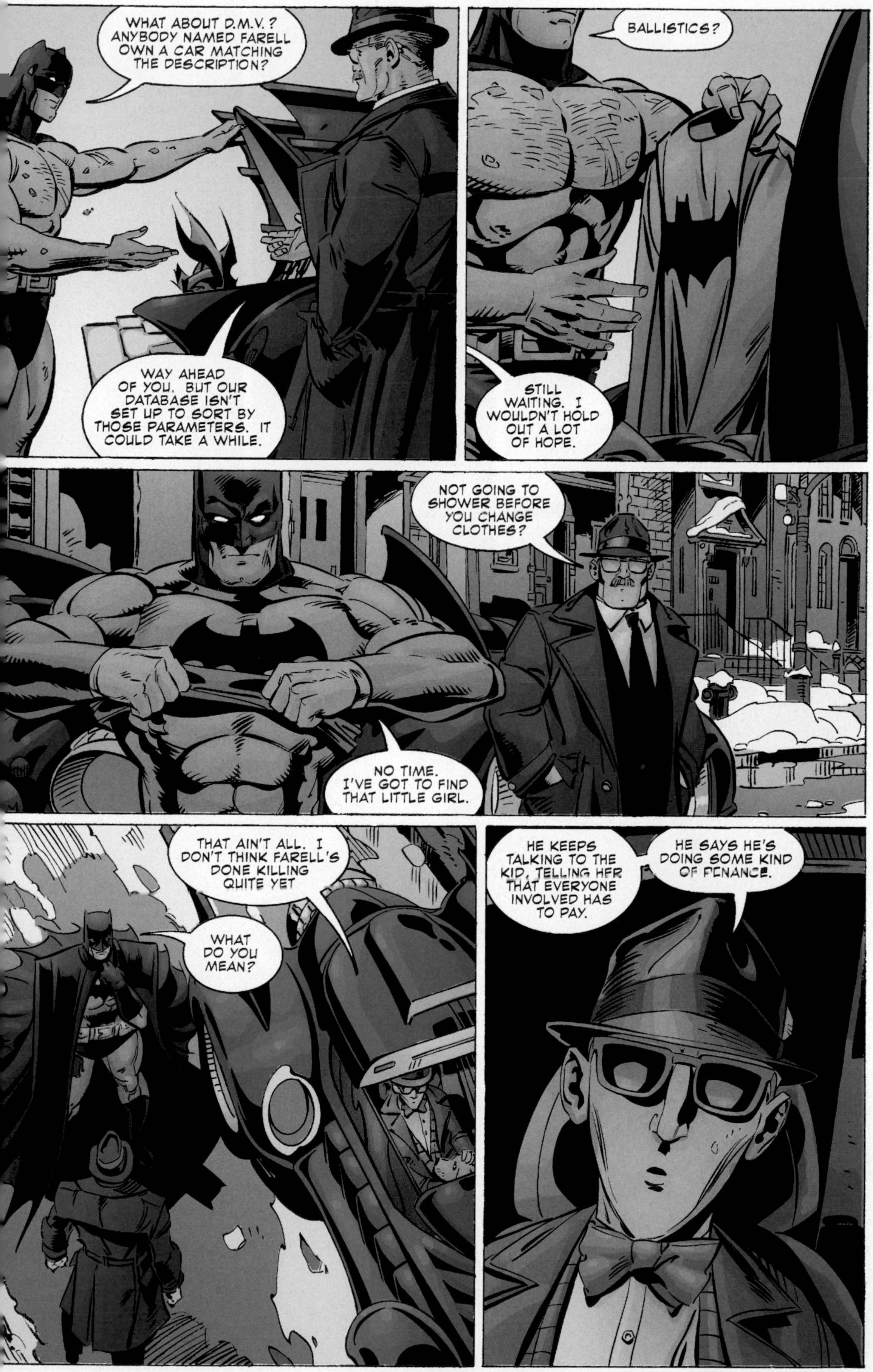
WHAT ABOUT D.M.V.? ANYBODY NAMED FARELL OWN A CAR MATCHING THE DESCRIPTION?
WAY AHEAD OF YOU. BUT OUR DATABASE ISN'T SET UP TO SORT BY THOSE PARAMETERS. IT COULD TAKE A WHILE.
BALLISTICS?
STILL WAITING. I WOULDN'T HOLD OUT A LOT OF HOPE.
NOT GOING TO SHOWER BEFORE YOU CHANGE CLOTHES?
NO TIME. I'VE GOT TO FIND THAT LITTLE GIRL.
THAT AIN'T ALL. I DON'T THINK FARELL'S DONE KILLING QUITE YET
WHAT DO YOU MEAN?
HE KEEPS TALKING TO THE KID, TELLING HER THAT EVERYONE INVOLVED HAS TO PAY.
HE SAYS HE'S DOING SOME KIND OF PENANCE.

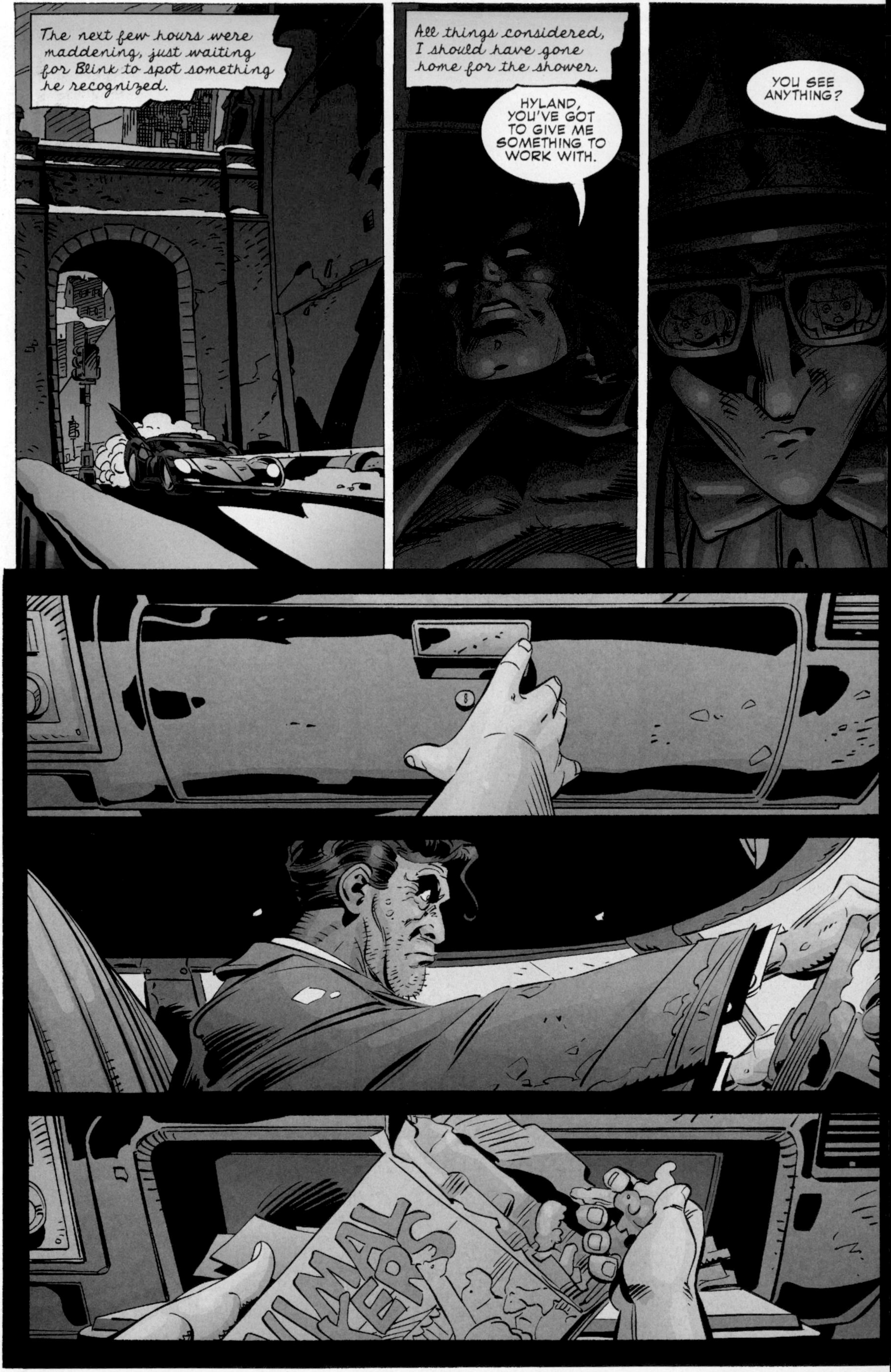
The next few hours were maddening, just waiting for Blink to spot something he recognized.
All things considered, I should have gone home for the shower.
HYLAND, YOU'VE GOT TO GIVE ME SOMETHING TO WORK WITH.
YOU SEE ANYTHING?

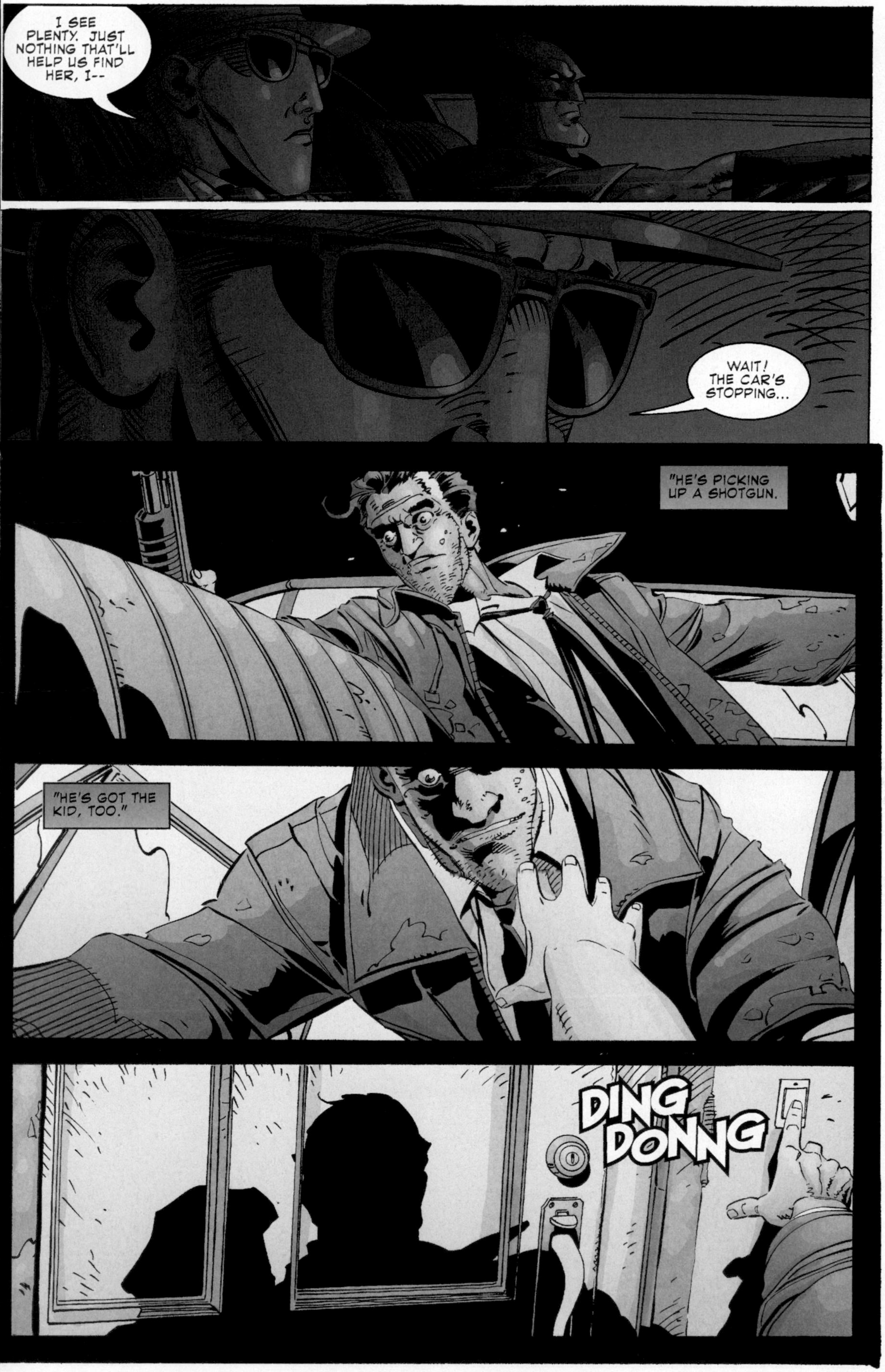
I SEE PLENTY. JUST NOTHING THAT'LL HELP US FIND HER, I--
WAIT! THE CAR'S STOPPING...
"HE'S PICKING UP A SHOTGUN.
"HE'S GOT THE KID, TOO."
DING DONNG

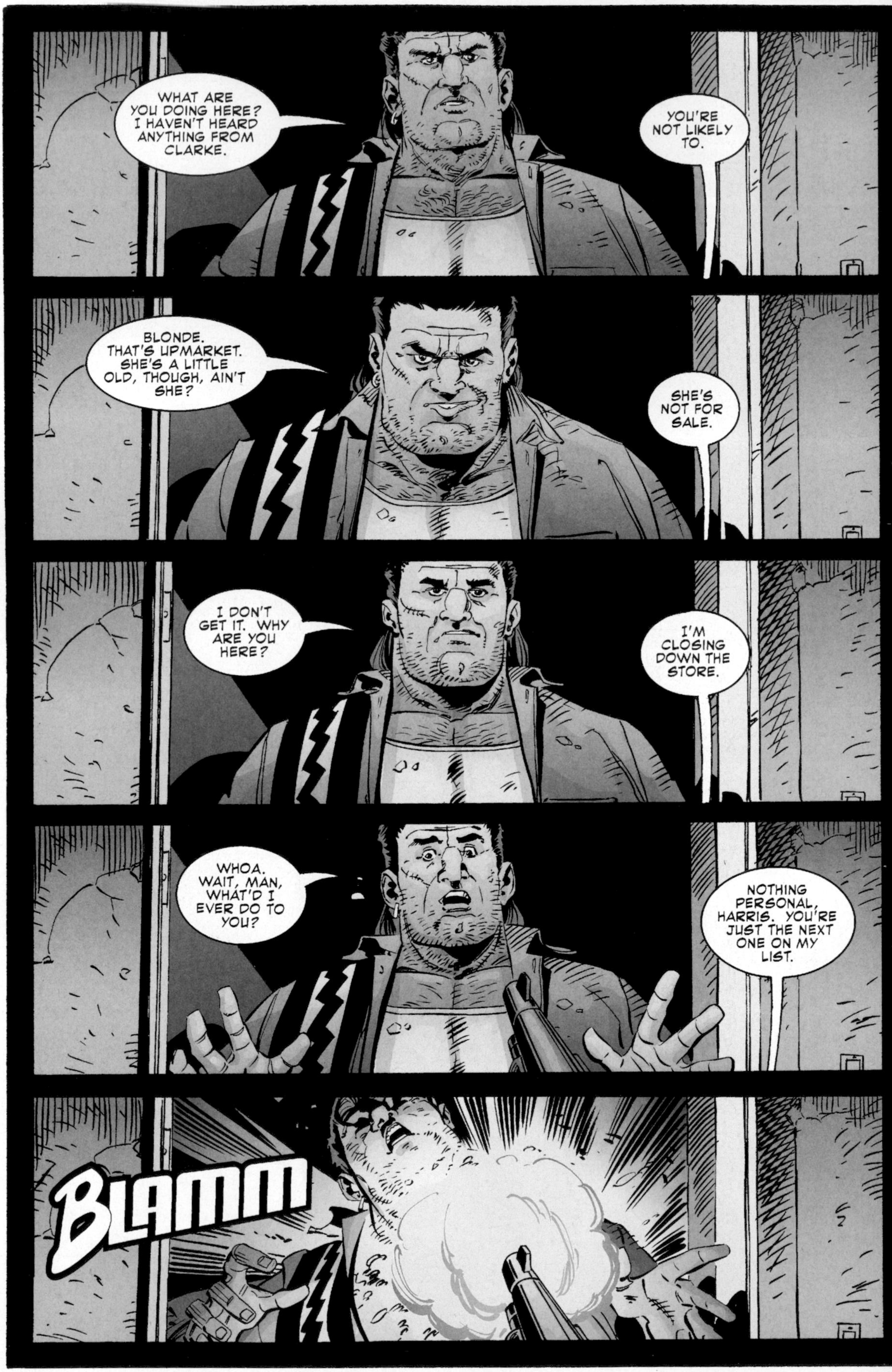
WHAT ARE YOU DOING HERE? I HAVEN'T HEARD ANYTHING FROM CLARKE.
YOU'RE NOT LIKELY TO.
BLONDE. THAT'S UPMARKET. SHE'S A LITTLE OLD, THOUGH, AIN'T SHE?
SHE'S NOT FOR SALE.
I DON'T GET IT. WHY ARE YOU HERE?
I'M CLOSING DOWN THE STORE.
WHOA. WAIT, MAN, WHAT'D I EVER DO TO YOU?
NOTHING PERSONAL, HARRIS. YOU'RE JUST THE NEXT ONE ON MY LIST.
BLAMM

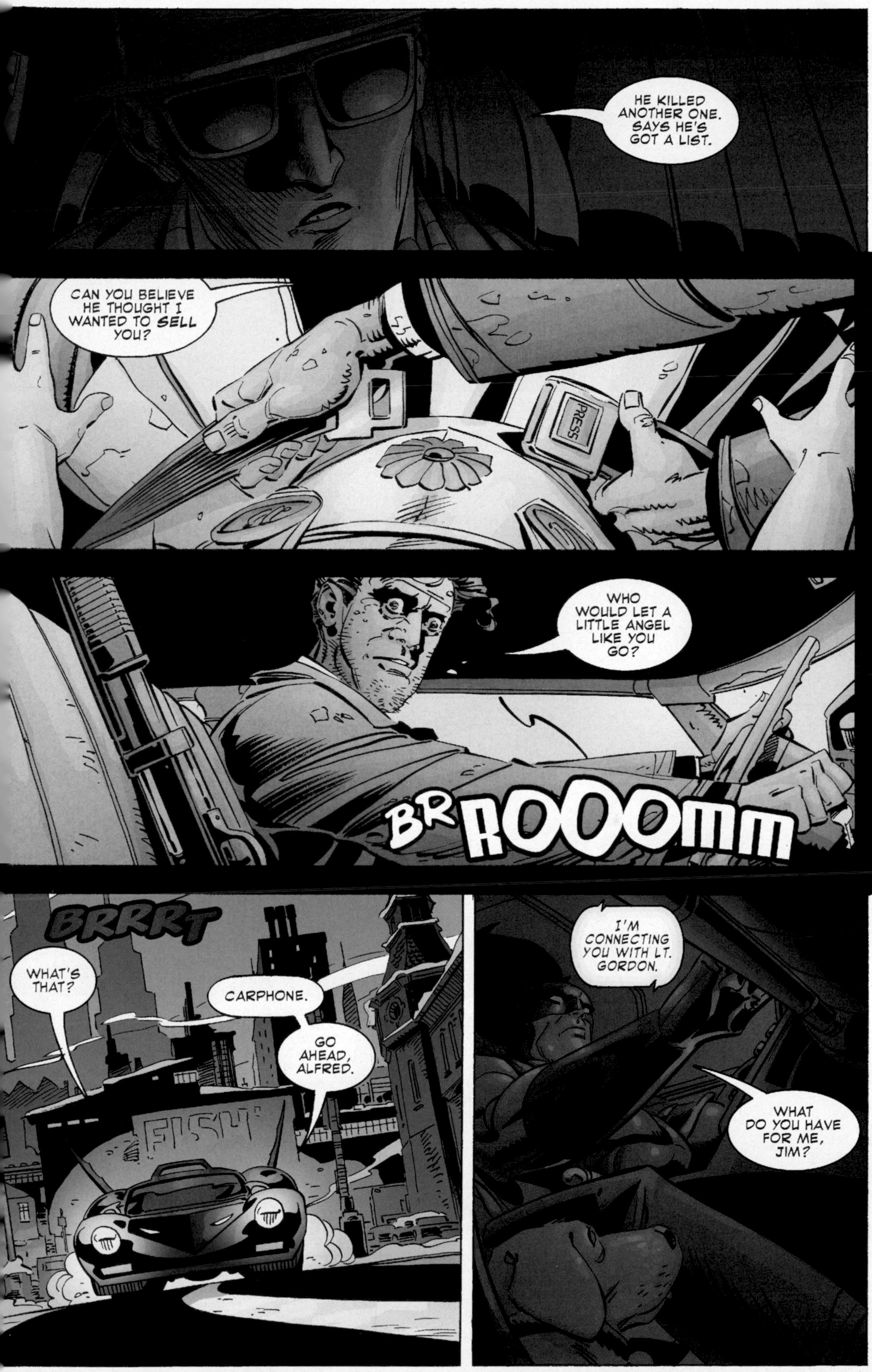
HE KILLED ANOTHER ONE. SAYS HE'S GOT A LIST.
CAN YOU BELIEVE HE THOUGHT I WANTED TO SELL YOU?
PRESS
WHO WOULD LET A LITTLE ANGEL LIKE YOU GO?
BRROOOMM
BRRRT
WHAT'S THAT?
CARPHONE.
GO AHEAD, ALFRED.
FISH
I'M CONNECTING YOU WITH LT. GORDON.
WHAT DO YOU HAVE FOR ME, JIM?

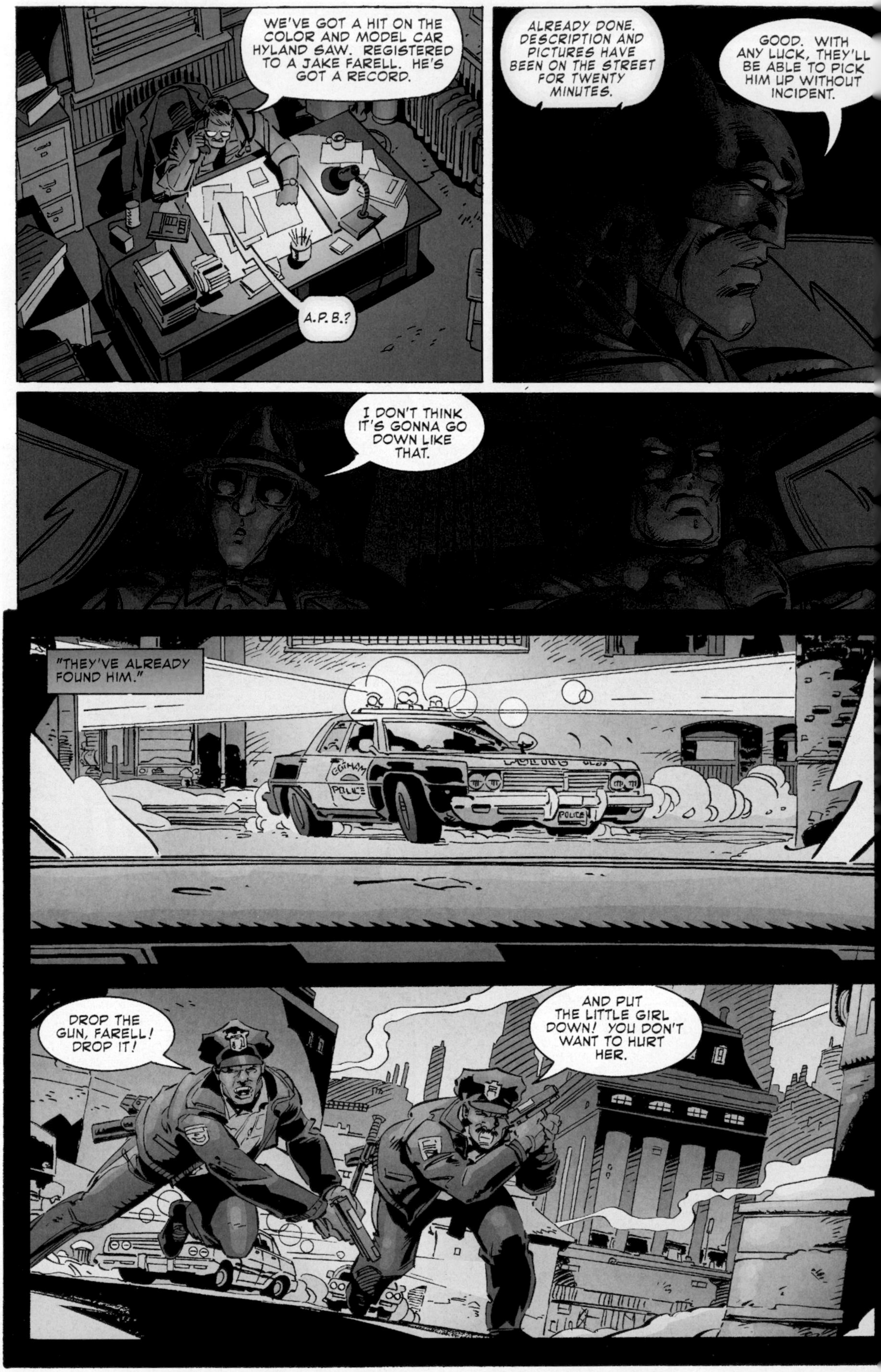
WE'VE GOT A HIT ON THE COLOR AND MODEL CAR HYLAND SAW. REGISTERED TO A JAKE FARELL. HE'S GOT A RECORD.
A.P.B.?
ALREADY DONE. DESCRIPTION AND PICTURES HAVE BEEN ON THE STREET FOR TWENTY MINUTES.
GOOD. WITH ANY LUCK, THEY'LL BE ABLE TO PICK HIM UP WITHOUT INCIDENT.
I DON'T THINK IT'S GONNA GO DOWN LIKE THAT.
"THEY'VE ALREADY FOUND HIM."
GOTHAM POLICE
POLICE
DROP THE GUN, FARELL! DROP IT!
AND PUT THE LITTLE GIRL DOWN! YOU DON'T WANT TO HURT HER.

HE'S SHOOTING. I CAN'T SEE IF HE HIT THEM.

THE OFFICERS CALLED FOR BACKUP, I'VE GOT A LOCATION.

SQUEEEL

ON OUR WAY.

WHAT'S HAPPENING HERE?

FARELL'S HOLED HIMSELF UP IN THAT WAREHOUSE. WE'RE WAITING FOR A SUPERVISOR BEFORE WE PROCEED.

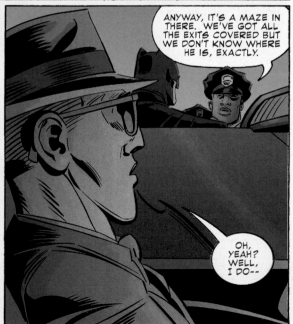

ANYWAY, IT'S A MAZE IN THERE. WE'VE GOT ALL THE EXITS COVERED BUT WE DON'T KNOW WHERE HE IS, EXACTLY.

OH, YEAH? WELL, I DO--

"--I'M LOOKING RIGHT AT HIM."

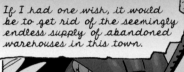

If I had one wish, it would be to get rid of the seemingly endless supply of abandoned warehouses in this town.

Have to stay away from the doors. He'll be watching them, and dodging buckshot isn't high on my list.

From Hyland's description, it has to be one of two rooms on the third floor in the southeast corner.

The lady or the tiger?

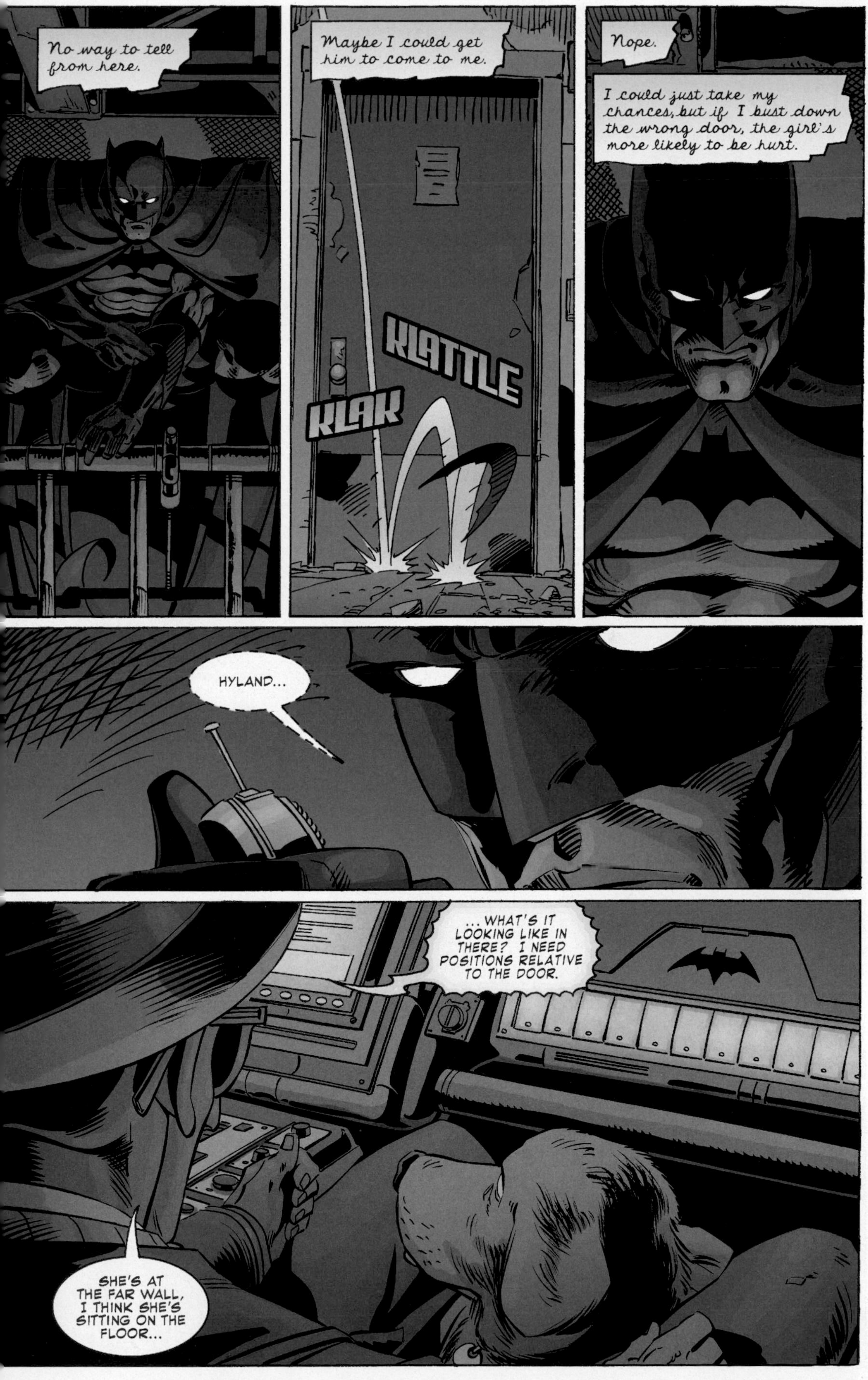
No way to tell from here.
Maybe I could get him to come to me.
KLATTLE
KLAK
Nope.
I could just take my chances, but if I bust down the wrong door, the girl's more likely to be hurt.
HYLAND...
...WHAT'S IT LOOKING LIKE IN THERE? I NEED POSITIONS RELATIVE TO THE DOOR.
SHE'S AT THE FAR WALL, I THINK SHE'S SITTING ON THE FLOOR...

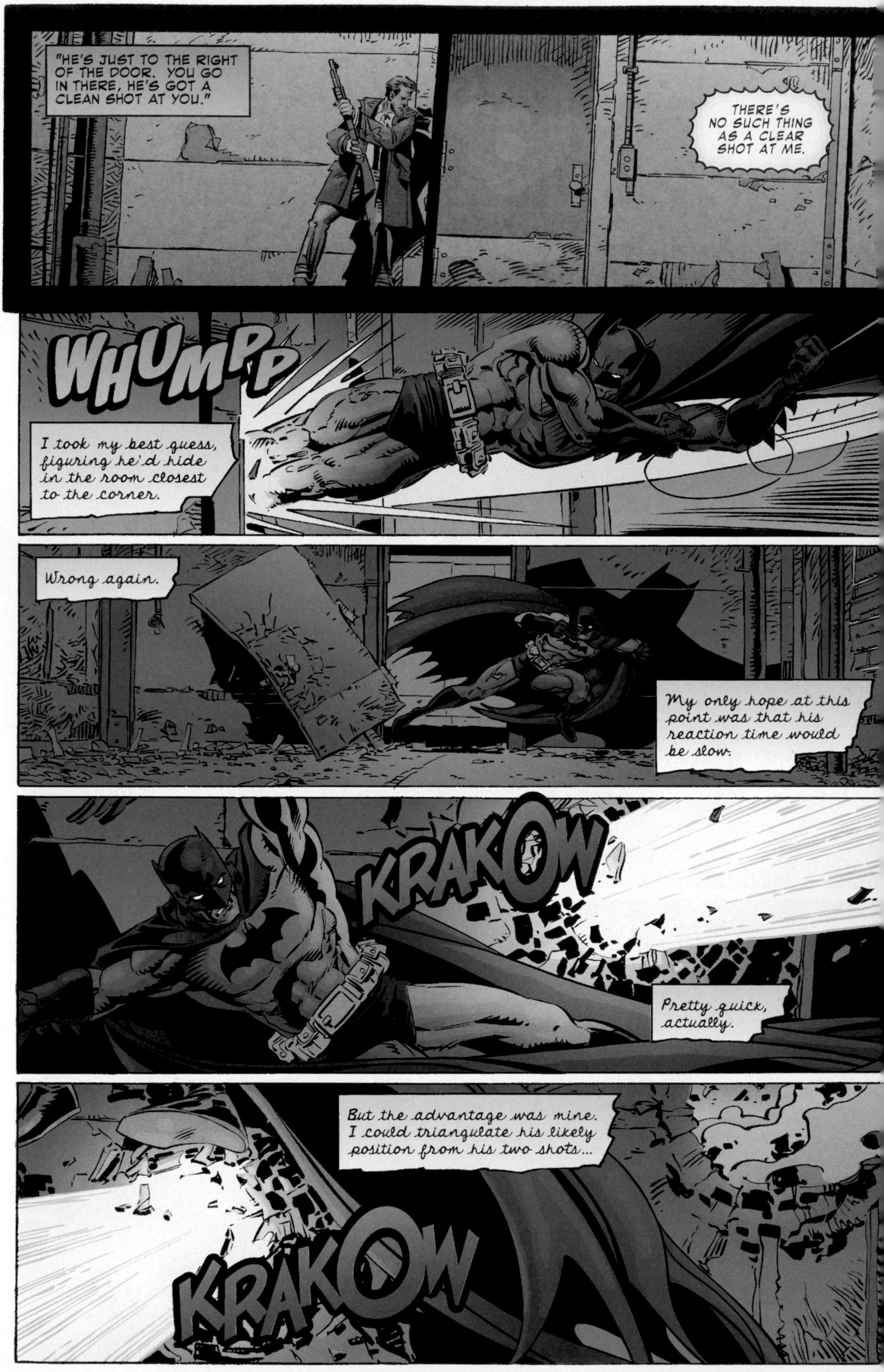
"HE'S JUST TO THE RIGHT OF THE DOOR. YOU GO IN THERE, HE'S GOT A CLEAN SHOT AT YOU."
THERE'S NO SUCH THING AS A CLEAR SHOT AT ME.
WHUMPP
I took my best guess, figuring he'd hide in the room closest to the corner.
Wrong again.
My only hope at this point was that his reaction time would be slow.
KRAKOW
Pretty quick, actually.
But the advantage was mine. I could triangulate his likely position from his two shots...
KRAKOW

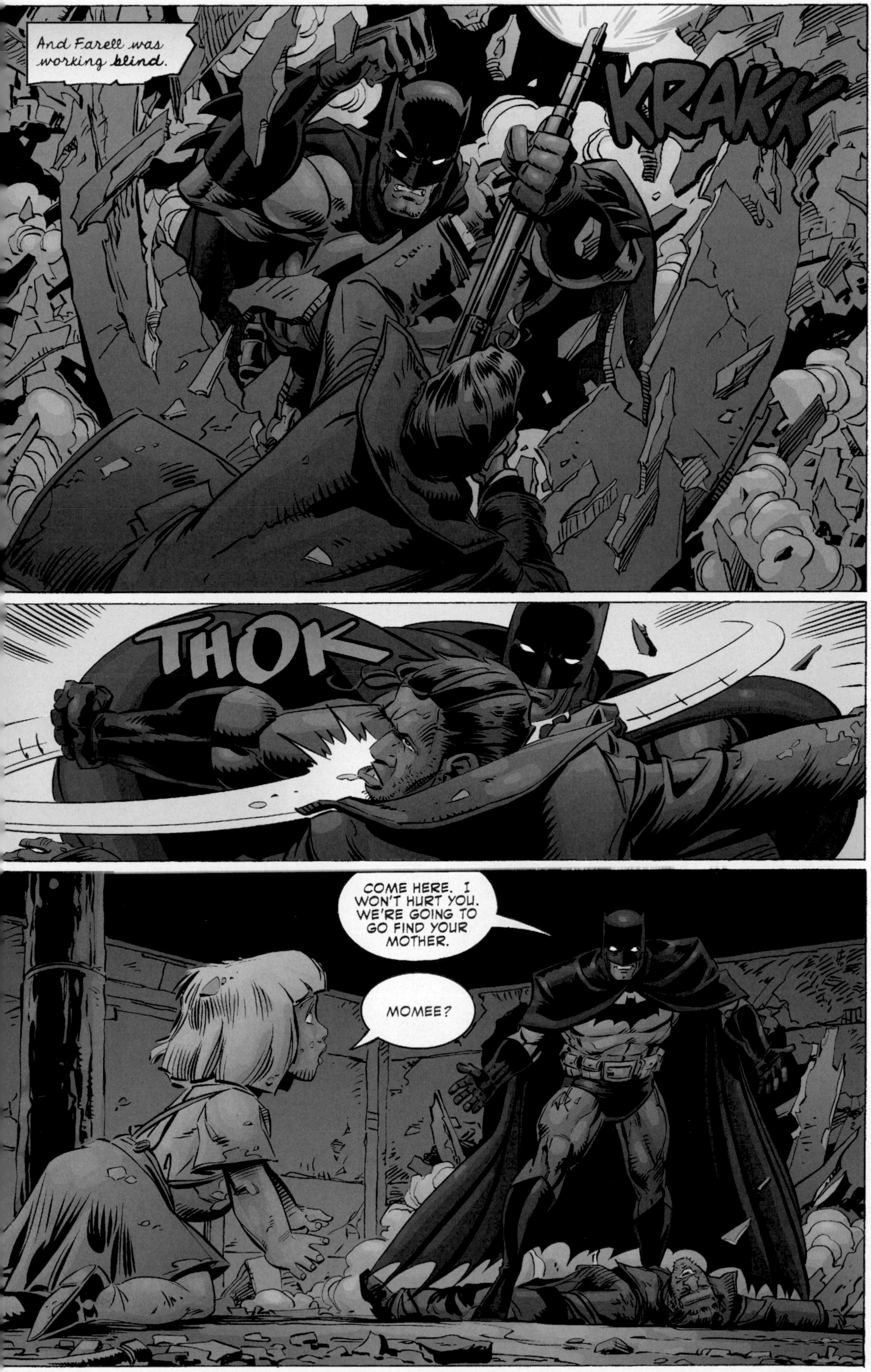
And Farell was working blind.
KRAKK
THOK
COME HERE. I WON'T HURT YOU. WE'RE GOING TO GO FIND YOUR MOTHER.
MOMEE?

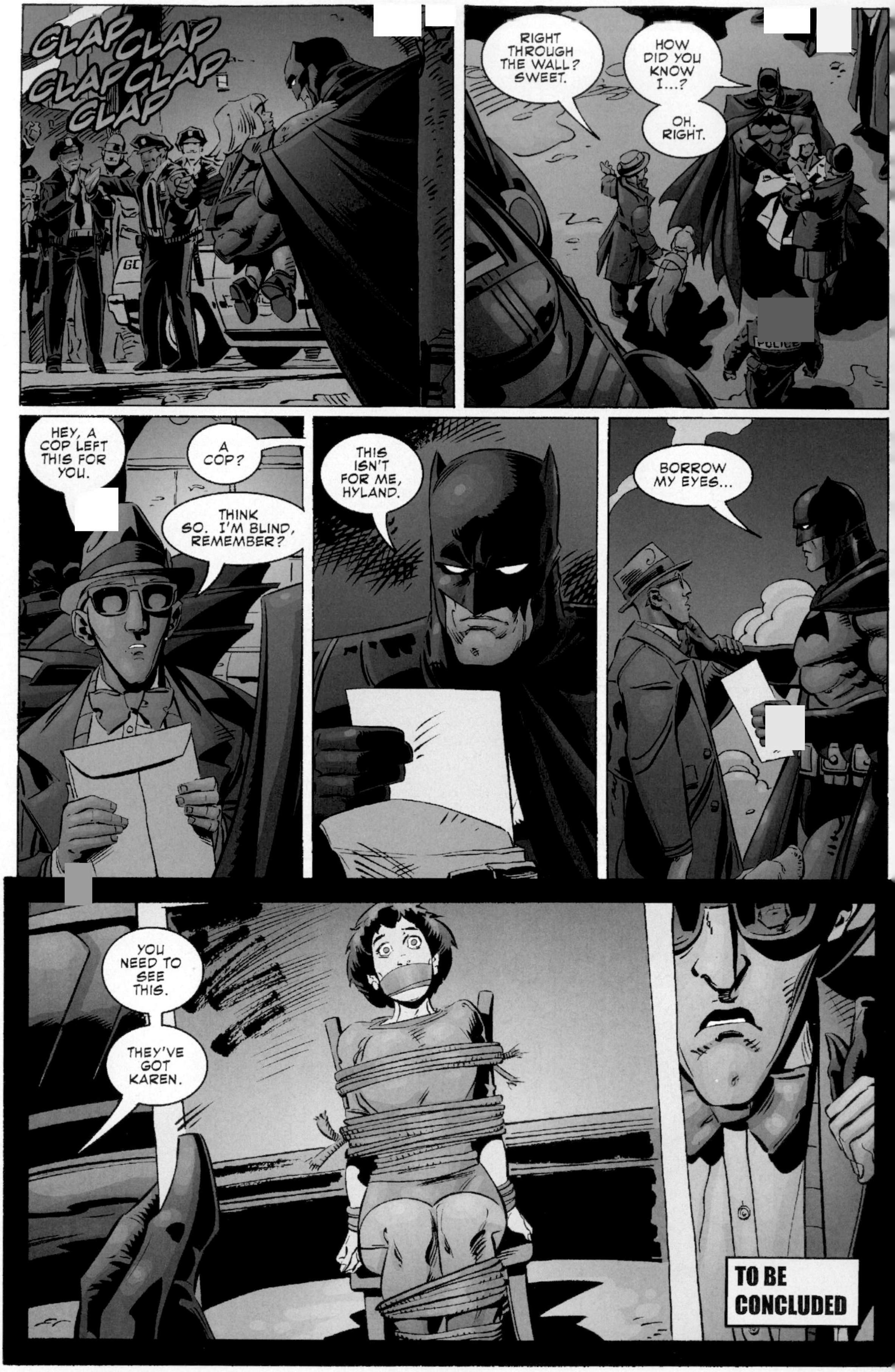
CLAP CLAP CLAP CLAP CLAP
RIGHT THROUGH THE WALL? SWEET.
HOW DID YOU KNOW I...?
OH. RIGHT.
HEY, A COP LEFT THIS FOR YOU.
A COP?
THINK SO. I'M BLIND, REMEMBER?
THIS ISN'T FOR ME, HYLAND.
BORROW MY EYES...
YOU NEED TO SEE THIS.
THEY'VE GOT KAREN.
TO BE CONCLUDED

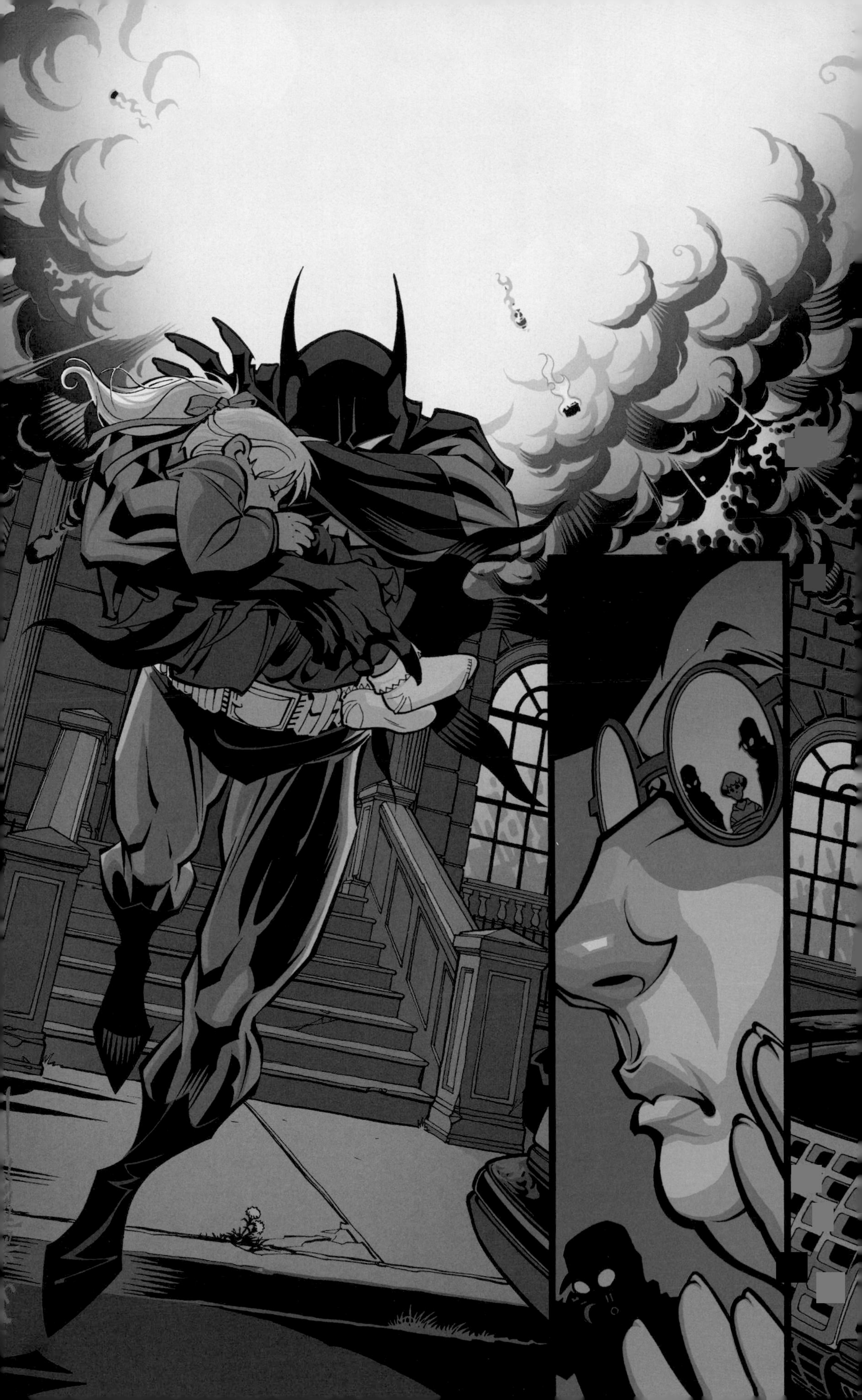

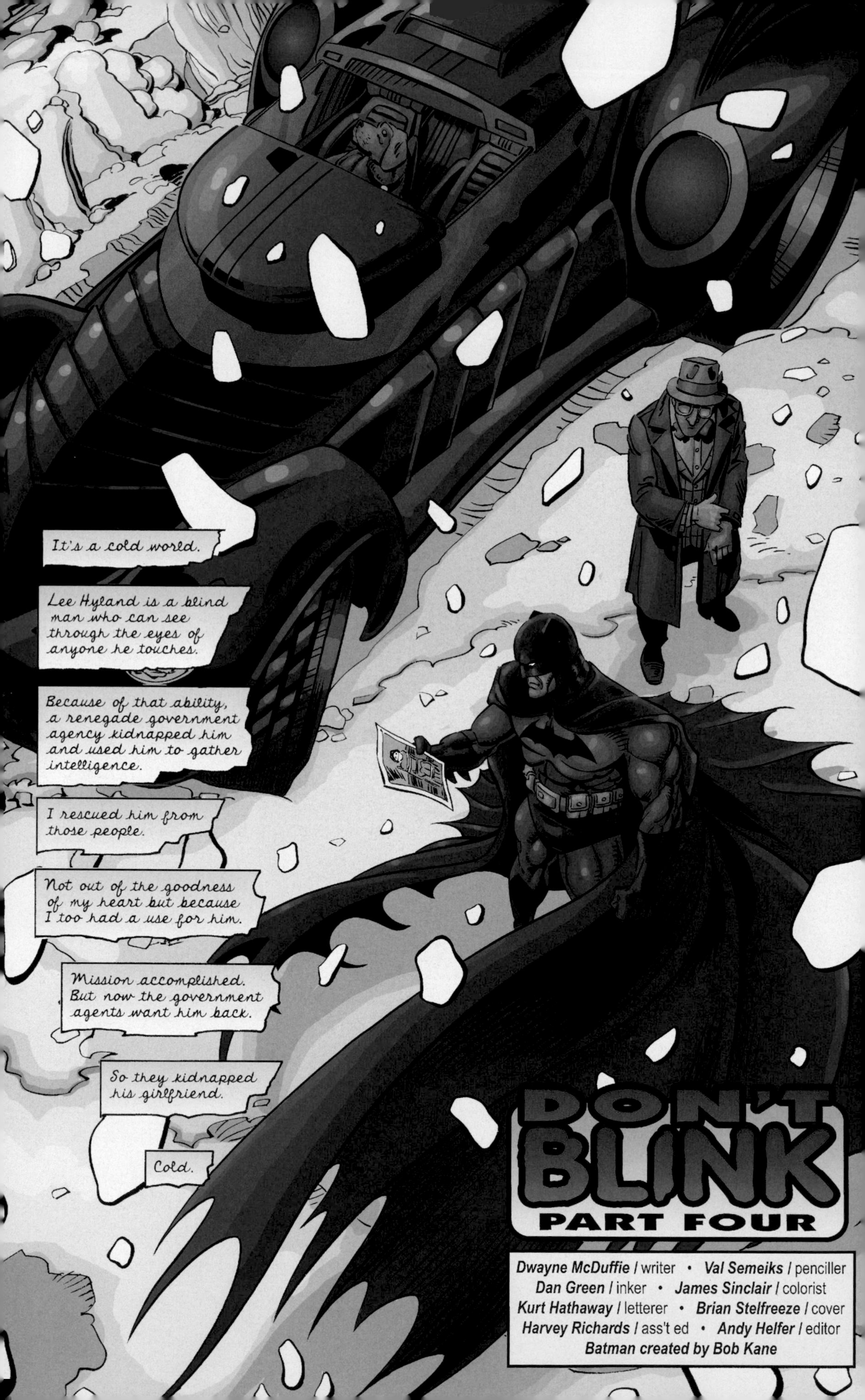

It's a cold world.
Lee Hyland is a blind man who can see through the eyes of anyone he touches.
Because of that ability, a renegade government agency kidnapped him and used him to gather intelligence.
I rescued him from those people.
Not out of the goodness of my heart but because I too had a use for him.
Mission accomplished. But now the government agents want him back.
So they kidnapped his girlfriend.
Cold.
DON'T BLINK
PART FOUR
Dwayne McDuffie / writer • Val Semeiks / penciller
Dan Green / inker • James Sinclair / colorist
Kurt Hathaway / letterer • Brian Stelfreeze / cover
Harvey Richards / ass't ed • Andy Helfer / editor
Batman created by Bob Kane

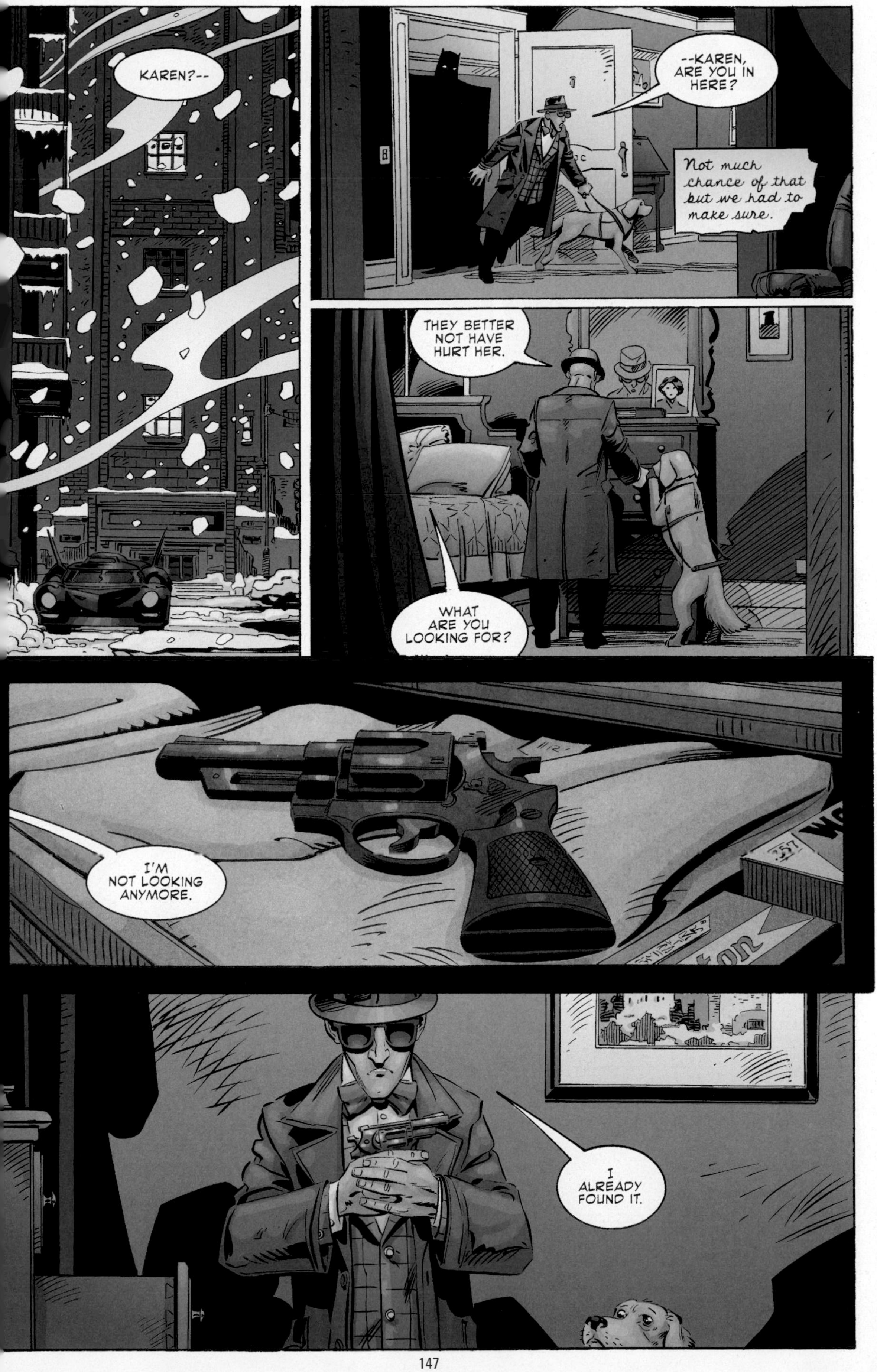
KAREN?--
--KAREN, ARE YOU IN HERE?
Not much chance of that but we had to make sure.
THEY BETTER NOT HAVE HURT HER.
WHAT ARE YOU LOOKING FOR?
I'M NOT LOOKING ANYMORE.
I ALREADY FOUND IT.

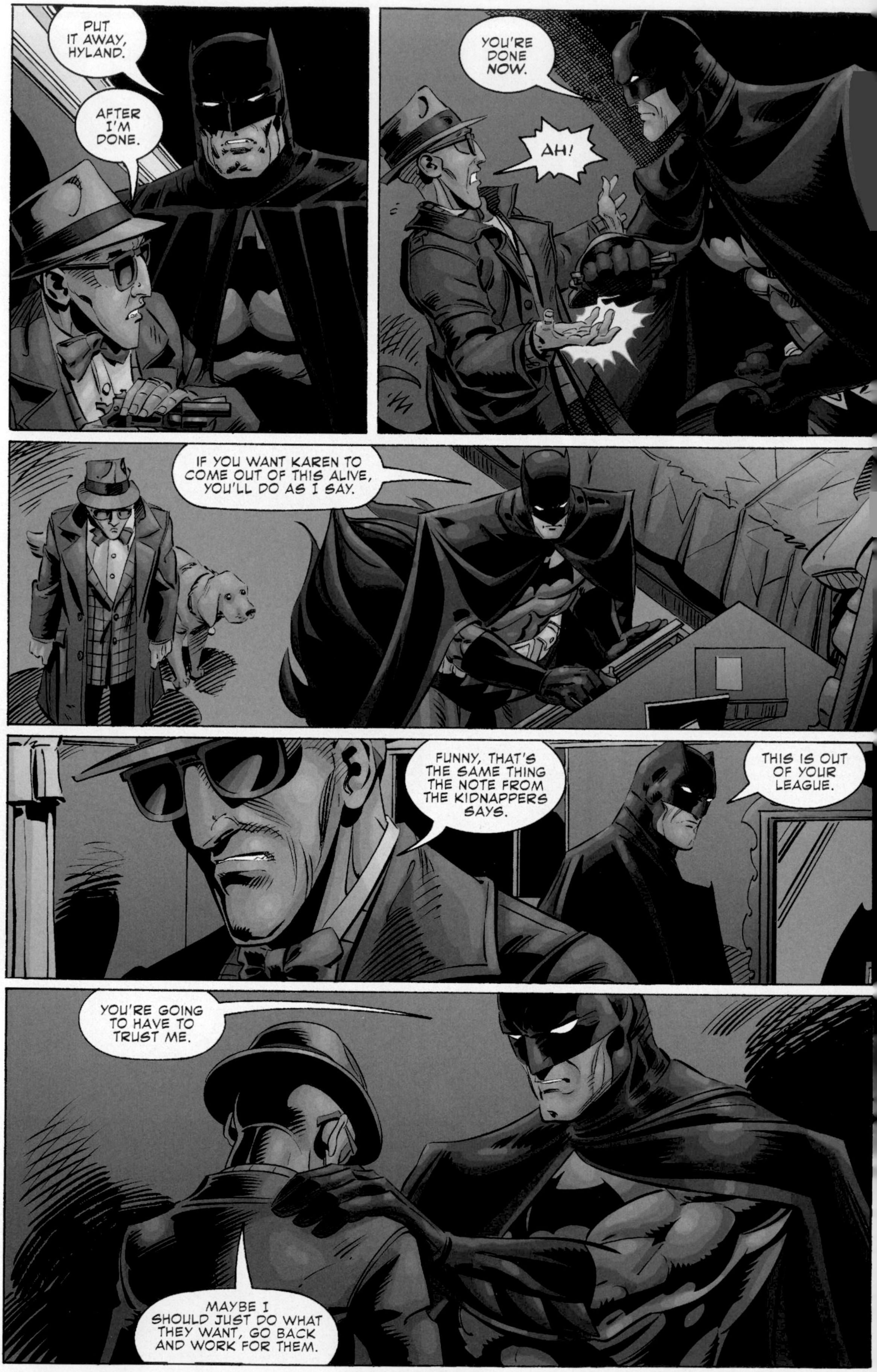
PUT IT AWAY, HYLAND.
AFTER I'M DONE.
YOU'RE DONE NOW.
AH!
IF YOU WANT KAREN TO COME OUT OF THIS ALIVE, YOU'LL DO AS I SAY.
FUNNY, THAT'S THE SAME THING THE NOTE FROM THE KIDNAPPERS SAYS.
THIS IS OUT OF YOUR LEAGUE.
YOU'RE GOING TO HAVE TO TRUST ME.
MAYBE I SHOULD JUST DO WHAT THEY WANT, GO BACK AND WORK FOR THEM.

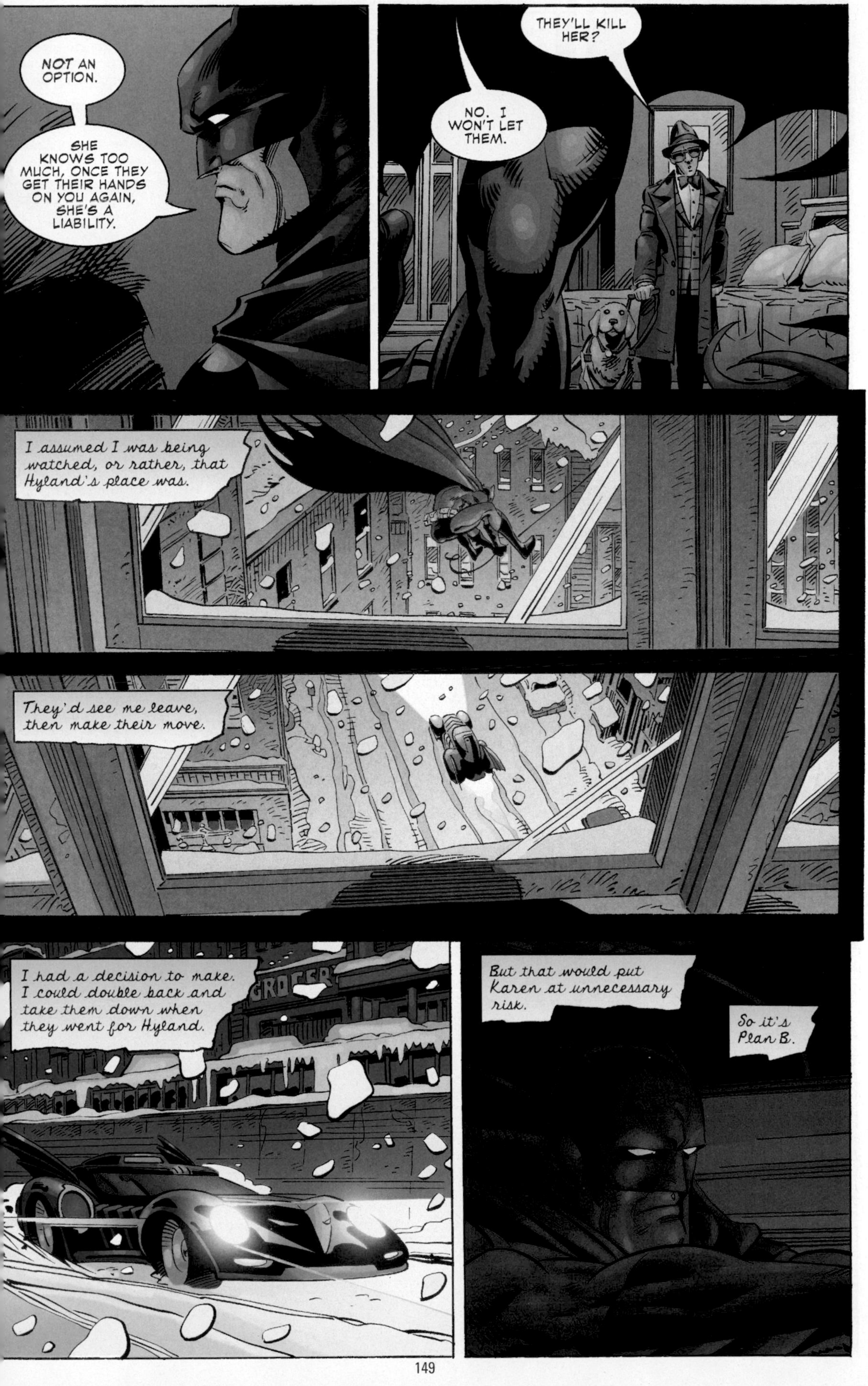
NOT AN OPTION.
SHE KNOWS TOO MUCH, ONCE THEY GET THEIR HANDS ON YOU AGAIN, SHE'S A LIABILITY.
THEY'LL KILL HER?
NO. I WON'T LET THEM.
I assumed I was being watched, or rather, that Hyland's place was.
They'd see me leave, then make their move.
I had a decision to make. I could double back and take them down when they went for Hyland.
GROCER
But that would put Karen at unnecessary risk.
So it's Plan B.

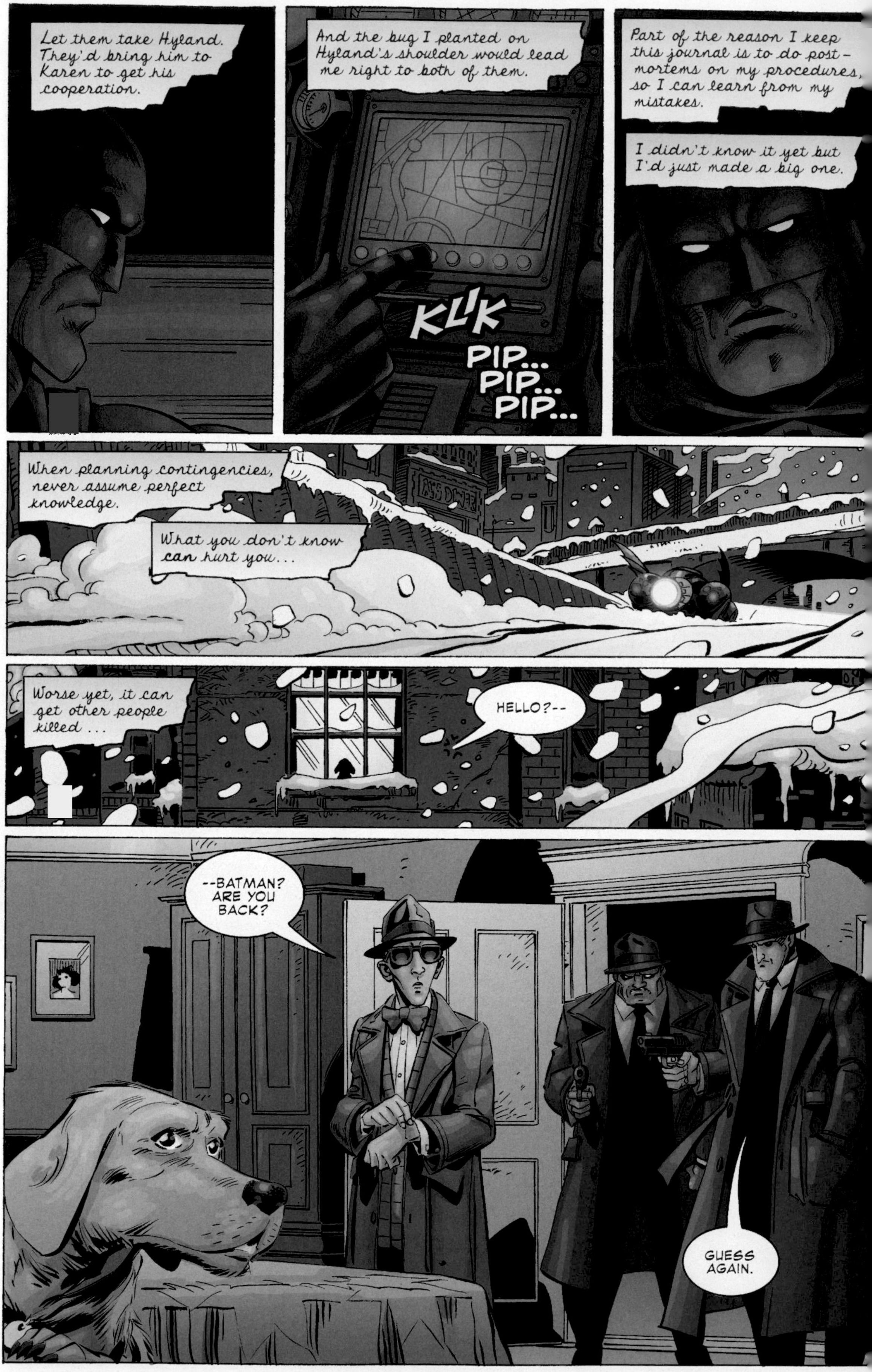
Let them take Hyland. They'd bring him to Karen to get his cooperation.
And the bug I planted on Hyland's shoulder would lead me right to both of them.
KLIK
PIP... PIP... PIP...
Part of the reason I keep this journal is to do post-mortems on my procedures, so I can learn from my mistakes.
I didn't know it yet but I'd just made a big one.
When planning contingencies, never assume perfect knowledge.
What you don't know can hurt you...
Worse yet, it can get other people killed...
HELLO?--
--BATMAN? ARE YOU BACK?
GUESS AGAIN.

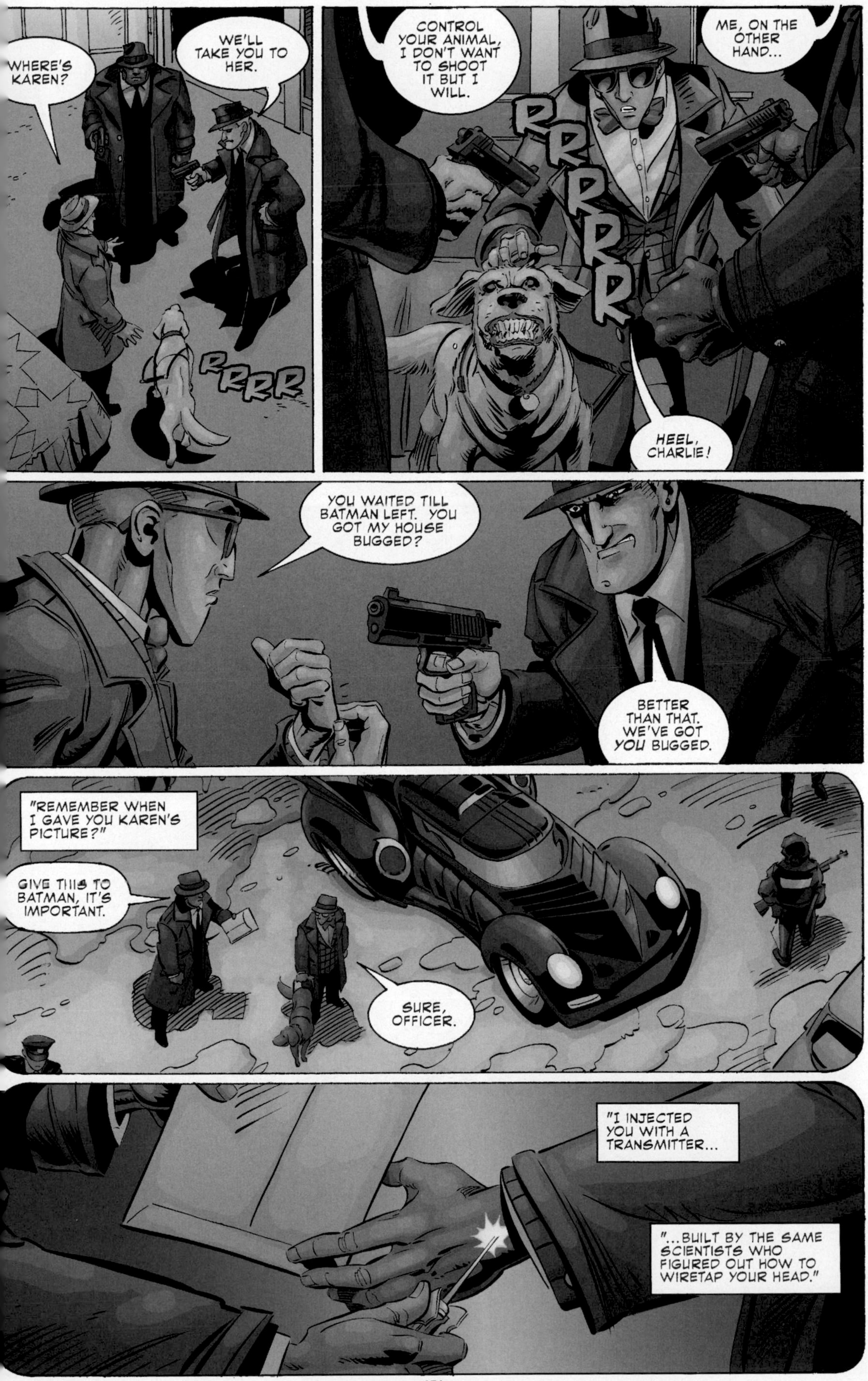

WHERE'S KAREN?
WE'LL TAKE YOU TO HER.
RRRR
CONTROL YOUR ANIMAL, I DON'T WANT TO SHOOT IT BUT I WILL.
ME, ON THE OTHER HAND...
RRRRRR
HEEL, CHARLIE!
YOU WAITED TILL BATMAN LEFT. YOU GOT MY HOUSE BUGGED?
BETTER THAN THAT. WE'VE GOT YOU BUGGED.
"REMEMBER WHEN I GAVE YOU KAREN'S PICTURE?"
GIVE THIS TO BATMAN, IT'S IMPORTANT.
SURE, OFFICER.
"I INJECTED YOU WITH A TRANSMITTER...
"...BUILT BY THE SAME SCIENTISTS WHO FIGURED OUT HOW TO WIRETAP YOUR HEAD."

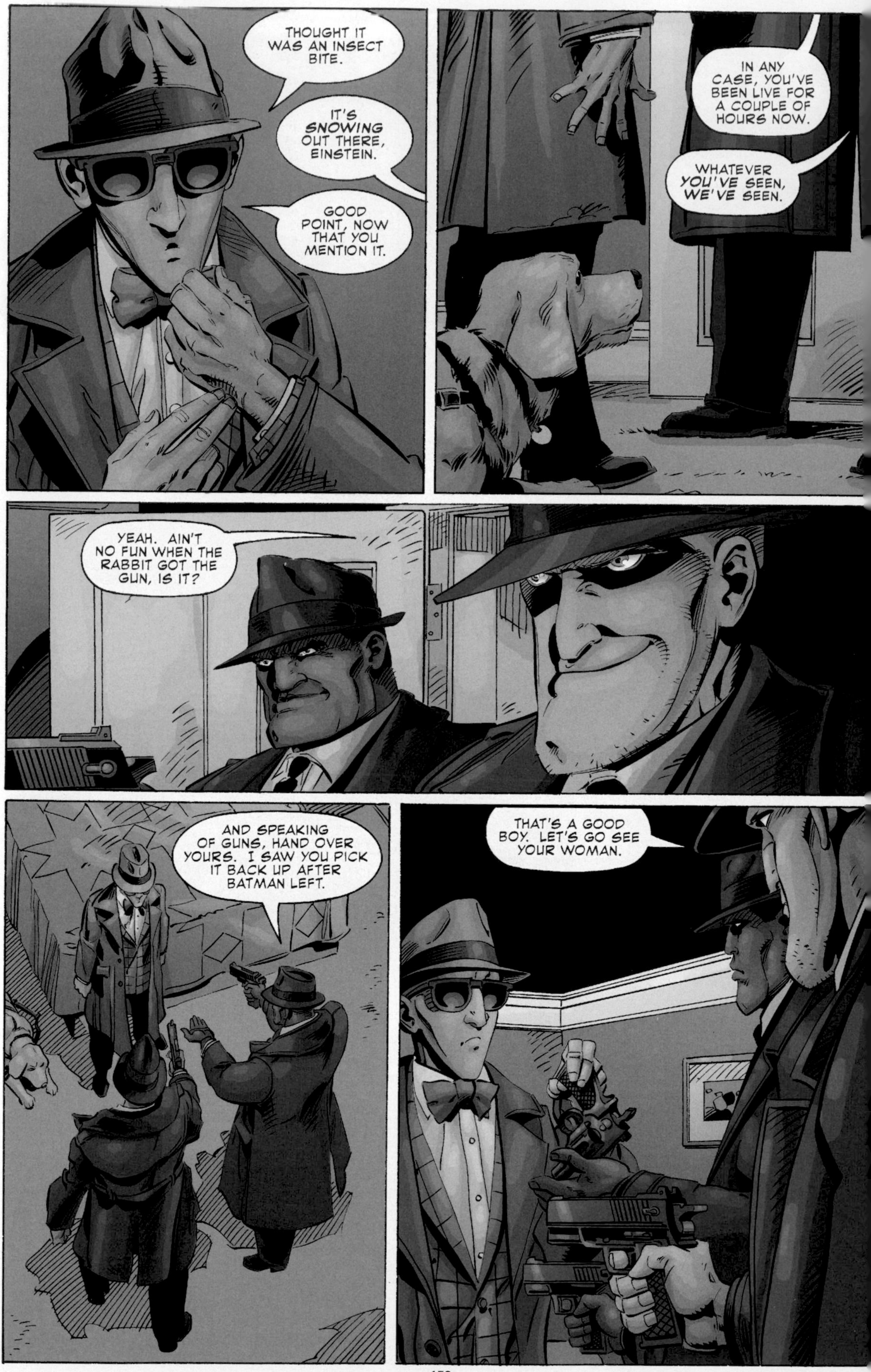
THOUGHT IT WAS AN INSECT BITE.
IT'S SNOWING OUT THERE, EINSTEIN.
GOOD POINT, NOW THAT YOU MENTION IT.
IN ANY CASE, YOU'VE BEEN LIVE FOR A COUPLE OF HOURS NOW.
WHATEVER YOU'VE SEEN, WE'VE SEEN.
YEAH. AIN'T NO FUN WHEN THE RABBIT GOT THE GUN, IS IT?
AND SPEAKING OF GUNS, HAND OVER YOURS. I SAW YOU PICK IT BACK UP AFTER BATMAN LEFT.
THAT'S A GOOD BOY. LET'S GO SEE YOUR WOMAN.

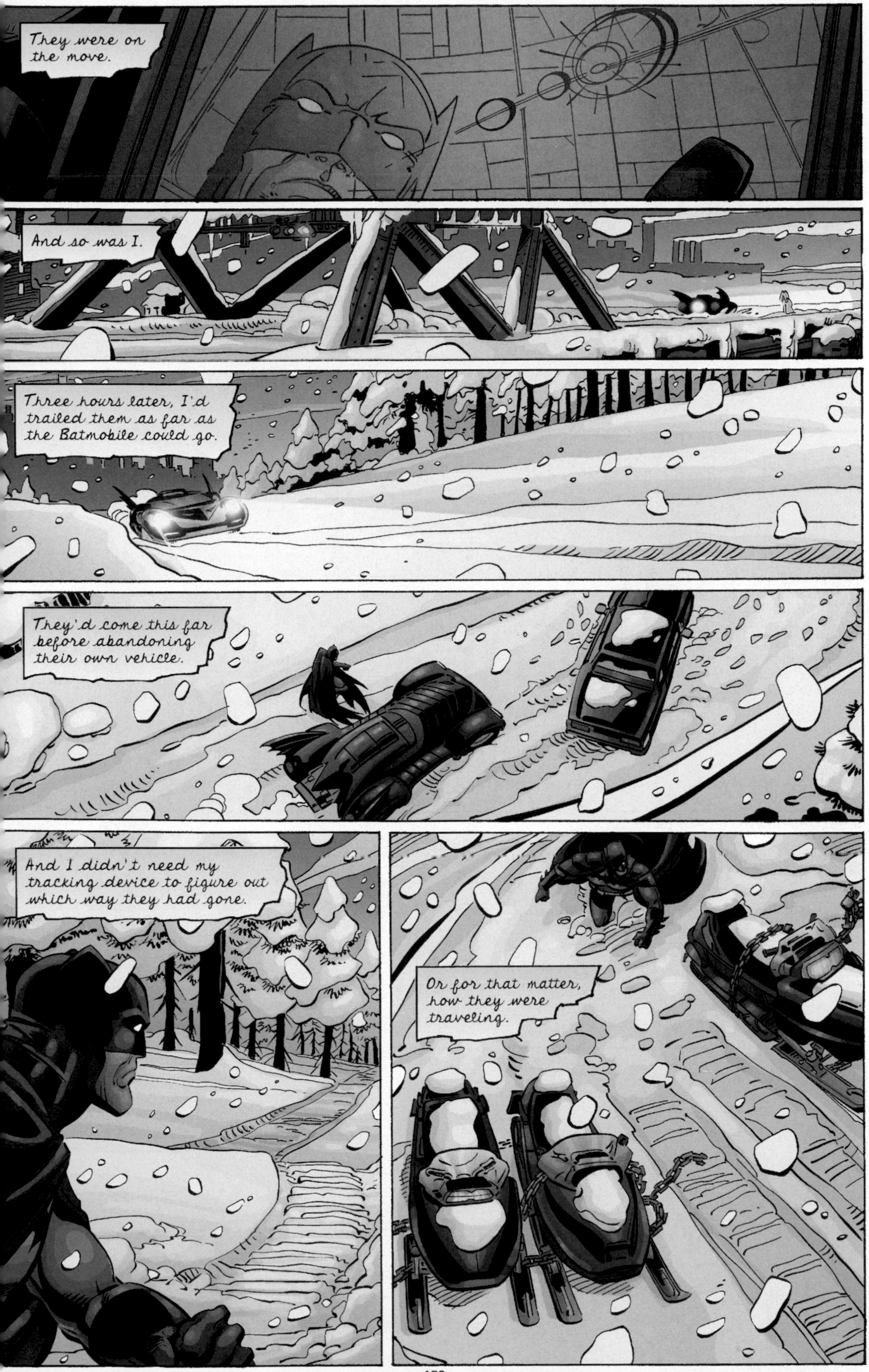
They were on the move.
And so was I.
Three hours later, I'd trailed them as far as the Batmobile could go.
They'd come this far before abandoning their own vehicle.
And I didn't need my tracking device to figure out which way they had gone.
Or for that matter, how they were traveling.

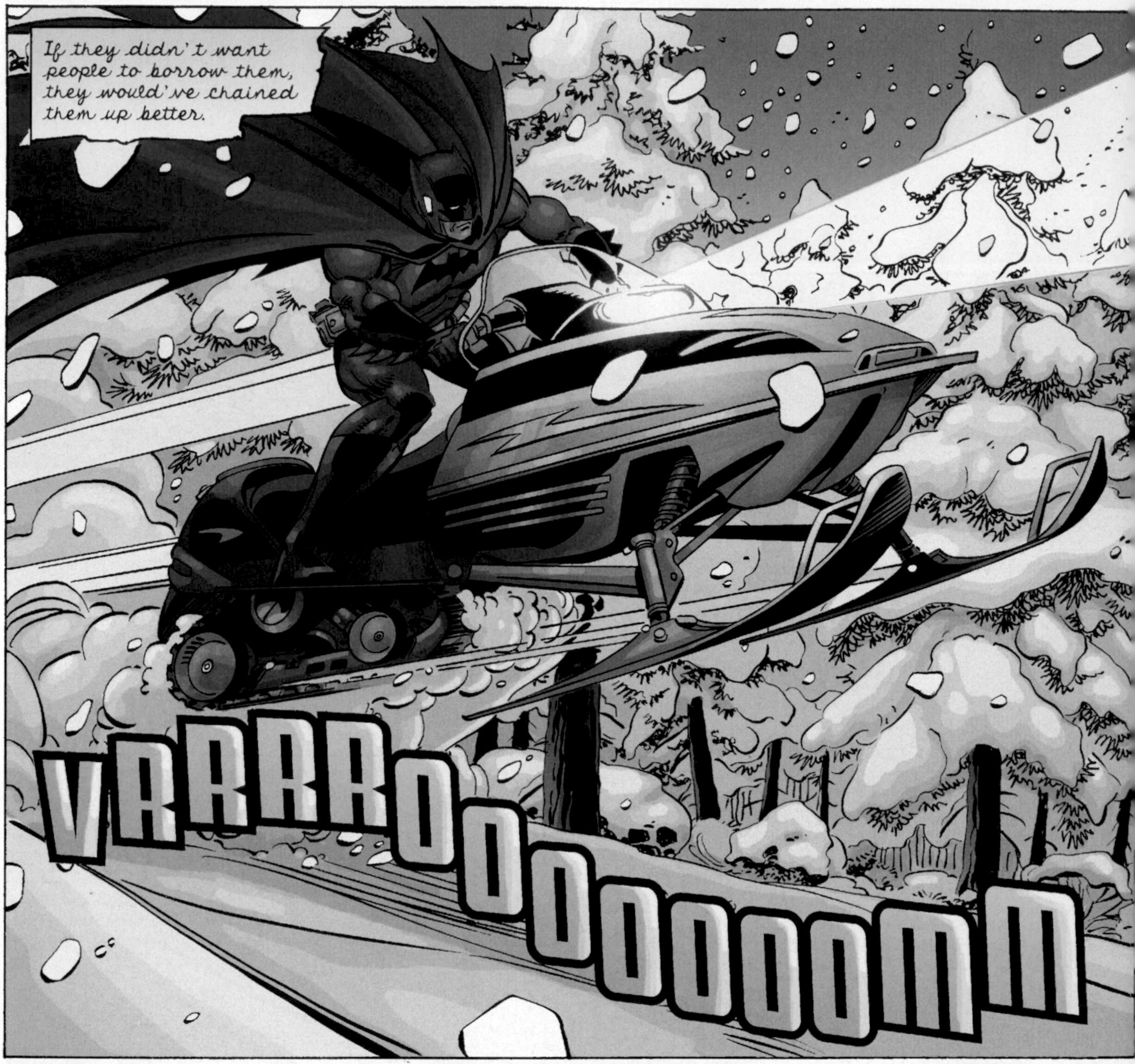
If they didn't want people to borrow them, they would've chained them up better.
VRRRROOOOOOOOMM

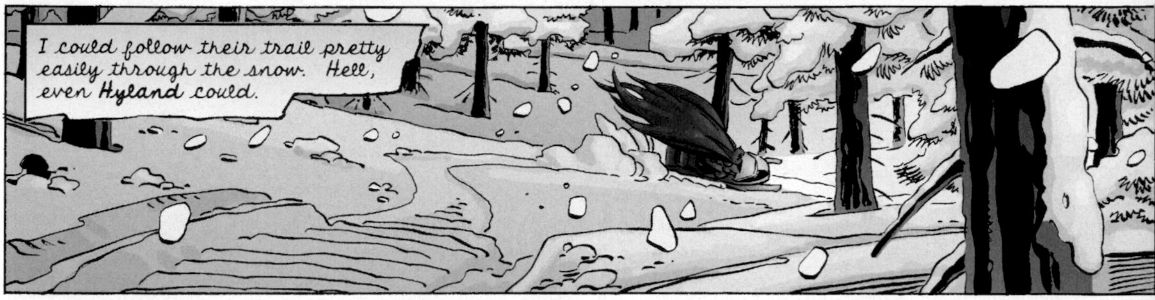
I could follow their trail pretty easily through the snow. Hell, even Hyland could.

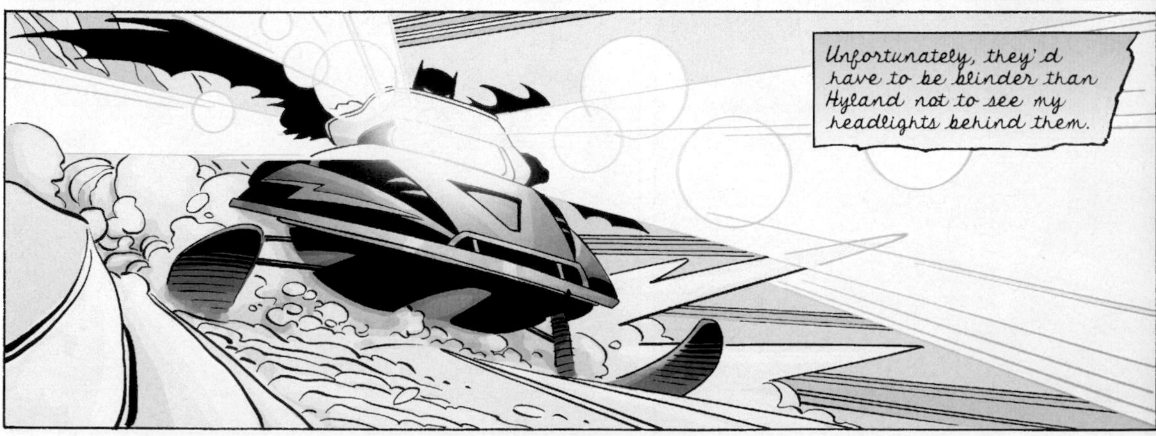
Unfortunately, they'd have to be blinder than Hyland not to see my headlights behind them.

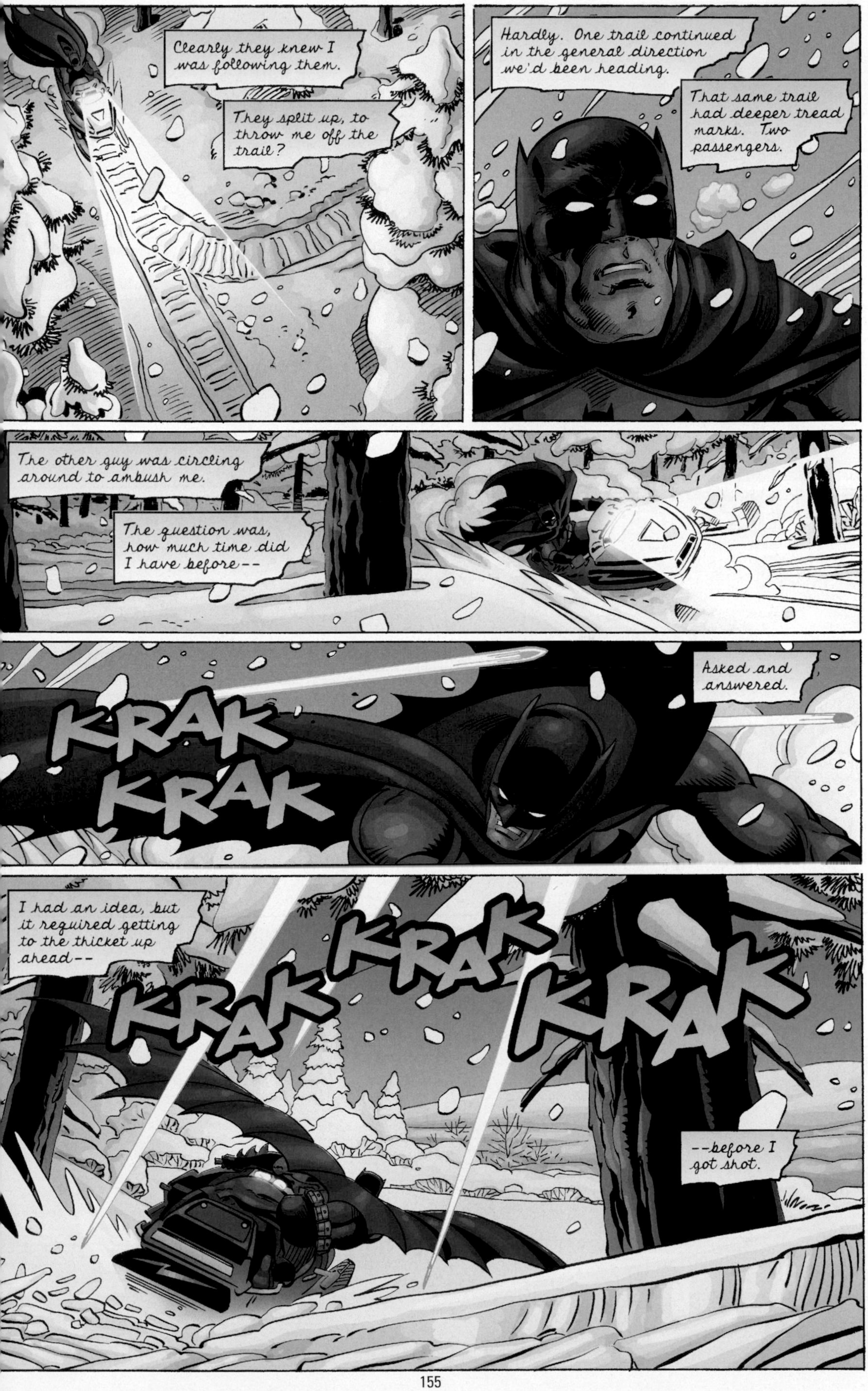
Clearly they knew I was following them.
They split up, to throw me off the trail?
Hardly. One trail continued in the general direction we'd been heading.
That same trail had deeper tread marks. Two passengers.
The other guy was circling around to ambush me.
The question was, how much time did I have before--
KRAK KRAK
Asked and answered.
I had an idea, but it required getting to the thicket up ahead--
KRAK KRAK KRAK
--before I got shot.

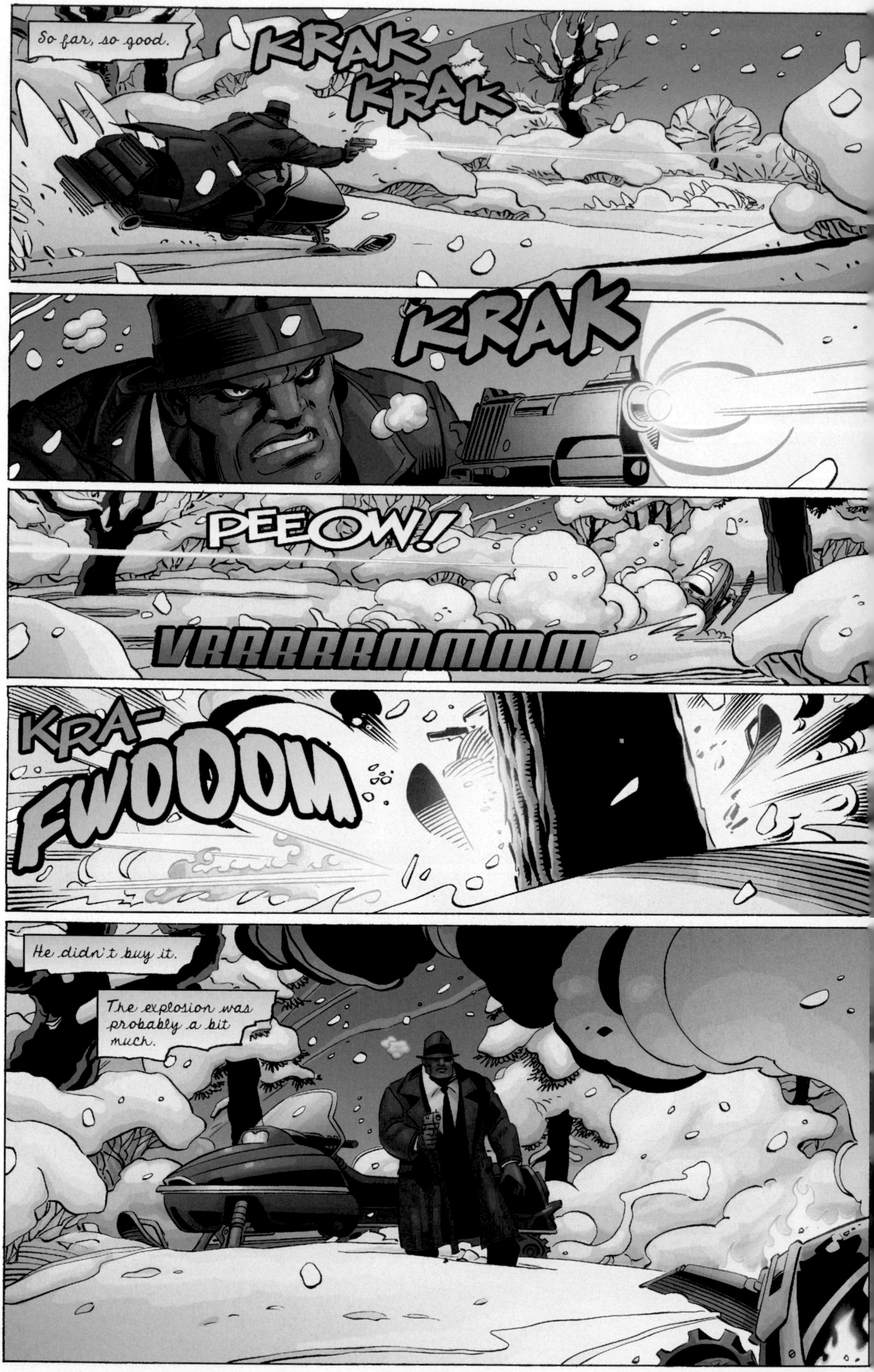
So far, so good.
KRAK
KRAK
KRAK
PEEOW!
VRRRRRMMMMM
KRA-
FWOOOM
He didn't buy it.
The explosion was probably a bit much.

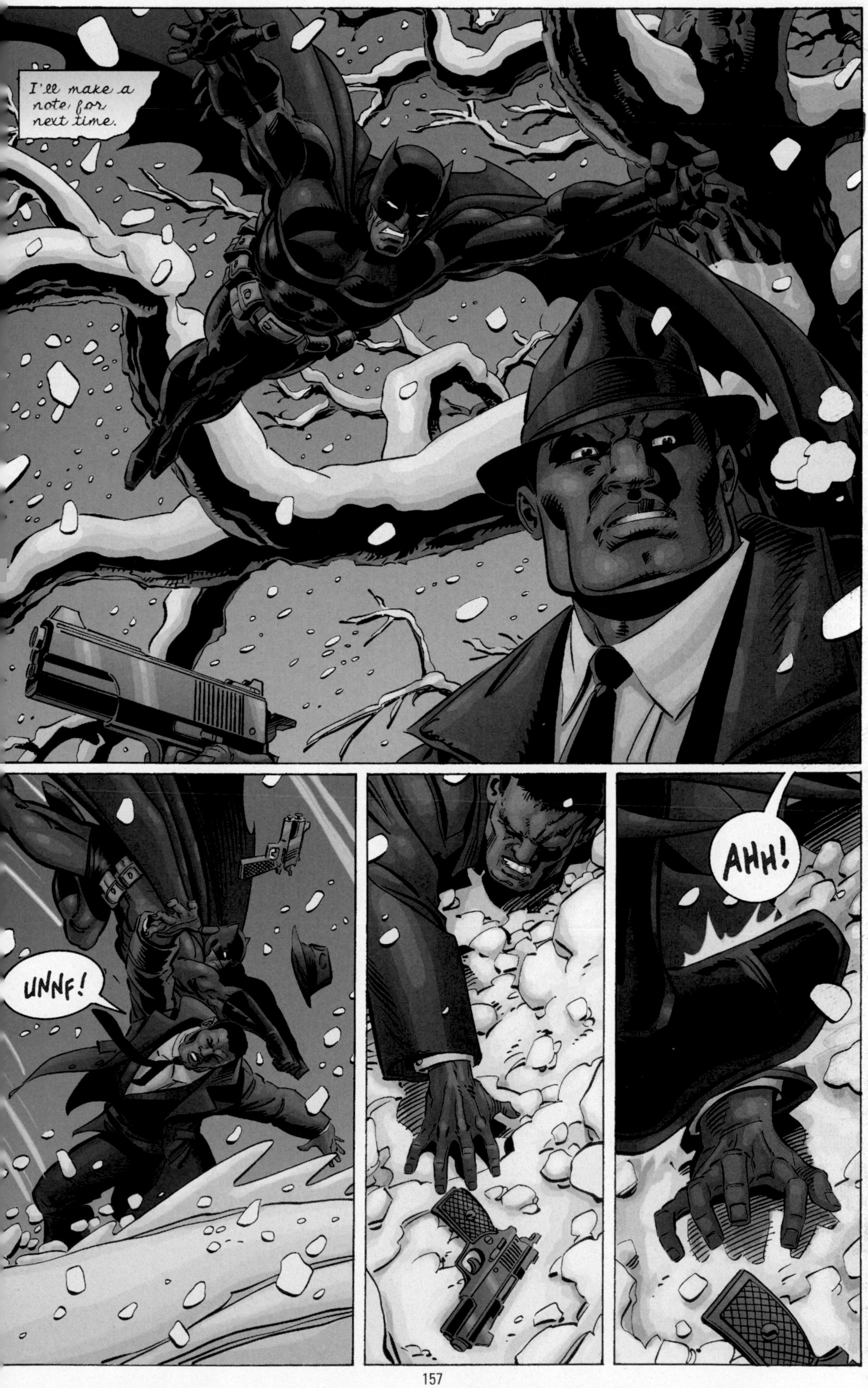
I'll make a note for next time.
UNNF!
AHH!

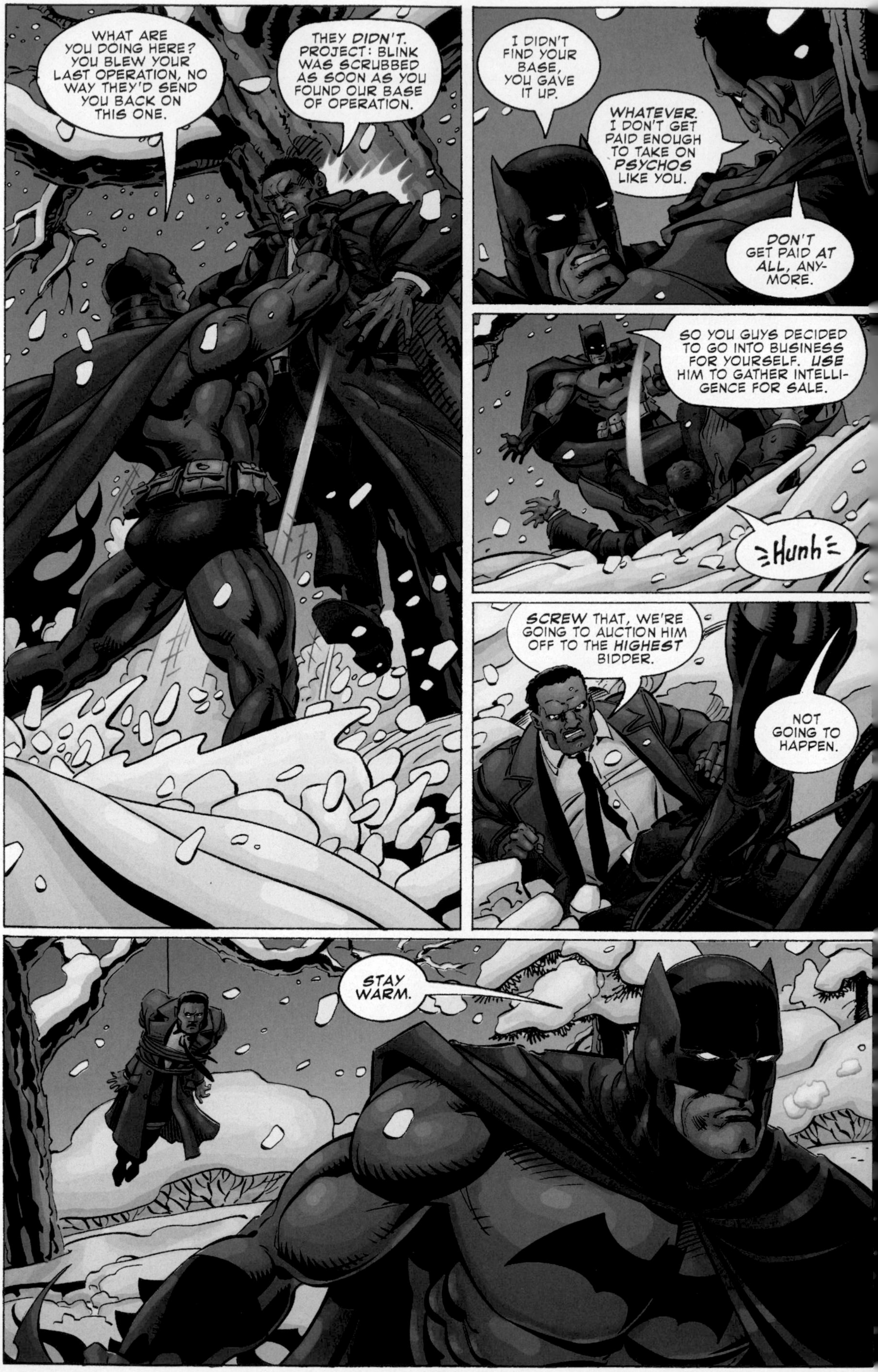
WHAT ARE YOU DOING HERE? YOU BLEW YOUR LAST OPERATION, NO WAY THEY'D SEND YOU BACK ON THIS ONE.
THEY DIDN'T. PROJECT: BLINK WAS SCRUBBED AS SOON AS YOU FOUND OUR BASE OF OPERATION.
I DIDN'T FIND YOUR BASE, YOU GAVE IT UP.
WHATEVER. I DON'T GET PAID ENOUGH TO TAKE ON PSYCHOS LIKE YOU.
DON'T GET PAID AT ALL, ANY-MORE.
SO YOU GUYS DECIDED TO GO INTO BUSINESS FOR YOURSELF. USE HIM TO GATHER INTELLI-GENCE FOR SALE.
Hunh
SCREW THAT, WE'RE GOING TO AUCTION HIM OFF TO THE HIGHEST BIDDER.
NOT GOING TO HAPPEN.
STAY WARM.

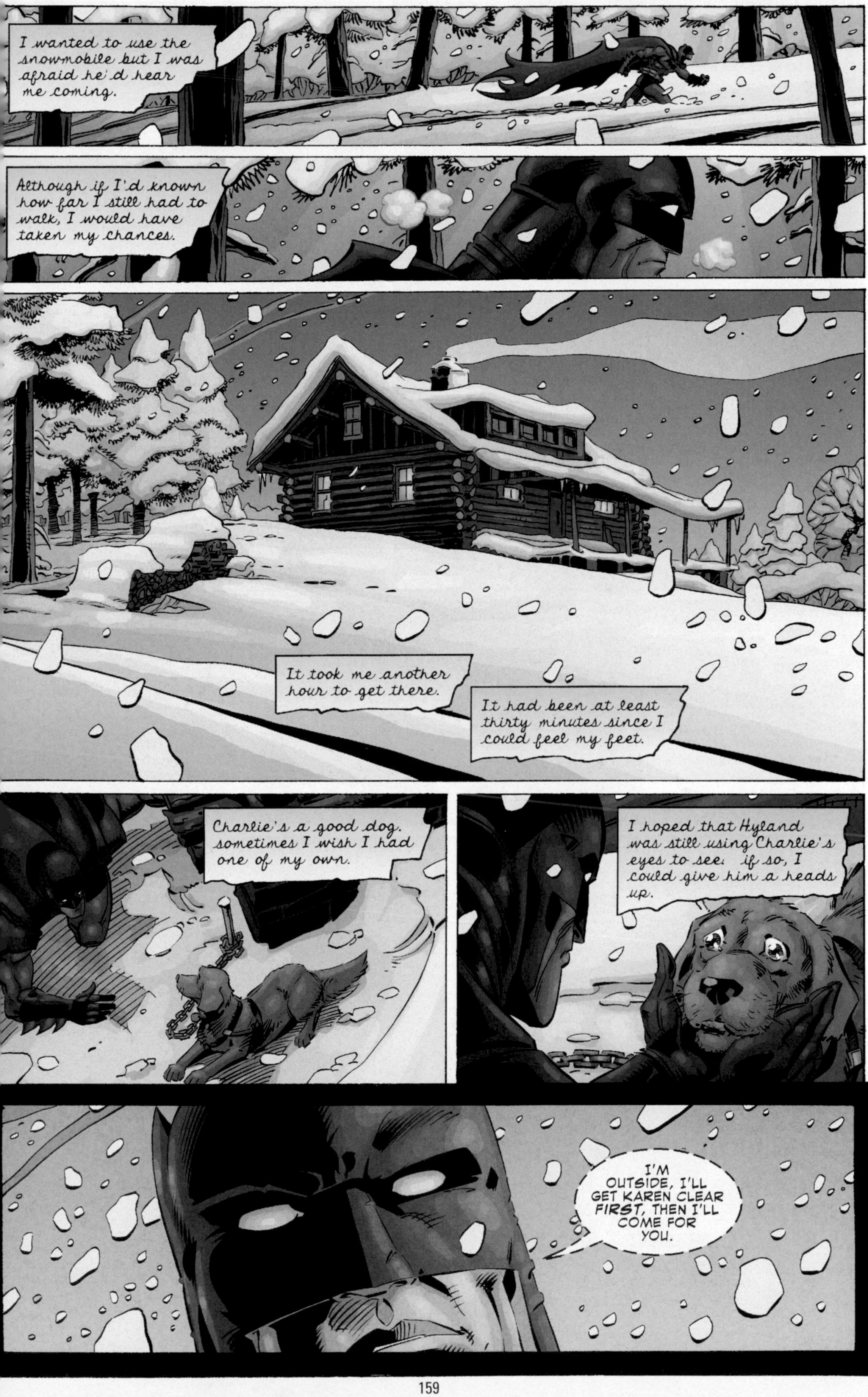
I wanted to use the snowmobile but I was afraid he'd hear me coming.
Although if I'd known how far I still had to walk, I would have taken my chances.
It took me another hour to get there.
It had been at least thirty minutes since I could feel my feet.
Charlie's a good dog. sometimes I wish I had one of my own.
I hoped that Hyland was still using Charlie's eyes to see. if so, I could give him a heads up.
I'M OUTSIDE, I'LL GET KAREN CLEAR FIRST, THEN I'LL COME FOR YOU.

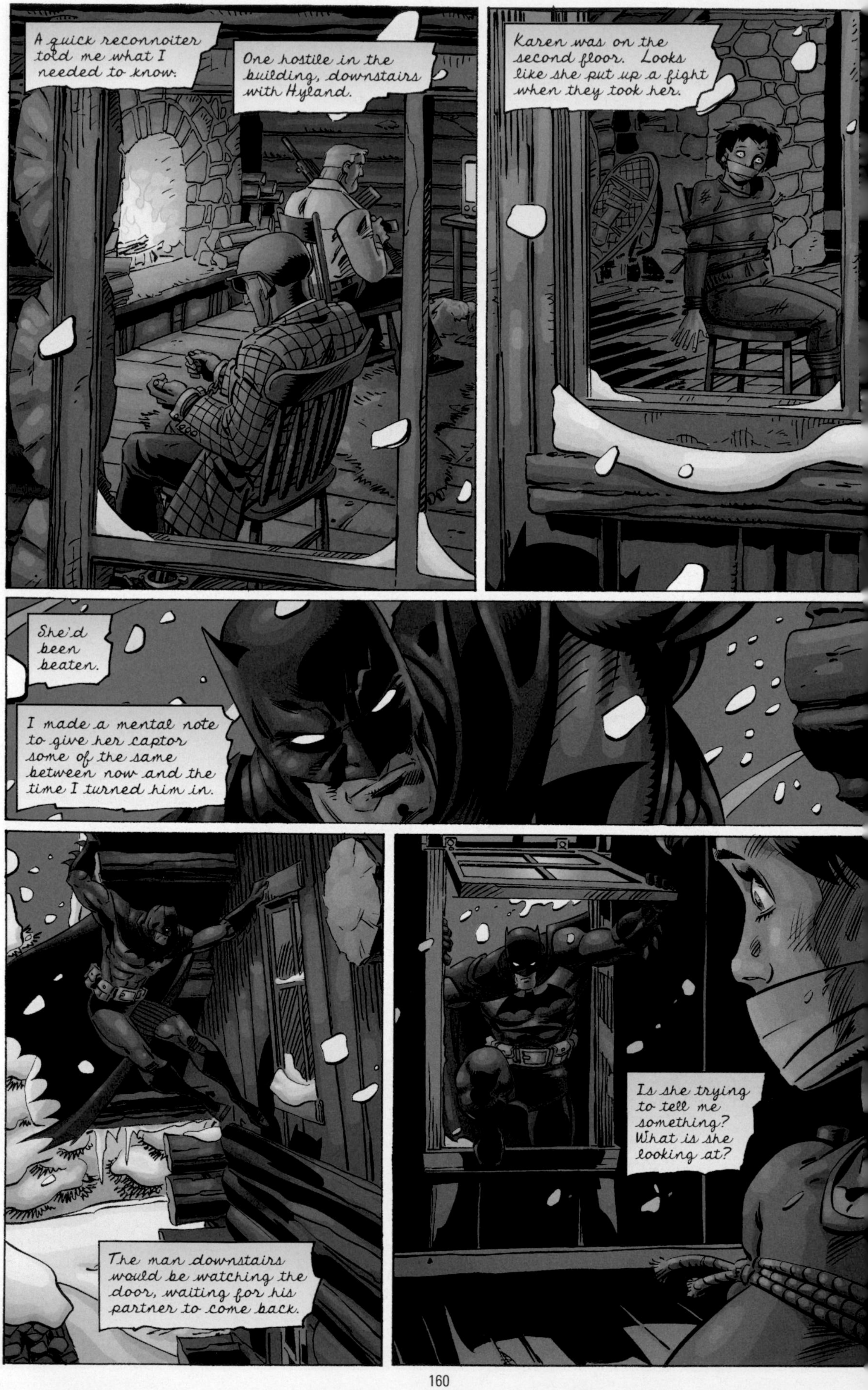
A quick reconnoiter told me what I needed to know.
One hostile in the building, downstairs with Hyland.
Karen was on the second floor. Looks like she put up a fight when they took her.
She'd been beaten.
I made a mental note to give her captor some of the same between now and the time I turned him in.
The man downstairs would be watching the door, waiting for his partner to come back.
Is she trying to tell me something? What is she looking at?

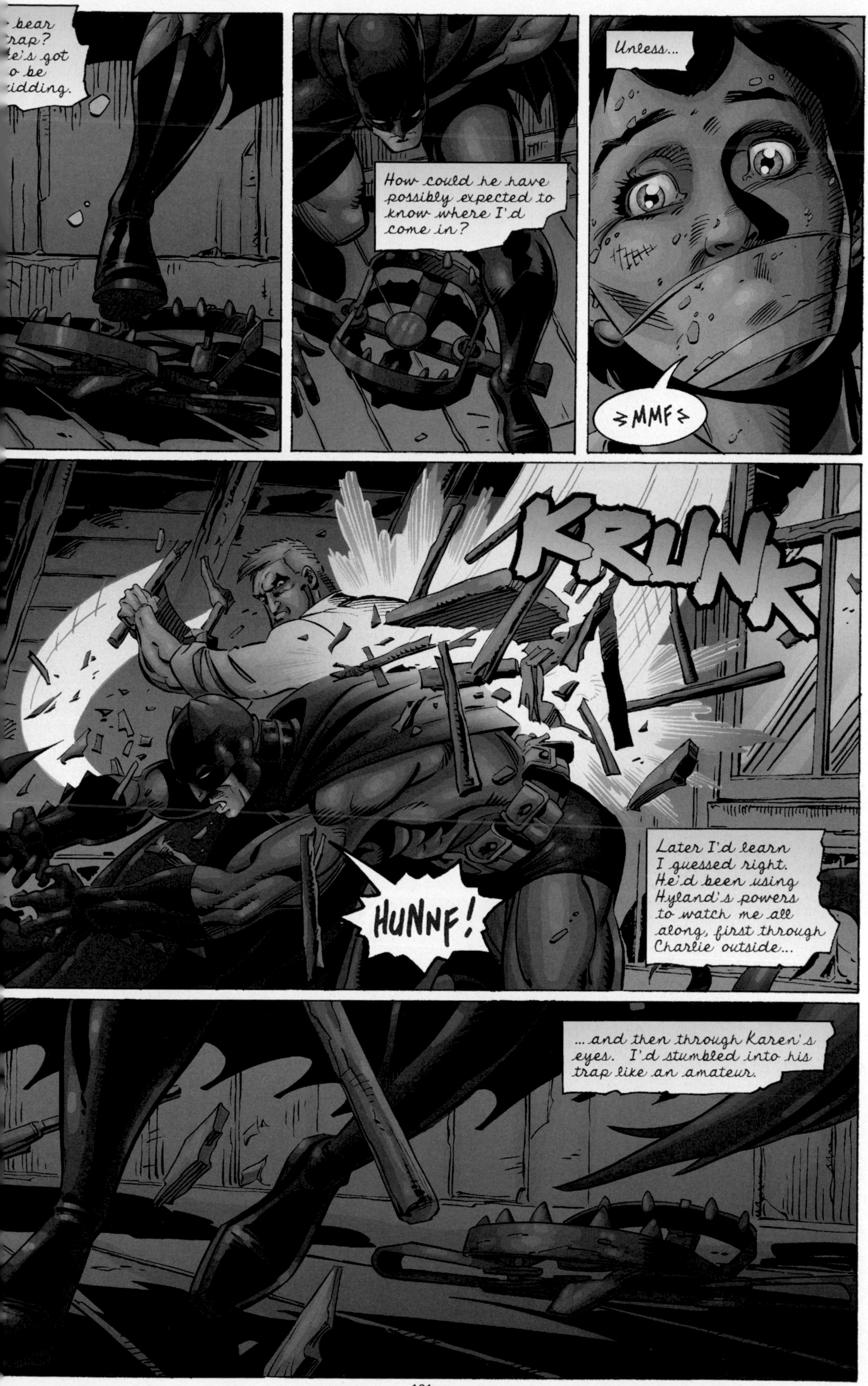
bear
rap?
e's got
o be
idding.
How could he have possibly expected to know where I'd come in?
Unless...
MMF
KRUNK
HUNNF!
Later I'd learn I guessed right. He'd been using Hyland's powers to watch me all along, first through Charlie outside...
...and then through Karen's eyes. I'd stumbled into his trap like an amateur.

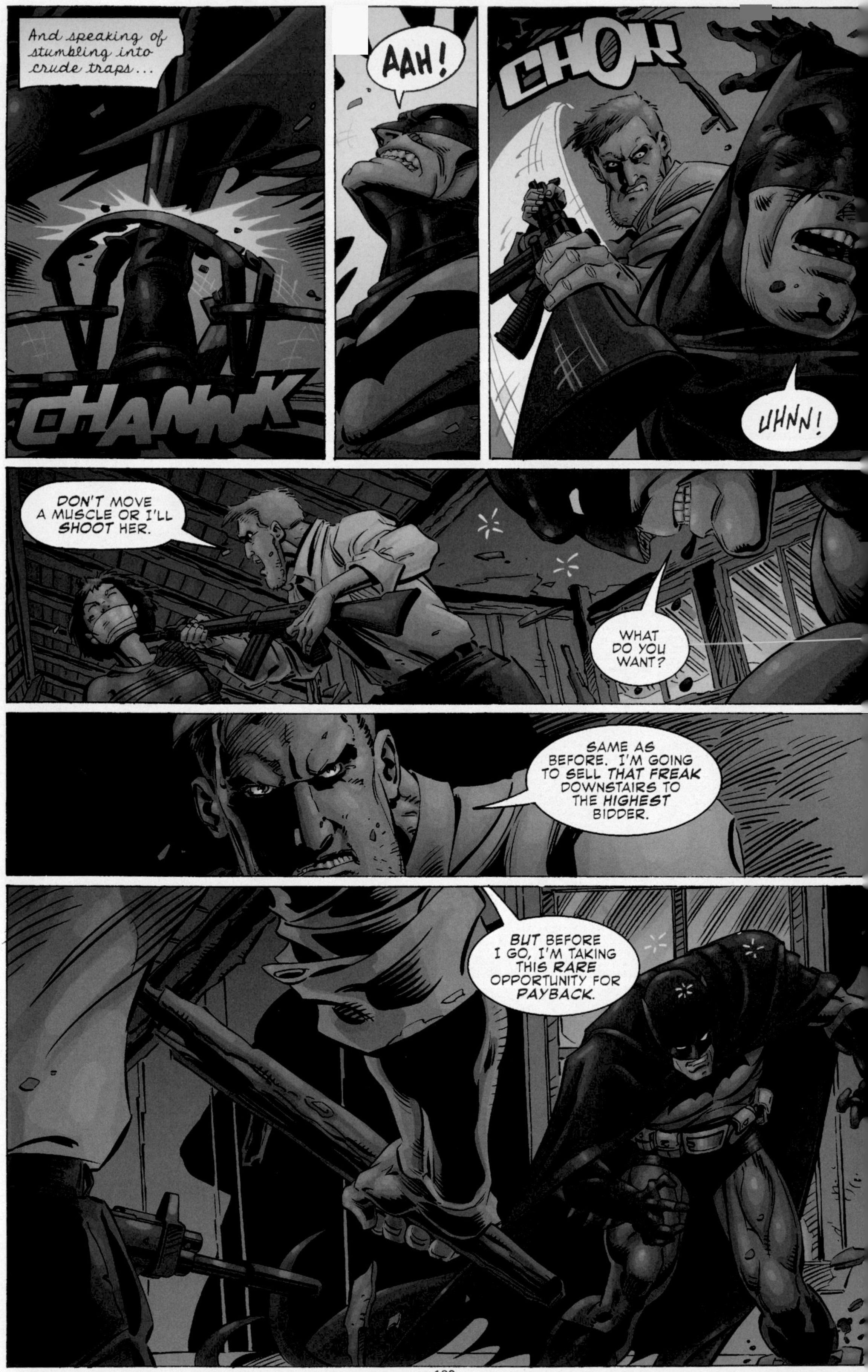

And speaking of stumbling into crude traps...
CHANNK
AAH!
CHOK
UHNN!
DON'T MOVE A MUSCLE OR I'LL SHOOT HER.
WHAT DO YOU WANT?
SAME AS BEFORE. I'M GOING TO SELL THAT FREAK DOWNSTAIRS TO THE HIGHEST BIDDER.
BUT BEFORE I GO, I'M TAKING THIS RARE OPPORTUNITY FOR PAYBACK.

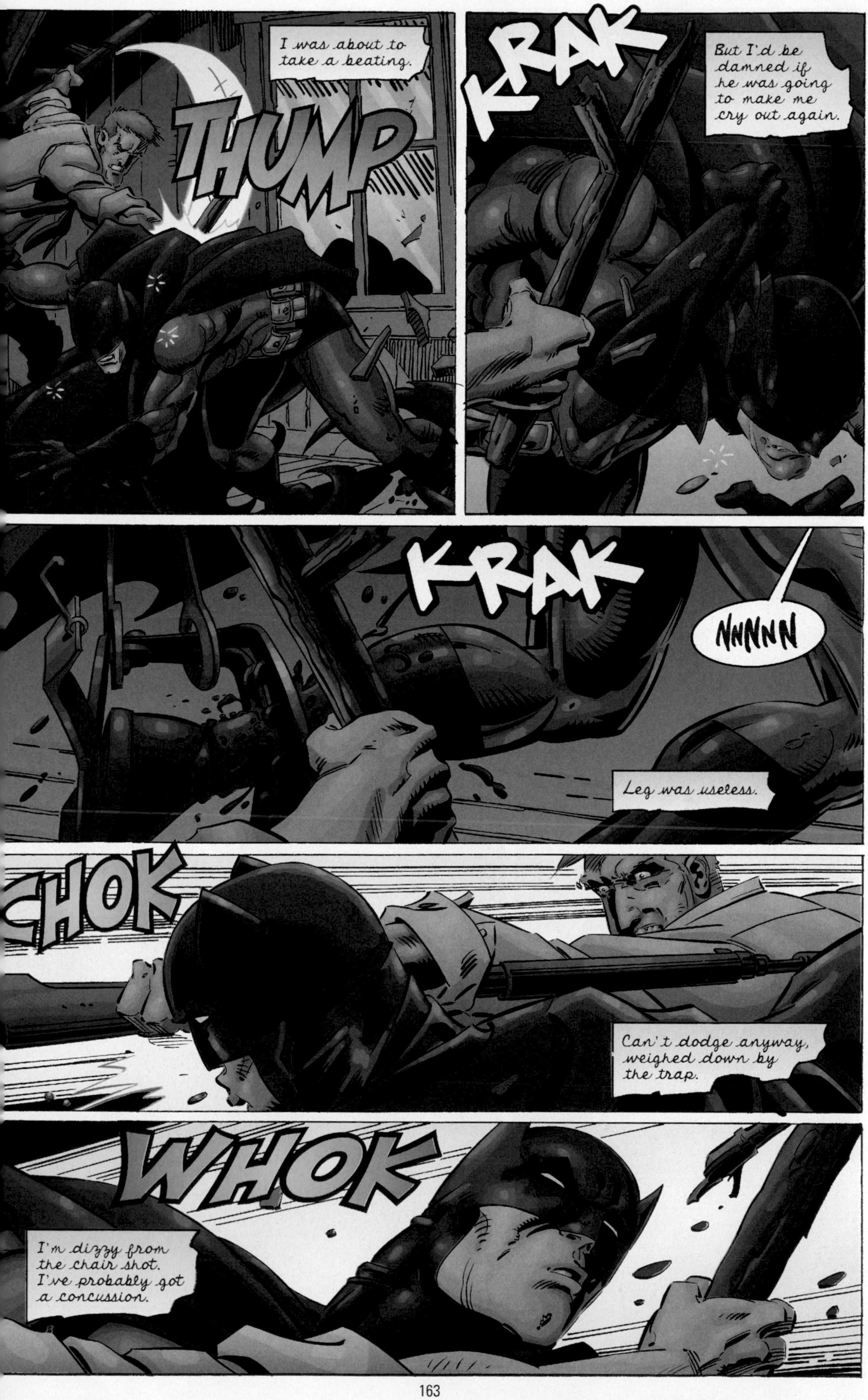
I was about to take a beating.
THUMP
KRAK
But I'd be damned if he was going to make me cry out again.
KRAK
NNNNN
Leg was useless.
CHOK
Can't dodge anyway, weighed down by the trap.
WHOK
I'm dizzy from the chair shot. I've probably got a concussion.

And this guy was tuning me up pretty good.

WHUNK

FWOO-O

Add it all up and one thing was clear...

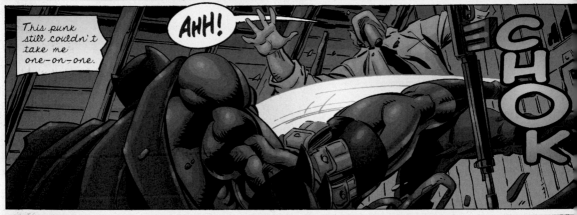

This punk still couldn't take me one-on-one.

AHH!

CHOK

MY GUN!

Although, I had to admit, I wasn't up for a footrace.

KRUNCH

WHOOLFF!

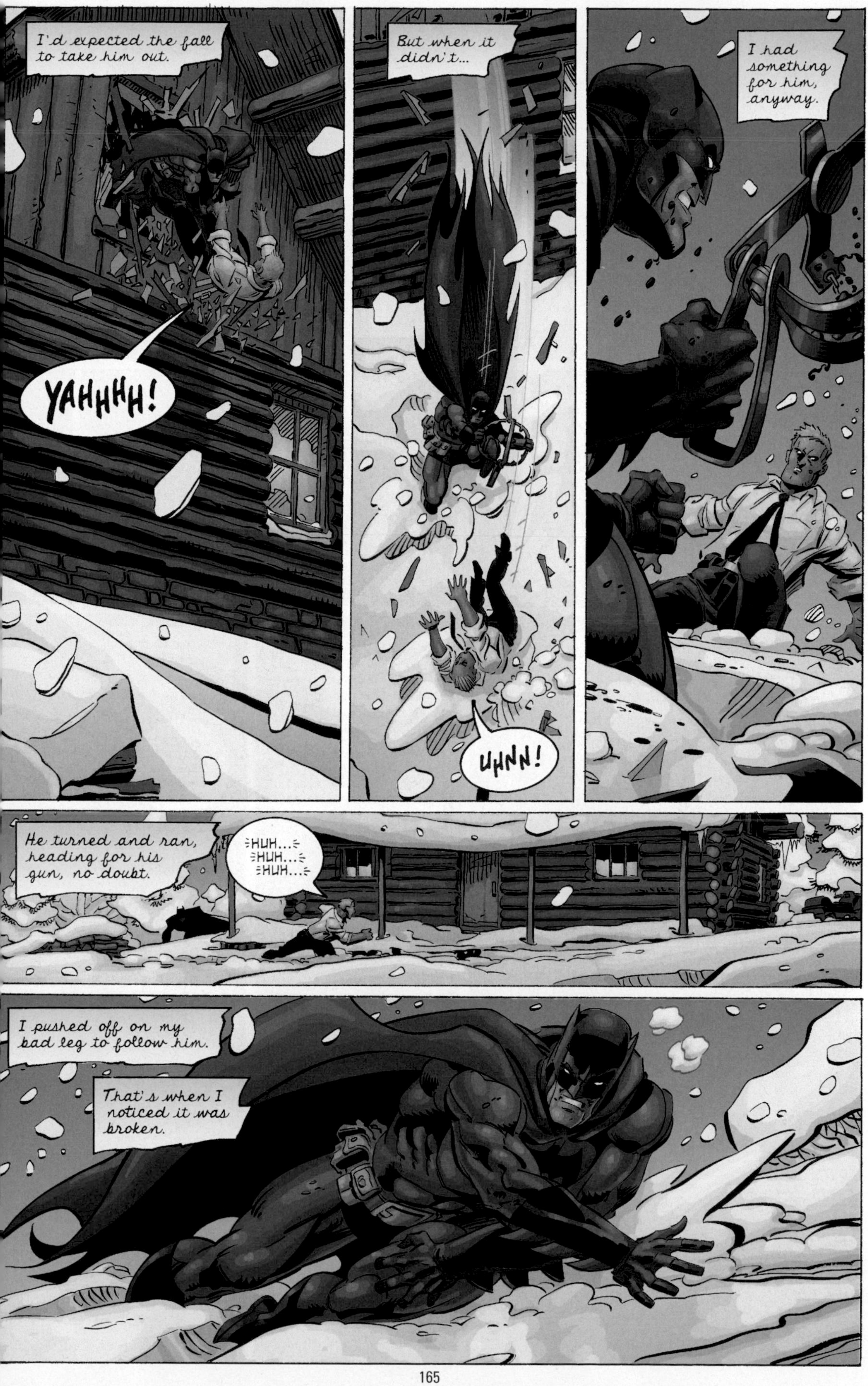
I'd expected the fall to take him out.
YAHHHH!
But when it didn't...
UHNN!
I had something for him, anyway.
He turned and ran, heading for his gun, no doubt.
HUH... HUH... HUH...
I pushed off on my bad leg to follow him.
That's when I noticed it was broken.

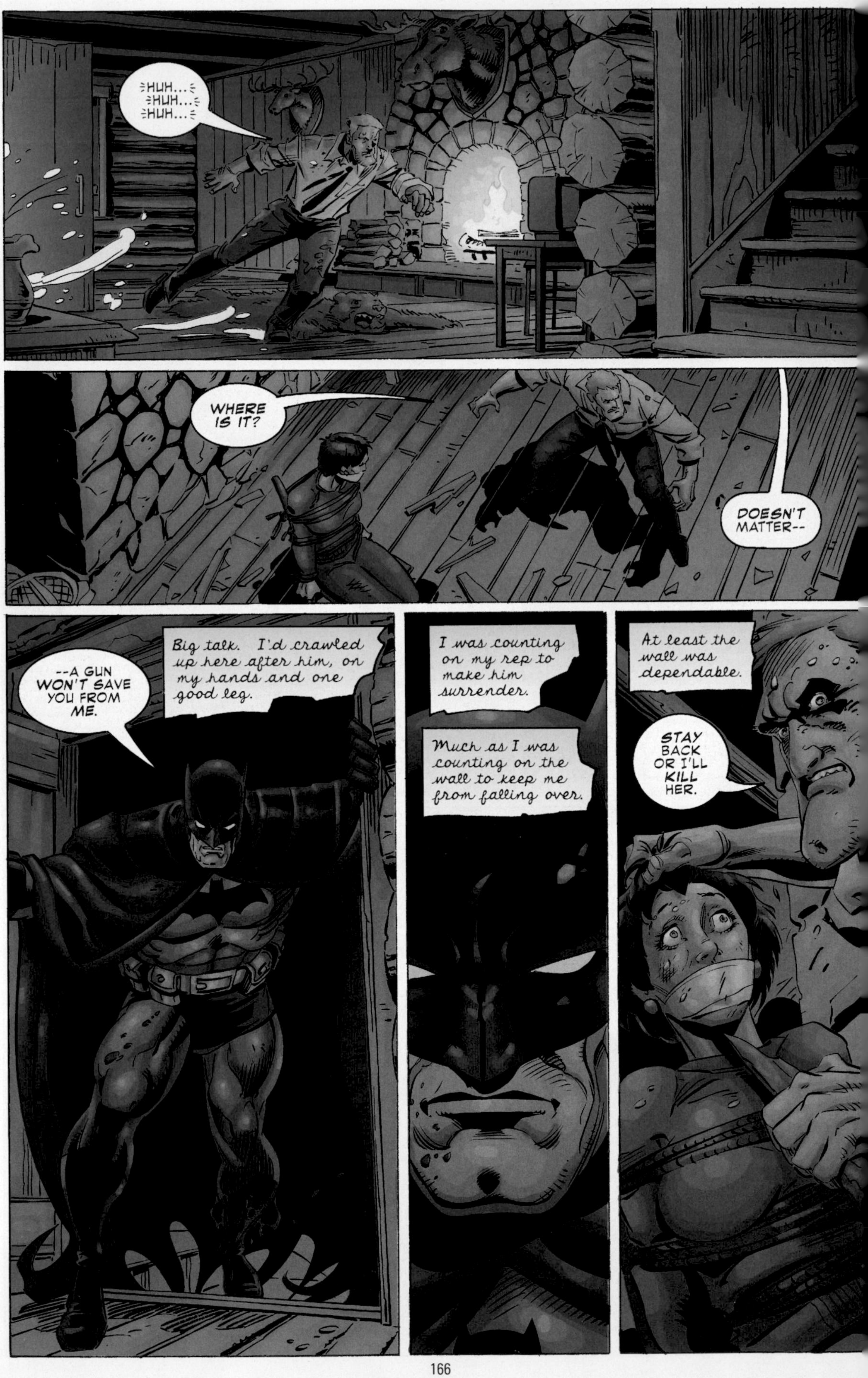
HUH... HUH... HUH...
WHERE IS IT?
DOESN'T MATTER--
--A GUN WON'T SAVE YOU FROM ME.
Big talk. I'd crawled up here after him, on my hands and one good leg.
I was counting on my rep to make him surrender.
Much as I was counting on the wall to keep me from falling over.
At least the wall was dependable.
STAY BACK OR I'LL KILL HER.

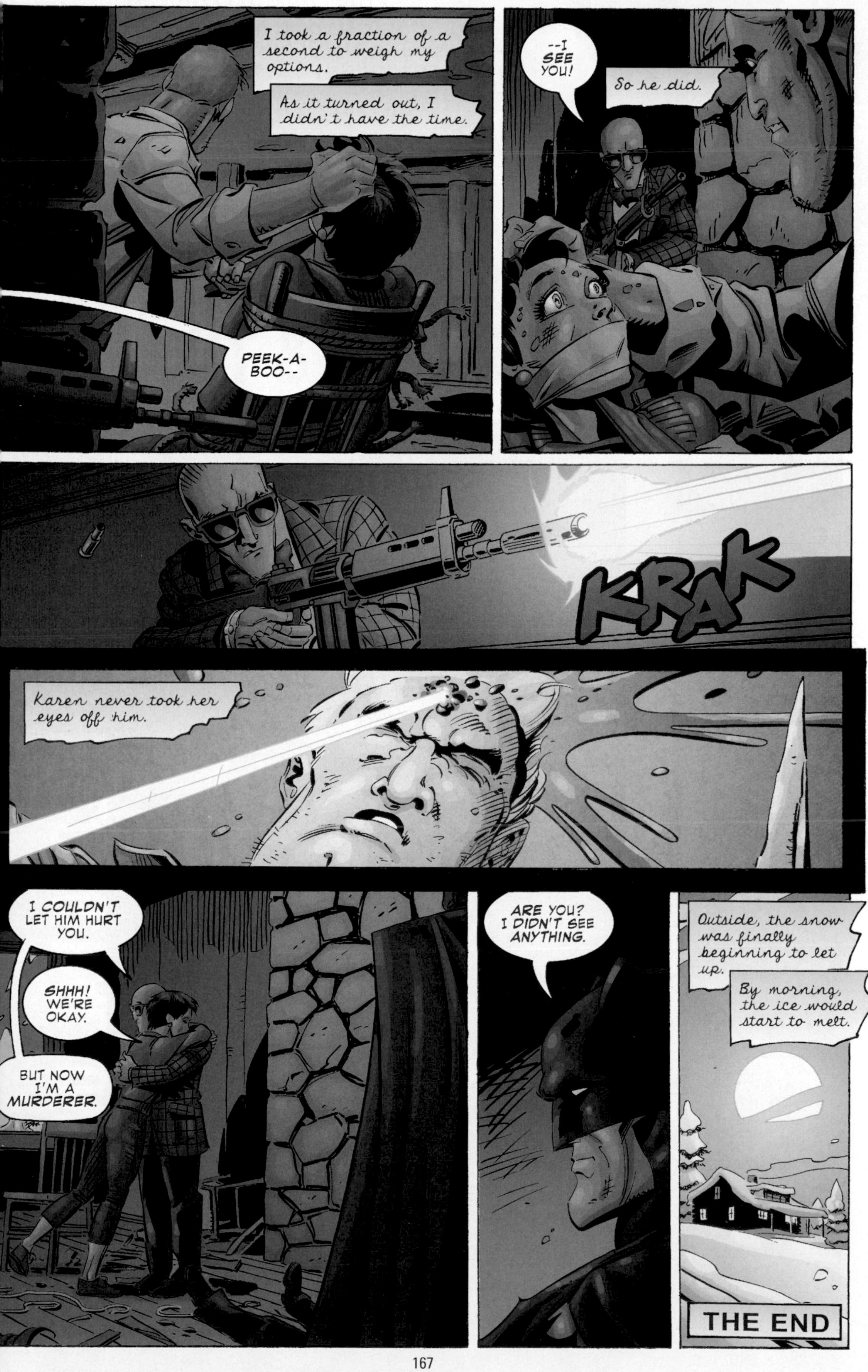
I took a fraction of a second to weigh my options.
As it turned out, I didn't have the time.
PEEK-A-BOO--
--I SEE YOU!
So he did.
KRAK
Karen never took her eyes off him.
I COULDN'T LET HIM HURT YOU.
SHHH! WE'RE OKAY.
BUT NOW I'M A MURDERER.
ARE YOU? I DIDN'T SEE ANYTHING.
Outside, the snow was finally beginning to let up.
By morning, the ice would start to melt.
THE END

DC COMICS™

"THE LONG HALLOWEEN is more than a comic book. It's an epic tragedy."
—Christopher Nolan (director of BATMAN BEGINS, THE DARK KNIGHT and THE DARK KNIGHT RISES)

"THE LONG HALLOWEEN is the preeminent influence on both movies [BATMAN BEGINS and THE DARK KNIGHT]."
—David Goyer (screenwriter of THE DARK KNIGHT RISES)

FROM THE AWARD-WINNING TEAM BEHIND *SUPERMAN: FOR ALL SEASONS*

JEPH LOEB & TIM SALE

BATMAN: DARK VICTORY

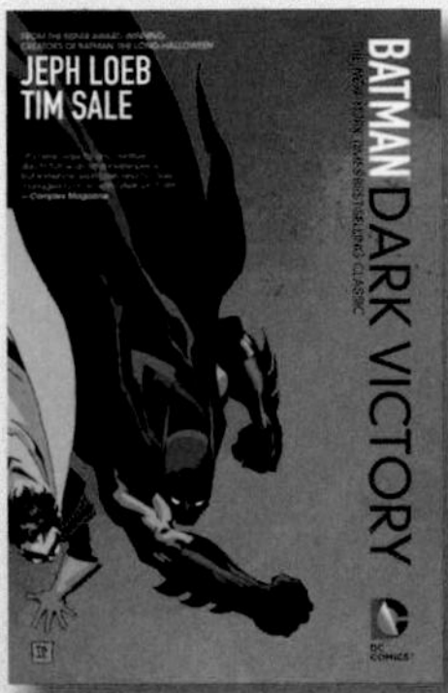
JEPH LOEB
TIM SALE
BATMAN DARK VICTORY

BATMAN: HAUNTED KNIGHT

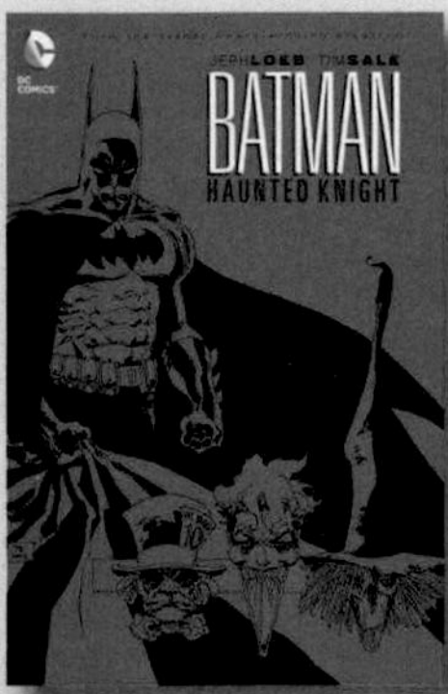
JEPH LOEB TIM SALE
BATMAN
HAUNTED KNIGHT

CATWOMAN: WHEN IN ROME

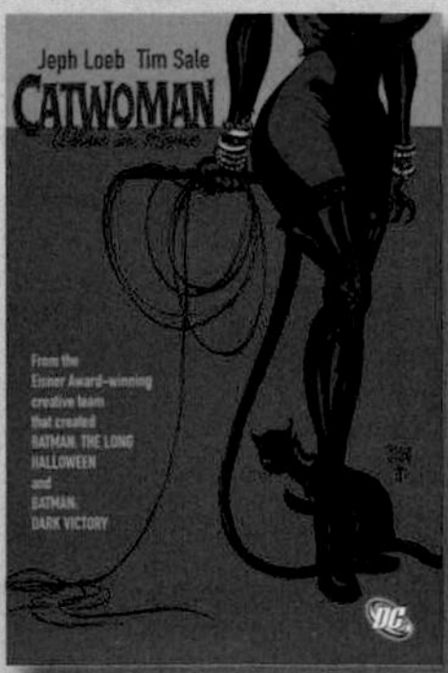
Jeph Loeb Tim Sale
CATWOMAN

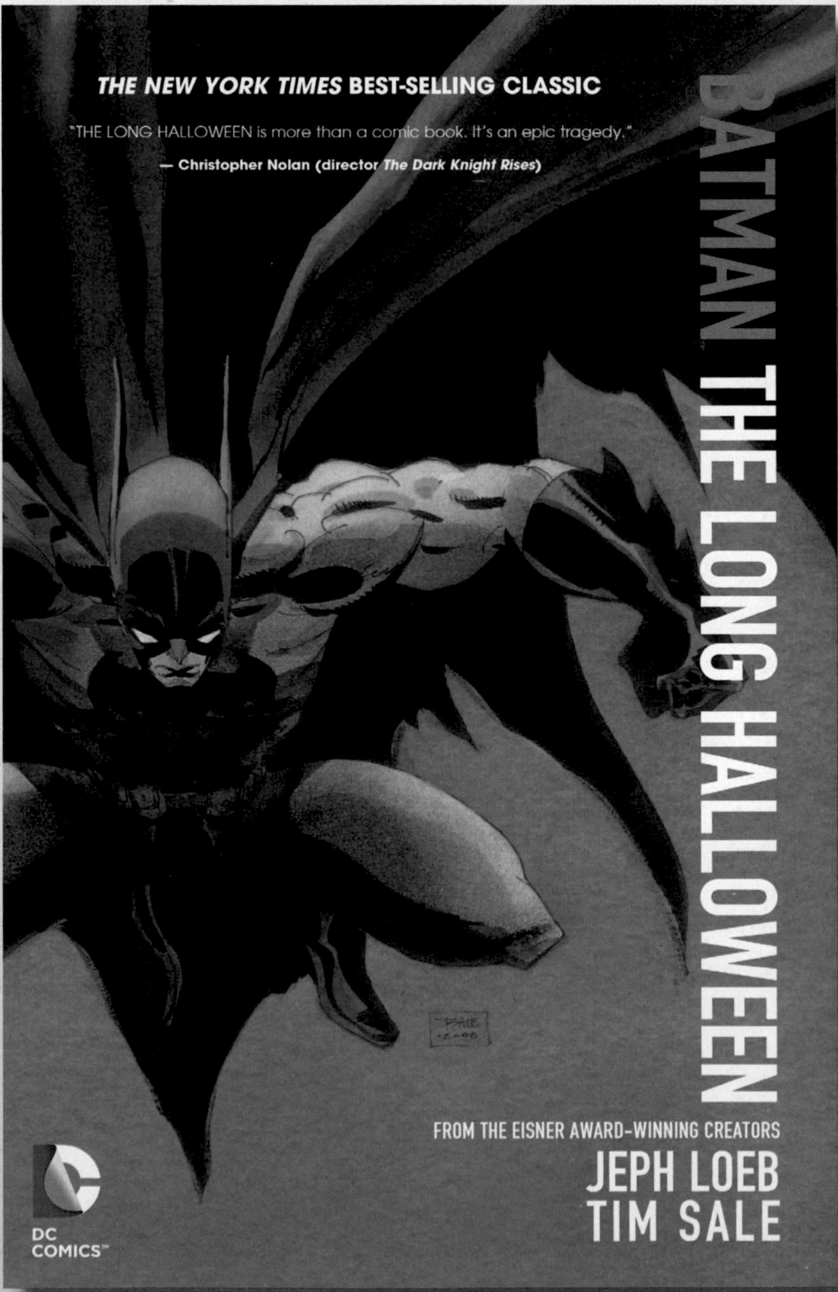
THE NEW YORK TIMES BEST-SELLING CLASSIC
"THE LONG HALLOWEEN is more than a comic book. It's an epic tragedy."
— Christopher Nolan (director The Dark Knight Rises)
BATMAN THE LONG HALLOWEEN
FROM THE EISNER AWARD-WINNING CREATORS
JEPH LOEB
TIM SALE
DC COMICS

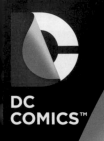